THE DOMESTICATION
OF MARTIN LUTHER KING JR.

The Domestication of Martin Luther King Jr.

Clarence B. Jones, Right-Wing Conservatism, and the Manipulation of the King Legacy

EDITED BY
Lewis V. Baldwin
and Rufus Burrow Jr.

FOREWORD BY
Adam Fairclough

CASCADE *Books* • Eugene, Oregon

THE DOMESTICATION OF MARTIN LUTHER KING JR.
Clarence B. Jones, Right-Wing Conservatism, and the Manipulation of the King Legacy

Copyright © 2013 Wipf and Stock Publishers. All rights reserved. Except for brief quotations in critical publications or reviews, no part of this book may be reproduced in any manner without prior written permission from the publisher. Write: Permissions, Wipf and Stock Publishers, 199 W. 8th Ave., Suite 3, Eugene, OR 97401.

Cascade Books
An Imprint of Wipf and Stock Publishers
199 W. 8th Ave., Suite 3
Eugene, OR 97401

www.wipfandstock.com

ISBN 13: 978-1-61097-954-2

Cataloging-in-Publication data:

The domestication of Martin Luther King Jr. : Clarence B. Jones, right-wing conservatism, and the manipulation of the King legacy / edited by Lewis V. Baldwin and Rufus Burrow Jr. ; foreword by Adam Fairclough.

xxxii + 268 p. 23 cm—Includes bibliographical references

ISBN 13: 978-1-61097-954-2

1. King, Martin Luther Jr. (1929–1968) 2. King, Martin Luther Jr. (1929–1968)—Social and political views. 3. United States—Social conditions—21st century. 4. United States—Politics and government—21st century. 5. Jones, Clarence B. I. Baldwin, Lewis V. (1949–). II. Burrow, Rufus (1951–). III. Fairclough, Adam. IV. Title.

E185.97 K5 D60 2013

Manufactured in the USA

For Morehouse College
a part of the center of Martin Luther King Jr.'s world

Contents

List of Contributors | ix
Foreword | *Adam Fairclough* | xiii
Acknowledgments | xvii
General Introduction | *Lewis V. Baldwin & Rufus Burrow Jr.* | xix

1. Distorted Characterizations: Images of Martin Luther King, Jr. in the Conservative Mind | *Lewis V. Baldwin* | 1

2. Who Is Clarence B. Jones's Martin Luther King Jr.: An Audacious Prophet or a Right-Wing Conservative? | *Lewis V. Baldwin* | 29

3. Leading in Challenging Times: Martin Luther King Jr., Ruby Hurley, and the Meaning of Black Leadership | *Rosetta E. Ross & Shirley T. Geiger* | 55

4. Looking for Martin: Black Leadership in an Era of Contested Postracism and Postblackness | *Walter E. Fluker* | 73

5. Drum Major for Justice or Dilettante of Dishonesty: Martin Luther King Jr., Moral Capital, and Hypocrisy of Embodied Messianic Myths | *Cheryl Kirk-Duggan* | 100

6. Ruminating about Martin Luther King Jr. and Sex | *Rufus Burrow Jr.* | 120

7. Gay Rights and the Misuse of Martin | *Traci C. West* | 141

8. What's Race Got to Do with It?: Anti-Semitism, Affirmative Action, and Illegal Immigration | *Lewis V. Baldwin* | 157

9. Nonviolence and a Moral Universe: What Martin Might Say about War and Terrorism | *Rufus Burrow Jr.* | 179

10. What Martin Might Say about Intracommunity Violence and Homicide among Young African American Males: An Extreme Emergency | *Rufus Burrow Jr.* | 202

11. Transforming Death: Life's Ultimate Tragedy and Hope for the Dawn | *Michael G. Long* | 219

12. A Prophet with Honor?: The Martin Luther King Jr. Holiday and the Making of a National Icon | *George R. Seay Jr.* | 236

Index | 261

Contributors

Lewis V. Baldwin is a historian in the Department of Religious Studies at Vanderbilt University in Nashville, Tennessee. He is the author of *There is a Balm in Gilead: The Cultural Roots of Martin Luther King, Jr.* (1991); *To Make the Wounded Whole: The Cultural Legacy of Martin Luther King, Jr.* (1992); *Toward the Beloved Community: Martin Luther King, Jr. and South Africa* (1995); *Between Cross and Crescent: Christian and Muslim Perspectives on Malcolm and Martin* (with Amiri YaSin Al-Hadid, 2002); *The Legacy of Martin Luther King, Jr.: The Boundaries of Law, Politics, and Religion* (with Rufus Burrow, Jr., Barbara A. Holmes, and Susan Holmes Winfield, 2002); *Never to Leave Us Alone: The Prayer Life of Martin Luther King, Jr.* (2010); *The Voice of Conscience: The Church in the Mind of Martin Luther King, Jr.* (2010); and *"Thou, Dear God": Prayers that Open Hearts and Spirits – The Reverend Dr. Martin Luther King, Jr.* (edited and introduced, 2012).

Rufus Burrow Jr. is the Indiana Professor of Christian Thought and Professor of Theological Social Ethics at Christian Theological Seminary in Indianapolis, Indiana. Among his publications are *Personalism: A Critical Introduction* (1999); *Daring to Speak in God's Name* (with Mary Alice Mulligan, 2002); *God and Human Responsibility: David Walker and Ethical Prophecy* (2003); *God and Human Dignity: The Personalism, Theology, and Ethics of Martin Luther King, Jr.* (2006); and *Martin Luther King, Jr. for Armchair Theologians* (2009).

Adam Fairclough is The Raymond and Beverly Sackler Professor of American History at Leiden University in the Netherlands. Among his publications are *To Redeem the Soul of America: The Southern Christian Leadership Conference and Martin Luther King, Jr.* (1987); *Martin Luther King, Jr.* (1990); *Race and Democracy: The Civil Rights Struggle in Louisiana, 1915-1972* (1995); *Teaching Equality: Black Schools in the Age of Jim Crow* (2001); and *Better Day Coming: Blacks and Equality, 1800-2000* (2002).

Walter Earl Fluker is the Martin Luther King, Jr. Professor of Ethical Leadership at Boston University, Boston, Massachusetts, and is editor of the Howard Thurman Papers Project. His publications include *They Looked for a City: A Comparative Analysis of the Ideal of Community in the Thought of Howard Thurman and Martin Luther King, Jr.* (1989); *Strange Freedom: The Best of Howard Thurman on Religious Experience and Public Life* (co-edited with Catherine Tumber, 1998); and *Ethical Leadership: The Quest for Character, Civility, and Community* (2009).

Shirley T. Geiger is a retired Professor of Political Science at Savannah State University, Savannah, Georgia, and the editor of "Race and Politics in the United States," in a special issue of the journal, *Politics and Policy* (2001). She is completing a biography, *Isaiah DeQuincey Newman and the Politics of Race in South Carolina, 1911–1985*. Her publications include *Understanding Gender at Historically Black Colleges and Universities* (2006); and *Black Women Mayors: Local Political Leadership at the Intersection of Race, Gender, and Class* (2004).

Cheryl A. Kirk-Duggan is a Professor of Theology and Women's Studies at Shaw University in Raleigh, North Carolina. Among her publications are *African American Special Days* (1996); *Exorcizing Evil: A Womanist Perspective on the Spirituals* (1997); *The Undivided Soul: Helping Congregations Connect Body and Spirit* (2001); *Misbegotten Anguish: A Theology and Ethics of Violence* (2001); *Refiner's Fire: A Religious Engagement with Violence* (2001); *Wising Up: Bible Study for Women on Proverbs* (2005); *Violence and Theology* (2006); *The Sky is Crying: Racism, Classism, and Natural Disaster* (editor, 2006); *The Africana Bible: Reading Israel's Scriptures from Africa and the African Diaspora* (co-edited with Hugh R. Page, Jr., Randall C. Bailey, Valerie Bridgeman, Stacy Davis, Madipoane Masenya, Nathaniel S. Murrell, and Rodney S. Sadler, 2009); *Women and Christianity* (2009); and *Wake Up!: Hip Hop Christianity and the Black Church* (2011).

Michael G. Long is an Associate Professor of Religious Studies and Peace and Conflict Studies at Elizabethtown College, Elizabethtown, Pennsylvania. Among his publications are *Against Us, But For Us: Martin Luther King, Jr. and the State* (2002); *Martin Luther King, Jr. on Creative Living* (2004); *Billy Graham and the Beloved Community: America's Evangelist and the Dream of Martin Luther King, Jr.* (2006); *Marshalling Justice: The Early Civil Rights Letters of Thurgood Marshall* (2010); *I Must Resist: Bayard Rustin's Life in Letters* (2012); and *Beyond Home Plate: Jackie Robinson on Life after Baseball* (2013).

Rosetta E. Ross is Professor of Religious Studies at Spelman College in Atlanta, Georgia. Her research and scholarship examine the role of religion in black women's activism, particularly in the civil rights movement. She is the author of *Witnessing and Testifying: Black Women, Religion, and Civil Rights* (2003); and *The Status of Racial and Ethnic Clergywomen in the United Methodist Church* (co-authored with Jung Ha Kim, 2004).

George Russell Seay Jr. is an Assistant Professor of Theology and Ethics at Oakwood College, Huntsville, Alabama. His PhD dissertation, titled "Theologian of Synthesis: The Dialectical Method of Martin Luther King, Jr. as Revealed in His Critical Thinking on Theology, History, and Ethics" (2010), is currently being revised for publication.

Traci C. West is Professor of Ethics and African American Studies at Drew Theological Seminary, Madison, New Jersey. She is the author of *Wounds of the Spirit: Black Women, Violence, and Resistance Ethics* (1999); *Disruptive Christian Ethics: When Racism and Women's Lives Matter* (2006); and *Defending Same-Sex Marriage: Our Family Values, Same-Sex Marriage and Religion* (editor, 2006).

Foreword

When President Barack H. Obama spoke at the official dedication of the Martin Luther King Jr. Memorial on October 16, 2011, the notion that King should be commemorated by a gigantic granite statue on the National Mall in Washington DC evoked little public opposition. Not that the monument failed to evoke controversy—far from it. But the most heated arguments swirled around the design of the monument, the nationality of the sculptor, and the financial demands of the King family, not the propriety of thus honoring the slain civil rights leader. This had not been the case twenty-eight years earlier, in October 1983, when Congress passed a bill designating the third Monday in January a federal holiday, or Martin Luther King Jr. Day. That proposal had evoked vocal opposition from influential politicians. President Ronald Reagan, who signed the bill through proverbially gritted teeth, had expressed skepticism. And for years after its passage, several states *dishonored* King by naming the holiday something else or, in the case of Virginia, calling it "Lee-Jackson-King Day," a title that gave priority to two white men, both slaveholders, who had waged war against the Union in a struggle to preserve human bondage.

As often happens in history, however, time cools political passions, and leaders once damned as radicals or traitors—and King was frequently called both—are absorbed into a patriotic narrative that stresses consensus rather than conflict. Abstracted from the specific circumstances of their history, they come to function as symbols of the nation as a whole. The iconic status testifies to the permanence of the changes they wrought and the broad acceptance of certain ideas and values, once bitterly resisted, that they had espoused. A mythologized Martin Luther King Jr. has been admitted to that select group of national heroes that peoples the pantheon of America's civil religion. The location of the King Memorial, on federal parkland near memorials to Thomas Jefferson and Franklin D. Roosevelt, underlines the fact that King stands in the company of the nation's demigods. "I Have a Dream" may well be the best known and the most widely quoted speech in American history. Like Abraham Lincoln's Gettysburg Address, which King consciously evoked, it has come to represent the quintessence of American democratic idealism.

This process of figurative and literal monument building, however, exacts a price in terms of historical understanding. The actual historical record is pruned and even sanitized. Mark Antony may have been right when, burying Caesar, he noted that "The evil men do lives after them; the good is oft interred with their bones." Historical commemoration, however, invariably entails the opposite kind of effect. We celebrate Thomas Jefferson the forward-seeing advocate of equality and liberty, not the pitiless slaveholder and hypocritical racist. We remember Winston Churchill the foe of Nazi tyranny, not the admirer of Mussolini and ruthless imperialist. Whatever evils King may have authored were minor when compared with Jefferson's practice of slavery or Churchill's indifference to millions of starving Indians. Nevertheless, the King of American civil religion is a highly selective version of King the historical actor. This is why conservatives can commemorate King with as much sincerity as liberals. Judging people "not by the color of their skin but by the content of their character" is entirely consistent with the individualism that provides the ideological underpinning of American capitalism. Conveniently forgotten is the man who berated America for its excessive materialism and militarism, who stated qualified admiration for Karl Marx and who regarded Sweden's social democracy as a model that the United States of America would do well to follow. This image of King is resurrected to a considerable degree on the pages of this work.

Serious students of King's life and work recognize the difference between the King of history and the King of American civil religion. They know, to quote Lewis V. Baldwin's essay in this collection, that to understand King demands "a serious engagement with King's own words, writings, and actions in the 1950s and 60s." By the same token, they appreciate that the memories of eyewitnesses must be subjected to the same critical analysis that scholars bring to bear on all historical documents. The memoirs of King's colleagues, such as Ralph D. Abernathy, Andrew J. Young, and Clarence B. Jones, provide valuable evidence, but each had a partial—in both senses of that word—view of King, and their testimony is filtered through the lens of time. Eyewitnesses to history they may have been, but, as any lawyer knows, the evidence of eyewitnesses is notoriously unreliable. Although Ralph Abernathy was King's constant companion throughout King's civil rights career, he was prone to nod off during staff meetings and strategy debates. Andrew Young did not join the staff until 1961. Clarence Jones, a member of King's circle of New York–based advisors, saw the civil rights leader close up; yet his main contact with King fell between the years 1962 and 1966. The man who might have shed the most light on King, his intimate friend and counselor Stanley Levison, who was also a member of King's New York circle, died in 1979 without writing a memoir or leaving a body of papers. Fortunately, and ironically, the transcripts of FBI wiretaps afford us a good idea of what these advisors said to King, and with whom King most often consulted.

It is with justifiable skepticism, therefore, that the contributors to this volume approach recent claims by Jones, published half a century after King's death, regarding the positions that King might take on present-day issues. To state the obvious: King died before women's liberation, the gay rights movement, the collapse of communism, and the end of the cold war. One can speculate how King, who described himself as "a realistic pacifist," might have judged US-led military interventions in Panama, Iraq, Serbia, and Kosovo, or the more recent Anglo-French-American intervention in Libya. But it would be only that: speculation. Given King's public and, particularly, his private statements, the left can claim him as a kindred spirit. Given King's search for coalitions and consensus, liberals can also regard him as one of their own. The truth is that we can only guess at King's political evolution had he lived on into the present. He might even have moved to the political right—highly unlikely, in this writer's opinion, but not beyond the realm of possibility. In short, any attempt to infer King's position on current issues is fraught with difficulty, and many would regard it as futile. Moreover, Jones's claim that his close relationship with King gives him a special, even unique, insight into "what Martin would say" cannot withstand serious scrutiny, as this volume concludes.

Nevertheless, we should be grateful to Clarence Jones for indirectly causing these essays to be written and published. As historian Hugh Trevor-Roper once observed, a fertile error can be more useful than a sterile truth. Bold claims, however dubious, provoke debate and stimulate research; knowledge and understanding are thereby advanced. It is a process that King himself, with his fondness for the Hegelian dialectic, fully appreciated. Relishing debate, he encouraged his staff to engage in spirited, even furious, argumentation. On any given issue—Vietnam, Black Power, poverty, presidential politics—King heard a variety of views, strongly expressed. One could never be certain, moreover, what position he would ultimately take, or which policy he would actually adopt. Moral principles were only a rough guide to action: King had to adapt those principles to politics and practicality. A coalition builder by both instinct and philosophy, King regarded compromise as creative synthesis, not betrayal. His ethics were guided by realism. All this underlines the difficulty in estimating where King might stand on the burning issues of today. This thought-provoking collection not only examines Jones's claims but also extends the debate over King's legacy.

Lewis V. Baldwin and Rufus Burrow Jr. are to be congratulated for commissioning and contributing, along with other scholars, to this interesting, timely, and provocative work.

Adam Fairclough
The Raymond and Beverly Sackler
Professor of American History
University of Leiden
The Netherlands

Acknowledgments

This volume would have never been completed without the help of colleagues and friends. We acknowledge with gratitude the assistance of Cynthia Lewis and Elaine Hall, who work in the library and archives at the Martin Luther King Jr. Center for Nonviolent Social Change, Inc. For years they have made the efforts of King scholars easier by providing sources and bibliographic information. Some of the chapters in this volume benefitted immensely from their help.

We are equally grateful for the contribution of Clayborne Carson, the Senior Editor of the Martin Luther King Jr. Papers Project, and his wonderful staff at Stanford University. Having collected, compiled, and published the six extant volumes of the King Papers, they provided a rich and enduring resource on which we could draw in advancing our many claims and conclusions.

Sincere thanks go to Peter J. Paris, the Elmer G. Homrighausen Professor of Christian Ethics Emeritus at Princeton Theological Seminary, for his kindness and encouragement. We had a number of contacts with Peter in the course of our research and writing, and he was always kind, considerate, and generous. Peter was particularly helpful when it came to the question of the organization of the chapters included in this book.

We appreciate the patient encouragement and editorial assistance of Christian Amondson and others at Cascade Books. Thanks for guiding us through the writing and formatting processes with sage advice and constant encouragement. You were most understanding and generous, even when we failed to grasp and follow instructions, asked the most difficult and probing questions, and failed miserably to meet the proper deadlines.

Particularly helpful in the final stages was Anthony Sandusky, a recent graduate of the Vanderbilt University Divinity School. Anthony helped prepare the book's manuscript for publication. This process included a lot of reading and some typing and formatting, and Anthony handled the challenge well. We hope he realizes his dream of becoming and finding a place among the next generation of King scholars.

A hearty word of gratitude is extended to Adam Fairclough, the British King scholar who teaches American history at Leiden University in the

Netherlands, for writing the foreword. We exchanged numerous e-mails with Dr. Fairclough while completing this work, and he was always willing to ask questions and to provide critical feedback. The first two chapters bear the marks of his influence at points.

A number of scholars in various disciplines contributed their time, resources, and expertise in the planning, researching, and writing of the chapters that comprise this volume. The twelve chapters in *The Domestication of Martin Luther King Jr.* were contributed by scholars who have taken the risk of thinking with King beyond King. They are not afraid or hesitant to think with King *in* and *beyond* his own time and space. They actually reevaluate King in his own day on into the twenty-first century. A special thanks to all of the contributors, for both your hard work and your willingness to donate the proceeds from this work to the Martin Luther King Jr. Collection at Morehouse College in Atlanta, Georgia. Consider yourselves worthy contributors to the promotion of the King legacy.

It was truly a delight to gather and edit these chapters, and to write the general introduction. As King scholars, we have long discussed the need for new and multidisciplinary approaches to the study of King. There is at present no single volume in which scholars from various fields explore King's meaning from the standpoint of sources on the religious and political right. Undoubtedly, this anthology fills a conspicuous gap in King studies, and we hope it will stimulate thoughtful discussion and debate, not only in academic settings, but in religious and political circles as well. We would be even more pleased and honored if it becomes a model for future scholarship on King. If any of this happens, everyone who contributed to *The Domestication of Martin Luther King Jr.* will have much for which to be thankful and to celebrate.

General Introduction

Martin Luther King Jr.'s name and image are currently being invoked in defense of every conceivable religious, political, and cultural agenda and point of view. Indeed, King has become a convenient symbol and resource for scholars, persons of faith, social activists, politicians, media moguls, TV hosts, radio personalities, and newspaper columnists, who routinely appeal to his authority when addressing the most pressing moral issues of this age. Polemicists and propagandists across the ideological spectrum frequently use King as a sort of blank screen onto which they project their own biases, insecurities, hopes, dreams, and aspirations. The many uses and abuses of King's legacy have become all too common, especially in right-wing, conservative circles, thus increasing the necessity for more accurate portrayals of the man and his ideas and activities.

This explains in part the publication of *The Domestication of Martin Luther King Jr.* The conceptual framework for this book developed gradually as we read and responded to Clarence B. Jones's *What Would Martin Say?* (2008), a work that makes sweeping claims about what would be King's perspectives on contemporary black civil rights leadership, affirmative action, illegal immigration, anti-Semitism, global terrorism, and the war in Iraq. Generally speaking, Jones suggests that King would be bitterly disappointed with the thinking and activities of present-day black civil rights leaders such as Jesse Jackson and Al Sharpton, that he would call for the abolishment of affirmative action as we know it, that he would oppose those who violate this country's immigration laws, that he would denounce anti-Semitism as the most virulent form of racism, and that he would ultimately support the use of violence as the most practical strategy in the struggle against Islamic terrorists and Saddam Hussein's Baathist regime in Iraq.

Knowing that Clarence Jones was one of King's legal advisors and confidants in the 1960s, we, as established King scholars, greeted such claims with a sudden feeling of wonder and, in some instances, even alarm, for they projected an image of King that has no resemblance to the Georgia-born black prophet who became "a drum major" for justice, peace, and righteousness. We were literally consumed with the urge to defend King against what we see as misrepresentation and distortion in many cases.

Jones's apparent mischaracterizations of King actually triggered reminders of William Styron's controversial, Pulitzer-Prize winning novel, *The Confessions of Nat Turner* (1966), which we had both read earlier. Styron, a white southerner, actually reduced the real historical Nat Turner, a black slave who led a revolt in Southampton County, Virginia in 1831, from an audacious prophet and rebel to an establishment Negro. In *William Styron's Nat Turner: Ten Black Writers Respond* (1968), edited by John Henrik Clarke, Clarke, Lerone Bennett Jr., Alvin F. Poussaint, Vincent Harding, John O. Killens, John A. Williams, Ernest Kaiser, Loyle Hairston, Charles V. Hamilton, and Mike Thelwell challenged Styron's domestication of Turner, and set out to restore Turner's rightful place as a slave insurrectionist and hero of his people. We have a similar purpose and mission in *The Domestication of Martin Luther King Jr.*, as we respond to Clarence Jones's portrayal of King. Although we are not driven by the deep anger that characterized the ten black respondents to Styron, we do feel a sense of urgency in challenging Jones's effort to make King's image more acceptable to the current status quo, and especially to the powerful religious and political establishments.

As we conceptualized *The Domestication of Martin Luther King Jr.*, Jones issued a second volume on King, titled *Behind the Dream: The Making of the Speech That Transformed a Nation* (2011). This book offers a behind-the-scenes account of the activities that culminated in the great March on Washington in 1963, and especially King's celebrated "I Have a Dream" speech. *Behind the Dream* further advances Jones's questionable image of King, suggesting at points that King would have much in common with the likes of Glenn Beck and the Tea Party phenomenon. We believe that Jones's *What Would Martin Say?* and *Behind the Dream*, which are exceptionally readable and engaging volumes, constitute an enormous challenge not only for King scholars and black intellectuals in general, but for all who honor King's memory and his rich and powerful legacy of ideas and struggle. We decided that we had a moral responsibility, as King scholars and as keepers of the dream, to subject Jones's image of and claims about King to historical scrutiny and rigorous analysis and critique. In this modern culture of deception and propaganda, we cannot afford to ignore or dismiss Jones's Martin Luther King Jr. out of hand. This would be not only a betrayal of King, but a blatant denial of the values for which he lived, struggled, and died.

We struggled with many questions as *The Domestication of Martin Luther King, Jr.* took shape in our minds: What should a book on this subject cover? What title should we use to best convey our thesis and purpose? How can we respond to Jones in ways that are charitable and also analytical and critical? Should Jones's claims about King be treated in isolation from those of that larger phenomenon of right-wing conservatism, or does it make more sense to approach them as an extension of what has too often been advanced by a certain highly visible and vocal cadre of religious and political conservatives? Is it really worthwhile for us, like Jones, to explore questions about what King *would* say about anything today, or would this be pure or fruitless conjecture, or perhaps even a waste of time? Is it really unfair for us, like Jones, to overburden King in a study of his life's work with the role of "the great man" with "the answers" to many of today's social problems? Should the book be a coauthored volume, or a collaborative effort involving a stellar cast of King scholars? Should only King scholars be involved, or should we make this a more inclusive effort involving black and white intellectuals who have a special interest in the study of King and the civil rights movement? Should we strive for a fifty-fifty male and female mix of contributors? We came to an agreement on how each of these questions should be answered before committing our ideas and thoughts to paper.

Inspired by John H. Clarke's edited piece on Nat Turner, we had initially planned to confine our focus to Clarence Jones's books on King, using, as a title for our work, *Clarence B. Jones's What Would Martin Say?: Ten King Scholars Respond*. But we decided against this approach for two important reasons. First, we felt that a book about Jones and his writings about King would be too narrowly focused and would not provide the nexus we need to struggle with the more general question of King's on-going relevance for contemporary times. In other words, we hoped to situate more accurately the content of this book on King and his legacy of ideas and activism, while also taking an approach that is both analytical and critical of parts of Jones' writings. It was clear to us that what is of the utmost significance is not so much what Jones says about King, but the fact that our nation as a whole is suffering from amnesia when it comes to the question of King's legacy, and particularly what he taught and believed. We are part of a culture that has been and continues to be unwilling to come to grips with the radicality of King's ideas and social praxis, and is therefore more comfortable with a domesticated King, or one who is harmless, gentle, and a symbol of our own confused sense of what it means to be Americans. This book's title, *The Domestication of Martin Luther King, Jr.*, is, in and of itself, really a commentary on what much of our society thinks and believes about King. It speaks to this nation's determination to make King something other than *who* and *what* he actually was. Our purpose is to somehow break through the mass public confusion and to present a more realistic King based on a careful study of his own words and actions.

Second, in the earliest stage of our research and writing, it occurred to us that Jones's portrayal of King squares in more precise ways with that put forth by many right-wing religious and political conservatives over the last three decades, beginning with Jerry Falwell's suggestion that he was acting in the tradition of King when he protested against abortion, homosexuality, pornography, and other so-called social ills in the early 1980s. From Jerry Falwell to Newt Gingrich, Dick Armey, Clint Bolick, Cal Thomas, Glenn Beck, and Sarah Palin, right-wing conservatives have manipulated King's image and words to fit their own narrow ideological and political agenda. This is not entirely surprising in a culture in which many different images of iconic figures like King are circulated, and in which heroes and "sheroes" (to use Maya Angelou's neologism) tend to remain mutable symbols. We understand the need for views of King that cover a wide span of diversity, and this, to be sure, is what scholarship should entail. Even so, no portrayal of King should go unexamined and unchallenged. With this in mind, we decided to go beyond the portrait of King provided by Jones to explore the larger question of how King is viewed and used by right-wing religious and political conservatives. It is our contention that Jones is part of this conglomerate of right-wing conservatives who are bent on making King's image more palatable, acceptable, and useful for their own self-serving purposes. Indeed, his books have done much to reinforce the right-wing, conservative use and abuse of King's words, image, and legacy.

Unlike Jones, we decided not to focus so much on what King *would say* about contemporary social issues and problems, but on what he *would be likely to say* based on words he spoke and positions he took in the 1950s and '60s. At the same time, we realize that both approaches require risk-taking and a venture into the realm of the unknowable. However, we are convinced that any discussion of how King might address contemporary social ills should be based not simply on conjecture or what was once the nature of one's relationship to King in King's own time, as is the case with Jones, but on a serious reading of King in his own time. For example, if King vehemently opposed violence in the 1950s and 1960s, then it is only logical to assume that he would take the same position today, especially in light of his oft-repeated contention that violence is intrinsically immoral and impractical, and that it no longer serves a useful purpose. We agree with Jones's insistence that King would have changed with the times, or that he would be in some ways a different person today, but it is highly doubtful that he would reach the point of abandoning his most sacred and cherished beliefs, especially in an age in which bigotry, intolerance, violence, and oppression have become even more corrosive or destructive in world cultures. As well-meaning as Jones is in his effort to contemporize King, he, despite his relationship to the civil rights leader, should not have the last word on the subject. This applies as well to others who interpret King through the lenses of a narrow, right-wing conservatism.

We abandoned our earlier plan to bring together a distinguished team of King scholars for the writing of this book. *The Domestication of Martin Luther King Jr.* is actually the product of a unique collaboration between scholars who have studied and written about King and various dimensions of the civil rights movement. They represent a range of academic disciplines and interests, which means that our approach to King is not only scholarly—with contributions from six male and four female scholars—but interdisciplinary as well. The issues treated range from right-wing, conservative images of King to Jones's relationship to King to the more general question of what King said and might still say today about black leadership, affirmative action, illegal immigration, anti-Semitism, and violence and human destruction. Some of the contributors also reflect on issues not raised by Jones, such as King's sex life, his relationship to women, and gay rights. Strangely enough, Jones, in both his books, says essentially nothing about positions King might take on issues such as women's liberation, classism, white supremacy, poverty, and gay rights—issues which figure prominently in both the national and global public consciousness in contemporary times.

This book consists of some twelve chapters. Chapter 1 traces images of King in right-wing religious and political circles from the 1950s and '60s to the present. Written by Lewis V. Baldwin, a historian by training and a King scholar, this chapter views right-wing religious and political conservatism as the source of so much of the distortion and manipulation surrounding King's image, words, and legacy. At the same time, Baldwin is sensitive to the fact that right-wing conservatives have never been monolithic or one-dimensional in their approaches to King; that some have categorically rejected and castigated King as a tool of communists and a symbol of un-Americanism, while others have distorted and manipulated his image and words to promote their own moral and political agenda for what they envision as the reform and ultimate salvation of America.

This first chapter concludes with a discussion of the mass rally led by the conservative radio and TV pundit Glenn Beck on 28 August 2010, the forty-seventh anniversary of the great march on Washington, which is most often associated with Martin Luther King Jr.'s "I Have a Dream" speech. Baldwin highlights the irony and absurdity surrounding Beck's and Sarah Palin's evocation of King's memory on that occasion, and carefully explains how the views and agenda of these right-wing conservatives conflict with the vision and mission of King. Baldwin concludes that the actions of Beck and Palin at the 2010 rally were actually a more glaring and massive effort to do what those on the right have always done with King; namely, distort and manipulate his image, words, and legacy. For Baldwin, praise for King by the likes of Beck and Palin, coupled with the conservative right's use of the civil rights leader to justify civil disobedience, and even uncivil disobedience, raise all sorts of questions, the most important of which are addressed in a very lucid fashion in this chapter. Baldwin's reflections are clearly a challenge to Clarence Jones's suggestion that King, were he alive today, would have no serious problem with the Beck rally and the larger right-wing conservative agenda.

Chapter 1 provides the criteria for assessing or making judgments about Clarence B. Jones and his works in chapter 2. Chapter 2 examines the question of Clarence B. Jones's relationship to King, and also Jones's effort to redefine King for this current age. This chapter is also provided by Baldwin, whose approach is highly analytical and critical. Baldwin concludes that Jones's treatment of King in both *What Would Martin Say?* and *Behind the Dream* does capture an important dimension of this fascinating figure; namely, his image as the face of the modern civil rights movement. The problem, Baldwin argues, is that Jones seemingly inflates his importance as part of King's inner circle, shows little appreciation for the moral and religious bases of King's thought, and actually echoes claims made over time by polemicists and propagandists on the right side of the religious and political spectrums, especially when it comes to issues such as the current black civil rights leadership, anti-Semitism, affirmative action, terrorism, and war. Baldwin also makes it clear that Jones goes much further than others on the right in his assessment of how King would address issues like illegal immigration, anti-Semitism, and violence and human destruction. Even so, Jones is treated as part of a much greater right-wing, conservative effort to use and misuse King for selfish purposes. This chapter, together with chapter 1, actually frames the general concern of *The Domestication of Martin Luther King Jr.*, and how it has arisen in relationship to the ideas put forth by both Jones and right-wing conservatives concerning King. These first two chapters also open the way to more topic specific concerns raised by the other contributors to this volume—concerns prompted primarily by a careful reading of Jones.

King and the question of black leadership is the focus of chapter 3. Here Rosetta E. Ross, an ethicist who has written extensively on women in the civil rights movement, and Shirley T. Geiger, a political scientist who specializes in race and politics, consider the current state of social and political leadership and make assertions about what King might say *to* and *about* African American leaders. For Ross and Geiger, the Congressional Black Caucus (CBC), which stemmed from the electoral political process during the civil rights movement, is the "logical representation of contemporary black leadership." They go on to establish points of agreement and disagreement between themselves and Jones around the question of what King *might* say about the qualities that current black leaders should embody.

Toward the end of chapter 3, Ross and Geiger explain what the life of King and of Ruby Hurley, a King contemporary who was active with the NAACP from the early 1940s until her death in 1980, might say to and mean for today's black leaders. Ross and Geiger maintain that excellence in both leadership and followership was characteristic of both King and Hurley to some extent, and that both consistently demonstrated vision, commitment, and responsibility. Even so, Ross and Geiger conclude that a leadership model different from King's and more like Hurley's, who advocated and represented a more group-centered leadership model, is needed today. This conclusion evidently undermines Jones's suggestion that King remains the quintessential model of leadership for our times. In any case, much of the strength and appeal of this chapter rest in Ross and Geiger's own definition of *leadership*, and in how they use the leadership qualities highlighted by Clarence Jones as a lens through which to examine the life and contributions of King and Hurley.

Walter E. Fluker, an ethicist, King scholar, and authority in the area of ethical leadership, takes up the question of King and black leadership from yet another angle in chapter 4. Inspired by his reading of Touré's *Who's Afraid of Post-Blackness?: What It Really Means to Be Black Now* (2011), Fluker explores how we might understand King and his style of and attitude toward leadership in this age of postmodernism and postblackness. Fluker is particularly concerned about how Clarence Jones appropriates King in defense of what he sees as the essential black leadership qualities for this current age. Fluker concludes that leadership today must be understood as *global*, and we have to determine what this means in this postmodern, postblack era. Fluker goes on to critique Jones for his failure to understand this, and for being trapped in the discourse of the civil rights period, a discourse limited by race and identity politics.

Fluker's chapter really confronts us with new ways of thinking not only about King but also about blackness and black leadership in this new century and millennium. In a provocative conclusion, Fluker argues that King's concept of the "great world house," set forth in his *Where Do We Go from Here: Chaos or Community?* (1967), still has some meaning, particularly as we develop a sense of leadership that is logical, timely, and relevant in this age of globalization. The point is that we must not be constrained by Jones's understanding and definition of black leadership, which is based on the model passed down from the civil rights movement. Indeed, the shifting realities of race and racial expectations demand something different.

Chapter 5 was written by Cheryl A. Kirk-Duggan, a theologian and authority in womanist and feminist studies, who is widely known for her scholarship on the intersection of theology, justice, and violence. Here Kirk-Duggan examines moral capital amid King's plagiarism and acts of adultery, with some attention to the problematics these pose in the context of African American leadership. Kirk-Duggan takes a fourfold approach. First, she provides an overview of celebratory moments and of acts of plagiarism and adultery in King's life. Second, she explores notions of moral capital and how power, prestige, and vulnerability perpetrate corruption. Third, Kirk-Duggan, with King in mind, analyzes the practice of putting people on pedestals, or of raising them to the space of messianic complex, as problematic for black leadership. Finally, she exposes the problems that arise when these exaggerated notions of leadership become paradigmatic for pastoral leadership in the black community.

Kirk-Duggan is highly critical of King while recognizing, at the same time, that he brought certain unique gifts and talents to black leadership during his time. Maintaining that "people who live large often have large flaws," Kirk-Duggan reminds us that King was "human" and thus "a flawed person." One finds here an insightful critique of both King's person and leadership, dimensions that get lost in Clarence Jones's tendency to highlight King's strengths while minimizing or ignoring his moral weaknesses and failures.

In chapter 6, Rufus Burrow Jr., a theological ethicist and King scholar, ruminates about King's sexual excursions as well as his sexism toward movement women such as Ella Baker and Septima Clark, a subject about which Clarence Jones is silent in his books. Using a somewhat different approach from that of Kirk-Duggan, Burrow treats King's philandering in light of his theological and ethical claims. Having grown up in a fundamentalist Christian household, King was taught the ethic of marital fidelity and seemed to accept it in principle throughout his life, notwithstanding behavior that contradicted it. Moreover, as a personalist theologian, he was committed to an ethic of human dignity, which, according to Burrow, should have buttressed his ethic of marital fidelity such that he should have been able to remain faithful to his spouse. Burrow proposes no answers for King's persistent infidelity, but considers possible reasons for it, noting particularly that in his ethical outlook King, like thinkers such as Walter Rauschenbusch and Reinhold Niebuhr, who influenced his intellectual development, focused more on social than personal morality. Moreover, Burrow reminds us that King was thoroughly human and flawed in one way or another like every other human being. Thus, if sexual misconduct had not been his Achilles' heel, something else likely would have been.

Burrow devotes special attention to King's sermon, "Unfulfilled Dreams," preached at Atlanta's Ebenezer Baptist Church a month and a day before his assassination, and concludes that whatever else King was grappling with in that sermon, he was, in a round about way, struggling with his conscience because of his womanizing. In that sermon, Burrow argues, King seemed to be struggling to confess his failings to his home church family, but could not quite do it. Burrow also touches on Coretta King's reaction to her husband's stance on women, and also her essential failure to address allegations, made in Ralph D. Abernathy's autobiography, *And the Walls Came Tumbling Down* (1989), that King engaged in sexual relations the night before he was assassinated. Burrow's treatment of King serves as a necessary challenge to the hagiographical tone that marks many of Clarence Jones' claims about the civil rights leader.

In chapter 7, Traci C. West, an ethicist and specialist in African American studies, treats the misuse of King in relation to the gay rights cause. West discusses the political use of King by supporters and opponents of same-gender marriage, both of which make King the moral authority and compass for their own particular viewpoints, agenda, and causes. West finds the use of King in both cases to be highly problematic and even unjustifiable. Perhaps more than any other contributor to this volume, she is highly critical of those who deify King in continuous efforts to decipher what he would say today about gay rights, same-sex marriage, or any other issue that sparks widespread political debate. Indeed, West, in a scathing critique of Clarence Jones and advocates for and against same-sex marriage, discourages the very idea of setting King up as "the great man" with the answer to virtually every social concern we confront and address. For West, this is really the misuse of the King legacy at its worst.

West acknowledges Jones's failure to include gay rights in his discussion of what King *would say* about contemporary social and political causes. At the same time, she makes it clear that King is not a moral authority when it comes to gay rights and same-gender marriage in our times. West concedes, however, that speculation about King's views on gay rights does provide space for a closer examination of the 1950s and 1960s civil rights movement and the role assumed by Bayard Rustin, a black gay man and important freedom fighter. In other words, the case of Rustin provides a major point of reference for understanding how King and the civil rights movement responded to gays. By raising and addressing probing questions about the political use of King, West actually affords hard insights into how we might properly view and appropriate King in both his time and our time.

Chapter 8 highlights some of the questions surrounding Clarence Jones's treatment of King in relation to the ongoing realities of race in

America. Here Lewis V. Baldwin declares that Jones's claims about what King *would say* today about issues like anti-Semitism, affirmative action, and illegal immigration are tainted by a rather limited and distorted view of race, and also by the baseless assumption that we now live in a postracial society. Baldwin agrees with Jones's contention that King still has something substantive to contribute to the discourse on and discussions about race, but he concludes that Jones and King could not be further apart on this issue. Baldwin also questions Jones's tendency to use race as the lens through which to assess what King *would say* about anti-Semitism, affirmative action, and illegal immigration.

On another level, Baldwin feels that Jones is too wedded to the racial concepts and roles of the civil rights era of the 1960s to provide a serious and reliable analysis of King's relevance for the contemporary age, especially when it comes to the connections between race, anti-Semitism, affirmative action, and illegal immigration. Baldwin feels that the contemporary dialogue around issues of race must be reframed and expanded beyond the black-white paradigm. Even so, Baldwin concedes that King was far ahead of his time in addressing issues like anti-Semitism and affirmative action, and their potential impact on the continuing quest for the beloved community. Thus, Baldwin writes about the enduring power of King's thought and how King's ideas, to a greater degree than Jones's, might build on and enrich current discussion and debate about how to respond to present challenges confronting "the least of these," or those who suffer on grounds of race and economics.

Chapter 9 focuses on King, nonviolence, and the moral universe. Here Rufus Burrow Jr. convincingly argues for King's belief in the existence of an objective moral order in the universe, created and sustained by God, grounded his belief in and practice of nonviolence, a topic he explores at much greater length in his *Personalism: A Critical Introduction* (1999) and *God and Human Dignity: The Personalism, Theology, and Ethics of Martin Luther King Jr.* (2006). Nonviolence for King was love in action and the most moral and effective principle for social action, especially since it is in deep accord with the essence of the moral order and the human desire for freedom, justice, peace, dignity, and community. Burrow makes this point emphatically while highlighting King's rejection of violence as both immoral and impractical. Burrow stresses the moral dimensions of King's nonviolence, and particularly its consistency with the Christian ethic, as part of his trenchant critique of Clarence Jones's claim that King would be open in some cases to the employment of violence as both a personal and social ethic today. Burrow categorically rejects Jones's suggestion that King would possibly be open to military options in dealing with Iraq and Islamic terrorists.

Burrow develops this subject from another angle in chapter 10, as he discusses King and the tragic phenomenon of black against black violence and crime. Jones hints at the problem at points in his *What Would Martin Say?*, but, unlike Burrow, fails to bring a depth of critical and analytical insight and perspective to it. According to Burrow, King was familiar with the problem as far back as the Montgomery bus boycott (1955–56), as King's writings indicate. King wrote and spoke against black intracommunity violence and crime then as well as in the later stages of the civil rights movement (e.g., during the Chicago campaign). Burrow contends that Jones's discussion of the tragedy of intracommunity violence and homicide among young black males does not go far enough, and that Jones implies, by omission, that King was not aware of this phenomenon. Burrow goes on to show that the magnitude of that problem is such that the Center for Disease Control characterized young black males as "an endangered species" in the 1980s. Burrow confronts us with a sense of the urgency of the moment as it relates to the need to reclaim certain of King's ideas in order to avoid the possibility of intra-community genocide.

The problem of black-on-black violence has worsened since the eighties, as the homicide rate in places like Chicago, Illinois, indicates, and Burrow struggles with questions about the viability of applying King's ethic of nonviolent resistance to this epidemic. Burrow concludes that although King did not schedule or lead nonviolent demonstrations against the problem of black-on-black violence, it is difficult to imagine that he would not have done so had he lived longer. This observation is certainly consistent with King's conviction that social evil in all forms should necessarily be exposed and challenged. In a striking conclusion, Burrow argues that there may be possibilities for the application of King's nonviolent ethic to black intracommunity violence and crime, but he also maintains that, because of the nature of this tragic phenomenon, it may be necessary to first get bloodied in order to prepare the way for nonviolence. For Burrow, this is a provocative idea, and he is certain that King would not agree with such a proposal. Because he likens intracommunity violence and homicide among young black boys to a *borderline situation* (i.e., a situation in which there seems to be no possible solution), Burrow believes that his proposal remains a viable option.

Chapter 11 is essentially a well-crafted and insightful response to chapter 7 in Clarence Jones's *What Would Martin Say?*," which is entitled, "What Martin Would Say about Who Killed Him?" Written by Michael G. Long, a King scholar and professor of religion, this chapter begins on a critical note, dismissing Jones's claims as "groundless" and "unknowable." Long contends that predictions about what King would say today about death or anything else cannot be established with certainty, a point that is taken seriously throughout *The Domestication of Martin Luther King Jr.*, despite its many claims and conclusions. Long chooses to stress what King *did* say about death in general, and, more specifically, about the possibility of his own death. Long concludes that King ultimately conquered the fear of death and deeply believed that the power of death would be defeated in the universe.

King's approach to both life and death was philosophical and theological, and Long makes this abundantly clear. As a philosopher, King entertained the question of the reality and inevitability of death, particularly in light of his activities as an audacious prophet, and as a theologian he affirmed the realness of God's presence in the midst of death, and of salvation and immortality after death. Long's chapter reminds us that King never separated living well from dying well, a point that Long develops at much greater length in his fine volume, *Martin Luther King Jr. on Creative Living* (2004). After reading the Long chapter, one is likely to read both King and Jones with fresh eyes.

In chapter 12, the last in this volume, George Russell Seay Jr., a theologian and emerging King scholar, raises and explores questions surrounding the symbolic meanings of both the Martin Luther King, Jr. annual birthday celebration and the Martin Luther King Jr. memorial on the National Mall in Washington DC. Seay argues that both are a reminder of how the guardianship of the King legacy has been turned over to the American governmental establishment and other forces that will use this for self-serving purposes. Seay goes on to associate the King holiday and the King memorial with what he calls "icon making," which places King in the pantheon of American saints who serve the best interests of American civil religion. In other words, these honors are a part of a carefully calculated effort to sanitize King's image and legacy; to purge these of their prophetic posture. Consequently, the prophetic King who attacked capitalism, criticized America's foreign policy, and warned of God's judgment upon the nation is replaced by a harmless, gentle pastor who merely preached love and nonviolence while calling for racial integration.

Seay believes that there is yet another motive behind the annual King Day celebration and the King national memorial. He contends that both are part of a greater strategy to convince Americans that we now live in a postracial society, especially when considered in relationship to Barack Obama's rise to the US presidency. Seay wants us to realize that the King holiday and the King memorial carry little positive meaning as long as white privilege and discrimination against blacks and other people of color are still functioning and actively blocking equal opportunity to the material and immaterial goods of the society. Clearly, Seay provides suggestions here for advancing the race debate to new levels of intensity and sophistication.

Seay wonders if Americans, even black Americans, are prepared to rethink the symbolism behind the King holiday and the King national memorial. Seay recognizes that celebrations of King can either cause us to rededicate ourselves to the unfinished agenda of his holy crusade, or to continue to devote ourselves to honoring King without any commitment to the goals for which he struggled and gave his life. The choice, Seay concludes, is ours, and the decision we make will inevitably impact both the future of race relations and the nation's capacity to live out the true meaning of her democratic creed. Here Seay takes on an issue that is essentially ignored by Clarence B. Jones, namely, King symbolism and how it is to be properly understood and interpreted in our culture.

The contributors to this volume approach King afresh, from their own viewpoints as academics in the early twenty-first century. If there is a single, unifying theme in this book, it centers on the nuances of King's thought, and on how he should be understood in relationship to many of the issues raised by Clarence B. Jones and the conservative right. We have tried to be very careful in recasting King as an idealist and activist for our times. As suggested earlier, the general idea is to critique Jones and right-wing approaches to King, while also contributing to a more informed, thoughtful, and balanced portrayal of King and his legacy. Each contributor understands that there was a prophetic quality to so much of what King said and did, and that this must be understood and treated in historically astute and literarily sensitive ways. The chapters combined lend credence to the idea that King remains not only a civil rights leader and a social activist with a global vision, but also a theologian and an ethicist who continues to provoke and challenge us on topics ranging from religion to spirituality, from politics to economics, and from national social policy to globalization theory and praxis.

Almost a half century has elapsed since King's voice was silenced. Also, the ranks of former civil rights activists who actually knew and worked closely with King are rapidly depleting, and there should be more of a sense of urgency in terms of gathering more of their testimonies. After all, this is essential to any discussion of King's significance and relevance in this modern era of globalization. These testimonies, as a supplementary source that builds on what King himself left us in terms of his social witness and praxis, can make it easier for us to at least make certain claims about how King would address the annoying and seemingly invincible moral, political, and spiritual problems that still haunt our society and world.

Much is evident today in terms of the shifting scholarly terrain as it relates to King studies. All the contributors to this volume are mindful of this trend, for they have contributed to it through their own teaching, research, and scholarship. But *The Domestication of Martin Luther King, Jr.* is not a conscious effort on our part to fundamentally reconfigure the landscape of King studies. However, we do hope this book will contribute, in some small way, to the marking of a turning point in the appropriation of King's important, complex, and often misunderstood legacy. If this happens, our objective will be more than sufficiently realized.

Lewis V. Baldwin
Vanderbilt University
Nashville, Tennessee

Rufus Burrow Jr.
Christian Theological Seminary
Indianapolis, Indiana

1

Distorted Characterizations
Images of Martin Luther King Jr. in the Conservative Mind

LEWIS V. BALDWIN

Current streams of the religious and political right originated as essentially a conservative reaction to the civil rights crusade of the 1950s and 1960s. Martin Luther King Jr. spoke about "the fanaticism of the Right" in the sixties, and he lamented "the marriage between the Radical Right and the segregationists." King included in his portrait of right-wing conservatism white politicians from both political parties and even white Christian fundamentalists and evangelicals who were, as he saw it, determined "to turn back the tide of history." He urged these elements to swallow "their prejudices in the interest of progress, prosperity, and world peace."[1] Little did King know that "the Radical Right" of his day would prepare much of the ground for the blossoming of a New Right in the 1970s and 1980s, as the Moral Majority, Inc., political organizers like Richard Viguerie, the politically charged preachers and programs of the electronic church, and scores of rigid pro-life groups, anti-gay and anti-ERA movements, pro-family advocates, pro–prayer in the public schools proponents, and anti–sex education and anti-pornography

---

1. Martin Luther King Jr., "Address at the Meeting of the Southern Association of Political Scientists" (13 November 1964), unpublished version, The Library and Archives of the Martin Luther King Jr. Center for Nonviolent Social Change, Inc., Atlanta, Georgia, 1–2.

constituencies joined forces in a struggle against their liberal counterparts for the soul of America.[2]

This chapter traces developments in the right-wing conservative assault on King's image, ideas, and dream of equality, from the 1950s and 1960s up to the present time. It maintains that the various portraits of King created by parties on the right over time have virtually no resemblance to the civil rights leader assassinated in Memphis, Tennessee, on April 4, 1968. It further contends that since King's death, the New Right forces have been consistently involved in calculated efforts to either destroy or domesticate King's image. At the very least, they are responsible for much of the confusion that surrounds King's identity and the ideas, values, and causes for which he gave his life.

Prophet without Honor: The Radical Right and the Vilification of King, 1955–1968

Right-wing conservatives were largely united in their views on Martin Luther King Jr. during the civil rights years. From the time of the Montgomery bus boycott in 1955–56, conservative voices in the churches and in the Republican and Democratic Parties were suspicious of the civil rights leader, his methods, and his vision of the beloved community, or a truly integrated society. Although King endured remarkably few public, verbal attacks from white church leaders in the late fifties, or "in the early stages of his ascendancy as the nation's most prominent civil rights preacher,"[3] he was perceived by many white fundamentalists and evangelicals, especially in the South, as a misguided religious extremist who, by his very involvement in "transitory social problems," was renouncing Scripture and the true gospel of Jesus Christ. In Montgomery, E. Stanley Frazier, minister of the St. James Methodist Church, and Henry L. Lyons Jr., pastor of the Highland Avenue Baptist Church, were among the first religious conservatives to judge King in these terms. In their minds, King's integrationist philosophy and nonviolent methods were not only unbiblical and lacking in theological substance but also morally indefensible and socially disruptive.[4]

---

2. Gabriel Fackre, *The Religious Right and Christian Right* (Grand Rapids: Eerdmans, 1982), 1–3.

3. Andrew M. Manis, "'Dying from the Neck Up': Southern Baptist Resistance to the Civil Rights Movement," *Baptist History and Heritage* 34/1 (1999) 36–38; and Bill J. Leonard, "A Theology for Racism: Southern Fundamentalists and the Civil Rights Movement," in ibid., 52–53.

4. Donald E. Collins, *When the Church Bell Rang Racist: The Methodist Church and*

On the political side of the spectrum, figures such as Governor John Patterson of Alabama, Senator James O. Eastland of Mississippi, Senator Herman E. Talmadge of Georgia, and Governor Orval Faubus of Arkansas appeared less interested in King's biblicism and theology, and more concerned about his challenge to the Southern values and ways of life. They regarded King as a public nuisance, and sought to use their power and prestige to limit his effectiveness and to defeat or hinder the civil rights cause.[5] More extreme factions in the radical right, such as the Ku Klux Klan (KKK) and the White Citizens Council (WCC), went even further, occasionally threatening King's life and the lives of those who joined him in the Montgomery bus boycott and other nonviolent activities. Attacks on King from these smaller but more rabid elements of the radical right escalated as the Montgomery bus protest moved toward a successful climax, and as King became increasingly identified as the chief symbol of the civil rights movement as a whole.[6] The widespread belief in these circles was that King was a self-serving, publicity-seeking troublemaker who had to be silenced completely. In any case, King, committed to a crusade that required much energy, resources, and sacrifice, chose to devote little time to responding to his opponents on the radical right in the late 1950s.

Conservative opposition to King had crystallized by 1960, as the civil rights leader sought to expand the reach of his nonviolent direct action beyond the focus on bus segregation to an assault on the broader structures of southern Jim Crow. King had become a well-known fixture in the popular imagination by this time, and even a few white religious conservatives made overtures toward him, at the risk of their own reputations. The widely known evangelist Billy Graham, the high priest of American evangelicalism, invited King to pray at his crusade in Madison Square Garden in New York in July 1957, a decision that brought a wave of harsh criticism from both religious and political conservatives, especially in the white South.[7] When the

---

the Civil Rights Movement in Alabama (Macon, GA: Mercer University Press, 1998), 27–28; Martin Luther King Jr., Stride toward Freedom: The Montgomery Story (New York: Harper & Row, 1958), 115–16; and Manis, "'Dying from the Neck Up,'" 38.

5. James M. Washington, ed., A Testament of Hope: The Essential Writings and Speeches of Martin Luther King, Jr. (New York: HarperCollins, 1991), 93, 320; Clayborne Carson, ed., The Autobiography of Martin Luther King, Jr. (New York: Warner, 1998), 109; Clayborne Carson, et al., eds., The Papers of Martin Luther King Jr., vol. 5, Threshold of a New Decade, January 1959–December 1960 (Berkeley: University of California Press, 2005), 25, 264, and 484.

6. King himself offered a probing analysis of these methods of opposition from the right. See King, Stride toward Freedom, 108–50.

7. Soon after King's appearance at Graham's crusade, Graham preached a sermon denouncing "the structural methods of the civil rights movement in favor of individual

social ethicist Henlee Barnette and some of his colleagues invited King to speak at the Southern Baptist Theological Seminary in Louisville, Kentucky, in April 1961, criticism came from the leadership and laypersons in many of the local congregations of the Southern Baptist Convention (SBC). More than thirty of its congregations in Alabama voted to cease sending financial contributions to the seminary.[8]

Needless to say, most on the right, and especially what King called "the Radical Right," associated the civil rights leader with values that they considered un-Christian, immoral, and un-American. This was most certainly the case for Robert H. W. Welch of the John Birch Society, who described King, in a pamphlet titled, *Two Revolutions at Once*, as "a troublemaker pushing pro-communist programs."[9] For factions in the Ku Klux Klan (KKK), King represented something considerably worse, especially since he had drawn gullible and misguided whites into his movement. Thus, Klansmen consistently denounced "Martin Lucifer Coon" and his "Jew-conspiracy of race mixing."[10]

The Birmingham campaign of 1963, perhaps more than any other during the civil rights era, exposed the glaring tensions between King and white religious conservatives. Launched against the business community, with the goal of eliminating segregation at lunch counters and in hiring practices in department stores, the campaign drew comments from the most moderate and the most radical right wing voices. In April 1963, Billy Graham questioned the timing of the activities spearheaded by King and his Southern

---

conversion," which proved that he, despite what appeared to be his friendly gestures toward King, held essentially the same position as King's fundamentalist detractors. See Clayborne Carson et al., eds., *The Papers of Martin Luther King, Jr.*, vol. 4 *Symbol of the Movement, January 1957—December 1958* (Berkeley: University of California Press, 2000), 238 and 264–66; Edward Lee Moore, "Billy Graham and Martin Luther King Jr.: An Inquiry into White and Black Revivalistic Traditions" (PhD diss., Vanderbilt University, 1979), 454–56; and Michael G. Long, *Billy Graham and the Beloved Community: America's Evangelist and the Dream of Martin Luther King Jr.* (New York: Palgrave Macmillan, 2006), 22.

8. Interestingly enough, King was well received at the Southern Baptist Seminary, and some of the faculty and administrators approached him about the possibility of teaching homiletics there. King, of course, graciously declined the offer due to heavy civil rights commitments and concerns about what would inevitably be the hostile reaction of many Southern Baptists. See Manis, "'Dying from the Neck Up,'" 40.

9. Robert Welch, "Two Revolutions at Once," reprinted in *The New Americanism, and Other Speeches and Essays* (Boston: Western Island, 1966), 203; and Daniel Levitas, *The Terrorist Next Door: The Militia Movement and the Radical Right* (New York: Dunne, 2002), 71.

10. David M. Chalmers, *Hooded Americanism: The History of the Ku Klux Klan*, 2nd ed. (New York: New Viewpoints, 1981), 379.

Christian Leadership Conference (SCLC), and in response to King's call for civil disobedience, urged his "good personal friend" to "put on the brakes a little bit."[11] A similar challenge came from eight Alabama clergymen in a letter to the *Birmingham News*, which labeled King an "outsider" and his activities "unwise and untimely." These clergymen saw King's "extreme measures," which involved acts of civil disobedience, as a threat to "the principles of law and order and common sense." Like Graham, they also believed that the civil rights cause could be better "pressed in the courts."[12] King responded in his *Letter from the Birmingham City Jail* (1963), which affirmed on moral and rational grounds his right to protest anywhere injustice exists,[13] but this accomplished little in terms of checking the conservative tendency to vilify King. By this time, many on both the religious and political right had become unalterably convinced that King was indeed a communist, and therefore a monumental threat to the national security.[14] For many on the most extreme right of the religious and political continuum, this alone justified any action to silence and perhaps even destroy King.

The fundamentalist preacher Jerry Falwell, who would later figure prominently in the rise of the New Right, suggested as much and more in his sermon, "Ministers and Marches," preached from the pulpit of his Thomas Road Baptist Church in Lynchburg, Virginia, in March 1965. Already known for his "scriptural defenses of segregation,"[15] Falwell questioned "the sincerity and nonviolent intentions" of King and other "civil rights leaders" who, as he put it, "are known to have left-wing associations." Falwell felt that King was a tool of the communists, and that "the Communists, as they do in all parts of the world," were "taking advantage of a tense situation in our land" and "exploiting every incident to bring about violence and bloodshed." Falwell went on to challenge King's view of the proper role of the Christian minister in the church and society, and also King's reading of the biblical exodus as the story of every people struggling for liberation. The minister is called to "preach the Word," Falwell declared, and he insisted that the

11. "Billy Graham Urges Restraint in Sit-Ins," *The New York Times*, April 18, 1963, 21.

12. S. Jonathan Bass, *Blessed Are the Peacemakers: Martin Luther King Jr., Eight White Religious Leaders, and the "Letter from Birmingham Jail"* (Baton Rouge: Louisiana State University Press, 2001), 2–8.

13. Martin Luther King Jr., *Why We Can't Wait* (New York: The New American Library Association, 1963), 76–95.

14. Probably in response to this senseless charge, King wrote and published his sermon, "How Should a Christian View Communism," in Martin Luther King Jr., *Strength to Love* (1963; reprinted, Philadelphia: Fortress, 1981), 96–105.

15. Leo P. Ribuffo, *The Old Christian Right: The Protestant Far Right from the Great Depression to the Cold War* (Philadelphia: Temple University Press, 1983), 264.

exodus is actually "a type of the sinners experience before he is converted."[16] Falwell epitomized the growing conservative tendency to question both King's knowledge of the Bible and his devotion to Christian orthodoxy.

King's growing public critiques of capitalism and the United States' military adventure in Vietnam in the mid- to late sixties led some on the right to question not only his judgment and motives but his patriotism as well. Such actions reinforced the image of King as a communist, a charge that evoked much emotion, particularly in this period of lingering McCarthyite hysteria. Gerald L. K. Smith, the conservative clergyman and political agitator, cast King in the image of "a Moscow-trained revolutionist."[17] The sheer hatred of King reached fever pitch among some on the radical right, as church leaders like the fundamentalist Jerry Falwell, politicians such as the Republican senator Barry Goldwater of Arizona, and officials in the John Birch Society warned their fellow Americans of the danger posed by the radical, left-wing ties of leading civil rights activists.[18] King was demonized in white ecclesiastical circles, in the political arena and in much of the public square, and the threats against his life, which were already quite serious, became even more ominous.

Fundamentalists in the Southern Baptist Convention, who equated the Christian ethic with capitalism and strongly endorsed the Vietnam War as a struggle against communism, were known to attack King with the ferocity of wild animals. John R. Rice, the Baptist fundamentalist, evangelist, and editor of the *Sword of the Lord*, headquartered in Murfreesboro, Tennessee, argued that "although religious infidels boost him as a Christian, Dr. Martin Luther King has openly declared that he does not believe the Bible. He is not a Christian in the historic sense of holding to the great essentials of the Christian faith; he is 'a minster' who doesn't preach the gospel, doesn't save

---

16. See Perry D. Young, *God's Bullies: Native Reflections on Preachers and Politics* (New York: Holt, Rinehart & Winston, 1982), 310–17; and Flo Conway and Jim Siegelman, *Holy Terror: The Fundamentalist War on America's Freedoms in Religion, Politics and Our Private Lives* (New York: Dell, 1984), 85–86.

17. Ribuffo, *The Old Christian Right*, 234.

18. Young, *God's Bullies*, 310–11; and Michael K. Honey, *Going Down Jericho Road: The Memphis Strike, Martin Luther King's Last Campaign* (New York: Norton, 2007), 46. Goldwater's strongest statement on King's supposed links with Communism is uttered in *The Promised Land, 1968*, a film in the Eyes on the Prize Series. Goldwater voted against the Civil Rights Bill of 1964, and actively encouraged "conservative southern defections from the Democratic Party." See David L. Chappell, *Inside Agitators: White Southerners in the Civil Rights Movement* (Baltimore: Johns Hopkins University Press, 1994), 205.

souls... He does not believe in the Christian faith nor trust in the virgin-born Savior."[19]

Archer Weniger, a fundamentalist Baptist pastor from California, had made essentially the same comments in an earlier statement in Rice's *Sword of the Lord*. He called King "a modernist" and "a pro-communist," and contended that King was "by definition an apostate" because he denies that hell is "a place of literal burning fire."[20] While deploring King's rejection of "the virgin birth of Christ," Noel Smith, a Tennessean and the editor of the *Baptist Bible Tribune*, located in Springfield, Missouri, also maintained that King was "guilty of a palpable falsehood when he implies that the New Testament and the practices of the early Christians authenticate his objectives and methods." "The preaching of the physical resurrection of Christ—which Dr. King must logically deny—was the Christian's power against the Roman Empire," Smith continued, "not negative sit-ins, sit-downs, lie-downs, and marches." Smith went on to conclude that "Dr. King has nothing in common with the Christ of the Bible"—that "Dr. King's objective and methods have nothing in common with the early Christians."[21] Clearly, Smith's reading of Scripture, history, and tradition was not as careful and perceptive as King's, for the early Christians' practice of nonviolent civil disobedience is firmly established in all of these sources. At any rate, King's theological and biblical liberalism proved easy prey for white fundamentalist Christians, who bitterly opposed his structural methods of nonviolent direct action in favor of revivalism and individual conversion, and who adamantly refused to accept his definition of *agape* love as central to the Christian religion.[22]

---

19. *Sword of the Lord* August 19, 1964, 3; and Leonard, "A Theology for Racism," 51, 59, and 61.

20. G. Archer Weniger, "Martin Luther King, Negro Pro-Communist, Modernist," *Sword of the Lord*, November 9, 1962; and Leonard, "A Theology for Racism," 63.

21. Noel Smith, "Martin Luther King Wants a Revolution," *Baptist Bible Tribune*, April 23, 1965; and Leonard, "A Theology for Racism," 61 and 63.

22. Bill J. Leonard is right in saying that these fundamentalists were unable to accept the civil rights movement "as a national social crisis," so they dismissed it as an unwelcome "challenge to certain unchanging truths in Holy Scripture... required of all true Christians." See Leonard, "A Theology for Racism," 50. King's critics were right in noting that he rejected many orthodox views regarding the virgin birth, the afterlife, and the resurrection. But King never understood the Christian faith in terms of a subscription to doctrine, and nor did he associate it with a sense of missionary urgency and compassion. What mattered most to King was not doctrinal Christianity or missionary Christianity, but practical or applied Christianity, the very kind that his fundamentalist and evangelical opponents wished to ignore. See Lee E. Dirks, "The Essence is Love: The Theology of Martin Luther King Jr.," *National Observer* (30 December 1963), 1 and 12; and Robert James "Be" Scofield, "King's God: The Unknown Faith of Dr. Martin Luther King Jr.," *Tikkun* (December 2009).

Most white fundamentalists and evangelicals throughout the country espoused what Bill J. Leonard terms "a theology for racism," and they were simply ill prepared to deal with King's social message and theological challenge, let alone his acts of protest. Thus, they joined right-wing politicians in variously charging that the civil rights leader was motivated by an insatiable thirst for power and recognition; that he meddled too much in temporal affairs; that he was employing the rhetoric of Christianity, civil rights, and racial integration for personal glory and self-gain; that he was forsaking biblical orthodoxy for some alien philosophy; that his protest methods encouraged social and political anarchy; and that he was desperately trying to transform the gospel of Jesus Christ into some revolutionary ideology.[23]

The attacks on King by right-wing conservatives did not cease with his assassination in April 1968, as evidenced by their responses to the tragedy. Many of the hundreds of letters sent by conservatives to James Earl Ray, the alleged assassin, praised him for killing "a Coon," "a nigger Communist imposter," and "a troublemaker."[24] A group of young white evangelicals at Los Angeles Baptist College cheered loudly when informed of King's death.[25] The same occurred at the fundamentalist Bob Jones University in Greenville, South Carolina, where its president, Bob Jones Jr., denounced King as "an apostate," dismissed his social gospel as "a joke," and refused to honor President Lyndon B. Johnson's order to lower his university's flag to half-mast in memory of the civil rights leader.[26]

Many fundamentalist and evangelical clergymen either refused to mention King from their pulpits in the immediate aftermath of his death, or they underscored the lessons to be learned from the tragedy, as if to drive home the point that his tactics were self-defeating and ill advised. Echoing the thoughts of political conservatives like Senator Jesse Helms of North Carolina and Senator Strom Thurmond of South Carolina, Noel Smith declared that "King's own actions created the 'climate'" that resulted in "his death." Bob Spencer, a fundamentalist Baptist pastor from Alabama, concluded that

---

23. Manis, "'Dying from the Neck Up,'" 41 and 43; Leonard, "A Theology for Racism," 57, 61, and 63; and Lewis V. Baldwin, *The Voice of Conscience: The Church in the Mind of Martin Luther King Jr.* (New York: Oxford University Press, 2010), 156.

24. See William B. Huie, *He Slew the Dreamer: My Search, with James Earl Ray, for the Truth about the Murder of Martin Luther King* (New York: Delacorte, 1970), 207–12.

25. Stephen E. Berk, *A Time to Heal: John Perkins, Community Development, and Racial Reconciliation* (Grand Rapids: Baker, 1997), 150 and 197.

26. Leonard, "A Theology for Racism," 63. Jones maintained that "promoters of a 'social gospel' were distorting the biblical message." "There is no such thing as a social Gospel," he declared. "The Lord's message is always a message to the individual." See Martin E. Marty and R. Scott Appleby, *The Glory and the Power: The Fundamentalist Challenge to the Modern World* (Boston: Beacon, 1992), 49–50.

King "loaded the gun of his own destruction by making himself the symbol of resistance to law and order." King's efforts were "anti-Christian" because "Jesus Christ was not and is not a 'revolutionary,'" Spencer added. Spencer went on to question whether "Bible-believing Christians should mourn the making of a martyr of one who 'rejected the cardinal tenets of Biblical Christianity for the heathen philosophy of Mahatma Gandhi.'"[27]

Unlike other white fundamentalists and evangelicals, Billy Graham responded to King's death with alarm and sadness. Graham was a rare exception in this regard. Involved in a crusade in Brisbane, Australia, at the time of King's murder, Graham "led his listeners in a prayer for the slain civil rights leader," and his "bereaved family." On the surface, it appears to have been a thoughtful gesture on the part of a conservative evangelist "for a person whose philosophy and strategy he had ceased to understand, much less condone."[28] In 1957, Graham had said to a journalist that ministers had to follow King's "example of Christian love" in order to solve the race problem;[29] but the evangelist, confused by King's turn toward more radical forms of nonviolence and massive civil disobedience in the sixties, had essentially broken ties with King when King was killed. It is hard to avoid the impression that Graham's refusal to attend King's funeral in Atlanta, Georgia, on April 9, 1968, was really an indication of his unwillingness to be identified with the civil rights leader and the values for which he stood. Graham knew that any close association with King, especially in those latter years, would have put at risk his broad evangelical base in the white churches, his standing in the seductive halls of governmental power, and his special role as the de facto chaplain for Washington's elite.[30]

The right-wing conservatives about whom King spoke in 1961 remained amazingly stubborn and unified in their condemnation of and

---

27. Ibid., 63; Bob Spencer, "Dr. Martin Luther King Died by the Lawlessness He Encouraged," *Sword of the Word* (14 June 1968); Manis, "'Dying from the Neck Up,'" 38; and Lewis V. Baldwin et al., *The Legacy of Martin Luther King Jr.: The Boundaries of Law, Politics, and Religion* (Notre Dame: University of Notre Dame Press, 2002), 101 2.

28. Moore, "Billy Graham and Martin Luther King Jr.," 54 and 465–66; "Graham Sees Moral 'Sickness,'" *The San Francisco Examiner* (7 April 1968) 2; and "Crusade Information Service News" (7 April 1968) 1. It was much easier for Graham to make such a modest statement about King in another country and, hence, one should be hesitant to give him even moderate praise for this. E-mail from Peter Paris to Lewis V. Baldwin, 8 August 2011.

29. Stanley Rowland Jr., "As Billy Graham Sees His Role," *The New York Times Magazine* (21 April 1957) 19; and Moore, "Billy Graham and Martin Luther King Jr.," 454.

30. Baldwin, *The Voice of Conscience*, 162. Michael Long is right in saying that "by the time of the assassination, Graham had also sniffed at King's pie-on-the-earth theology." See Long, *Billy Graham and the Beloved Community*, 2.

rejection of the civil rights leader and his gospel of freedom. Evidently their devotion to the status quo overshadowed any inclination they may have had to look favorably on King, and to throw the weight of their financial, moral, and physical support behind his efforts. The Religious and Political Right that emerged after King's death would be similar in terms of their biblicism, theological conservatism, and approach to issues of racial injustice, but different on other levels. First, those who would constitute this New Right would be more identified with a particular wing of evangelical Christianity and the Republican Party. Second, they would be much more open than their predecessors to bringing faith claims into politics, and introducing religious language into the public discourse. Third, they would embrace a far more progressive landscape of Christian thought and practice, albeit in distorted and misdirected ways. Fourth, the Religious and Political Right that blossomed in the late 1970s and the 1980s would converge and become virtually indistinguishable, particularly in terms of mixing politics and religion in pursuit of a selective moral, social, and political agenda. Finally, the representatives of this New Right would be less united than their forerunners in their images of and approaches to King and his mission and legacy.[31] King would be rediscovered, transformed, manipulated, distorted, and used by some on the right in defense of their own protest activities and political and public policy goals, while others on the right would continue to vehemently denounce King as a meaningless and undesirable symbol in American life and culture.

Can the Dream Live? The New Right and the Meaning of the King Legacy

The vitality of religion in public life should be accounted as a fundamental aspect of the legacy of Martin Luther King Jr. In the 1950s and '60s, King and other liberal clergy brought the resources of the Christian faith and tradition to bear on public policy matters, political decision making, and the practical problems of daily life. King believed that religious convictions could play a positive and constructive role in politics and in other matters of public consequence. The church-centered movement he led encouraged public expressions of faith, while also reintroducing the themes of freedom, sacrifice, redemptive suffering, hope, and deliverance into the nation's public faith.[32] The conversation about how religion should function in public

31. Lewis V. Baldwin, "The Perversion of Public Religion," *Orbis* 5/7 (April 2006) 12.

32. John Dixon Elder, "Martin Luther King and American Civil Religion," *Harvard*

life was advanced to new levels of sophistication and intensity, and many questions that so often emerge at the interface of religion and politics were answered. The New Right that emerged in the 1970s and '80s benefitted enormously from this dimension of the legacy of King and the civil rights movement, even as it opposed the continuing efforts toward the completion of the unfinished agenda of King's sacred crusade.[33] In other words, King and the civil rights movement inadvertently strengthened the more conservative strands of American Christianity, particularly evangelicalism and certain facets of fundamentalism, by enabling them to shed the image of segregationists while becoming mainstream, and by providing a model of how to use religion as a form of political mobilization and activism.[34]

Opinions about King on the conservative right had begun to shift and splinter when the Moral Majority Inc., "the centerpiece of the Religious Right,"[35] was founded in 1979. Jerry Falwell, a staunch King critic in the 1960s, was the founder of this organization of politically active Christian fundamentalists, which also included a few conservative Catholics and orthodox Jews. In launching the Moral Majority's crusade against abortion rights, pornography, gay rights, the Equal Rights Amendment (ERA), and other perceived threats to the traditional family structure, Falwell, perhaps with King's challenge to unjust laws in mind, emphatically stated that his ultimate loyalty was to a higher moral law.[36] In a stunning statement in 1980, Falwell publicly rejected his 1965 sermon, "Ministers and Marches," which questioned the legitimacy of King's civil disobedience and nonviolent direct action campaigns, and declared, "In recent months, God has been calling me to do more than just preach—He has called me to take action. I have a divine mandate to go right into the halls of Congress and fight for laws that will save America."[37] A year later, Falwell evoked the memory of the civil rights leader, noting that "I feel that what King was doing is exactly what we are doing."[38] An evangelical scholar speculated that "given the change in"

Divinity Bulletin, new ser. 1/3 (Spring 1968) 17–18; and Baldwin, "The Perversion of Public Religion," 12.

33. Baldwin, et al., *The Legacy of Martin Luther King Jr.*, 102.

34. I am indebted to the British King scholar Adam Fairclough for much of this insight. See e-mail from Adam Fairclough to Lewis V. Baldwin, 23 August 2011.

35. Fackre, *The Religious Right and Christian Right*, 1.

36. Ibid., 1–2, 14, and 28; and "Falwell Shaped Religion, Politics," *The Tennessean* (16 May 2007) 1A and 11A.

37. Quoted in Conway and Siegelman, *Holy Terror*, 86. Also see Richard J. Neuhaus and Michael Cromartie, eds., *Piety and Politics: Evangelicals and Fundamentalists Confront the World* (Lanham, MD: University Press of America, 1987), 12.

38. Quoted in John J. Ansbro, *Martin Luther King Jr.: Nonviolent Strategies and*

Falwell's "views toward Martin Luther King's methods, it is possible that acts of nonviolence and civil disobedience will be entertained by the Religious Right, a violation of civil law under the claims of a higher moral law."[39]

Unquestionably, Falwell was transformed by his encounter with the Christian public testimony and activism of King, and he became a prime example of how King continued to live in the right-wing conservative imagination, albeit in a strange and distorted fashion. The fundamentalist leader's "acknowledged about-face on the validity of church involvement in civil affairs" testified to the conservative revision of the historical image of King, at least on some levels.[40] Falwell's revised perspective on King and the civil rights movement was echoed by Cal Thomas, the Moral Majority's director of public relations, who suggested that "if the abortion problem is not solved through legal means," then "radical action" similar to that taken by King would be inevitable: "The strength of Martin Luther King came through his willingness to go to jail. By dramatizing his belief in black equality, he went to work on the conscience of the nation. Those who regard abortion as infanticide have got to show that this is not just a bunch of philosophic beliefs they are holding—that they are prepared to suffer in order to stop the killing."[41]

In rare cases, figures on the Religious Right also acknowledged the legitimacy of King's legacy as it related to the continuing struggle against racial inequality. In 1989, the Reverend Richard Land, director of the Southern Baptist Convention's Christian Life Commission, mildly condemned the problem of racism while offering a tribute to King. Land praised King "for articulating themes of liberty and justice that are embodied in age-old Sunday school lessons and the Pledge of Allegiance."[42] However, Land's widely known opposition to affirmative action and to public policy initiatives that benefited the poor and outcast inevitably raised questions about the sincerity of his statements.

Writing in the 1980s, Daniel C. Maguire, the internationally known ethicist and social analyst, maintained that it was "an obscenity to compare" the project of Jerry Falwell, Tim LaHaye, and others on the Religious Right

---

Tactics for Social Change (New York: Madison, 2000), 315 n115.

39. Fackre, *The Religious Right and Christian Right*, 27.
40. Ibid., 14.
41. Neuhaus and Cromartie, eds., *Piety and Politics*, 89.
42. Ray Waddle, "Critic of King Should Resign, Baptists Urge," *The Tennessean* (18 January 1989) 3B.

"with the work of Martin Luther King, Jr."[43] In a statement that merits extended quotation, Maguire insisted that the Religious Right's

> objections that they are just doing what King and others did is wrong. That both King and they are attempting to bring religiously affiliated ideas into politics is true. So far, so good. The issue is not whether religion has its legitimate place under the political sun. Surely it does. The question is: *how is religion being used?* To disempower and disable or to empower and enable? The former use of religion is anti-political and subversive. People get hurt when the power of religion is thus abused. There is all the difference imaginable between what Martin Luther King, Jr., brought to the political order and what the Falwells and LaHayes bring. When King left his pulpit and ceased his political activism, many who had lacked rights before had come to possess those rights. People were voting who could not vote before, were getting hired and educated who would have only known rejection, and were finding decent housing who could not before. In short, King's interventions in politics were *enabling* and *empowering*. However, when the Falwells of the New Right leave their pulpits and end their political activism, inasmuch as they are successful, people who had rights will have lost them. Their interventions are *disabling* and *disempowering*. Also, depending on their success, the most wholesome elements of the American dream will have been undermined.[44]

Maguire went on to note that the Religious Right's "ferocious resistance" to the ERA and its failure to support affirmative action and aid for the poor could not have suggested a more glaring contrast to King: "Here again is the difference between a religiously motivated Martin Luther King, Jr., and the New Right. The Hebrew and Christian scriptures from which King drank are obsessed with the needs of the poor and the powerless in society. How the New Right can read those scriptures and support elitist monopolies, weaken civil rights enforcement, and cut back on aid to poor children is an epic of hypocrisy that must be called by its name."[45]

The more positive assessments of the meaning of King's legacy, provided in the 1980s by Falwell, Thomas, and Land, were not shared by most on the right. In the early 1980s, Senator Jesse Helms of North Carolina, a major Political Right figure, staged essentially a one-man crusade in the halls of the

43. Daniel C. Maguire, *The New Subversives: Anti-Americanism of the Religious Right* (New York: Continuum, 1982), 39–41.

44. Ibid.

45. Ibid., 40 and 42.

US Congress against the idea of a Martin Luther King Jr. national holiday, charging that King was virtually a symbol of un-Americanism in his time. But despite such efforts, the US Senate voted overwhelmingly, on October 19, 1983, to designate the third Monday in January as a federal holiday in honor of the civil rights leader. Ironically, the King holiday bill was signed into law by President Ronald Reagan, another major voice on the Political Right, and one of the key personalities in the wedding between the Political and Religious Right in the 1980s.[46] This action, while historic, did not end the conservative assault on King and the holiday. In the late eighties, the Republican governor Evan Mecham of Arizona epitomized this assault as he resisted "the rising tide of public support" for the recognition of the King holiday in his state. Mecham's efforts ultimately failed as Arizona joined the other states in officializing the holiday in honor of King.[47]

Certain parties on the right could not resist the urge to attack King's personality, his moral integrity, and his place in history. In 1989, Dr. Curtis Caine of Jackson, Mississippi, a physician, local John Birch Society leader, and member of the Southern Baptist Convention, called King "a communist" and "a fraud."[48] Also in 1989, Patrick Buchanan, the conservative newspaper columnist, television personality, and US presidential candidate, suggested that King's philandering undermined his "status as a saint." Buchanan went on to assert that King, despite his achievements in the civil rights field, "was not remotely so great a man or historic figure as George Washington, who led the army of independence, presided at our constitutional convention, and became our first president." "To raise Dr. King to a niche in the pantheon of American heroes alongside our founding father," continued Buchanan, "is affirmative action at its most absurd."[49] As troubling as this

46. "A National Holiday for King: But Not without Rancor," *Time* (October 31, 1983) 32; "Behind the King Debate," *Newsweek* (31 October 1983) 32; Eric Breindel, "King's Communist Associates," *The New Republic* (30 January 1984) 14; David J. Garrow, "The Helms Attack on King," *Southern Exposure* 12/2 (1984) 12–15; and Lewis V. Baldwin, *To Make the Wounded Whole: The Cultural Legacy of Martin Luther King, Jr.* (Minneapolis: Fortress, 1992), 291 and 294–95.

47. "Arizona Governor's Stance on King Holiday May Cost State $18 Million Loss," *Jet* 72/13 (22 June 1987) 36; "Arizona Finally Gets a M. L. King State Holiday," *Jet* 77/1 (9 October 1989) 18; and Baldwin, *To Make the Wounded Whole*, 295.

48. Waddle, "Critic of King Should Resign," 1B.

49. Patrick Buchanan, "A Rascal's Bedroom Escapades Diminish His Status as a Saint," *The Tennessean*, October 22, 1989, 5G; and Baldwin, *To Make the Wounded Whole*, 297. It is difficult to avoid the conclusion that Buchanan's image of King reflects his own racist tendencies, especially since he has tried for years "to pass off white supremacist ideology as legitimate mainstream political ideology." See Matt Lockshin, "Keep the Pressure on MSNBC to Fire Pat Buchanan," *Credo Action: More than a Network, a Movement*. Online: http://act.credoaction.com/call/report/index.

seemed, the most disturbing portrayals of King still came from extremists on what Gabriel Fackre calls "the Radical Right,"[50] and particularly the KKK. For the Klan, the idea of a national holiday for King defied even the most elementary standards of logic. Angered by the interracial character of the annual celebrations of King, elements within its ranks began to hold its own street demonstrations on King Day to spread racist propaganda.

The ambivalent approach to King's legacy on the part of the New Right continued into the 1990s and beyond, with some using King as a kind of sacred aura for their own political ends, and others denouncing the civil rights leader for some of his greatest personal and moral failures. King remained morally and politically relevant for those right-wing forces that opposed abortion and what was perceived to be an assault on the traditional family structure. The Jewish rabbi Yehuda Levin "and others in the pro-life movement" claimed that "their protests follow in the tradition of Martin Luther King, Jr.'s civil rights movement."[51] The conservative political activist Ralph Reed seemed most conscious of this when he was jailed for acts of civil disobedience and street protests against abortion. Reed found King useful in a number of ways. First, he used the name of King's Southern Christian Leadership Conference (SCLC) "to justify the name *Christian* Coalition," which was the political action group he and Pat Robertson established in 1989. As the first director of Christian Coalition, serving up to 1997, Reed also turned to King as he set the blueprint for the organization: "During his speech at the 1995 'Road to Victory' conference, Reed distributed a seven point 'Christian Coalition Pledge Card.' This pledge was supposedly based on one drafted by Martin Luther King, Jr. for the Southern Christian Leadership Conference. Citing the seventh point of the pledge, Reed urged CC members to 'Refrain from the violence of fist, tongue, or heart.' Reed argued that King's healing and inclusive rhetoric was crucial for the success of the civil rights movement. According to Reed, the pro-family movement has needed a similar rhetoric."[52]

Finally, Reed "appealed to the precedent" of King's "religiously based civil rights movement to justify the political activism of religious conservatives," especially in response to liberals who questioned his blend of faith and politics. One of the principal complaints of Reed and others on the right was that they were being criticized for doing essentially what liberal

---

html?tg=779.783&cp_id=166/.

50. Fackre, *The Religious Right and Christian Right*, 5.

51. Quoted in James D. Hunter, *Culture Wars: The Struggle to Define America* (New York: Basic Books, 1991), 17.

52. Justin Watson, *The Christian Coalition: Dreams of Restoration, Demands for Recognition* (New York: St. Martin's, 1999), 45, 79, and 136.

religionists had always done; namely, mixing religion and politics. King, they argued, went from the pulpit to the street corners to the polling booths, and he took the ideals grounded in the Bible, evangelical piety, and the American Constitution and made them the basis of a crusade for social and political justice.[53] For Reed, then, liberals who honored King while castigating the Religious Right were simply "using a double standard when it comes to conservative faith-based political activism."[54]

Throughout the 1990s, voices on the Political Right used some of King's most famous words in arguments against government-sponsored public policy for the benefit of minorities and the poor, maintaining, for example, that King's call for a nation in which persons are judged by character rather than skin color suggested that he would be opposed to affirmative action. Rabid anti-affirmative-action advocates like Newt Gingrich, Dick Armey, and Clint Bolick actually invoked "King's struggle in support of their specious arguments."[55] This distortion and manipulation of King's words would have been expected but still difficult to grasp, particularly in view of King's position on what he termed "special" or "compensatory measures" for "the deprived" and "the disadvantaged," a topic to be explored at greater length in chapter 2. But this was yet another indication of how King had become a useful symbol in a protracted campaign by the New Right to promote a conservative social and political platform.

The KKK remained the most vocal among right wing extremists when it came to attacks on King's legacy in the 1990s. They had become widely known by this time for their annual marches on King Day. On King Day 1992, the Grand Wizard Thomas Robb and members of the Knights of the KKK met on the steps of the Colorado State Capitol in Denver to denounce what they called "this horrible holiday." Ironically, Robb, confronted with white and black King marchers, spoke to a TV news commentator about the evils of hate and violence, while also declaring, "To hell with Martin Luther King and what he tried to teach America." The confrontation embodied clear but painful proof of a clash of messages between those who wished to destroy King's memory and dream for America, and those committed to preserving King's iconic status and the civil rights gains for which he struggled and ultimately gave his life.[56] Evidently, the aftershocks of the 1950s and '60s continued to resound in the lives of Americans throughout

---

53. Maguire, *The New Subversives*, 39.

54. Watson, *The Christian Coalition*, 79 and 136.

55. Baldwin, et al., *The Legacy of Martin Luther King Jr.*, 104.

56. For interesting comments on Robb and the Colorado KKK, see "The Girl Next Door," *Denver Westword News*, December 29, 2011, 1–4. Online: http://www.westword.com/1994-03-16/news/the-girl-next-door/.

the 1990s, from the most right wing conservative extremist to the most flaming liberal.

A number of factors have coalesced in these early years of the twenty-first century to impact images of King and the King legacy in the minds of Americans. These include the increasing streams of diversity in America, the rise of new patterns of right wing extremism during and after the George W. Bush years, and the election of Barack Obama. The extent to which these trends signal a continuing movement toward the fulfillment of King's vision for this nation is questionable and most certainly debatable. What is most important in this chapter is how the New Right is interpreting King in light of these developments. Clearly, Clarence B. Jones's *What Would Martin Say?* (2008), a work mentioned at many points in this volume, is relevant to any serious engagement with these considerations.[57] Jones's work actually increases the possibilities for parties on the right-wing conservative side to create a King in their own image—a King whose position on matters such as diversity, the New Right agenda, and the role of government would be essentially the same as that of any evangelical Christian or member of the Republican Party today.

Shortly before Jones's book was published, Carolyn Garris, in a piece titled, "Martin Luther King's Conservative Legacy," strongly implied that King would fit better into the New Right than within contemporary liberalism. In January 2006, as the nation remembered its fallen hero, Garris wrote: "It is time for conservatives to lay claim to the legacy of the Rev. Martin Luther King, Jr. King was no stalwart conservative, yet his core beliefs, such as the power and necessity of faith-based association and self-government based on absolute truth and moral law, are profoundly conservative. Modern liberalism rejects these ideas, while conservatives place them at the center of their philosophy. Despite decades of appropriation by liberals, King's message was fundamentally conservative."[58]

In October, 2006, the National Black Republican Association (NBRA), an African American conservative group, went even further in a radio ad, claiming that King "was a Republican." The ad brought swift and even angry reactions from a few who had known and struggled with King. "To suggest that Martin could identify with a party that affirms preemptive, predatory war, and whose religious partners hint that God affirms war and favors the rich at the expense of the poor," declared Joseph E. Lowery, "is to revile Martin." Congressman John Lewis of Georgia called the ad "an insult to the

57. Fairclough e-mail to Baldwin (23 August 2011).

58. Carolyn Garris, "Martin Luther King's Conservative Legacy" (12 January 2006). Online: http://www.heritage.org/research/reports/2006/01/martin-luther-kings-conservative-legacy?renderforprin/.

legacy and the memory of Martin Luther King, Jr.," and also "an affront to all that he stood for." Even a former spokesperson for the NBRA, Christopher Arps, labeled the ad "a joke," and added, "Anyone with any sense knows that most black people were Republican at one time. But it's a far stretch to think that in the '60s Martin Luther King was a Republican."[59]

It is troubling that claims like those made by Carolyn Garris and the NBRA would surface at a time when a new surge of King's influence needs to be felt not only across the religious and political spectrums, but in the public domain as a whole. But this is all part of a surreptitious design to make King's image palatable or acceptable to the religious and political establishments, which are apparently uncomfortable with the prophetic King; the King who decried the racism of the white churches, called America "the greatest purveyor of violence in the world today," and declared, in a moment of stern prophecy, that God would "rise up and break the backbone of her power and put it in the hands of a nation that doesn't even know my name."[60] By turning this prophetic King into a fierce conservative, or the high priest of Americanism, in his *What Would Martin Say?*, Clarence B. Jones has contributed immeasurably to the New Right's effort to domesticate this phenomenal figure. Obviously, the adjective *conservative* associated with the name of King seems so oxymoronic, in both a religious and political sense. Those on the right who package King in ways that justify their own moral crusade and political ends cannot honestly deny the depth of his prophetic critique and challenge to the nation and the world. Nor can they overlook his ethic of risk and his willingness to pursue radical discipleship to the point of martyrdom.

But the need to reshape, control, and even identify with King's image seems almost obsessive in some circles of the New Right, but this is understandable in a nation that has too long refused to face the sinister side of its history. Jerry Falwell virtually epitomized this tendency when speaking of King's civil disobedience, the greatness of the American past, and his own determination to obey God rather than manmade laws in the same breath. In a CNN *Crossfire* debate over displaying the Ten Commandments in government buildings in 2003, Falwell shockingly recounted: "You know, I supported Martin Luther King, Jr., who did practice his civil disobedience."[61]

59. Darryl Fears, "Controversial Ad Links MLK, GOP," *Washington Post* October 19, 2006. Online: http://www.washingtonpost.com/wp-dyn/content/article/2006/10/18/AR2006101801754.html/.

60. Washington, ed., *A Testament of Hope*, 233; and excerpts of a sermon delivered at Ebenezer Baptist Church, Atlanta, Georgia (11 April 1967) in *Dr. Martin Luther King Jr.: An Amazing Grace*, a film presentation (Del Mar, CA: McGraw Hill Films, 1978).

61. Quoted in Baldwin, *The Voice of Conscience*, 322 n48.

Here Falwell was apparently denying the nature of his response to the real, historical King, while projecting an image of the civil rights leader purely out of response to his own needs and aspirations. King needs to be rediscovered, not transformed to fit neatly into popular notions or for the purpose of promoting a particular ideology or socio-political agenda.

Extremists on the Radical Right continue to play their part by making King the symbol in their racist attacks on African Americans. On the night before Martin Luther King Jr. Day 2011, fifteen "neo-Nazis demonstrated near a civil rights center in Coeur d'Alene, Idaho," some thirty-five miles from Spokane, Washington. Kevin Harpham, a longtime member of the KKK and other white-supremacist groups, was arrested and "charged with planting a powerful homemade bomb along the route" of Spokane's King Day parade.[62] Harpham was convicted and imprisoned in 2011. Also, an editorial on King by neo-Nazi Kevin A. Strom was read on a radio show in Colorado, in which King was dismissed as "a sexual degenerate, an America-hating communist, and a criminal betrayer of even the interest of his own people."[63] This seemingly endless cacophony of mean-spirited, derogatory, and divisive rhetoric will undoubtedly be heard from the Radical Right during future King Day celebrations, and it will continue to be a reminder that there are those on the right who are determined not to come to terms with the true meaning of King and his legacy.

The portrayals of King across the spectrum of the New Right are deliberate and certainly not surprising, particularly in a culture in which King's image and legacy have been distorted and manipulated to fit the purposes and agenda of so many individuals and groups. The decades since King's death have afforded ample time for his admirers and detractors to form their impressions about *who* and *what* King was, and about what we might expect of him and he of us today. For today's New Right, images of the civil rights leader range from that of "convenient hero" to that of "convenient villain," both of which emerge out of a misunderstanding of who and what King was all about. So much of what is passed for King's message is actually in opposition to that message. The King of the New Right is one who is not really interested in challenging and eliminating white supremacy, poverty and economic justice, and war and human destruction. He is not the King who proclaimed "the interrelated structure of all reality," and who felt that

---

62. Southern Poverty Law Center, "MLK Day Bomb Suspect Has Extensive White Supremacist Background," *Intelligence Report* 142 (Summer 2011) 6–7.

63. "Hate in the Mainstream: Intelligence Briefs," in ibid., 4.

"injustice anywhere is a threat to justice everywhere."[64] In short, the King of the New Right is the antithesis of the real, historical King.

But the problem is greater than simply misinterpretations and misappropriations of King and his legacy. The right is actually dominating the faith and politics debate in contemporary society, and this alone makes their use of King disturbing and even frightening in some ways. Most of what we see today, in terms of the wedding of religion and politics, is not the kind of healthy mixture King represented but rather "a perversion of public religion."[65] In other words, religion is used to sanction the status quo, or to bless things as they are, and is not an instrument in swaying the workings of democracy in the direction of greater rights and privileges for the despised, the rejected, the exploited, and the outcast in society. King's moral and political sensibilities and goals were so radically different from those of today's New Right, and this is not likely to change in the future.

In a culture in which right wing conservatives are leaving a deep imprint on popular understandings and presentations of King, one wonders if the dream can still live, let alone achieve full realization. The question becomes all the more pressing when one considers the impact that the New Right and its agenda are having on sectors of the African American community. The possible impact of Clarence B. Jones's *What Would Martin Say?* on right-wing conservative images of King has already been noted, but one must also consider the degree to which the content of Jones's book has been influenced by the ideology and agenda of a certain wing of the New Right. The mere thought of Jones, a black friend and aide of King in the civil rights struggle in the 1960s, being impacted by right wing conservatism is hard to accept but difficult nonetheless to relinquish.[66]

Equally disturbing is the fact that too many black churches, and especially mega churches and their gurus, have capitulated to the ideology and platform of the New Right. Apparently, forces on the New Right are using the black megachurches to control black religious leadership and to impose its rigid moral and political agenda on African Americans. This has been evident from the time that Bishop Eddie Long, Bishop Harry R. Jackson Jr., and other black megachurch pastors aligned themselves with President George W. Bush after the 2000 presidential election.[67] Like their white

---

64. Martin Luther King Jr., *The Trumpet of Conscience* (New York: Harper & Row, 1986; originally published in 1967), 69–70; and King, *Why We Can't Wait*, 77.

65. Baldwin, "The Perversion of Public Religion," 12–13 and 18.

66. Clarence B. Jones and Joel Engel, *What Would Martin Say?* (New York: HarperCollins, 2008), 69–178.

67. Neela Banerjee, "More Black Clergy Embracing GOP Ideals, Creating Division," *The Tennessean*, March 6, 2005, 17A.

partners, these leaders have turned to abortion, same-sex marriage, and other issues of personal morality as the nation's greatest sins, while virtually ignoring racism, the structures that cause poverty and economic injustice, the subordination of women and gays, religious bigotry and intolerance, and the evils of US aggression and war. Given these circumstances, black communities, and especially the churches, could potentially become willing partners in the conservative drive to distort, manipulate, and ultimately domesticate Martin Luther King Jr.'s image and legacy. Much of the prophetic King has already gotten lost in the so-called new black church, and this in itself may reveal something of the influence that the New Right has already had on that institution.[68]

King belongs to the entire nation and indeed the whole world, and conservatives have as much right as liberals to honor and celebrate him, and to offer their own perspectives on how his words and actions might still impact our approaches to social and public policy concerns. But misrepresenting King's image and legacy solely for personal and political purposes violates the very moral standards that the New Right claims to cherish and uphold. In his *I May Not Get There with You: The True Martin Luther King Jr.* (2000), Michael E. Dyson cautions us against ceding control of King's image to not only "the right," but to "the federal government and its holiday, and even the King family themselves."[69] The aim should never be to control or own King's image, words, and legacy, but, rather, to make these sources of insight and inspiration for these times.

From King's Dream to Beck's Scheme: Reclaiming the Great March on Washington

Exactly forty-seven years to the day after Martin Luther King Jr. delivered his celebrated "I Have a Dream" speech on the steps of the Lincoln Memorial in Washington DC, Glenn Beck, the conservative radio and TV pundit, led a rally that drew tens of thousands to that same location. The date was 28 August 2010, and memories of King and his electrifying speech were strong nationwide and in other parts of the world. Standing before "the leading luminaries of the tea party movement," Beck casually evoked King's legacy, spoke emphatically of "the content of our character," and called for

---

68. Baldwin, *The Voice of Conscience*, 220–45; and Paula L. McGee, "Pastor or CEO?: The New Black Church Leaders," *The National Baptist Voice* (Summer 2006) 64–65.

69. Michael E. Dyson, *I May Not Get There with You: The True Martin Luther King, Jr.* (New York: Free Press, 2000), x (preface).

"a troubled nation" to reclaim its greatness.[70] It was here that the use and abuse of King's image and legacy by the Radical Right reached new levels of irony and absurdity, especially since Beck had become very well known for his racist attacks against President Barack Obama,[71] his openness to and encouragement of violence among right-wing extremists,[72] his strong and unwavering support for the radical agenda of the Tea Party movement,[73] his constant tirades against liberals,[74] his offensive remarks against blacks and

70. Erika Bolstad and James Rosen, "Beck, Sharpton Rallies Trade Chants," *The Tennessean*, August 29, 2010, 4A; Mimi Hall, "Beck Supporters Head for D.C. Rally: Event Site, Date Disturb Civil Rights Leaders," *USA Today*, August 27, 2010, 4A; and "Civil Rights Groups Set for Showdown with Tea Party on MLK March Anniversary," Online: http://www.thegrio.com/politics/civil-rights-groups-set-for-showdown-with-tea-party-on-... (14 July 2010).

71. Beck unjustifiably accused Obama of "a deep-seated hatred for white people or the white culture," and called him "a fascist, a Nazi, and a Marxist." Obviously, such claims reveal more about Beck than about Obama, whose life story is actually a testimony against bigotry and intolerance. See "Going Mainstream," in *Intelligence Report*, The Southern Poverty Law Center, Issue 135 (Fall 2009) 38; Southern Poverty Law Center, "Hate in the Mainstream: Intelligence Briefs," *Intelligence Report* 136 (Winter 2009) 4; Southern Poverty Law Center, "The Ringmaster, Glenn Beck 46," *Intelligence Report* 138 (Summer 2010) 28; and Southern Poverty Law Center, "Fox News Personalities Reaching New Lows," *Intelligence Report* 139 (Fall 2010) 7.

72. Beck's "charismatic and sometimes end-times focused diatribes" have inspired "right-wing fanatics" "to murder" and engage in "threats of violence" at times, but Beck always denies that this is the case. See Southern Poverty Law Center, "Going Feral," *Intelligence Report* (Fall 2009) 34; Southern Poverty Law Center, "Once Again, Glenn Beck's Views Invoked Extremists," *Intelligence Report* 141 (Spring 2011) 5–6.

73. Beck actually gave the Tea Party movement "a jumpstart by urging viewers to attend the gatherings and broadcasting from rallies." See "The Ringmaster, Glenn Beck 46," 28; and Kate Zernike and Carl Hulse, "At the Lincoln Memorial, a Call for Religious Rebirth," *New York Times* (29 August 2010) 15.

74. Beck has been especially critical of what he labels "the extreme left," whom he also calls "the oppressors." His attacks on the American Civil Liberties Union (ACLU) and the Tides Foundation, a "San Francisco-based foundation" that provides financial support and "other services around the world 'to individuals and institutions committed to accelerating positive social change through philanthropy,'" are also widely known. See Southern Poverty Law Center, "Hate in the Mainstream: Intelligence Briefs," *Intelligence Report* 139 (Fall 2010) 4; "Man Accused of Shooting at Police Allegedly Targeted Liberals," Southern Poverty Law Center, *Intelligence Report* 140 (Winter 2010) 5–6; and "Once Again, Glenn Beck's Views Invoked by Extremists," 6.

Jews,⁷⁵ and his steady stream of race baiting, conspiracy rants, and exercises in fearmongering.⁷⁶

When pressed about his decision to hold his rally on the anniversary of King's famous speech, Beck offered a number of explanations. He initially claimed that the effort was designed to "pick up Martin Luther King's dream," which "has been distorted" and even "massively perverted." Beck also complained that "the U. S. civil rights movement had been 'co-opted' by progressives," and that "this is a moment, quite honestly, that I think we can reclaim the civil rights movement."⁷⁷ At other times, Beck asserted that his rally "is about supporting the troops, not about politics."⁷⁸ On still other occasions, he insisted that the aim was to "turn to the values of the Founding Fathers to restore honor to America." In Beck's terms, "restoring honor" meant agitating against the federal government, which he feels is leading Americans "down the path to ruin," and "taking back the control of our country,"⁷⁹ a quest with disturbing implications since the president of the United States, Barack Obama, is an African American. Beck's failure to offer a clear rationale for the Washington rally only added to the growing perception that he was an attention-craving lunatic without any real substance.

Beck's explanations simply were not accepted by many in the civil rights community. Marc H. Morial, the president of the National Urban League (NUL), criticized the timing of Beck's rally and accused him of "deception and trickery," particularly for "trying to take the imagery of Dr. King and Abraham Lincoln and somehow wrap his agenda of intolerance and division around it." "Dr. King stood for a unified America around civil rights, cooperation and tolerance," Morial added. "Glenn Beck stands for something very different."⁸⁰ Stefanie Brown, national field director for the

---

75. Beck's praise for Nazi sympathizer Elizabeth Dilling and his tendency to trivialize black experiences in slavery, for example, are most disturbing. Southern Poverty Law Center, "Fox News Personalities Reaching for New Lows," 7; and Southern Poverty Law Center, "Hate in the Mainstream: Intelligence Briefs" *Intelligence Report* (Winter 2010) 4.

76. "Going Mainstream," 38; "Once Again, Glenn Beck's Views Invoked by Extremists," 5–6; and Leah Nelson, "End of Time: Fox News Host Glenn Beck Fretted Endlessly about the End Times, but It was Really Beck's Hourglass that was Running Out," *Intelligence Report* (Summer 2011) 49.

77. Southern Poverty Law Center, "Fox News Personalities Reaching for New Lows," 7–8; and Phillip Elliot, "Beck: Rally to Reclaim Civil Rights," *The Tennessean* August 27, 2010, 4A.

78. Hall, "Beck's Supporters Head for D.C. Rally," 4A.

79. Bolstad and Rosen, "Beck, Sharpton Rallies Trade Chants," 4A; "The Ringmaster: Glenn Beck, 46," 28–29; and Hall, "Beck Supporters Head for D.C. Rally," 4A.

80. Beck repeatedly mentioned King and Lincoln, and "at one point read excerpts

National Association for the Advancement of Colored People (NAACP), said that Beck's decision to schedule "his 'Restoring Honor' event on the same date and location of the March on Washington was a way to manipulate King's legacy and that of the civil rights movement for his own benefit."[81] The Reverend Al Sharpton of the National Action Network (NAN), who was leading another march that began at Dunbar High School in northeast Washington at the same time as Beck's, charged that "It is just an outright attempt to flip the imagery of Dr. King and the imagery of that march, and distort it for some opposite purposes." "They want to disgrace this day," Sharpton continued. "We ain't giving them this day! This is our day." Images of a classic conflict between right-wing conservatives and keepers of the dream shimmered before onlookers, as Beck's marchers, wearing "'Proud to Be American!' shirts," hoisting "American flags," and chanting "USA! USA!," were confronted by Sharpton and other King marchers who "waved photos of the civil rights leader at them" while shouting "MLK! MLK!"[82]

Beck's political opportunism was far more evident than any inclination he may have had to honor King. Noting in a CNN television interview that "black people don't own Martin Luther King Jr.," Beck, like Falwell, Gingrich, and others before him, simply used King as a kind of sacred endorsement for the advancement of his own political and moral agenda. Indeed, the tone of Beck's message, imbued with "references to God and a need for a religious revival,"[83] made this abundantly clear. Denying that his was "a gathering of a bunch of hatemongers," Beck declared that "something that is beyond man is happening. . . . America today begins to turn back to God." His initial plan, he reported, was to have a march on Washington that would "be political," but "then I kind of feel that God dropped a giant sandbag on my head." "My role, as I see it," Beck added, "is to wake America up to the backsliding of principles and values and most of all of God. We are a country of God. As I look at the problems in our country, quite honestly, I think the hot breath of destruction is breathing on our necks and to fix it politically is a figure that I don't see anywhere."[84] And in language

---

from the Gettysburg Address." "Civil Rights Groups Set for Showdown with Tea Party," 2; Hall, "Beck Supporters Head for D.C. Rally," 4A; and Bolstad and Rosen, "Beck, Sharpton Rallies Trade Chants," 4A.

81. "Civil Rights Groups Set for Showdown with Tea Party," 2.

82. "Going Mainstream," 38; "Civil Rights Groups Set for Showdown with Tea Party," 1; Hall, "Beck Supporters Head for D.C. Rally," 4A; and Bolstad and Rosen, "Beck, Sharpton Rallies Trade Chants," 4A.

83. Zernike and Hulse, "At the Lincoln Memorial, a Call for Religious Rebirth," 15.

84. Hall, "Beck Supporters Head for D.C. Rally," 4A; and Zernike and Hulse, "At the Lincoln Memorial, a Call for Religious Rebirth," 15.

that contrasted sharply with the content of King's "I Have a Dream" oration, Beck went on to assert: "For too long, this country has wandered in darkness, and we have wandered in darkness in periods from the beginning. We have had moments of brilliance and moments of darkness. But this country has spent far too long worried about scars and thinking about the scars and concentrating on the scars. Today we are going to concentrate on the good things in America, the things we have accomplished and the things we can do tomorrow."[85]

Sarah Palin, the former Alaska governor and Republican vice-presidential candidate, who headlined the event with Beck, gave the keynote speech, making references to God and patriotism. Interestingly enough, Palin later recalled "feeling the spirit of Dr. Martin Luther King, Jr." on that occasion. One of the great ironies is that both Palin and Beck seemed to think of themselves as the new face of the civil rights movement, despite Beck's claim that "social justice is not in the Bible."[86] Neither of them had previously shown any interest in King and civil rights,[87] and their carefully concocted scheme in the nation's capitol was designed to give them nationwide and even worldwide exposure at a time when the spotlight was supposed to be on the legacy of King and his great march on Washington forty-seven years earlier. In short, both Beck and Palin actually showed that they are potential killers of the dream, not keepers of the dream.

Strangely enough, this assessment does not square with that of Clarence B. Jones, a friend and confidant of King, and the author of *What Would Martin Say?* (2008) and *Behind the Dream: The Making of the Speech that Changed a Nation* (2011). While characterizing Beck's march "clearly as political theater," or as "an attempt to further invigorate the far-right Republican 'Tea Party' base through an evangelical call," Jones seems to reject the contention that the event was "a fundamentalist, conservative, and yes, *white* co-opting" of an "iconic moment in the black struggle."[88] He calls Beck's rally "a peaceful airing of political grievances and desired changes,"

---

85. Bolstad and Rosen, "Beck, Sharpton Rallies Trade Chants," 4A.

86. "Can Conservative Populists Claim King as Their Own?," *CNN Sunday* August 29, 2010; Southern Poverty Law Center, "Fox News Personalities Reaching for New Lows," 8; and Serene Jones, "An Open Letter to Glenn Beck: We're Sending You Bibles." Online: http://www.huffingtonpost.com/serene-jones/an-open-letter-to-glenn-b_b_650604.html/.

87. Southern Poverty Law Center, "Fox News Personalities Reaching for New Lows," 8.

88. Clarence B. Jones, *Behind the Dream: The Making of the Speech that Transformed a Nation*, with Stuart Connelly (New York: Palgrave Macmillan, 2011), 169–70.

and suggests that the event should "be commended."[89] Similar sentiments were put forth by King's niece, Alveda King, who opined that King "would love Glenn Beck." King would indeed love Beck and declare his right to stage a rally, but Beck's self-serving, publicity-seeking, political opportunism and misplacement of the nation's problems conflict with what King considered noble and morally defensible. In any case, such opinions about Beck, coming from Jones, Alveda King, and other sources who supposedly represent and value the legacy of King and the civil rights movement, are very difficult to dissect and understand. But they are also important in assessing the possible impact of right wing conservatism on black attitudes toward King and the problems that African Americans still encounter today.

Surprisingly, Jones appears oblivious to the fact that Beck's overwhelmingly white Tea Party crowd, unlike the significantly smaller numbers of whites who were present at the 1963 march on Washington, were fiercely opposed to affirmative action and the current civil rights agenda. There would have been no need to take a poll to prove this. Moreover, Jones seems to think that the whites at Beck's rally were really there to honor King. He says that "every time King's name was spoken or the 'Dream' was referenced," they "cheered," and "They applauded Dr. King's legacy at every turn."[90] There is every reason to believe that the Beck crowd, considering their political ties and tendencies, was actually cheering and applauding Beck and Palin, not King and his dream. The notion that these people could reasonably cheer and applaud King, while obviously disagreeing with much of what he actually stood for, is grossly misguided, to say the least.[91]

In trying to explain what he terms the "Beck-versus-Sharpton aftermath," Jones attempts what is essentially impossible; namely, "to look at this all from Martin's perspective."[92] Jones feels that King would see Sharpton's attack on Beck's rally as tantamount to a "turning off of potential allies," and that the civil rights leader would suggest instead that the rally be viewed as "a litmus test" of the levels of "dissatisfaction" with the Obama administration and its policies.[93] It is hard to imagine anyone, including King, speaking

---

89. Ibid., 170–71.

90. Ibid., 171.

91. Strangely enough, there are right-wingers who actually believe that King's civil rights campaigns had much in common with today's Tea Party rallies. See William Haupt III, "MLK's and Tea Party Rallies Have a Lot in Common: Letters to the Editor," *The Tennessean* (31 August 2011) 9A; and Robert Judkins, "MLK's Perspective Could Not be Further from Tea Party's: Letters to the Editor," *The Tennessean* September 2, 2011, 11A.

92. Jones, *Behind the Dream*, 171.

93. Ibid., 171–72.

of "potential allies" for the civil rights cause among Tea Party people and other radical right-wing groups. King was always very realistic about what he *could* and *could not* expect from what he called "the Radical Right" in his own times, and, based on his assessment of that phenomenon, it is doubtful that he would be so naïve as to expect support from today's Radical Right. While one might take seriously Jones's suggestion that the Beck march mirrored much "dissatisfaction with the presidency of Barack Obama,"[94] the possibility that the event was also staged to undermine King and to further turn back the clock on civil rights should also be seriously entertained. Our knowledge of the whole history of the Radical Right and its attitude toward King and civil rights demands nothing less than this.

The great march on Washington of 1963 was not an old-fashioned religious camp meeting or a revival at which throngs of faithful whites gathered to praise America and to call for a return to God. Punctuated by the dynamism and profundity of King's "I Have a Dream" speech, it was more of an interracial movement aimed at justice, peace, and equality of opportunity for all Americans. King's march on Washington also took what had essentially been a southern-based civil rights crusade and gave it a national identity and international significance. Moreover, that march became the principal model for subsequent generations of social activists who wished to dramatize legitimate social, political, economic, and public policy issues or problems before the entire nation and world.

The need to reclaim King and the great march on Washington of 1963 could not be more pressing in this age of peril and uncertainty, when there is a raw resurgence of bigotry and intolerance, the erosion of basic rights and civil liberties, and growing cycles of violence and human destruction. At the same time, it would be unwise to freeze King on the steps of the Lincoln Memorial. Perhaps more important, we must also reclaim the King who became more radical in the five years after his famous "I Have a Dream" speech. That was the King who looked beyond a nation in which little white boys and girls hold hands with little black boys and girls to envision a world free of racial oppression, economic exploitation, religious bigotry and intolerance, and war and human destruction. As Vincent Harding has indicated, this King is not as "comfortable," especially for those on the right, as "the triumphant King of the March on Washington," who challenged us with "a magnificent dream of human solidarity."[95]

---

94. Ibid., 172.

95. There is no better statement of this pressing need than Vincent Harding, *Martin Luther King Jr.: The Inconvenient Hero* (Maryknoll, NY: Orbis, 2008), 67.

It would be a mistake of astronomic proportions to allow parties on the right to remake King in their own image, thus robbing him of his prophetic posture, message, vision, and activism. At the same time, we must understand that King will remain what Richard Lentz calls "a mutable symbol"[96] in our culture. In other words, no fixed, one-dimensional image of the civil rights leader can survive unchallenged, especially in a nation and world in which his memory is still greeted with a mixture of respect and disdain.[97] Some will continue to admire and imitate King, and others will castigate and seek to render him meaningless for today and tomorrow. Whatever the case, King's persona and the meaning of his legacy should always be protected and sustained, and never surrendered to the short-sighted, narrow-minded, and uncommitted among us.

---

96. Richard Lentz, *Symbols, the News Magazines, and Martin Luther King* (Baton Rouge: Louisiana State University Press, 1990), 237.

97. Baldwin, *To Make the Wounded Whole*, 301.

2

Who Is Clarence B. Jones's Martin Luther King Jr.

An Audacious Prophet or a Right-Wing Conservative?

LEWIS V. BALDWIN

Clarence B. Jones's *What Would Martin Say* (2008) and *Behind the Dream: The Making of the Speech that Transformed a Nation* (2011) challenge much that is commonly known and accepted about Martin Luther King Jr. In these volumes, and especially in *What Would Martin Say?*, Jones makes numerous controversial and questionable claims about King's legacy and about what King would say today about civil rights leadership, affirmative action, illegal immigration, anti-Semitism, war, and other social and public policy issues.[1] This chapter approaches those claims in the spirit of erudition, setting forth essentially a three dimensional thesis. First, Jones's description of his relationship to King raises as many questions as it answers, especially when one considers his reflections on what would be King's positions on many of the intractable moral, social, political, economic, and spiritual

---

1. Amazingly, most King scholars have greeted Jones's claims and conclusions with an abysmal silence. An exception is Rufus Burrow Jr., whose short but critical review of Jones's *What Would Martin Say?* appears in *Encounter* 70/1 (Winter 2009) 67–69. The reluctance to challenge Jones on the part of even the most highly reputable King scholars probably stems from a sense of the nature of his relationship to King. In any case, this is another example of how we, according to Michael Dyson, are ceding control of King's image and ideas to those who would sanitize them. See Michael Eric Dyson, *I May Not Get There with You: The True Martin Luther King Jr.* (New York: Simon & Shuster, 2000), xv–xvi (preface).

problems that still threaten human welfare and survival in this society. Second, the question of what King would say about any current issue ultimately calls for conjecture, and it warrants a much closer and careful examination than that provided by Jones. Finally, the answer to this question is best determined not by what Jones or anyone else thinks or believes today, but, rather, through a serious engagement with King's own words, writings, and actions in the 1950s and '60s. In other words, King himself is the best and only source for making any determination of how he might address contemporary problems and challenges.[2] And even when the necessary task of examining King's ideas and activities has occurred, we are still essentially left with speculation about what he might actually say were he alive today, for we cannot be certain as to how King would be affected by the changed events of the last half century. However, we have no reason to really doubt that he would still respond based on his most fundamental and deeply held moral and spiritual principles.

Much of what is said and written about King in contemporary times amounts to a distortion or manipulation of history and of fact.[3] This is why King is too often misunderstood by critics and admirers alike. Luther D. Ivory has alluded to the "multiple and competing images," which "continue to generate" not only "ambiguity about" King's "vocational identity," but also "mass public confusion about King's life and thought" in "both academia and the public square."[4] In a similar vein, Vincent Harding has written at length about "the profound sense of national amnesia that has distorted so much of America's approach to Martin Luther King, our national hero."[5] In such a climate, Clarence B. Jones's image of the civil rights leader, like that of any other King interpreter, should be subjected to serious, critical scrutiny.

---

2. This contention is shared by all of the contributors to this volume, and it is reflected in their different treatments of King.

3. John A. Williams brilliantly makes this point regarding William Styron's treatment of the slave rebel Nat Turner, and I have clearly benefitted from a close reading of his essay. See John A. Williams, "The Manipulation of History and of Fact: An Ex-Southerner's Apologist Tract for Slavery and the Life of Nat Turner; or William Styron's Faked Confessions," in John Henrik Clarke, ed., *William Styron's Nat Turner: Ten Black Writers Respond* (Boston: Beacon, 1968), 45.

4. Luther D. Ivory, *Toward a Theology of Radical Involvement: The Theological Legacy of Martin Luther King Jr.* (Nashville: Abingdon, 1997), 14–15.

5. See Vincent Harding, *Martin Luther King Jr.: The Inconvenient Hero* (Maryknoll: Orbis, 2008; originally published in 1996), ix (introduction). Another source that makes a similar observation is Dyson, *I May Not Get There with You*, 284–306. Dyson discusses our celebration of King in the context of what he calls a "reverential amnesia," a "repentant amnesia," a "revisionist amnesia," a "recalcitrant amnesia," and a "resistant amnesia."

Nothing less is acceptable for the millions who honor King's memory and his rich legacy of ideas and struggle.

In the Circle of Civil Rights Leadership: Jones's Relationship to King

Clarence B. Jones is becoming increasingly recognized as one of the personal lawyers, draft speechwriters, and principal advisors and confidants to Martin Luther King Jr. in the 1960s. Jones actually met King in 1960, after the civil rights leader was unjustly indicted in Alabama for perjury and tax evasion. King visited with Jones at his home in Los Angeles, and solicited the involvement of Jones in his struggle to successfully beat the charges. Convinced that Jones "was not, at present," putting his talents "to their highest and best use," King also enlisted his involvement in "his war," or what he called "the movement." Jones recounts that he initially resisted all efforts on the part of King and his associates to get involved in any way, but changed his mind after hearing King preach a sermon at a Baptist Church in Los Angeles. The sermon, parts of which were supposedly directed at Jones personally, brought tears to the young lawyer's eyes, and he subsequently joined King and his staff. This was apparently the beginning of a relationship that supposedly lasted up to King's assassination in April 1968.[6] Jones's account of what happened is not only very interesting but deeply touching, and it is quite unlike the recollections of other activists who have shared their accounts of meeting and working with King.

Jones discusses this growing relationship at some length in "What Did Martin Say About Me?," the title of the first chapter in his interesting and provocative book, *What Would Martin Say?* There is no question that Jones knew and worked with King, for the civil rights leader stated the following in a letter to the New York Bar Association in 1962: "Ever since I have known Mr. Jones, I have always seen him as a man of sound judgment, deep insight, and great dedication. I am also convinced that he is a man of great integrity."[7] In his *Why We Can't Wait* (1963), King also referred to Jones as "my friend and lawyer," and he noted how Jones's words "lifted a thousand pounds from my heart" when the SCLC needed money to make bail for activists who had been arrested in Birmingham in 1963. Jones reported to King: "Harry Belafonte has been able to raise fifty thousand dollars for bail

---

6. Clarence B. Jones and Joel Engel, *What Would Martin Say?* (New York: HarperCollins, 2008), 1–21; and Clayborne Carson, et al., eds., *The Martin Luther King Jr. Encyclopedia* (Westport, CT: Greenwood, 2008), 164–65.

7. Quoted in Carson, et al., eds., *The Martin Luther King Jr. Encyclopedia*, 164.

bonds. It is available immediately. And he says that whatever else you need, he will raise it."[8] King apparently viewed this as further evidence that he had divine favor in the movement, and that God was using figures like Jones to advance the freedom cause:

> I found it hard to say what I felt. Jones's message had brought me more than relief from the immediate concern about money; more than gratitude for the loyalty of friends far away; more than confirmation that the life of the movement could not be snuffed out. What silenced me was a profound sense of awe. I was aware of a feeling that had been present all along below the surface of consciousness, pressed down under the weight of concern for the movement; God's companionship does not stop at the door of a jail cell. I don't know whether the sun was shining at that moment. But I know that once again I could see the light.[9]

These statements alone probably reveal as much if not more about what King thought of Jones than Jones himself relates in his chapter, "What Did Martin Say about Me."[10] The impelling moral, spiritual, and intellectual power that united the two men in a common struggle to eliminate racial injustice seemed genuine and far-reaching, despite their different backgrounds and professions. There is no reason to doubt that King included Jones among the great "winter soldiers"[11] in the movement, thus assigning him a place alongside Stanley Levison, Fred D. Gray, Orzell Billingsley, Arthur Shores, and other attorneys who put their reputations and even their lives on the line for a more just, inclusive, and peaceful society.

King often talked about the potential contributions that lawyers like Jones could and should make to the quest for civil rights and liberties. Jones vividly recalls King's "belief that the greatest weapon against civil rights was not a fire hose but a lawyer on the wrong side of history."[12] Statements like this were possibly made by King at times, especially when he was conversing

---

8. Martin Luther King Jr., *Why We Can't Wait* (New York: New American Library, 1963), 75. Jones's name also surfaces in Clayborne Carson et al., *The Papers of Martin Luther King Jr.* vol. 5, *Threshold of a New Decade, January 1959—December 1960* (Berkeley: University of California Press, 2005), 518 and 634.

9. King, *Why We Can't Wait*, 75.

10. Jones reflects a lot on some of what King said to him and how he viewed King, but he should have gone into greater depth about what King actually said and thought about him. Even so, much can be concluded or inferred from what Jones actually shares in this chapter. See Jones and Engel, *What Would Martin Say?*, 1–27.

11. Ibid., 26–27.

12. Ibid., 22.

with or in the presence of lawyers like Jones, or when he thought in terms of the great contributions of Supreme Court Justice Thurgood Marshall. But King actually felt that any person "on the wrong side of history" was potentially a formidable threat to civil rights. He never meant to suggest that lawyers were more important to his crusade than people in other walks of life. He placed equal value on politicians, preachers, teachers, students, scientists, social critics and activists, cooks, maids, and janitors, because he was convinced that it took people in every field of endeavor to wage a successful battle against the forces of evil, injustice, and retrogression.[13] Thus, when King spoke of "the grand alliance" or "a real coalition of conscience,"[14] he had in mind not only lawyers such as Jones, but even Mother Pollard, the "elderly Negro woman" in Montgomery, who was "poverty-stricken and uneducated," and who walked until her feet were tired and sore.[15] King frequently made it clear that the civil rights movement was not about him personally, nor anyone else for that matter, but about the extraordinary power of ordinary people struggling together to accomplish much-needed goals, and to translate an ethical ideal into practical action and practical reality.

In both *What Would Martin Say?* and *Behind the Dream*, Jones repeatedly reminds us that he knew and worked closely with King, whom he variously describes as "a moral architect," "a secular saint," "a realist," "a dreamer," as "divinely sent," "the commander of a righteous army," and a master preacher with a marvelous "speaking voice," "a natural storyteller's ease," and a capacity of "transfixing the listener."[16] Jones also writes in glowing terms about King's outstanding leadership qualities, his keen intellect, the depth of his vision, and the genuineness of his humility, and he even calls King "a friend of mine."[17] Clearly, Jones sees King as the moving spirit behind the movement, but he maintains that King depended on him for advice, and for many of the handwritten and typed versions of the speeches he so often delivered during his civil rights campaigns. In *Behind the Dream*, Jones describes his role in drafting and finalizing King's celebrated "I Have a

13. Martin Luther King Jr., "Address at the Meeting of the Southern Association of Political Scientists" (13 November 1964), unpublished version, The Library and Archives of the Martin Luther King Jr. Center for Nonviolent Social Change, Inc. Atlanta, Georgia, 1–3.

14. Ibid., 2–3; and Martin Luther King Jr., *Where Do We Go from Here: Chaos or Community?* (Boston: Beacon, 1967), 9.

15. Clayborne Carson, et al., eds., *The Papers of Martin Luther King Jr.*, vol. 6, *Advocate of the Social Gospel, September 1948—March 1963* (Berkeley: University of California Press, 2007), 544.

16. Jones and Engel, *What Would Martin Say?*, xv–xvi (introduction), 11–12, 41, 45, and 83.

17. Ibid., xv (introduction).

Dream" speech, and in giving shape to the March on Washington in August 1963.[18] To be sure, Jones's accounts of his collaborative efforts with King, Stanley Levison, A Philip Randolph, Bayard Rustin, and others on the civil rights front are interesting and should be valued and treated as sources of insight and inspiration, but it is difficult to avoid the conclusion that Jones is seeking to establish his own special place in history. There is nothing inherently wrong with this, as long as historical facts and truth telling are not sacrificed on the altar of mythmaking.

Jones was a witness in the grand old-fashioned sense to so much of what King said and did in the context of the freedom struggle, and he is clearly on track in terms of his delineation of certain traits of King's personality. But questions inevitably arise when Jones claims that he "was privy to" King's "innermost thoughts," that he "knew" King's "mind as well as anyone," that he "did indeed often put words" in King's "mouth," and that he thinks he understands what King "would have to say, and what he would advise, on the issues of the day."[19] At points in his two books, Jones actually prefaces sentences with comments like, "Were he here now, Martin would . . . ," "Martin would likely conclude, as I have . . . ," and "Being fair-minded, if that's all Martin saw, he'd declare," etc.,[20] all of which suggests not only pride, and rightly so, but also some level of arrogance and audacity. It is almost impossible to fathom that even King's own parents, wife, and children knew his mind or innermost thoughts, let alone someone who was not one of his relatives. King was too complex a figure for anyone except God, or his "divine companion," to actually know exactly what was going on in his mind as he pondered and responded to the day-to-day challenges of the movement.

Jones's relationship with King might easily be redefined, and, ironically, his two books, *What Would Martin Say?* and *Behind the Dream*, are among the very sources that can make this possible. It appears that Jones's

---

18. Ibid., 25; and Clarence B. Jones and Stuart Connelly, *Behind the Dream: The Making of the Speech That Transformed a Nation* (New York: Palgrave Macmillan, 2011), xiv–xv and 56–62.

19. Jones and Engel, *What Would Martin Say?*, xv–xvi (introduction). Because his schedule was always so crowded, King had his ghostwriters, among whom were also Al Duckett, Harris Wofford, Stanley Levison, and Bayard Rustin, but this does not mean that King accepted their words and not his own. I have argued that "In cases where ghostwriters prepared King's books, essays, and speeches, they took words out of his mouth instead of putting words into his mouth." Jones's claims obviously go against this statement, but I stand by it nonetheless. See Lewis V. Baldwin, *There Is a Balm in Gilead: The Cultural Roots of Martin Luther King Jr.* (Minneapolis: Fortress, 1991), 13.

20. Jones and Engel, *What Would Martin Say?*, 53 and 81; and Jones and Connelly, *Behind the Dream*, 176.

relationship to King consisted primarily in his role as legal advisor, and there was no one more qualified than he for that task in the 1960s.[21] Jones's books hold some importance when King is studied through the lens of his associations and interactions, and from the standpoint of his human and pastoral sides, but they offer essentially no strong evidence that Jones was one of King's closest conversation partners when it came to matters of philosophy, theology, and ethics. Also, there is no solid indication that Jones carefully read King's six books and the many essays King wrote, all of which reveal much about King as person, thinker, and activist. There is no way to know anything about King's mind and person apart from a serious reading of his *Stride toward Freedom: The Montgomery Story* (1958), *The Measure of a Man* (1959), *Strength to Love* (1963), *Why We Can't Wait* (1963), *Where Do We Go from Here: Chaos or Community?* (1967), and *The Trumpet of Conscience* (1967).

The names of figures such as Georg Hegel, Mohandas K. Gandhi, and Reinhold Niebuhr briefly surface in Jones's discussion of King,[22] but one wonders if Jones, whose specialty is obviously legal studies, has a workable knowledge of these and other major intellectual sources of King. Evidently, he has not brought a sharpened awareness of personalism, social gospelism, Christian realism, Gandhian nonviolence, and other intellectual disciplines to his treatment of who King was, and to his reflections on his relationship with the civil rights leader. Jones's apparent unfamiliarity with the complex and dynamic world of King's intellectual life makes it virtually impossible, and understandably so, for him to discern King's innermost thoughts, let alone to place King in a coherent intellectual and religious context in which

---

21. The British King scholar Adam Fairclough agrees to a point. He endorses the need "to question Jones's relationship to King," noting that "He was one of a group of speechwriters, ghostwriters, fundraisers, advisers, and 'Mr. Fixits' who constituted King's informal inner circle. I refer to the New York-based group that in 1964 gave itself the title of 'Research Committee.' Among those advisers, he (Jones) was less important than Levison, Rustin, or Andrew Young. I think he became closest to King during the period 1963–65 when King distanced himself from Levison. After 1965 his activities on behalf of King declined, and by 1967–68 his participation in King's 'kitchen cabinet' or 'research committee' was far less significant. The FBI wiretaps, which record most of the conference calls that King had with his advisers, reflect this. Jones is rarely included after 1966. Of course, he may have had informal contacts with King that left no record. I haven't read the FBI file on Jones himself, if it is available." Fairclough added: "I don't think Jones was primarily valuable to King as a lawyer. The Gandhi Society never really got off the ground, and in 1964 King made an agreement with the NAACP that the LDF, headed by Jack Greenberg, would represent him. I think King valued Jones as a friend, advisor, and general source of help." E-mail from Adam Fairclough to Lewis V. Baldwin 23 August 2011.

22. See Jones and Engel, *What Would Martin Say?*, 19, 91–92, 106, and 156–58.

he can be much better appreciated as a person and activist. This will become increasingly apparent in the next section of this chapter, which focuses a critical eye on Jones's claims about what King would say and do about the most pressing issues and concerns of our time.

What Would Martin Say?: The Jones Version of King's Gospel

In his *Letter from the Birmingham City Jail* (1963), Martin Luther King Jr. spoke of being "compelled to carry the gospel of freedom" to the far corners of the earth.[23] That gospel, as King understood and proclaimed it, affirmed the personal God of love and reason, the essential dignity and worth of all human personality, the redemptive power of love, the existence of a moral order in the universe, the moral obligation to resist individual and collective evil, the social roles of the Christian church, and the morality and practicality of nonviolence versus the immorality and impracticality of violence;[24] and it also freed and empowered people of all backgrounds to realize the fullness of their personalities, hopes, dreams, and aspirations. Unfortunately, King's "gospel of freedom" gets lost at many points in Clarence B. Jones's *What Would Martin Say?* and *Behind the Dream*. Jones is right in suggesting that King has some relevance in our astoundingly altered society today, but many of his claims about what King would say about black leadership, affirmative action, illegal immigration, anti-Semitism, terrorism and the war in Iraq, and certain parties in the federal government should not go unchallenged.

Jones believes that much of King's message today would be directed at black civil rights leadership, and he is right. Jones devotes the second chapter of *What Would Martin Say?* to the issue, insisting that black leadership fails to pass what he terms "the Martin Luther King test of integrity." Jones suggests that King would be bitterly disappointed with today's black leaders, who are easily manipulated by politicians in the Democratic Party, who "pimp the best interests" of their people for personal gain, who engage in "the propagation of fear," who ignore the call to responsible action, who are lacking in moral authority, who overplay the race card while raising the

---

23. King, *Why We Can't Wait*, 77.

24. For the very best treatments of these ideas, see John J. Ansbro, *Martin Luther King Jr.: Nonviolent Strategies and Tactics for Social Change* (Lanham, MD: Madison, 2000); and Rufus Burrow Jr., *God and Human Dignity: The Personalism, Theology, and Ethics of Martin Luther King Jr.* (Notre Dame: University of Notre Dame Press, 2006), 17–265.

banner of "black victimhood," who are at times "appallingly disingenuous" in raising racial concerns, and who "have strayed off course from the beliefs and precepts that guided Martin Luther King and therefore the movement four decades ago."[25] Strangely enough, some of the criticisms that Jones levels against figures like Jesse Jackson and Al Sharpton are basically the same as those made against King by right-wing conservatives in the 1950s and '60s. The image of black leaders as self-serving, publicity-seeking crusaders who fail to insist on an ethic of personal responsibility for their people has long been advanced by critics on the right of the religious and political spectrums, and Jones himself, however well-meaning in his critique of Jackson and Sharpton, fits well into these categories.

No one can conclude with certainty what King would say about black leadership in America today. However, it is possible to establish, with some degree of reasonableness and conviction, what he *would not* say. In contrast to Jones, King would be far less likely to reduce the current black leadership in America to merely public figures such as Jackson and Sharpton.[26] When it came to leadership qualities and potential among his own people, King turned first and foremost to the church, where "the Negro minister" is "freer, more independent than any other person in the community." In more contemporary terms, this evidently means that not only Jackson and Sharpton, but pastors throughout the nation, and especially T. D. Jakes, Creflo Dollar, Eddie Long, Paul Morton, and other megachurch gurus, are essentially called and thus obligated to provide what King termed "strong, firm leadership."[27] Jones says nothing about these powerful megachurch personalities; who are rich in material resources; who are able to speak to, reach, and help millions; and who have the moral responsibility King himself took on in terms of speaking truth to power and uplifting and empowering the exploited, rejected, and marginalized.[28] This absence of any serious attention to full-time pastors in black churches today, or what King labeled "spiritual leaders,"[29] is a major omission in *What Would Martin Say?*,

25. Jones and Engel, *What Would Martin Say?*, 30–34, 42, 44–45, 49, 55–57, 63–64, and 67.

26. While it is clear at points that Jones has a broader sense of contemporary black leadership, he essentially confines his focus in chapter 2 to Jackson and Sharpton. See ibid., 48–50, and 55–58.

27. King, *Why We Can't Wait*, 67; and James M. Washington, ed., *A Testament of Hope: The Essential Writings and Speeches of Martin Luther King Jr.* (New York: HarperCollins, 1991), 346.

28. King's enduring challenge to the mega church pastors and other religious leaders is treated extensively in Lewis V. Baldwin, *The Voice of Conscience: The Church in the Mind of Martin Luther King Jr.* (New York: Oxford University Press, 2010), 217–49.

29. King, *Why We Can't Wait*, 67; and Washington, ed., *A Testament of Hope*, 346.

and it is really inexcusable since King himself was fundamentally a pastor and man of the church.

It is difficult to imagine King endorsing Jones's ringing critique of current black leaders like Jackson and Sharpton, who, despite their shortcomings, continue to provide a prophetic word on behalf of the poor and oppressed. It is also important to note that King, unlike Jones today, was not known in his time for public, scathing attacks on other black leaders, in part because he knew that the movement had nothing to gain from this. A strong believer in the kind of "group unity" that "necessarily involves group trust and reconciliation,"[30] King tended to be far more charitable and objective than Jones, even when voicing his concerns about figures like Malcolm X, who bitterly denounced King's Christian ethics, and especially his views on *agape* love, integration, and nonviolence. Despite his deep disagreements with Malcolm on matters ranging from religion to morality to politics, King, determined not to "sound self-righteous or absolutist," conceded that the Muslim leader had "some of the answers" to the problems afflicting his people.[31] This kind of humility and open mindedness appears lacking in Jones's account of what King would say to and about black civil rights leaders in our times.

One wonders if King would have a critique of Jones himself, who is not known for strong and prophetic leadership in the continuing struggle against bigotry and intolerance, and who has apparently drifted, ideologically, toward the very right-wing forces that King abhorred.[32] King often highlighted the need for self-criticism, and he was never hesitant to subject himself to the same critique that he visited upon others. Here King was very much in line with personalist methodology, which requires a constant openness to being critical, including self-criticism. Also, King's high regard for Mohandas K. Gandhi resulted largely from Gandhi's insistence on subjecting himself and his ideas to self-critique.[33] There are lessons here for Jones and others who are quick to lament the state of contemporary black leadership. King questioned whether Jones was putting his talents to "their highest and best use"[34] when he met him in 1960, and King might well raise

30. King, *Where Do We Go from Here*, 123–24; and King, *Why We Can't Wait*, 71.

31. Washington, ed., *A Testament of Hope*, 364–65. Also see King's very moving account of Malcolm's life in Clayborne Carson, ed., *The Autobiography of Martin Luther King Jr.* (New York: Warner, 1998), 265–69.

32. King, "Address at the Meeting of the Southern Association of Political Scientists," 1–2.

33. King spoke of Gandhi's "amazing capacity for internal criticism." See Carson, et al., eds., *The Papers of Martin Luther King Jr.*, 5:152–53.

34. Jones and Engel, *What Would Martin Say?*, 3 and 13.

the same question today. Does Jones himself, an accomplished lawyer and "winter soldier" from the struggle for civil rights in the 1960s, represent the best of what King would call strong and effective black leadership today? Indeed, this is a question that each of us should ask about ourselves, and it reminds us that any constructive critique of others must be aimed at ourselves as well. For King, true leadership often demanded a painful journey of self-critique and examination.[35] The chapters by Rosetta Ross and Shirley Geiger, Walter Fluker, and Cheryl Kirk-Duggan will provide considerably more on this question of King and leadership from moral and/or ethical standpoints.

Jones's characterization of King as "the right man at the right time"[36] seems quite logical, and King, with a slightly concealed but genuine modesty, suggested the same about himself at times. King occasionally asserted that he was "the victim of what the Germans call a *Zeitgeist*," or the spirit of the times, but his humility was such that he understood that leadership in the movement was not all about him. King held that the civil rights crusade would have occurred even if he had never been born, and he insisted that he stood where he was "because others helped me to stand there and because the forces of history projected me there."[37] King never accepted uncritically the messianic aura that many of his people sought to impose upon him. He knew that there were scores of black leaders, especially at the grassroots level, who were virtually unknown and unheralded, and who never got "their names in the papers and in the headlines."[38] Jones's failure to seriously consider King's thinking at this level further complicates his judgments about what the civil rights leader might say about and expect of black leaders in these times.

Jones's thoughts on what King might contribute to the continuing debate over affirmative action, set forth in the third chapter of *What Would Martin Say?*, are clearly defensible in some cases and quite disputable in others. As Jones points out, King addressed the fact that his people had been enslaved, robbed, and denied the basic right to make a living in America, and he was very "committed to the concept of fairness" and "achieving that level playing field we speak of today."[39] Jones also recalls King's insightful discussion of "special, compensatory measures" in *Why We Can't Wait* (1963), in which the civil rights leader highlighted the nation's principle of

---

35. Baldwin, *The Voice of Conscience*, 245.
36. Jones and Engel, *What Would Martin Say?*, 2.
37. Carson, ed., *The Autobiography of Martin Luther King Jr.*, 105.
38. Ibid.
39. Jones and Engel, *What Would Martin Say?*, 72 and 78.

compensating those who have been historically deprived of certain rights and opportunities.[40] King readily conceded that "all the wealth of this affluent society" was insufficient to adequately compensate "for the exploitation and humiliation of the Negro down through the centuries," but he insisted, at the same time, that "equal opportunity" for "the Negro" had to also come with "the practical, realistic aid which will equip him to seize it."[41] Jones is quite sensitive to the logicality and morality of King's reflections around these matters.

But Jones's claim that King mistakenly packaged "a black reparations argument" with his call for a "Bill of Rights for the Disadvantaged," thereby inadvertently undermining "the eloquent justice of reparations for black America,"[42] is highly questionable. King was enough of a realist to understand that because of the circumstances of history and the racial climate of the 1960s, any workable, economic aid program for the benefit of the disadvantaged had to be both *race-based* and *need-based*, so that the poor and deprived of *all* races could be included. For King, this was only "logical and moral,"[43] and, of course, quite consistent with his beloved community vision. Obviously, Jones is unmindful of this, concluding that if King were alive today, he would "look back" and realize that his "moral arguments for reparations" would "have been better confined" to his own race, whose "four-hundred-year history" in America merited "unique consideration from at least the U.S. Treasury."[44] But the very idea of advancing moral arguments in defense of reparations for blacks to the exclusion of calls for economic aid for poor and deprived whites was alien to King's philosophy and methods.

Jones suggests that what King said about "compensatory measures" almost a half century ago is irrelevant to any careful debate about what he would say about reparations in the form of affirmative action today.[45] Convinced that the terms of the debate have changed, Jones contends that King would oppose affirmative action as it is presently conceived and

40. Ibid., 73; and King, *Why We Can't Wait*, 136–41.

41. King, *Why We Can't Wait*, 136–37.

42. Jones and Engel, *What Would Martin Say?*, 75.

43. King, *Why We Can't Wait*, 136. As with all complex matters of this nature, King took a *both-and* rather than an *either-or* approach to reasoning. When approaching the question of economic benefits for the deprived and disadvantaged in both races, King was a dialectical thinker in the best sense of the word. Jones seems not to realize this, despite his claim to have shared King's fascination for Hegel's "unifying theory of history." See Jones and Engel, *What Would Martin Say?*, 75 and 91.

44. Jones and Engel, *What Would Martin Say?*, 77.

45. Ibid., 79.

implemented because white racism is no longer a very serious problem in America, and, consequently, "the only thing in the way of a black man's aspirations is himself."[46] Once again, Jones is echoing exactly what has come from the mouths of parties on the religious and political right over the last three or more decades. Like Newt Gingrich, Dick Armey, Clint Bolick, and other rabid anti-affirmative action advocates, Jones opposes reparations. This opposition seems to be rooted in the false premise that affirmative action as currently administered is merely a raced-based policy that mostly benefits blacks. Jones appears oblivious to the fact that the greatest beneficiaries of affirmative action up to this point have been white women.

Perhaps most disturbing is Jones's tendency to trivialize the problems stemming from white supremacy in the United States. Convinced that "this may be the least prejudiced country in history," he points to "an astonishing amount" of progress, "a robust and rising black middle class," and a few successful and powerful figures such as Oprah Winfrey as proof, and he denounces those who still speak of a continuing, haunting race problem as "race pimps."[47] There has indeed been progress on many levels in this nation, but white racism is far more pervasive than Jones is prepared to admit. The election of Barack Obama to the presidency, the lingering economic crisis, and concerns over immigration have led to a resurgence of raw racism in America,[48] and the failure to acknowledge this could lead to tragic consequences.

Even a casual glancing at the intelligence reports and newsletters of the Southern Poverty Law Center (SPLC) supports this view. The number of hate groups such as the Ku Klux Klan, Neo-Nazis, the Aryan Nations, Skinheads, and anti-government militia had exceeded one thousand in early 2011, and incidents of hate crimes and hate group activities still occur almost daily in every state in the Union.[49] Overtly racist elements exist in

46. Ibid., 77 and 92–93.

47. Ibid., 79–80 and 92–93.

48. Richard Cohen, "Racism Rears Ugly Head in Tough Economic Times," *SPLC Report* 38/3 (Fall 2008), 2; Mark Potok, "After the Election," *Intelligence Report* 132 (Winter 2008), 1; "Authorities Smash alleged Obama Assassination Plots," in ibid., 3–4; Jesse Washington, "Election Spurs Racial Backlash: Obama's Win Raises Incidents of Hate Crimes in Nation," *The Tennessean* (November 16, 2008) 3A; and Jennifer Brooks, "Obama's Popular, but So Are Racist Jokes," *The Tennessean* (March 4, 2009) 1A and 8A.

49. "U.S. Hate Groups Top 1,000: Numbers Reflect Explosive Growth of Radical Right," *SPLC Report* 41/1 (Spring 2011) 1 and 3; Richard Cohen, "Despite Obama Victory, Strong Racial Divide Remains," *SPLC Report* 38/4 (Winter, 2008), 2; "Fighting Hate—Terror from the Radical Right: SPLC, Homeland Security Warned of Rising Right-Wing Extremism," *Intelligence Report*, 38/2 (Summer 2009), 1–2; "All-White Jury Finds Teens Not Guilty of Immigrant's Murder," *Intelligence Report* 135 (Fall 2009)

the Republican Party and the Tea Party movement,[50] a reality Jones refuses to underscore in his *Behind the Dream*.[51] Racial profiling and the insults and occasional violence routinely aimed at blacks and other minorities in predominantly white settings are not merely momentary lapses of prejudice but signs of a culture that still sanctions racism.[52] Apparently, those who envisioned the advent of a postracial society with the election of Obama, the first African American president of the United States, were sadly mistaken.[53] As Tim Wise points out in his writings, white privilege and discrimination against persons of color are still functional and are actively thwarting opportunities, despite the successes of a few individuals like Obama. Obama's ascendancy to the office of United States president has further angered and emboldened the forces of white supremacy, even at the highest levels of this nation's political and economic life, and it is destined to elevate the race debate to new levels of intensity.[54]

Unwilling to engage the race problem in America in provocative, challenging, and constructive ways, conservative black voices like Jones, knowingly or unknowingly, have united in spirit and purpose with right wingers, who resort to the politics of denial while continuing to invest in the rightness of whiteness. Jones functions among a small black conservative elite that commonly moves in white circles, where they are not exposed to the most blatant racism, personally and institutionally, and they assume

---

11; "Armed Neo-Nazis 'Helping' Law Enforcement on Border," *Intelligence Report* 140 (Winter 2010) 8; "Major Police Cover-Up Alleged in Hate Murder of Immigrant," *Intelligence Report* (special issue) 137 (Spring 2010) 10–11; "For the Record," *Intelligence Report*, Issue 138 (Summer, 2010) 46–48; "Active Hate Groups in the United States," *SPLC Report* (special issue) 141 (Spring 2011) 43–49; and DeWayne Wickham, "Hate Groups Escalate Since Obama's Election," *The Tennessean* (16 June 2009) 7A.

50. "GOP Presses White Supremacists to Quit Party Posts," *Intelligence Report* (Winter 2008), 8 and 10; Chas Sisk, "GOP Aide Rebuked for Racist E-Mail," *The Tennessean* (June 16, 2009) 1B and 6B; Kathleen Parker, "GOP Needs to Be Purged of Entrenched Racism," *The Tennessean* (23 June 2009), 9A; Darrell S. Freeman, "Racial Ideology is a Roadblock to Any Future GOP Success," *The Tennessean* (June 24, 2009) 13A; and DeWayne Wickham, "Tea Party Is Today's 'Know Nothing' Movement," *USA Today* (September 7, 2010) 11A.

51. Surprisingly enough, Jones's references to Glenn Beck and the Tea Party really suggest that he has no sense of the depths of their racism. See Jones and Connelly, *Behind the Dream*, 169–72.

52. Jones takes the opposite view. See Jones and Engel, *What Would Martin Say?*, 92.

53. Frederick Wine, "The Rev. King's Dream has Finally Come True: Letters to the Editor," *The Tennessean* (November 6, 2008) 15A; and Dylan Lovan, "Church Revisits Interracial Ban after Uproar," *The Tennessean* (December 3, 2011) 5A.

54. See Tim Wise, *Between Barack and a Hard Place: Racism and White Denial in the Age of Obama* (San Francisco: City Lights, 2009), 7–149.

that their reality is the reality of all minorities in this country. They not only deny the pervasiveness of white racism, which in effect absolves them of the responsibility for doing something about it, but they also misplace the problem by blaming the victims.[55] The problem for black conservatives, then, is not white supremacy but the failure of blacks and other minorities to "pursue excellence" or to take advantages of hard-earned opportunities.[56] It should be clear to the perceptive mind that the problem involves both to some extent. As a dialectical thinker, King understood this well, and this is why he called for both government-sponsored "compensatory measures" and a vital ethic of personal responsibility.

Unfortunately, this is a point at which King surpassed even contemporary black leaders such as Jesse Jackson and Al Sharpton. King not only put forth a strong social critique of the structural causes of injustice and inequality, but he also insisted on the need for personal moral responsibility and self-determination on the part of blacks. Jackson and Sharpton are not placing proper emphasis on the personal element as an essential ingredient in black self-uplift and empowerment. Whatever the case, we are still moral agents, and if nothing else, we can decide how to respond to what systems are doing to undermine and victimize us. This should be central to Jackson's and Sharpton's social critique. The personal responsibility critique advanced by the likes of Bill Cosby should never be trivialized or ignored, even as stress is placed on the need for government initiatives through affirmative action.

Contrary to Jones's claims, black progress has not eliminated affirmative action's raison d'etre. Sadly, Jones is now identified with hard-core conservatives who are mounting what George E. Curry calls "a campaign to foist their agenda on the American public."[57] Over the last two decades, more than twenty public policy law firms and anti-civil rights think tanks, such as the Landmark Legal Foundation and the Institute for Justice, have emerged to "systematically attack affirmative action at all levels." The assault on affirmative action is mainly occurring in the areas of higher education, employment, and government contracting. Curry is right to include these anti–affirmative action advocates among the new opponents of civil rights. "Instead of acknowledging their strident opposition to civil rights

---

55. Robert Terry identifies the major marks of a racist society, including the "misplacement of the problem." When it comes to questions about racism or white supremacy today, the "misplacement of the problem" is very much an aspect of the politics of denial. See Robert W. Terry, *For Whites Only* (Grand Rapids: Eerdmans, 1970), 16–67.

56. Jones and Engel, *What Would Martin Say?*, 90–93.

57. George E. Curry, "The Real Conservative Agenda: Editor's Note," *Emerge* 11/ 2 (November 1999) 8.

gains," writes Curry, "they cleverly present a more palpable package, claiming to actually be pro-civil rights."[58] In a nation weary of charges of racism, increasing numbers are likely to listen to and accept the anti-affirmative-action rhetoric of these conservative voices, especially if they, like Jones, are able to manipulate King's words in defense of their ideas. The last thing America needs is a misrepresentation of what King, its celebrated national hero, said about affirmative action, especially at a time when the issue, due to the recent lifting of Michigan's ban on sex- and race-based preferences in government and public education, "appears headed for a return engagement before the U. S. Supreme Court."[59]

King had a keen sense of the complex social, political, and economic structures of this society, and he knew that it would take generations before they yielded equal opportunity and "a level playing field" for all Americans. We have not yet reached what King called "the promised land" in the spheres of race relations and economic opportunity and equality, and if King were with us today, it is highly doubtful that he would advocate and support the erosion of affirmative action initiatives and guidelines.[60] Unlike Jones, he would be more apt to argue that the problems that have attended the implementation of affirmative action up to this point are no justification for eliminating the policy altogether. The most logical step would be to find better and more effective ways of implementing this still much-needed policy. One could expect nothing less of King in these times, because bigotry and intolerance remain a threat to equal opportunity, there is still a glaring racial divide, the income gap between rich and poor is growing ever wider, and there are still too few inspiring possibilities for reconciliation and community.

Illegal immigration is another problem that Jones thinks King would address if he was with us today. Jones devotes much attention to the problem in chapter 4 of *What Would Martin Say?* King did speak to the immigration issue from time to time, noting how "the situation of the Negro" differed from "other immigrant groups," who came to America "voluntarily." He stressed the fact that immigrants from Europe did not come to America in

---

58. Curry, "The Real Conservative Agenda," 8; and "Profiling the Assault on Affirmative Action," in ibid., 54–56. For further insights into the debate over reparations and affirmative action initiatives, see Raymond A. Winbush, ed., *Should America Pay?: Slavery and the Raging Debate on Reparations* (New York: Amistad, 2003); Howard Fineman and Tamara Lipper, "Spinning Race," *Newsweek*, (27 January 2003) 26–29.

59. David Ashenfelter et. al., "Affirmative Action Battle Likely to Return before Supreme Court," *The Tennessean* (July 2, 2011) 4A.

60. This point stands as an enduring challenge to Wine, "The Rev. King's Dream has Finally Come True," 15A.

chains and "with the stigma of color," nor were they enslaved, nor did they suffer the deliberate disintegration of their "family structure."⁶¹ But even as King spoke of the unique experiences of the various immigrant groups, he was not known to even use the term "illegal immigration," and there is reason to believe that, in the case of immigration, moral considerations would be ultimately more important to him than what federal law and the various state laws mandate. He understood America to be a nation of immigrants, and in this situation no human being really has the right to say who should and should not live here. King occasionally quoted Psalms 24:1: "The earth is the Lord's and the fullness thereof; the world, and they that dwell therein."⁶² The civil rights leader deeply believed that humans are *dwellers and caretakers* of God's earth but not *owners* of God's earth; that we are the earth's sojourners, and that all of God's children ideally have the right to inhabit any part of it.⁶³ Furthermore, the very concept of an "illegal alien" would seem to call into question King's concepts of the interrelated structure of all reality," the social nature of human existence, and the necessity for a truly integrated society and world.⁶⁴

Jones cleverly, forcefully, and audaciously projects a different image on King, suggesting that he would see "our immigration laws and policies" as not "inherently racist" but consistent with "God's law," that he would be very concerned about the potential threat immigrants might pose in this post- 9/11 age, that he would insist that every one who enters this country "go through the legal channels," and that he would be open to some type of penalties for illegal immigrants. Jones uses the "saga of Elvira Arellano," a twenty-two-year-old Mexican woman who took every means at her disposal to remain in the United States illegally, to explain how King would approach this issue legally and morally. For Jones, Elvira becomes the typical illegal alien. But there are obviously problems here. Jones portrays Elvira as one who unjustifiably violates both legal and moral laws to live in America, as a burden to the nation's taxpayers, and as one who potentially takes jobs that should go to someone black, and, because of this, she has no rights and

61. King, *Where Do We Go from Here*, 103.

62. See, King, "The Meaning of Hope," unpublished version of a sermon, Dexter Avenue Baptist Church, Montgomery, Alabama (10 December 1967), King Center Library and Archives, 11.

63. Interestingly enough, King, in his celebrated "Letter from the Birmingham City Jail" (1963), established the right of the prophet of God to go "far beyond the boundaries of their home towns," to go and proclaim God's word wherever it was needed. It is difficult to imagine King being of this opinion while, simultaneously, denying the right of immigrants to live where they wish. See King, *Why We Can't Wait*, 77.

64. Martin Luther King Jr., *The Trumpet of Conscience* (New York: Harper & Row, 1987), 69–70.

deserves to be treated like a thief. Jones's account is further complicated by his heavy focus on illegal immigrants from Mexico, with no major attention to the many who may have come from some other country or even Europe.[65] Such views do not square with King's *agape* love ethic and his concept of the dignity and worth of all human personality. They are far more in line with what one might expect today from some Christian fundamentalist or politician with Republican or Tea Party connections. The thought of King joining those who protest today against the racist, new immigration laws in states like Arizona, Alabama, and South Carolina, over the objections of right-wing religious and political extremists, is really not difficult to fathom, for he understood the need for immigration in light of the pervasive impact of racial and economic imperialism worldwide.[66]

Jones has made an honest attempt to explain what King would say about illegal immigration, but he comes frighteningly close to lending credence to "the right wing vitriol and demonizing propaganda" that too often target Hispanics and other immigrants of color.[67] The immigration issue actually exposes our unresolved effort to come to terms with the realities of racial and cultural diversity, and this is good in some sense. Moreover, we are being forced to reframe the discourse and dialogue on race and diversity, beyond the issues of black-white relations, and this, too, should be appreciated, because it could yield more possibilities for the creation of the kind of society that King envisioned. Immigration just may be part of God's plan to force us to live out the true meaning of King's dream, particularly as it relates to a genuinely integrated society, characterized by brotherhood and sisterhood, mutual acceptance, interpersonal and intergroup living, and shared power across the boundaries of human differences. In a later chapter in this work, I will more fully explain how King might be understood in relation to the issue of illegal immigration in our times.

Strangely, Jones takes up the issues of race and diversity with a little more sophistication in chapter 5 of *What Would Martin Say?*, which explores what King would say about anti-Semitism. This topic is well worth the attention Jones devotes to it, because King highly respected Jewish people and their faith, and he also conversed, prayed, sang, and marched with Jewish

---

65. Jones and Engel, *What Would Martin Say?*, 110–24.

66. This suggestion is made with the knowledge that most of the demonstrations against the immigration laws already passed have targeted their openness to racial profiling, which "creates an unwelcome environment for people of color" ("Thousands Rally against Immigration Law," *The Tennessean* [July 3, 2011] 3A).

67. Mark Potok, "The Arizonification of America," *Intelligence Report* (special issue) 141 (Spring 2011) 1; and "Nativist Leader Charged in Double Murder, Tied to Aryan Nations," *Intelligence Report* 135 (Fall 2009) 7.

leaders like Rabbi Abraham J. Heschel and Rabbi Everett Gendler in civil rights campaigns across the South. As Jones notes, King would undoubtedly speak out, in the strongest terms possible, against anti-Semitism, though he would be less prone than Jones, for reasons already mentioned, to single out particular persons, like a Louis Farakhan, Jesse Jackson, and Al Sharpton, to make his points.[68] King saw anti-Semitism as a great social evil, but, realizing that Jews were not the only victims, he considered it in the larger context of racism as a world phenomenon. Also, King viewed the struggle against anti-Semitism, not so much in terms of a clash between individuals or individuals and groups, but as a tension between justice and injustice.

Jones should have perhaps framed his thoughts around what King would say today about the more general problem of racism, while treating anti-Semitism as one expression of that problem. King was more apt to do this, even when speaking to Jewish audiences. After all, anti-Semitism is not the only form of racism, and Jews are not the only victims of racism. Jones also essentially ignores the racism that some Jews practice toward blacks and other persons of color, including the Palestinians, which rarely gets attention in books, the media, and other sources. King denounced racism in all forms, and he, unlike Jones, was much more objective in his position on the Israeli-Palestinian crisis. Knowing that both Israelis and Palestinians had legitimate goals, and that both were guilty at times of acts of aggression against each other,[69] King would be less likely to suggest, as does Jones, that "there would be peace tomorrow if today the Palestinians put down their rocks, stones, guns, and bombs."[70] Statements like this are expected to come from right-wingers and Christian Zionists such as Gary Bauer, Tim LaHaye, and John Hagee, but not from a legal mind who worked with King, and who contributed so much to free this nation. King never affirmed Israel's "territorial integrity" and "right to exist as a state in security," without also stressing the need for the Palestinians and all Arabs to be freed from "a state of imposed poverty and backwardness."[71] This was the profundity of King's

68. Jones stops short of calling Farrakhan, Jackson, and Sharpton anti-Semites, but he does accuse them of anti-Semitic actions and, perhaps unjustly, of refusing to speak and act against the problem. See Jones and Engel, *What Would Martin Say?*, 136–41.

69. See King's strong statement to this effect in "Conversation with Martin Luther King," in Washington, ed., *A Testament of Hope*, 670–71. This conversation took place on 25 March 1968 at the invitation of Jewish rabbis.

70. "Draft of a Statement Regarding SCLC's Participation at the National Conference on New Politics," Chicago, Illinois (September, 1967), King Center Library and Archives, 1; Lewis V. Baldwin and Amiri YaSin Al-Hadid, *Between Cross and Crescent: Christian and Muslim Perspectives on Malcolm and Martin* (Gainesville: University Press of Florida, 2002), 344–45; and Jones and Engel, *What Would Martin Say?*, 139.

71. "Draft of a Statement Regarding SCLC's Participation," 1; "Interview with

communitarian ethic and ideal, as we will see in the more extensive discussion of King and racism in chapter 8.

Jones's reflections on what King would say concerning Islamic terrorism and the war in Iraq call into question much of what King said about the morality and practicality of nonviolence and the immorality and impracticality of violence. The subject is examined in the sixth chapter of *What Would Martin Say?*. Jones suggests that King would have backed the preemptive war policy that led to the fall of Saddam Hussein, especially since he was a brutal dictator, a potential threat to world peace, and one who refused to listen to the voice of reason when it came to weapons of mass destruction. Jones leads us to believe that Hussein's recalcitrance and the very thought of his bombs exploding in America's major cities would have compelled King to see war as the only alternative, but, Jones adds, "once the war started, he'd want the killing and bloodshed ended as soon as possible."[72] In an equally stunning conclusion, Jones maintains that King would be pleased with America's military campaign in Afghanistan, for it freed the country from the Taliban's brand of radical Islam and its oppression of women, guerrilla skirmishes, and the further advance of Islamic terrorism.[73] From Jones's point of view, King's stands on these matters would be essentially no different from the positions taken by George W. Bush, Jerry Falwell, and Pat Robertson, who falsely posited a link between Hussein and Islamic terrorism, and who defended America's aggression against both Iraq and Afghanistan on moral and humanitarian grounds.

The mere thought of King supporting the use of violence for any reason whatsoever is virtually impossible to entertain, especially in view of what he consistently wrote and passionately proclaimed. King, by his own admission, went "through a kind of intellectual pilgrimage on the whole question of war and the pacifist position,"[74] and he concluded over time that "wisdom born of experience should tell us that war is obsolete"—that "the destructive power of modern weapons eliminates even the possibility that war may serve any good at all."[75] In fact, King dismissed violence in all

---

Martin Luther King Jr. on 'Issues and Answers,'" an ABC Radio and Television Program, by Tom Jerriel, ABC Atlanta Bureau Chief, and John Casserly, ABC Washington Correspondent (18 June 1967), King Center Library and Archives, 13–14; and Baldwin and Al-Hadid, *Between Cross and Crescent*, 344–45.

72. Jones and Engel, *What Would Martin Say?*, 175–77.

73. Ibid., 169–73.

74. "Interview with Martin Luther King Jr. on World Peace," unpublished version prepared for *Red Book Magazine* (November 1964), King Center Library and Archives, 3–7.

75. King, *Where Do We Go from Here*, 183.

forms as both impractical and immoral because it is rooted in hatred rather than love, it leads to more violence, it tends to destroy rather than redeem relationships, and it is antithetical to creativity, wholeness, and the creation of community.[76]

Jones's image of a King who would endorse interpersonal violence and war under certain conditions is difficult to reconcile with this King, and with the King who placed love and nonviolence at the core of the Christian ethic. King was not known to compromise his convictions, and there is really no reason to assume that he would move from an unwavering commitment to nonviolent resolution of conflict to a support for war if he lived among us today, especially since weapons of mass destruction are far more pervasive and the potential for human self-destruction considerably greater than in his own time. It appears safer to say that King would be even more passionate in denouncing any justification for war as morally repulsive and practically unsound. Jones's claim that King would shift positions in the face of brutal dictatorships and the immense spiral of global terrorism raises even more doubt about whether he knew King's mind "as well as anyone."[77] Rufus Burrow's chapters will further elaborate these and other concerns, while placing King's views about various forms of violence in proper context.

The problem with Jones's reinvented image of King is further complicated by his tendency to only associate Islam with violence and terrorism. King knew that there were persons susceptible to violence in all the great religions, and he said in 1964 that "some of the most tragic wars in the world have been religious wars."[78] He did not exclude Christianity from his analysis of the problem, for he knew that much of the violence and terrorism used against blacks in the South over generations came from whites who professed to be Bible-believing Christians. Furthermore, King had a much greater respect for the Muslim faith than is suggested in Jones's *What Would Martin Say?* King held that Islam, like Christianity, Judaism, Hinduism, and Buddhism, embraces love "as the supreme unifying principle," and "has always sought to promote peace and good will among men."[79] There is nothing in King's writings or speeches which suggest that he would agree with Jones's indictment against Islam based on the violent actions of Osama Bin Laden and other self-proclaimed Muslim extremists, who constitute such a minority in the faith. Jones's tendency to identify Islam, and not groups like

76. Ansbro, *Martin Luther King Jr.*, 231–32.

77. Jones and Engel, *What Would Martin Say?*, xvi (introduction).

78. "Interview with Martin Luther King Jr. on World Peace," 2; and Baldwin, *The Voice of Conscience*, 214–15.

79. King, *Where Do We Go from Here*, 190–91; Washington, ed., *A Testament of Hope*, 242; and "Interview with Martin Luther King Jr. on World Peace," 1–2.

the Aryan Churches in America, with violence actually feeds into the religious bigotry and intolerance so widespread today,[80] and that King found entirely unacceptable in his own time. The emerging patterns of Islamophobia, or the anti-Islamic, anti-Arab sensibilities, in our contemporary society can never be rightfully associated with the King legacy.

In the seventh and last chapter of *What Would Martin Say?*, Jones explores what he thinks would be King's views on who assassinated him. Jones is convinced that James Earl Ray killed King, and he strongly suggests that King would agree. Although Jones discusses the tensions that increasingly surfaced between King and elements in the federal government, and especially the Federal Bureau of Investigation (FBI), he never entertains the real possibility that the civil rights leader's death resulted from a conspiracy that included government officials. In Jones's opinion, King would have much to say to Ray but not to parties in the federal government, who at least share some moral responsibility for King's murder.[81] No one actually knows what King would say today about these matters, but one can be fairly certain that he would not hesitate to criticize the government when it fails to protect prophetic, social activists who risk all in the defense of values that stand at the heart of the nation's creed and interests. Michael G. Long has far more to say about this later in this volume.

Jones missed a great opportunity in the last chapter of *What Would Martin Say?*, and also in *Behind the Dream*, to discuss what might be King's prophetic word to the federal government today. King most certainly believed in speaking truth to power, even when it meant being isolated and persecuted. It is not hard to imagine him speaking to those at the highest levels of this nation's political life about war and peace, economic justice, and the need to ensure that all Americans enjoy life, liberty, and the pursuit of happiness. There is no way to ignore such a profound and enduring challenge, especially if Jones, driven by "a profound sense of responsibility to the past and the future," is really serious about interpreting "what contributions" King "would add to his singular legacy if he were alive today."[82]

If Jones "put words in" King's mouth,[83] as he claims, then we need to know why King's words on paper sound so different from Jones's words on paper. We also need to understand why there is such a contrast between the two men, philosophically and in terms of methods designed to eliminate

80. The assumption that Islam breeds violence is pervasive even at the highest levels of America's political life. See Eileen Sullivan, "Congress Gets Sidetracked on Islam Debate," *The Tennessean* (16 June 2011) 4A.

81. Jones and Engel, *What Would Martin Say?*, 206–12.

82. Ibid., xii (author's note).

83. Ibid., xvi (introduction).

social evil. Moreover, we need some explanation as to how King could be so prophetic in the 1960s, and Jones so defensive of the status quo today. This is a real enigma, particularly in light of the clear and important role Jones played as one of King's closest aides. Without answers to these and other questions, it is virtually impossible to make sense of much of Jones's *What Would Martin Say?*

It is obvious that the words in both *What Would Martin Say?* and *Behind the Dream* are Jones's words and not those of King. In explaining how King's ideas and message would take on new hues and pertinence in our perilous society, Jones essentially attributes his own words to King, and, in the process, uses the civil rights leader to convey his own thoughts on problems that still afflict society and how they might best be addressed. Jones has been less than careful here, and he actually reinvents King in the image of a present day right wing conservative. Unfortunately, this is the product of Jones's lively but seemingly misinformed zeal to make King's legacy a source of insight and inspiration for this current age, but King is undeserving of this. Jones seeks to justify his claims with the assertion that King, "had he lived, would've changed with the times."[84] This is one of the basic assumptions behind Jones's treatment of King as a spokesperson for today. But it is better to say that King had a tremendous capacity to grow and develop in positive or constructive ways, but he was not known to embrace the kind of change that required him to surrender his most cherished beliefs and values, especially when this also necessitated a break with the essentials of the Christian faith.

Can King Survive Jones?: A Final Word

Clarence B. Jones notes that he frequently becomes highly annoyed by persons who take King's "words out of their spoken and written context to prove" their points, "knowing that Martin's supposed opinion will lend credibility to any argument." "Martin Luther King, Jr. was no Rorschach test," Jones continues, "allowing the beholder to see whatever he chooses to see and believe."[85] Ironically, Jones's words are actually an indictment against himself, because he is guilty of the very tendency that vexes him about others who manipulate and distort King's words in defense of their own points of view. Jones does not appear to be the kind of person who would consciously or purposely falsify King's words, but he does have the overbearingly proud sense that he, due to his association and friendship

---

84. Ibid., 27.
85. Ibid., xv (introduction).

with King, is in a better position than most people to decide what words would come out of King's mouth today. Nothing could be more problematic in these times, when all too many Americans are confused about King and the principles and values for which he gave his life.

Jones creates an image of King not based on what the civil rights leader said, but purely as a response to the needs and aspirations of our times. This obviously requires risk-taking and a venture into the horizon of the unknown. Any venture into the unfamiliar is fraught with risks, but the tragedy in this case is that there are those who will accept Jones's picture of King as authoritative, especially since it is projected in books written by one of King's personal friends and lawyers. We simply must insist on the need for people to know what King actually said and what his actual ideas and practices were, instead of easily and uncritically allowing Jones and others on the right to misappropriate and domesticate his words, ideas, and legacy. As stated previously, the keys to what King might say on any contemporary issue or problem rest not with Jones's claims, but, rather, in an intense and profound study of King's own words, which are accessible to us in unusual fullness.[86] Casting a fresh eye on King's legacy should translate into a more careful examination of the substance of what King expressed in his own words. Thus, Jones's image of King should be contested by admirers of the King legacy, and by all who understand the need to treat King in historically astute and sensitive ways. Jones knew King in the 1960s, more than a half century ago, but there is no way that he or anyone else can, with certitude, speak the mind of this prophet of peace today.

The full impact of what Jones has written about King is not yet evident, but this will undoubtedly change as more and more religious and political conservatives become familiar with *What Would Martin Say?* and *Behind the Dream*. Conservative voices like Richard Land of the Southern Baptist Convention (SBC) are already using words similar to those used by Jones to attack the continuing civil rights leadership and involvements of Jesse Jackson and Al Sharpton. This was most evident in the recent national protests surrounding the death of Trayvon Martin, an unarmed seventeen-year-old black youth in Florida, in which Jackson and Sharpton figured prominently. Land strongly defended the shooter, George Zimmerman, while denouncing Jackson and Sharpton as "race hustlers."[87] Land went on to charge that Sharpton was "a provocateur and a racial ambulance chaser of the first order."[88] It is difficult to avoid the conclusion that African Americans like

86. Fairclough e-mail to Baldwin (23 August 2011).

87. Heidi Hall, "Land Rant Stings Some Southern Baptists: Radio Host Blasts Black Leaders over Trayvon Martin Case," *The Tennessean* (5 April 2012) 1A and 8A.

88. Ibid.; William W. McDermet III, "Land Remarks in Martin Case Show Lack of

Jones are doing much, consciously or unconsciously, to create the kind of climate in which white religious and political conservatives can feel comfortable in making attacks like this on Jackson, Sharpton, and any other black civil rights leader who dares to take steps that King himself often took in the interest of racial justice.[89]

A similar problem surfaces when the lingering effects of Jones's attacks on affirmative action are considered. Recent statistics show that the average annual income of whites far exceeds that of African Americans, Latinos, and other minorities, and that women are paid considerably less than men for the same work routines, thus highlighting the continuing need for affirmative action in some forms. In light of these disturbing trends, Jones's use of King in a blistering assault on affirmative action will obviously do more harm than good. It means that King is being used to justify the disabling and disempowering of the very persons whom King labeled "the least of these."

Jones's claims about what King would say about race will only reinforce the thinking and actions of conservatives who have long been determined to ignore and even deny the existence of the problem. The attacks on President Barack Obama, from virtually every segment of conservative white society, should remind even casual observers that we do not live in a postracial society, that white supremacy is alive and well. Contrary to what Jones would have us believe, anti-Semitism, while painfully present in some circles, is not the only form of racism that haunts the nation. White supremacy is still the most virulent and destructive form of racism in America. King himself understood that it takes more than the passage of time and a few pieces of legislation to eliminate white supremacist policies and practices. It is ultimately about changing the hearts and minds of people. The challenge to eliminate every vestige of racism from the society remains quite evident, and those who think otherwise are sadly trapped in the politics of denial. Apparently, Jones is ill prepared to accept this analysis of America's continuing racial climate.

In a real sense, Jones emerges from both *What Would Martin Say?* and *Behind the Dream* as essentially an uncritical enthusiast for King, failing to

---

Understanding," *The Tennessean* (April 8, 2012) 17A; Bob Smietana, "Critics Call for Land to Resign: Baptist Ethicist's Radio Show Canceled over Racial Comments," *The Tennessean* (2 June 2012), 1A and 4A; and Bob Smietana, "Radio Executive Defends Baptist Ethicist Land," *The Tennessean* (June 3, 2012) 2B.

89. Equally disturbing were the comments of the Reverend C. L. Bryant, a conservative black pastor who once headed the Garland, Texas, chapter of the NAACP. Bryant also referred to Jackson and Sharpton as "race hustlers," and accused them of "exploiting" the tragic death of Trayvon Martin. See "Former NAACP Leader Blasts Jackson and Sharpton as 'Race Hustlers,'" in *Catholic Online News Consortium*, http://www.catholic.org/national/national_story.php?id=45427/.

sufficiently explain those cases in which King's words may not be relevant or meaningful for our age. Interestingly enough, Jones also provides nothing important on what King might say about the Christian Church, youth, the status of women, the issue of gay rights, environmental protection, and other concerns currently in the forefront of public thinking. It is only natural to assume that King, who was always on the cutting edge of current events, would be speaking to these concerns.

Jones actually fails to weave together the complex facets of King's life and thought into a vivid, absorbing portrait for our times, but the question is, *"Can King survive Jones?"* Much of the answer to this question lingers with the *true* bearers of the King legacy, who cannot afford to remain silent in the face of efforts to domesticate King. One of King's last sermons, "A Drum Major Instinct," delivered at his Ebenezer Baptist Church in Atlanta, Georgia, on February 4, 1968, is still a timely warning against any effort to turn him into the likes of a Jerry Falwell or Pat Robertson, an establishment Negro, or someone other than who he really *was*. King declared that after his death, he would like for somebody to simply say that he was "a drum major for justice," "a drum major for peace," and "a drum major for righteousness," "and all of the other shallow things will not matter."[90] These are the words of an audacious prophet, not a right-wing conservative or a status-quo-seeking Negro. They are words that will forever separate the historical King from the King that Clarence B. Jones re-creates on paper.

Past associations with King have spawned a notable variety of images of the civil rights leader and his legacy. This is clear proof that King has transcended his own person and time. Jones's books, *What Would Martin Say?* and *Behind the Dream*, however controversial, are a reminder of how the different images might encourage us to approach King afresh, and from our own viewpoints in these early years of the twenty-first century. But we must also be careful not to overlook or trivialize the prophetic zeal and greatness that characterized King's life, that indelibly mark his legacy, and that still endear him to so many freedom-loving people worldwide.

---

90. Clayborne Carson and Peter Holloran, eds., *A Knock at Midnight: Inspiration from the Great Sermons of Reverend Martin Luther King Jr.* (New York: Warner, 1998), 185.

3

Leading in Challenging Times
Martin Luther King Jr., Ruby Hurley, and the Meaning of Black Leadership

ROSETTA E. ROSS & SHIRLEY T. GEIGER

On January 21, 2010, the *New York Times* reported the Supreme Court's ruling that the federal government may not ban political spending by corporations in candidate elections. This decision in the *Citizens United v. Federal Elections Commission* case represents a major departure from historic judicial and legislative efforts to safeguard democratic processes by placing restrictions on campaign financing. The ruling does not allow corporations to make direct contributions to candidates; however, it does allow unlimited corporate expenditures "in candidate elections." Because of the extraordinary resources at corporate disposal, the ruling appears to offer the possibility of inordinate corporate influence on candidates for elected office, on the outcomes of elections and, ultimately, on decisions made by elected officials. Dissenting from the majority opinion, Supreme Court Justice John Paul Stevens argued that, contrary to political rhetoric, there is not a substantial difference between selling votes and selling access to candidates. "And selling access," Stevens wrote, "is not qualitatively different from giving special preference to those who spent money on one's behalf."[1] Stevens, the other two justices who joined his dissent, and the community of those concerned about the undue influence of money on our political system worry that the *Citizens United* decision will obscure or obstruct elected leaders' ability to

---

1. Adam Liptak, "Justices, 5–4, Reject Corporate Spending Limit," *New York Times*, January 22, 2010, httpp:www.nytimes.com/.

make choices that benefit the entire country and all its citizens. The decision appears to reflect the trend toward widespread loss of honorable and effective leadership across social and political life in the United States.

In Clarence B. Jones's recent book about Dr. Martin Luther King Jr. (for whom Attorney Jones worked as "principal advisor" from 1960 to 1968), Jones expresses a related concern about the ability of contemporary leaders, specifically black leaders, to make decisions and choices that benefit their constituencies.[2] The book's second essay, "What Would Martin Say about Today's Black Leadership?," laments that contemporary black leaders are being manipulated, that they squander moral capital, and that they are stuck in one paradigm of analysis. When the goal of personal aggrandizement seems written into political and corporate leadership manuals, what is to be made of contrary admonitions to those who would be leaders? In this essay, we consider the current state of social and political leadership and make assertions about what Martin Luther King Jr. might say to, and not simply about, leaders, especially today's black leaders.

In what follows, we first offer an overview of an article on corporate fundraising and members of the Congressional Black Caucus (CBC) that appeared in the *New York Times* on February 14, 2010. Since the CBC substantially symbolizes and is an outgrowth of the electoral political emphasis during the Civil Rights Movement, and since at its launch in 1971, the CBC was described "as a single unified group representing the 'national Black community,'" we consider it one logical representation of contemporary black leadership.[3] The second section of the essay presents a critical reading of Jones's chapter, "What Would Martin Say about Today's Black Leadership?" In the chapter, Attorney Jones identifies his ideal characteristics of or goals for black leadership by naming well-known individuals and groups and then laying out his view of their shortcomings and faults. When framed positively, these characteristics may be seen as what, according to Jones, Dr. King would say *to* today's black leaders: Be independent; act with integrity; be responsive to what people need; have a vision of a just, unsegregated society; be prepared; demonstrate moral authority; be relevant; and, finally, reject being a victim. Jones asserts that, "judged by these clear standards, few black leaders of today pass the Martin Luther King test of integrity."[4] While we cannot disagree with the eight qualities of honorable leadership

---

2. Clarence B. Jones and Joel Engel, *What Would Martin Say?* (New York: Harper Collins, 2008), 32–33.

3. Marguerite Ross Barnett, "The Congressional Black Caucus: Illusions and Realities of Power," in *The New Black Politics: The Search for Political Power*, ed. Michael B. Preston et al. (New York: Longman, 1982), 33.

4. Jones and Engel, *What Would Martin Say?*, 34.

to which Jones alludes, we question the liberty he takes in making some assertions about Dr. King's likely positions on contemporary issues. In several instances, we suggest that Jones's view appears to contradict the legacy and spirit of Dr. King's leadership as described by Jones and others. Most prominently, Jones suggests that King would oppose undocumented workers, "insisting that the border be closed and everyone sent home," and Jones implies that Dr. King would affirm Jones's negative and sometimes erroneous characterization of other leaders and groups.

Before moving to the final section of the essay, we include a discussion of the meaning of *leadership* and develop our own definition to show how leadership includes a critical relationship between leaders and followers in King's time and today. In this interlude, we explore how such leadership is exemplified in the life of one of King's contemporaries, Mrs. Ruby Hurley. The final section of the essay links our definition of *leadership* with the qualities identified by attorney Jones to create a lens through which to examine the life and contributions of Hurley, whose career as an organizer and administrator for the National Association for the Advancement of Colored People (NAACP) was recently honored by the United States Postal Service on a commemorative stamp. Consistent with King's leadership style, which was wise and confident enough to integrate leading and following, Hurley demonstrated vision, commitment, courage, and responsibility. We conclude with an assessment of contemporary black leadership and offer modest assertions about where we go from here.

The Citizens United Ruling and the Congressional Black Caucus

Just three weeks after its coverage of the *Citizens United v. Federal Elections Commission* decision, the *New York Times* ran on its front page a story on the methods by which corporations are already able to secure access to lawmakers when it reported that the Congressional Black Caucus (CBC) has become a "fund-raising powerhouse" through a network of nonprofit organizations, including the Congressional Black Caucus Foundation.[5] Noting what may be perceived as lavish spending on its headquarters, golf outings, casino visits, and parties, the *Times* article says the CBC sometimes is forced to defend itself against criticism of ties to companies that have businesses "seen by some as detrimental to its black constituents." This, the *Times* suggests, is ethically ambiguous since the CBC "has used its status

---

5. Eric Lipton and Eric Lichtblau, "In Black Caucus, a Fund-Raising Powerhouse," *New York Times*, February 13, 2010. Online: http:www.nytimes.com/.

as a *civil rights* organization to become a fund-raising power in Washington." The article's identification of the CBC as a "civil rights organization" likely derives from the Caucus's emergence as a direct consequence of the increased number of blacks elected to Congress in the wake of gains made during the Civil Rights Movement. However, in the context of an article examining corporate influence on lawmakers, using the appellation "civil rights organization" to characterize the CBC in 2010 likely carries the additional innuendo that the CBC's relationship to corporations departs from one legacy associated with the Civil Rights Movement: occupying the moral high ground. When one recalls the commitment to accepting consequences for engaging in civil disobedience, or examples like the exoneration of Dr. King on income tax evasion charges because of his meticulous circumspection in recording travel expenses, contributions, and speaking fees,[6] identification of the Civil Rights Movement with high moral ground (at least the social and political moral high ground) is not unwarranted. This appears to be the standard by which *New York Times* reporters Lipton and Lichtblau judged the CBC in the story.

The fundraising power of the Congressional Black Caucus derives, the *Times* reported, from corporate contributions to its main nonprofit arm, the Congressional Black Caucus Foundation (CBCF). Then-CBC Chair, Representative Barbara Lee, responded to the story by saying, "It was a severe disservice to the CBC and to other legal entities written about ... to mistakenly and recklessly lump these organizations together in a way that demeans each of these organizations and their work."[7] President and chief executive of the Congressional Black Caucus Foundation, Ms. Elsie Scott, told the *Times* that corporations who contribute "are trying to get the attention of CBC members ... I don't think there is anything wrong with that. They're in business and they want to deal with people who have influence and power."[8] Ms. Scott also published a letter challenging the *Times*' charge that the Congressional Black Caucus Foundation's spending is "lavish and ethically ambiguous." Noting the number of internships, community conference opportunities, food-for-the-homeless programs, health-screening programs, and comparably low administrative costs, Ms. Scott defended the CBCF as an organization bringing racial changes to "the landscape on Capitol Hill," and "giving future leaders the experience and foundation they need

---

6. See Taylor Branch's discussion of tax specialist Chauncey Eskridge's audit of King's finances in *Parting the Waters: America in the King Years, 1954–1963* (New York: Simon & Schuster, 1988), 294–97.

7. "Congressional Black Caucus Rips New York Times Piece." Online: http:/politico.com/news/stories/0210/33141.html/.

8. Ibid.

to have successful careers in public service." She especially noted the *Times'* misrepresentation of an expenditure of funds for food for a four-day meeting ($693,137) as the cost for a single banquet. In general, Ms. Scott asserted a defense of the CBC similar to that of Congresswoman Barbara Lee: "The *Times* article," Ms. Scott wrote, "blurs the lines between the Congressional Black Caucus Foundation (CBCF), the Congressional Black Caucus (CBC), the Congressional Black Caucus Institute (CBCI), and the Congressional Black Caucus Political Action Committee (CBC PAC)."[9]

The possibility of "blurring the lines," not only in the identities of organizations, but also in influence on elections and, most importantly, in decisions of lawmakers, is just what alarmed the dissenting Supreme Court justices and others in the *Citizens United v. Federal Elections Commission* case. The social and moral context that produced nonviolent civil disobedience and moral circumspection during the Civil Rights Movement is a far cry from the morally hazardous territory to which Justice Stevens referred in his dissenting opinion. The Congressional Black Caucus's practices, similar to those of lawmakers across Capitol Hill, reflect the morally fuzzy (and, therefore, challenging) nature of the current social and political context as indicated by the majority opinion in the *Citizens United* case: as long as they do not give funds directly to candidates, corporations may spend as much as they want in whatever ways they want in candidate elections. In light of this ruling, it could well be argued that current legal campaign financing practices in the United States pose a challenge to the character of its democracy. Institutionalizing a system of campaign finance that carries with it the implied right of access to elected political leaders, whether because of spending on elections or contributions to nonprofit organizations supporting candidates, makes greater the moral hazard that economic opportunity will trump all other options during electoral and legislative processes.

Does the role of money subvert the will of the people and, hence, derail the possibility of a true democracy in which the people and their leaders can function cooperatively? Should rank-and-file citizens cynically dismiss all politicians as crooks, and choose apathy, passivity, and noninvolvement? What is the role of leaders and of the people, especially the people less well represented than those holding extraordinary economic wealth? Could the people assume a role as co-leaders with power to hold elected officials accountable to adopt behaviors that ensure that money in politics does not subvert the commonweal? What is the meaning of leadership in a context in which such questions arise? The eight qualities of honorable leadership

9. Elsie M. Scott e-mail: The New York Times Article on CBC. BookerRising.net. Online: http://www.bookerrising.net/2010/03/email-new-york-times-article-on-the cbc.html/.

gleaned from Jones may be identified as important to leading with integrity in any setting; however, given the racial and historical circumstances within which Jones discusses these qualities, they may be seen as especially important for honorable black leadership. In what follows, we explicate the eight qualities identified by Jones.

What Jones Says Martin Would Say about Black Leadership

Jones identifies his first three qualities of honorable leadership in an intersecting discussion of autonomy, character, and intention. Emerging in the introductory section of the essay, through these first three qualities, Jones urges black leaders to "Be independent, act with integrity, and be responsive to what people need." Jones agues that black leadership (and rank-and-file black persons) cannot be independent so long as they demonstrate uncritical and unwavering loyalty to any one political party, as is substantially the case with the Democratic Party. Arguing that this unquestioning loyalty does not require Democratic candidates to respect or listen to black communities, Jones challenges black leaders to act with autonomy and pragmatism by recognizing the loss of bargaining power as well as the potential loss of access when black people give themselves so wholeheartedly to one political party. Related to this discussion of independence, Jones disputes the possibility that black leaders act with integrity as they participate in what may be called the dance of disrespect of black communities. In this dance, Democratic candidates partner with many black leaders who pledge to deliver black votes while the leaders look out "less for the people's interest than their own."[10] Jones writes, "For them money and publicity appear to trump justice, humanity is an abstraction with little connection to human beings, and the greatness of their egos often supersedes or obscures the righteousness of their cause."[11] In contrast to what he might call the codependent and dishonorable practices of some black leaders, Jones says Martin Luther King Jr. identified "Doing for others" as the most important and persistent life question."[12] In this regard, a third quality of honorable leadership Jones identifies is responsiveness to the people's needs.

In addition to this cluster of three primary traits of honorable leadership, Jones identifies five additional qualities: "Have a vision of a just, unsegregated society," "Be prepared," "Demonstrate moral authority," "Be relevant," and "Reject being a victim." The vision of the "new generation

---

10. Jones and Engel, *What Would Martin Say?*, 32–33.
11. Ibid., 34-35. See also ibid., 31–34.
12. Ibid., 34.

of African American leaders," Jones says, is limited by the apparent belief that propagating fear is the only way for them to succeed. Jones argues that King's vision of truth and hope (not fear) inspired others to join and follow him. In contrast, Jones says some contemporary black leaders appear unable to move beyond seeking to convince African Americans that they are severely disadvantaged, or threatening white organizations and businesses with potential boycotts or other demonstrations. Suggesting that the propagation of fear results from a lack of vision and preparation, Jones asserts that Martin Luther King Jr. met leadership moments he encountered with the preparation needed to set a course for change. Because King was prepared, Jones writes, he "found himself in the right place at the right time with the right tools to deliver the right message for the right cause."[13]

Jones's understanding of King's preparation includes King's willingness to subject himself to the practices and consequences to which he called others. This, Jones writes, was the basis of King's moral authority. King "never asked, never encouraged, never even suggested that someone else engage in a battle that he himself was not prepared to lead personally." Consistently, Jones continues, King recognized and bore the consequences of the nonviolent civil disobedience to which he called others.[14] Although contemporary times present different challenges, Jones calls contemporary black leaders to demonstrate moral authority. He also calls contemporary black leaders to relevancy, noting the tendency of some leaders to express outrage about "apparent racial injustices while neglecting larger, more pressing issues confronting black communities."

Examining the 2006 Duke University lacrosse team debacle and the 2007 Jena (Louisiana) Six demonstrations, Jones concludes that contemporary black leaders sometimes look for racial injustice where it does not exist, while overlooking real challenges to black communities that do not appear overtly related to racial oppression. "At a time when the nation's streets are black killing fields," Jones writes, "with blacks killing blacks by the dozens every week with no rational reason the leadership appears only concerned with what might get on television."[15] The numbers of black persons dying to black-on-black violence, Jones argues, is as relevant, and in many cases is more relevant, than interracial offenses within specific contexts. Finally, Jones encourages black leaders to reject the temptation to persistently identify themselves and black people as victims. Jones calls current black leaders to "have the nerve and political courage to suggest that sometimes, even just

13. Ibid., 41.
14. Ibid., 45, 46.
15. Ibid., 49.

sometimes, blacks are the masters of their own fates."[16] The failure to face this reality, Jones says, often hurts black persons instead of helping.

Before turning to our own assertions about leadership, we offer the following assessment of Jones's discussion in his chapter, "What Would Martin Say about Today's Black Leadership?" We agree with the importance of these eight qualities of honorable leadership to which Jones's discussion points. While there certainly are examples of black leaders who persistently demonstrate vision, commitment, and responsibility (e.g., Marian Wright Edelman of the Children's Defense Fund, Geoffrey Canada of the Harlem Children's Zone, Congressman John Lewis of Georgia, and First Lady Michelle Obama, to name just a few), we agree with Jones's general assertion that there is a leadership crisis in black communities, and we find this can be stated of the larger society as well. For much of the first decade of the twenty-first century, citizens of the United States have witnessed unconscionable failures of leadership in the public and private sectors. These failures brought the financial system to near collapse and led to dramatic loss of working class wealth (held largely in homes and retirement funds). In New Orleans, millions were traumatized, displaced, and left homeless because leaders did not ensure quality construction and maintenance of levees that might have protected the city from waters brought by Hurricane Katrina. This leadership failure was compounded as the whole world watched the spectacle of inept and uninspired governmental response to the crisis. Leadership failure involved the United States in two wars, neither of which seems worth the cost in human lives, money, or time. Most recently, failure of leadership has resulted in environmental degradation of the US Gulf Coast at a level that surpasses the 1989 Exxon Valdez oil spill, which had long stood as one of the most devastating human-caused environmental catastrophes in US history. Without a doubt, the risk and ambiguity regarding campaign financing affirmed in the *Citizens United* decision and the apparent ordinary selling of access to elected officials also figure among recent failures of leadership.

We join with Jones's admonition that all leaders, especially black leaders, should be independent, act with integrity, be responsive to what people need, have a vision of a just and nonsegregated society, be prepared, demonstrate moral authority, be relevant, and reject being victims. However, some assertions Jones makes as he discusses black leadership appear out of step and even in conflict with what Dr. King might say about some contemporary issues. For example, in an essay discussing what Martin Luther King Jr. would say about illegal immigration, Jones's inclusion of a recommendation

16. Ibid., 63.

that blacks use their political power in the Democratic Party to insist that "the border be closed and everyone sent home," and his prediction that "overnight jobs would be freed and wages would rise, especially for those at the lower end,"[17] seem contrary to Dr. King's vision. Further, it requires an extraordinary leap backwards to believe that King would advocate our borders be closed to poor brown people so that poor black people can have exclusive rights to perform the low wage, backbreaking, dehumanizing tasks reserved for those lowest on the economic ladder. By Jones's own description, King advocated a "human rights," not just a "civil rights" agenda: "Martin had become the commander of a righteous army that included all human beings, not just blacks."[18] Since King engaged those institutions (business and government) and persons whose policies and practices cause injustice, it seems more likely that King would urge close scrutiny of the ways in which businesses, the US government, and ordinary US citizens benefit from the labor of undocumented persons, and would seek an appropriate response to the issues of fair wages and immigration.

Jones's generalization in identifying the NAACP, the National Urban League, and the National Baptist Convention as organizations that would "go along to get along"[19] with the federal government seems mean spirited and historically uninformed. It is unfair to criticize an entire organization because of the failure of one or even many individuals. In particular, the historic work of the entire NAACP has included persistently challenging the federal government, on all fronts, to enforce the laws; to redress stresses caused by local, state, and national discriminatory policies; and generally to put our democratic principles into action. The National Urban League continues to press for addressing the issues of African Americans in the nation's cities. And any investigation of their financial statements would attest to the role of ordinary people making these organizations the center of their volunteer efforts. These organizations, with their legacies of service, are not the corporations about which Justice Stevens expressed concern for their inordinate economic power in the political arena. Finally, we feel it unlikely that, in general, King would affirm Jones's negative identification and characterization of other leaders and groups.

17. Ibid., 63.
18. Ibid., 45.
19. Ibid., 44.

An Interlude: So, What Is Leadership?

Adopting a definition and approach to leadership focused on select persons based on their positions in an organizational or societal hierarchy, and expecting them to solve our problems, is destined to result in our disappointment and their failure. "Ethical leadership," Walter Earl Fluker writes, arises from "moral traditions that have shaped the character and shared meanings of a people." Ethical leaders, Fluker says, do not emerge ex nihilo, without a context or background. An ethical leader arises, he continues, "from the life worlds of particular traditions and speaks authoritatively and acts responsibly with the aim of serving the collective good."[20] Fluker's definition and discussion of ethical leadership points beyond identifying leaders simply as individuals with certain characteristics; instead, he sees leaders as persons who emerge from among the people and their traditions, and as persons whose authenticity and actions (leadership) are judged by whether they remain engaged with the communities of which they are leaders. "The assumption here," Fluker writes,

> is that leaders are a part of living traditions that are also parts of ongoing narratives that are at once personal and communal. The identification of particular traditions and institutions that are bearers of memory and perpetuators of habits and practices provides leaders with opportunities to look at the role that certain values have played in the formation of leaders in communities; and how leaders within those traditions have dealt with complex issues and challenges over time. The significance of this approach of returning to memory and retrieving substantive discourse is that it also creates space for reframing of beliefs and assumptions, as well as learning from these experiences so that there is a continuous creative cycle of remembering, reframing, and learning. In this process, values that have been the long stay of a said tradition find resonance in new contexts of meaning and are enabled because of their "plasticity" to inform and guide the leader in discerning, deliberating, and deciding on the appropriate course of action.[21]

Similarly, John Gardner suggests that the entire society/community is responsible for leading. However, rather than viewing leaders as a distinct class, Gardner maintains that leaders must be "dispersed among all levels of society and down through all levels[,] and the system simply won't work as it

---

20. Walter Earl Fluker, *Ethical Leadership: The Quest for Character, Civility, and Community* (Minneapolis: Fortress, 2009), 33.

21. Ibid., 54–55.

should unless large numbers of people throughout our society are prepared to take leader-like action to make things work at their level."[22] Gardner's assertion that responsibility for leading requires "large numbers of people throughout . . . society . . . to take leader-like action" conforms to Fluker's argument that ethical leadership emerges from ongoing engagement with community traditions, discourse, and values. We join with Gardner in suggesting that the training of leaders prescribed by Fluker must not be offered only to the select, but must be extended to each citizen and integrated into what it means to become a person in a democratic society.

Rather than pinning all hope *and blame* on "leaders," everyone has a responsibility for sustaining leadership. This point was captured in the pithy words of Civil Rights Movement leader Ella Baker who said, "Strong people don't need strong leaders." Baker argued for building the abilities of everyone in the communities. When this is done, Baker said, people will act together to make changes they need. We suggest here that looking to a few individuals designated as "the leadership" is likely to prove insufficient to meet challenges affecting Americans in general, and the African American community in particular, as we embark upon the second decade of the twenty-first century. Following Fluker, Gardner, Baker, and others who argue that, in a democratic society, each of us, as citizens, must be prepared to lead, we assert that any message to today's black leadership should speak at once to those whom we typically regard as leaders and to those in the rank-and-file (followers), for they are engaged in a collaboration in which both must be prepared to "take leader-like action to make things work." So defined, leaders and followers are partners linked in a dance in which both must be prepared to take the lead, while, at the same time, participating as competent or exemplary followers. Neither can succeed without the other, and both can be held equally responsible for the success or failure of the common good. Excellence in both leadership *and* followership are required in any efforts to address the challenging needs of our communities today, and to provide hope and a future for our children. To that end, an effective leader must emerge from and be accountable to serious followers.

In spite of King's allegiance to black Baptist forms of governance, with emphasis on pastoral authority and autonomy, history shows that Dr. King was a leader in touch with the community he served as leader. His being catapulted into the national and international spotlight during the Montgomery bus boycott resulted as much, if not more, from the community's

22. John Gardner, Remarks to the National Association of Schools of Public Affairs and Administration, Seattle, Washington, October 23, 1987, cited in Robert Denhardt et al., *Managing Human Behavior in Public and Nonprofit Organizations*, 2nd ed. (Los Angeles: Sage, 2009), 182–83.

determination that the time and cause were ripe for action as it did from King's ability and willingness to head the ad hoc Montgomery Improvement Association (MIA). In her autobiography, civil rights activist JoAnn Robinson recalls that when Mrs. Parks was arrested, for example, it was the women of the Women's Political Caucus (WPC), who swung into action first. "I made some notes on the back of an envelope: 'The Women's Political Council will not wait for Mrs. Parks' consent to call for a boycott of city buses. On Friday, December 2, 1955, the women of Montgomery will call for a boycott to take place on Monday, December 5.'"[23] The black ministers, including Martin Luther King Jr., met for the first time the night *after* the WPC had distributed 52,500 leaflets to the African American community calling for the boycott. "It was then that the ministers decided that it was time for them, the leaders, to catch up with the masses . . . Had they not done so, they might have alienated themselves from their congregations . . . for the masses were ready, and they were united!"[24] Similarly, in Memphis, Tennessee, the garbage strike was called by the sanitation workers themselves, not by their leaders. This truth was affirmed by sanitation striker Taylor Rogers's statement: "We just got together, and we decided to stand up and be men, and that's what we did."[25] Memphis's black community members, such as Cornelia Crenshaw, observed and took pride in the workers' initiatives. "We were so proud of the fact that the sanitation folk has stood as men . . . and they showed a kind of togetherness that maybe some of us had never shown . . . When you are very poor and you don't have very much to lose anyway, just maybe you can get together a little better."[26] Dr. King's response to the actions and calls for action from others, in Montgomery, Memphis, and elsewhere, demonstrates the dance of leading and following as central to King's leadership style, notwithstanding the fact that Dr. King also initiated projects, which others joined and followed.

Mrs. Ruby Hurley, whose work is less well known, is also an example of a leader who, like King, behaved in a manner that flowed from their respect for and accountability to their followers—ordinary people—who were prepared and willing to take the lead when necessary and whose character and integrity, as Fluker might say, helped leaders live up to their calling. Leadership is evident in the sense of urgency with which King and Hurley

23. Jo Ann Robinson, *The Montgomery Bus Boycott and the Women Who Started It: The Memoir of Jo Ann Gibson Robinson*, ed. David J. Garrow (Knoxville: University of Tennessee Press, 1987), 45.

24. Ibid., 53–54.

25. Michael K. Honey, *Going Down Jericho Road: The Memphis Strike, Martin Luther King's Last Campaign* (New York: Norton, 2007), 98.

26. Ibid.

engaged the Movement, in the demonstration that they each had a vision of a just society that resonated with the community's longing, in their long-term commitment to Movement work, and in their responsiveness to the people for whom they worked. An important difference between King and Hurley was the purposeful way through which Hurley responded to others by intentionally seeking to train followers to be leaders. In what follows, we introduce Ruby Hurley and briefly examine her sense of urgency, vision, commitment, and responsiveness as an important and exemplary leader during the Civil Rights Movement era.

What Ruby Hurley's Work Might Say to and about Today's Black Leaders

As a result of serving on the committee that organized Marian Anderson's 1939 Easter concert at the Lincoln Memorial, Ruby Hurley (1909–1980) helped reorganize the local Washington DC branch of the NAACP. She served on the branch executive committee and began directing its youth work. Hurley was thirty years old.[27] Her appointment as National Youth Secretary for the NAACP in 1943 marked the beginning of a career as an administrator within the NAACP bureaucracy that would span nearly four decades. Under Hurley's direction, the NAACP youth memberships grew to more that twenty-five thousand by 1947. The success of Hurley's work with youth led to her appointment in 1950 as coordinator of membership campaigns in five southern states. In 1951, Hurley was named NAACP Southeast Regional Secretary, and in 1952 she was appointed Southeast Regional Director. When Hurley left NAACP headquarters in New York to set up her office in Birmingham, Alabama, she had the distinction of opening the first full-time NAACP national office in the Deep South, and developing, in the Southeast, the first regional structure of the NAACP. In 1955, Hurley investigated the murder of Emmett Till, with her Mississippi staff member, Medgar Evers. In 1955, Hurley also helped prepare the lawsuit that allowed Autherine J. Lucy to register as the first black student at the University of Alabama. During 1956, Hurley was forced to relocate the Southeast Regional offices to Atlanta, Georgia, because the state of Alabama enjoined NAACP work there. She continued her activism in Atlanta for the next twenty-four years. Hurley helped coordinate legal and logistical support, including raising bail money for the Movement's intense work during

---

27. John H. Britton, Interview with Mrs. Ruby Hurley, director, Southeastern Regional Office of the National Association for the Advancement of Colored People, Atlanta, Georgia (January 26, 1968), 1–2.

the 1960s and 1970s. Hurley also had the unusual experience of supervising a group of persons who were recognized as among the nation's strongest advocates for civil rights, including Medgar Evers, director of branches in Mississippi; Isaiah DeQuincey Newman, field secretary in South Carolina; Vernon Jordan, field secretary in Georgia; L. C. Bates, field secretary in Tennessee; and Robert Saunders, field secretary in Florida. Hurley died in 1980.

In addition to performing long-term NAACP work, Ruby Hurley was an active Protestant churchwoman, similar to women contemporaries in the Civil Rights Movement, such as Septima Poinsett Clark and Ella Baker. She was an officer of the Methodist Episcopal Church Woman's Society of Christian Service (now United Methodist Women) at Warren Memorial Methodist Church in Atlanta, as well as a state and denominational leader of Methodist Women's activities. Hurley also engaged Methodism at various levels beyond her work with the Methodist women's group. She was active in her local congregation. She collaborated with and, on occasion, spoke in the place of her local church pastor. She organized and sometimes led Methodist youth excursions and made connections between church work and her civil rights activism. She was a founding leader of a once quite active Georgia State Legislative Day, during which church leaders and Georgia state legislators met to share information, concerns, and, sometimes, collaborate.[28] Former Field Secretary of the Florida NAACP, Robert Saunders, states, "Not enough is said today about Ruby Hurley. Not enough credit is given to her for her leadership during really tough times." [29] By Saunders's estimation, Hurley inspired a majority of the young men and women from the South who occupied leadership positions in the Movement.

Ruby Hurley recognized and exploited the opportunity of her time to change racial conditions in the United States. As NAACP youth director, Hurley sought to develop young people as leaders and to empower young people to act. She once observed, "I guess the biggest thrill that I've gotten out of not just working in the South, but working with the NAACP, is seeing people with whom I work move up and out and really give the kind of leadership I like to see."[30] Through her leadership in developing young people, Hurley helped shape persons such as the late federal judge A. Leon Higginbotham, who was the first president of the youth chapter Hurley

---

28. Rosetta E. Ross, Interview with Mrs. Thomasina Daugherty, October 29, 2009, Atlanta, Georgia; Rosetta E. Ross, Interview with Mrs. Lonnie Austin, March 25, 2010, Atlanta, Georgia.

29. Robert Saunders, *Bridging the Gap: Continuing the Florida NAACP Legacy of Henry T. Moore, 1952–1966* (Tampa: University of Tampa Press, 2000), 247.

30. Britton interview, 19.

organized at Antioch College.³¹ As she developed young people's leadership abilities, Hurley also encouraged them to take action. "I used to tell them," she said, "they could do anything they wanted to do, short of starting a race riot, in order to achieve their goals."³² Hurley also used her role as NAACP Youth Secretary to guide efforts to diversify the curriculum of schools by influencing textbook choices. Early NAACP youth, she said, tried "to get the kind of information into the schools that would let young people know that Negroes have made a contribution to American life and history and culture."³³ She encouraged work to overcome segregation, supporting youth who, "recognizing that the NAACP was against segregation or discrimination even then, said they would raise money to get smokes for the boys in camps and give them to both Negro and white soldiers." Indicating her participation in the dance of leading and following, Hurley noted that these ideas came from the youth she guided.

Although Hurley did not initiate her move South to coordinate regional work there, she, once assigned to the region, sought to respond to the issues African Americans confronted. "I found that when I came south that the Negroes, particularly in the smaller communities in Mississippi and Alabama, were very anxious to do something about their problems," she recalled.³⁴ Problems included treatment such as police brutality and murders in Mississippi and bombings in Birmingham, Alabama. In addition to responding to issues community members raised, Hurley sought to increase their understanding and awareness of issues they confronted. Recognizing the role Christianity played in the lives of African Americans, her work sometimes included using Christianity to encourage participation and activism. "I used the Bible a great deal," she said. "I found this effective in saying to our people, 'You go to church on Sunday, or you go every time the church doors are open. You say Amen before the minister has even had a word out of his mouth . . . Yet you tell me you're afraid. Now how can you be afraid and be honest when you say, 'My faith looks up to Thee,' or when you say, 'God's going to take care of you'? If you don't believe it, then you're not really being the Christian you say you are."³⁵ Once persons consented to participate in NAACP-sponsored activities, Hurley sought to provide support they needed to continue the work. She said, "In dealing with the school [integration] situation, for instance, after 1954, I always encouraged

31. Ibid.
32. Ibid., 6.
33. Ibid.
34. Ibid., 9.
35. Ibid., 15.

our branches to get as many parents as possible to apply for transfers so that one parent wouldn't be left out there alone."[36]

Hurley's concern that persons not be left alone in their civil rights activism may have grown from reflections of her own early work. As a woman civil rights activist negotiating the Southeast during the 1950s and 1960s, Hurley saw violent reprisals and knew the dangers black persons faced when they opposed racial subordination. Perhaps because she remembered the challenge of her own lonely work, Hurley tried to shield others: "When I was out there by myself, for instance, there were no TV cameras with me to give me any protection. There were no reporters traveling with me to give me protection because when the eye of the press or the eye of the camera was on the situation, it was different. It was differen . . . I had to be very defensive, very careful about what I said, what I did, and with whom I was seen . . . These are the kinds of things that took their toll inwardly, though I was able to, I think, effect at least a climate for some change."[37] By the time the Civil Rights Movement reached its heyday, solitary, groundbreaking work like Ruby Hurley's was forgotten. As her career began to ebb, Hurley found herself defending against the perceptions of the "old guard" as "taking it." Still she persisted in being responsive to what people needed. "I think young people need to know and some older people need to know, that it didn't all begin in 1960."[38] Hurley continued her work as director of the Southeastern Region of the NAACP until she retired at age 68 on March 21, 1978.

Conclusion

This essay began as a critical reading of Clarence Jones's chapter, "What Would Martin Say about Black Today's Black Leadership," in his recent book, *What Would Martin Say?* We find both common ground and important differences with Mr. Jones on what Dr. King would say about black leadership. One important difference is simply an approach that reflects our interest in surmising what Dr. King's message would be *to* black leaders, rather than focusing on what Dr. King would say *about* individual leaders. We further conclude that while Dr. King excelled on most leadership dimensions, his shortcomings were apparent when compared to the leadership style and heritage of a woman contemporary, Mrs. Ruby Hurley, who was working in

---

36. Ibid., 16.

37. Howell Raines, *My Soul Is Rested* (New York: Viking, 1983; originally published New York: Putnam, 1977), 136.

38. Ibid, 136–37.

Birmingham, Alabama, when Dr. King was called to pastor Dexter Avenue Baptist Church in Montgomery. As our discussion of Mrs. Hurley's leadership shows, like Ella Baker, she understood the importance of developing the leadership skills of followers.

As a regional director, Hurley understood that she was both a leader and a developer of leaders. At the height of the Movement, Hurley could be counted on to make sure NAACP field secretaries in the southeastern states had the resources, including her time and attention, required to do the work they needed to do, but because she was not overbearing or emotionally needy of the spotlight, each leader in her region was recognized nationally as outstanding in their own right. Hurley's admission that her greatest joy was in seeing people that she trained become really effective leaders reveals her strongest leadership skill: She was a leader who prepared others for leadership. She did this in a purposeful and intentional way, paralleled by few of her male contemporaries, including Dr. King.

In *Women in the Civil Rights Movement* (1990), Charles Payne asserts that the men led while the women organized. Ruby Hurley was the exceptional woman who depended on the community's vision and developed community resources to both organize and lead. Her life has much to say *about* leadership and *to* leaders who have a vision of the common good and seek to change things from the way they are to what they should be. Developing and maintaining a vision of the common good that belongs to the whole community, Fluker says, is central to the meaning of ethical leadership. "The primary questions are," he writes, "How do we create and maintain a responsible and respectful relationship with each other in the quest for community, and how does this model relate to the broader and critical issues of ethical leadership . . . ?"[39] John Gardner reminds us that, "Citizens must understand the possibilities and limitations of leadership . . . Understanding these things, we come to see that much of the responsibility for leaders and how they perform is in our hands. If we are lazy, self-indulgent, and wanting to be deceived; if we willingly follow corrupt leaders; if we allow our heritage of freedom to decay; if we fail to be faithful monitors of the public process, then we shall get and deserve the worst."[40] We agree with Fluker, Gardner, Hurley, and yes, Dr. King, who, in his last book, *Where Do We Go From Here?*, called on black people to "become sophisticated, intensive activists and educators in order to create a more conscious, alert,

---

39. Fluker, *Ethical Leadership*, 130.

40. Gardner speech. See also John W. Gardner, *On Leadership* (New York: Free Press, 1990), xviii.

and informed people."[41] That is the charge to each of us. For, ultimately, we are all called to leadership in challenging times.

---

41. Martin Luther King Jr., *Where Do We Go From Here: Chaos or Community?* (Boston: Beacon, 1967), 184.

4

Looking for Martin

Black Leadership in an Era of
Contested Postracism and Postblackness

WALTER EARL FLUKER

In this chapter, I respond to Clarence B. Jones's *What Would Martin Say?* (2008) within the context of debates on *postracism* and *postblackness* as metaphorical strategies for re-evaluating Martin Luther King Jr.'s leadership for twenty-first-century African American leadership, with particular emphasis on his distinctive place within black church traditions. Martin Luther King Jr. was a religious leader with strong social-political, theological-ethical, and aesthetic-existential commitments that provided him a unique platform from which to espouse his views on justice and peace in mid-twentieth-century American society and the world. Forty-five years after King's assassination, the ground has shifted, i.e., the essentialism that undergirded and informed his prophetic pronouncements on civil and human rights requires a reevaluation of his leadership in light of the premises and principles that shaped his distinctive leadership and heroic courage.

Jones's book offers insight into the quagmire of early twenty-first-century popular opinions of King's leadership and its relevance to the concrete social, political, economic, and existential problems of African Americans. However, it begs the question whether the basic presuppositions and language of Martin Luther King Jr. are adequate for an era of contested postracism and postblackness. In response to this challenge, I engage the idea that race is fluid and revisable (against postracism), using postblackness as a lens to reevaluate interpretations of Martin Luther King Jr.'s leadership within the context of the black church in the United States. Specifically, I consider how the major metaphors that have shaped the social-political, theological-ethical, and aesthetic-existential dimensions of black leadership in the previous century have become inadequate guiding paradigms in the twenty-first century. The root metaphor grounding this reevaluation of King's leadership is "the ground has shifted but ghosts still haunt us," which is a way of signaling to African American religious scholars and church leaders that they must engage a new time and rhythm, a shift of *lifeworlds* and *systems* in what is being called *a postracist, postblack world*.

What Would Martin Say?: Looking for Martin

Looking for Martin Luther King Jr. in an era of contested postracism and postblackness is akin to scavenging through a huge heap of postmodern, used, and reusable linguistic and cultural fragments and piecing together a quilted image of the man who has been lost in consumerism, conservatism, and conspiracy. This is not at all a disparagement of Martin Luther King Jr.'s witness and legacy for our times; rather it is a statement about ways in which history, culture, and, most notably, memories of great human beings, especially heroes like King, are recycled for cultural consumption, sometimes as charitable offerings, sometimes not. As Michael Eric Dyson claims, either "we have trapped King in romantic images or frozen his legacy in worship."[1]

Finding the "real" Martin among the ruins and debris of twenty-first-century cultural packaging and marketing strategies is even more difficult if it is delivered as a litany of aphorisms and diatribes against black leadership. The literature on black leadership, in general, tends to be extraordinarily harsh in its excoriations of the failure of African Americans in contemporary leadership roles to respond to the challenges of black life, which by any reasonable estimate are particularly difficult and foreshadow an even more dismal future for generations unborn. A sampling of titles on black leadership speaks volumes to the issues at stake. *Scam: How the Black Leadership Exploits Black America*; *The Rise and Fall of Modern Black Leadership: Chronicle of a Twentieth Century Tragedy*; *Losing the Race: Self-Sabotage in Black America*; *Transcending the Talented Tenth: Black Leaders and American Intellectuals*; *The Head Negro in Charge Syndrome: The Dead End of Black Politics*; *We Have No Leaders: African-Americans in the Post Civil Rights Era*; *Capitalist Nigger: The Road to Success*; and *Enough: The Phony Leaders, Dead-End Movements, and Culture of Failure That Are Undermining Black*

---

1. Michael E. Dyson, *I May Not Get There with You: The True Martin Luther King Jr.* (New York: Free Press, 2000), xv (preface).

America—and What We Can Do about It, are reflective of the self-critique that abounds with respect to post-civil-rights African American leadership.[2] In *What Would Martin Say?*, Clarence B. Jones joins this long procession of impassioned critics who use the civil rights movement as a backdrop for the assessment and expectations of contemporary leaders who are African American. Jones's treatise parallels the dominant themes from most of these works: the departure from the moral and political strategies of the civil rights movement; the greed and showmanship of black leaders; instilling and encouraging a "cult of victimization" in lower-class black communities; and the failure to emulate the heroic and self-sacrificial legacy of Martin Luther King Jr.[3]

Jones's book is part memoir and part ethical handbook, spiced with grave disappointment at the moral and civic laxity that he sees in post-civil-rights leadership and an alarming castigation of a generation of black youth, whom he is convinced has forgotten or never known the superhuman accomplishments of this great American leader. The failure of black leadership to follow the principled example of Martin Luther King Jr. is perhaps the greatest heartbreak for Jones. Naming the Reverends Jesse Jackson and Al Sharpton as America's "two most famous black leaders," he writes, "Intentionally or not, current black leaders seem to pursue policies that pimp the best interests of black people. Convincing blacks that they've been born with one foot in the grave, or are hopelessly disadvantaged in politics and economics, only works to make names and fortunes for power brokers perceived as being able to reliably deliver the black vote to the councilmen, aldermen, mayors, assemblymen, congressmen, senators, and presidents."[4] For Jones, the issues associated with black leadership are many, but among the most damning are the perceived collapse in the pursuit of moral and intellectual excellence that guided earlier generations of leaders

---

2. Walter Earl Fluker, ed., *The Stones That the Builders Rejected: The Development of Ethical Leadership from the Black Church Tradition* (Harrisburg, PA: Trinity, 1998), 8–9; Walter Earl Fluker and Catherine Tumber, eds., *A Strange Freedom: The Best of Howard Thurman on Religious Experience and Public Life* (Boston: Beacon, 1998), 8–11; Fluker, *Ethical Leadership: The Quest for Character, Civility, and Community* (Minneapolis: Fortress, 2009), 61–62.

3. This is not an exhaustive list of criticisms, not least being, the failure of contemporary black leaders to deal aggressively with issues of youth, sexuality, and gender, and the impact of the prison industrial complex on black life, to name a few. See Michelle Alexander, *The New Jim Crow: Mass Incarceration in the Age of Colorblindness* (New York: New Press, 2010), Chapters 1–2, 5; Melissa Harris-Perry, *Sister Citizen: Shame, Stereotypes, and Black Women in America* (New Haven: Yale University Press, 2011).

4. Clarence B. Jones and Joel Engel, *What Would Martin Say?* (New York: Harper & Row, 2008), 33.

like Martin (and by implication, himself); the utter incredulity of the moral licentiousness of the black poor and the disintegration of family structures that were assumed in the past; and the paralyzing apathy and pervasive truancy of contemporary generations of young black people engendered by low self-esteem combined with deep alienation from civil society and the consequences of such alienation for seizing opportunities that promote middle-class lifestyles and values. Such lifestyles and values were, Jones maintains, elements of Martin Luther King's dream for justice and fairness in American society. Jones, who spent much of his professional life as a confidant, speechwriter, and legal adviser to Martin, assures us that Martin would be appalled at these circumstances:

> Martin would not question the courage of today's black leaders, but he might very well wonder about their dedication to the cause that would be furthered, if not achieved, by an insistence that black people avoid the quicksand of victimization and instead pursue excellence regardless of barriers. In the twenty-first century moral leadership requires recognition that our worldwide economy is based on information, and that knowledge and the content of someone's character are clearly far more important than skin color. Let our black leadership lead by developing programs, strategies, and tactics that help our young people commit themselves to excellence.[5]

For instance, Jones thinks that Martin Luther King Jr. would have very little empathy for the leaders of the Free Jena Six Case. "For Martin, Jena and Jena 6 would exemplify just how far the African American community down South, and more explicitly, our civil rights leadership nationally has strayed off course from the beliefs and precepts that guided Martin Luther King and therefore the movement four decades ago."[6] The beating of a white student by six black male students, who were charged with attempted murder,[7] according to Jones, was morally indefensible and legally culpable. Unlike the black leaders who rushed to the defense of the Jena Six, "In Martin's time and on his watch, the Jena 6 would have never been celebrated for committing violence against their brother—yes, their brother, be he white or black."[8] The responsible leadership equation for Martin, Jones writes, would extend beyond the political and social drama surrounding the

---

5. Ibid., 65.

6. Ibid., 49.

7. The charges were later reduced, but Mychal Bell, who was accused of standing on the white student's head, was convicted of second-degree battery.

8. Ibid., 53.

case, and include the young men's parents: "But I am quite sure he (Martin) would have some penetrating questions, starting with the parents of the six black students: What kind of leaders were they to their own children? How did they raise their boys? What rules of moral conduct did they instill? Were they themselves good examples to their sons?"[9]

Similarly, according to Jones, Martin would lament the response of black leaders to the Duke University lacrosse incident, in which three white lacrosse players were charged with raping a young black woman who had performed for them as a stripper at a team party. Again, he singles out Jesse Jackson and Al Sharpton as eager publicity hounds who seized the opportunity for their own public aggrandizement. "If only the current crop of civil rights leaders understood that crying wolf—or supporting those who do—only hurts the people it's theoretically intended to help."[10] These leaders, according to Jones, were engaged in an anachronistically tragic view of the present that contributes to an acceptance of victimization, foolishly acting as if it were still 1913. He remarks that real issues have to do with the failure of African Americans to make progress politically and economically; and that black leaders should, therefore, provide strategies that change their dire contemporary situation, reflected in the fact "that most blacks in the early twenty-first century ha[ve] not achieved at least middle-class status through their own hard work and determination, with the top 20 percent of earners becoming the fastest growing segment. How belittling."[11] Jones relates the moral, political, and economic failure of black leadership to the embrace of the rhetoric of black consciousness movements of the late 1960s, which he argues became "associated with bloodshed and separation." Martin, says Jones, would find this approach as dangerous and ill advised today as it was in the past. In fact, Martin would repeat what he said regarding Black Power—that it was an imprudent strategy and a morally indefensible objective because means and ends must cohere. "We have never sought the moral goal of freedom and equality by immoral means. Black supremacy or aggressive black violence is as invested with evil as white supremacy or white violence."[12] If black leaders had the black community's interest at heart, they would address the "black killing fields" in our nation's streets.[13]

9. Ibid., 54.
10. Ibid., 60.
11. The original statement read, "that most blacks in the early twenty-first century had not achieved at least middle-class status through their own hard work and determination, with the top 20 percent of earners becoming the fastest growing segment. How belittling." See Jones and Engel, *What Would Martin Say?*, 61.
12. Ibid., 61.
13. Ibid., 49.

Remembered Pasts, Prevailing Presents

One can hardly disagree with Clarence Jones's stated objective in the writing of this book on the fortieth anniversary of Martin Luther King Jr.'s death: "to interpret what contributions he [Martin] would add to his singular legacy if he were alive today."[14] Nor can one dismiss Jones's own courageous and intellectual leadership within the civil rights movement and his support of our fallen hero. Nonetheless, Jones's observations and interpretations of Martin Luther King's legacy find resonance with a certain segment of the social, political, and economic environment of the country today. As we witness an emergent Christian nationalism buttressed by invectives against individuals of the "wrong" class, race, gender and sexual orientation, I am suspicious of the self-proclaimed "moral leaders" of America, who want to "take our country back," who advocate "family values," and who rail against the "entitlement society" and "welfare queens." What might some of these moral leaders say to Jones's book? Jones's emphasis on self-reliance, self-esteem, and individualism extends to his arguments for the dismissal of affirmative action as outdated and unhealthy for African American progress and to immigration policies (especially for Mexicans and Latin Americans) that he rallies against as being too liberal and harmful to American workers, especially to African Americans. In places Jones labels welfare recipients lazy, sex-crazed, and indulgent. In doing so, he comes perilously close to affirming the very same caricatures that recent conservative contenders for the 2012 Republican presidential nomination have made about African Americans and Mexican and Latin American immigrants—positions that Jones, and most certainly Martin Luther King Jr., would oppose.

It is ironic, at least, that Jones's criticism that contemporary black leaders live in the past mirrors his own argument. His close relationship with Martin Luther King Jr. and his memories of King's thoughtful responses to situations in the past are used to address supposed identical or similar problems of the present. These are strange times, very complex and slippery times indeed, for African American leadership. The most powerful leader in the world, the first African American president of the United States of America, is caught at the center of the many intricate and eliding ideological differences and debates about the future of American society—from sweeping matters of war, economic recovery, religious liberty, morality, and poverty to specific questions about the state of black America. Against this backdrop, reading Jones's interpretation of the relevance of Martin Luther King for our time begs for critical reflection on what is at stake in reading

14. Ibid., xii.

King through a particular set of lenses that looks back to a time remembered, maybe a time swept under the rug, and that misses some important lessons and dangers that confront us as a nation and as African American citizens.

The challenge of remembering the past through lenses that are still in the past is that we never leave the situation that gave birth to the problem, nor do we quite grasp the historical complexity and our complicity in the contests of the present. There is an inherent danger in combining ideological admixtures of the experienced past with moral solutions to the prevailing present. Barack Obama suggests that "values are faithfully applied to the facts before us, while ideology overrides whatever facts call theory into question."[15] Jones's criticisms of black leaders (though many are accurate) commit this frequent error of misplaced reasoning. What Martin would say in 1960 probably is not what he would say in 2008 or 2012; and even if his words are carefully selected to reflect what needs to be said, the vain and often destructive fallacy of believing that the truth that was spoken in a particular place and time to a particular situation reflects the truth for all times and places, relies more on ideology than on the facts. This is especially true in an era of contested postracism and postblackness, in which a larger conversation about Martin Luther King Jr.'s contribution to leadership and African Americans must be undertaken.

The Shape-Shifting Ghost of Postracism and Postblackness

At stake in Jones's discussion of what Martin would say to black leadership is not simply a question of ideology and morality in America, but a grander revelation of how deeply *race* is embedded in American culture; and of the ways in which race as a *cultural and social ghost shape-shifts and reinvents itself in myriad figurations. In this sense it has formal affinity with postblackness as a quest for identity, authenticity, and agency in Black cultural life and practices.* Touré writes that "Blackness is a completely liquid shape-shifter that can take any form, just like the chameleonic agents in *The Matrix* or T-1000 or the TX in the *Terminator* sequels that are made of a mimetic polyalloy that allow them to take on any appearance. It's an unfortunate coincidence that both of those memorable examples of infinitely mutable figures are villains because for the shape-shifter that power equals freedom: Be anyone you want at any time. As the artist William Pope L says, 'Blackness is limited only by the courage to imagine it differently.'"[16]

15. Barack Obama, *The Audacity of Hope* (New York: Random House, 2006), 59.
16. Touré, *Who's Afraid of Post-Blackness?* (New York: Free Press, 2011), 6–7.

In this discussion, my use of the *shape-shifting* character of *race* and *blackness*,[17] however, is not as fluid as Touré's; it is rather a form of critical signification on how we understand the remembered past of Martin Luther King Jr. and his allegiances to black church traditions.[18] Historically, the black church has taken its metaphors, its parody, and its transformation of Western stories and ideas too literally. It has often mistaken these rhetorical devices for preordained things, essences. For example, I will argue that the idea of exodus as appropriated by King is not a fixed reality but a metaphorical device that must be revisable if the black church leadership is to survive and fulfill its mission in this century. Related to this usage, I am arguing that the notion of God as an unchangeable reality is better understood as a relational reality that participates in human experience.

Shape-shifting, in this sense, is a form of postmodern self-reflexive critique of all signs that claim to be Absolute, including race, blackness, and theological metaphors. In some respects, this method draws on the image of the trickster, as in *Ananse, Esu*, or *the Signifying Monkey*, as a shape shifter in terms of the indeterminacy of the meaning of language.[19] I am suggesting, therefore, that the interpretations of King and the black church remain open to revisability and remember the black church's own tradition of shape shifting, signifying, and reinterpreting in preaching and liturgy, and of playing

---

17. Unlike race, which will be discussed below, postblackness places emphasis on individuality, not individualism. Such individuality is rooted in the uniqueness of one's identity, hence there is a certain autonomy in blackness that does not necessarily exist in constructs of race. Dyson, for instance, names three dimensions of postblackness as accidental, incidental, and intentional. Touré refers to the themes introverted, ambiverted, and extroverted, respectively. The introverted mindset refers to a more private relationship with blackness. "I'm American, I am a human being. I happen to be Black." These are the Condoleeza Rice, Clarence Thomas variety. Ambiverted or incidental Blackness refers to a more fluid relationship to Blackness: Blackness is an important part of them but does not necessarily dominate their persona. Dyson says it's "people who more completely embrace Blackness—they aren't trying to avoid it—but it is not their total identification. "I love it, but it doesn't exhaust me." Representatives are Colin Powell, Barak Obama, and Will Smith. The third dimension is intentional or extroverted Blackness: "I be Black, that's what I do, that's what my struggle is about." Malcolm X, Jim Brown, Martin King, Jay Z, and so on. These different dimensions of Blackness play out in a variety of ways as strategies for survival, for authenticity, and for bartering for recognition, position, and status. See ibid., 9–10; and Michael Dyson, *Is Bill Cosby Right?* (New York: Basic Civitas, 2005), 41–45.

18. Henry Louis Gates Jr., "The 'Blackness of Blackness': A Critique of the Sign and the Signifying Monkey," *Critical Inquiry* 9/4 (1983) 686–93, 723; see also Henry Louis Gates Jr., *The Signifying Monkey: A Theory of African-American Literary Criticism* (New York: Oxford University Press, 1988).

19. Gates, "The 'Blackness of Blackness,'" 688.

on words. In this sense I am asking for a return to a type of process thinking that is already present in the traditions of the Black Atlantic and in Africa.[20]

Race as Fiction or Fact?

The metaphor of race as a ghost-like social entity that shape-shifts into different guises in order to adapt to changing cultural and sociopolitical situations is a hotly contested thesis in contemporary academic discourse. On the one hand, eliminativist philosophers such as Kwame Anthony Appiah argue that since the concept of a race is a biological fiction it is a meaningless term that should be discarded in academic, cultural, and sociopolitical life. To continue to employ the concept of race as though it were a scientific fact simply reinforces and encourages historical oppression and divisiveness on the basis of skin color. Describing the eliminativist thesis as an Enlightenment ideal, Richard Jones writes: "according to the eliminativists, if race is not a scientific fact, it must be a sociohistorical convention that can be eliminated by the construction of a counterconsciousness based on the delivery of the high egalitarian promises of the Enlightenment."[21]

On the other hand, conservationist thinkers such as Richard Jones, Lucius T. Outlaw, and Charles Mills argue that eliminating the concept of race will not lead to an egalitarian society. The opposite is actually true. If we eliminate the concept of race from our academic and socio-political discourse, we render racism and its consequences beyond rational critique.[22] The danger of postracial thinking is that it easily degenerates into an outright denial of racism—a theoretically sophisticated, mutated, shifting form of racism in the name of antiracism. This perspective reminds us of the proverbial ostrich that hides its head in the sand in the presence of imminent danger so as not to see what is happening. The danger of this position, of course, is that when we bury our heads in the sand, more is exposed than is hidden. Those who adopt this perspective must also attend to a type of double jeopardy to nonwhite oppressed classes. Philosopher Naomi Zack writes: "It's one thing to understand within a safe forum that race is a biological fiction. [But] in American culture at large, the fiction of race continues to operate as fact, and in situations of backlash against emancipatory progress, the victims of racial oppression, non-whites, are

20. Robert Pelton, *The Trickster in West Africa: A Study of Mythic Irony and Sacred Delight* (Berkeley: University of California Press, 1989).

21. Richard A. Jones, "Race and Revisability," *Journal of Black Studies* 35/5 (2005) 612–32.

22. Ibid., 621.

insulted and injured further for their progress against oppression. If those who practice such second-order oppression begin to employ the truth that race is a fiction, gains already secured against first-order oppression (or in redress of it) could be jeopardized."[23] So how do we employ the concept of race in academic and sociopolitical contexts without reinforcing it as biological fact or treating it is as social fiction? Here I follow Richard Jones in thinking about race as a resilient, shifting, and revisable historical reality that is constantly adapting to new social situations.

The Revisability of Race and Postblackness: Racing and Languaging

Drawing from American pragmatism and W. E. B. Du Bois, Richard Jones redefines race as a linguistic tool, infinitely revisable, that we use in a myriad of ways to ascribe meaning to ourselves and others. As it assigns difference and value to varying configurations of class, gender, sexuality, and tribalism, it also ascribes and inscribes notions of identity, otherness, and definitions of human flourishing as in postblackness. In this sense, race is ". . . a tool in a language game, or a tool for achieving viable forms of life—that is infinitely revisable as the dynamic relationships (processes) between frameworks (or environments) and agents (or organisms) [that] evolve over time as they work out internal inconsistencies. In this instrumentalist view, race as a linguistic concept can be seen diachronically as having been a tool for domination and subordination in 'master/slave' scripts; [and] it can be viewed synchronically as a developing linguistic instrument for human liberation."[24] Thus, positing race as a tool in the creation of meaning recognizes that race is not a biologically or historically fixed reality; rather it encourages us to be aware that it exists nevertheless in mutable social forms that constantly adapt and blend into new socio-political situations. As a shape-shifting social phenomenon, we may conceive of race as something *conjured* in our lives, and as *conjuring agents* we have the responsibility to discern whether or not we use race effectively as an emancipatory instrument in the exorcism of social evil or for demonic oppressive ends: *hence, the double jeopardy of racing as fact or fiction is simultaneously instrumental and revisable; and, therefore, potentially a tool of the spirit that can be used in the art of conjuring liberative practices.*

23. Naomi Zack, "Mixed Black and White Race in Public Policy," in Zack, et al., eds., *Race, Class, Gender, and Sexuality: The Big Questions* (Malden, MA: Blackwell, 1998), 83.

24. Richard Jones, "Race and Revisability," 627.

I apply this perspective of the revisability of race (against postracism) to interpretations of the leadership of Martin Luther King Jr. in the context of the black church in the United States, to consider how the major metaphors that have shaped the social-political, theological-ethical, and aesthetic-existential dimensions of this phenomenon in the previous century have become inadequate guiding paradigms for black leadership in the twenty-first century. Again, the meta-metaphor guiding this re-evaluation of black leadership is "the ground has shifted but ghosts still haunt us." "The ground has shifted but ghosts still haunt us" is a symbolic marker that pushes us to think together about ways African American religious scholars and church leadership must engage a new time and rhythm, a shift of *lifeworlds* and *systems* in what is being called a *postracial, postblack* world.

And Ghosts Will Drive Us On . . .

We died but you who live must do a harder thing than dying is . . . You must think and ghosts will drive you on.—Quoted by Howard Thurman[25]

As Clarence Jones's memoirs reflect on the legacy of our fallen friend and brother, Martin Luther King Jr., I am struck by the uncanny correspondence of "the house that race built"[26] and the ways in which we remember, retell, and relive our stories, especially the story of Martin Luther King Jr. *The ground has shifted* and memories like ghosts speak to us and drive us on! But memory without critical engagement and historical suspicion is dangerous and potentially destructive. James Baldwin wrote in *The Fire Next Time*: "To *accept* one's past—one's history—is not the same thing as *drowning* in it; it is learning how to use it."[27] How shall we then think together in what is being called a *postracist, postblack* world where African American religious scholars and church leadership must engage this new time and rhythm of lifeworlds and systems and their many deep-textured transitions, and transformations? I have written elsewhere, "More than any other American leader in the twentieth century, Martin Luther King Jr. stood at the intersection

---

25. From Howard Thurman's meditation in memory of James Reeb—a paraphrase from Hermann Hagedorn's "The Boy in Armor"—"Because you would not think we had to die . . . We died. And there you stand no step advanced." See *The Liberal Context* (Spring, 1965).

26. Wahneema Lubiano, ed., *The House That Race Built* (New York: Vintage, 1998).

27. James Baldwin, *The Fire Next Time* (New York: Dell, 1963), 95 and 111.

where worlds collided ... It was King's spiritual genius that provided for him the essential assets and tools to lead a revolution of values that expanded the moral grammar of American history and culture from parochially applied democratic principles to concrete proposals for inclusiveness and action ... In doing so, King also changed the leadership equation: public leadership no longer belonged to the strict province of position, power, and privilege, but also to the marginalized moral minority—those whom King labeled 'transformed nonconformists.'"[28] The idea of "transformed nonconformity" was the basis for King's dynamic interaction with fixity and change—always calling forth the new in situations that had become calcified and entrenched in past logic and ideologies that justified certain ways of viewing and living in the world. Such *transforming-nonconforming* leadership practices involve *balancing*; "a certain improvisational artistry, which yields without breaking and holds its central values without losing its integrity as it challenges recalcitrant structures of injustice and evil. Martin Luther King Jr.'s dialectical appropriation of knowledge and faith is another example of what is at stake in this perspective of ethical leadership. This approach enabled King to develop a methodology for dealing with conflict and struggle in both his personal and public life. More revealing, however, is the fact that dialectical thinking has long been a hallmark of the black church tradition."[29] King's dialectal method, however, is not without its own inherent challenges; while it is dialectic, it also involves a sense of determinacy that history is inevitably on the side of justice. Most postmodernist observers find this idealistic and essentialist version of history and human agency problematic and opt for a more pluralistic understanding of self, agency, and the world.

Thinking along the lines of King's transforming-nonconforming leadership practices, I would like to suggest experimentation with three dynamically and integrally related moments that speak to the shifting paradigms of African American life and culture that provide us with conceptual tools for re-evaluation and appropriation of Martin Luther King Jr.'s leadership legacy for our time: social-political, theological-ethical, and aesthetic-existential. I structure each moment respectively as *from* dilemma *to* Diaspora, *from* exodus *to* exile, and *from* "the frying pan *to* the fire."

---

28. Fluker, *Ethical Leadership*, 23–24.
29. Ibid., 55. For example, see my treatment of King's dialectical methodology in Fluker, "Transformed Nonconformity in the Thought of Martin Luther King Jr.," *Princeton Seminary Bulletin* (Spring 2004); Cornel West, *Prophesy Deliverance! An Afro-American Revolutionary Christianity* (Philadelphia: Westminster, 1982), 108–9.

From Dilemma to Diaspora: Social-Political Contexts of Black Church Leadership Practices

Clarence Jones's book arises out of a remembered past that was dealing with the struggle of "dilemma." Since Gunnar Myrdal's classic study, *An American Dilemma*,[30] the term "dilemma" has come to represent broad and conflicting ideologies in respect to African American life and culture.[31] The subtitle of Myrdal's work, however, underscored the fundamental character of the issues at stake. He characterized the *dilemma* as "The Negro Problem and Democracy." The Negro Problem (sometimes called the Negro Question) has been the staple ideological statement defining and representing the life and place of the African in American society since slavery. The Negro Problem, formulated by all sides of the male-dominated white power elite, was "What shall we do with the Negro?"[32] The dilemma is hardly resolved; it still exists at the heart of African American life and practices and has far-reaching implications for the ways in which African American church leaders understand and participate in civic life. Preoccupation with dilemma is unproductive and akin to riding two horses galloping in different directions, which is a strain on the anatomy. In recent years, a number of scholars working in critical race theory and in historical, literary, cultural, multicultural, and philosophical studies have addressed the problematic in other terms.[33] More progressive critiques look at the question of dilemma in respect to macroeconomic and political variables and their relationship to cultural and aesthetic meanings; and the place of the *body*.[34] Most relevant to the purposes of the present discussion is the treatment afforded

30. Gunnar Myrdal, *An American Dilemma: The Negro Problem and American Democracy* (New York: Harper & Brothers, 1944).

31. Harold Cruse, *The Crisis of the Negro Intellectual: A Historical Analysis of the Failure of Black Leadership* (New York: The New York Review of Books Classics, 1967); Kevin K. Gaines, *Uplifting the Race: Black Leadership, Politics, and Culture in the Twentieth Century* (Chapel Hill: University of North Carolina Press, 1996), 5.

32. Benjamin Quarles, *The Negro in the Making of America* (New York: Collier, 1964), 59 and 142; Sidney M. Wilhelm, *Who Needs the Negro?* (New York: Anchor, 1971); Ralph Luker, *The Social Gospel in Black and White* (Chapel Hill: University of North Carolina Press, 1991), 288.

33. C. Eric Lincoln, *Race, Religion, and the Continuing American Dilemma* (New York: Hill & Wang, 1984); Victor Anderson, *Beyond Ontological Blackness: An Essay on African-American Religious and Cultural Criticism* (New York: Continuum, 1995). See Cornel West's observations on "doubleness" in "Black Strivings in the Twilight of Civilization," in *The Cornel West Reader* (New York: Basic Civitas, 1999), specifically, its relationship to despair, destruction, and death using DuBois's metaphor.

34. Anthony B. Pinn and Dwight N. Hopkins, *Loving the Body: Black Religious Studies and the Erotic* (New York: Palgrave Macmillan, 2004).

by cultural critics who ask the question of dilemma as it pertains to binary oppositions in black life that grow out of adaptation to a North Atlantic aesthetic. These studies seek to understand the ways in which attachment to the heroic ideal of the European aesthete prevents and further complicates progressive critiques and strategies for agency and peoplehood. Victor Anderson, for instance, understands the cultural attachment to "the Apollonian rhetoric of heroic genius" as signifier on the legacy of Martin King and other notable black male leaders.[35]

Peter Paris pinpoints a problematic dimension of the moral anthropology that is a part of this cultural production as "autonomy in dilemma." The long-standing struggle within African American communities between loyalty to faith and loyalty to the nation is an example of dilemma: how to reconcile these contending demands for loyalty—the inclusive moral demand of faith *versus* the more particularized, and often self-annihilative demand, of the nation. These loyalties, he suggests, "represent, respectively, theories of politics and ecclesiology that imply moral conflicts in theory and practice."[36] Historically, we have tended not to reconcile them at all, but rather to acquiesce to the demands of the nation. Our participation in the two World Wars, in the Korean and Vietnam wars, and in the conflicts in Iraq and Afghanistan are illustrations of this position. Such a posture has stymied not only our "power" within the political scenario of the United States, but has prevented the black church leadership from authentically participating in the global community.

The notion of dilemma, I suggest, is the first moment in the movement toward reconstructing a political and ecclesiological ground for the black church leadership in a global perspective. The second movement within the paradigm is emerging into itself: a reconstructed notion of Diaspora. It has always been present within African American sociopolitical and cultural discourse in the illustrious examples of the call for Pan-Africanism by Robert Alexander Young, David Walker, Henry Highland Garnet, Anna Julia Cooper, Ida B. Wells-Barnett, Martin Delany, Marcus Garvey, W. E. B. DuBois, and Malcolm X. In another tradition within the African American Christian community, it was ably articulated by King in his excoriation of the Vietnam War and the call for a "world house." King wrote: "We have inherited a large house, a great 'world house' in which we have to live together—black and white, Easterner and Westerner, Gentile and Jew, Catholic and Protestant, Moslem and Hindu—a family unduly separated in ideas,

---

35. Victor Anderson, *Creative Exchange: A Constructive Theology of African American Religious Experience* (Minneapolis: Fortress, 2008), 151-57.

36. Peter J. Paris, *The Social Teaching of the Black Churches* (Philadelphia: Fortress, 1985), 29.

culture and interest, who, because we can never again live apart, must learn somehow to live together with each other in peace."[37]

"Diaspora" emerges from "dilemma" as a way of addressing issues of identity that are not confined to nationalistic ideologies that bind one to potentially narrow visions of peoplehood. Rather, "Diaspora" places African Americans within the world context as global citizens. What Diaspora ultimately does is give the black church leadership a more appropriate paradigm from which to talk about ministry in global perspective; and it affords a prophetic position relative to the loyalty-to-nation motif that has in many respects prevented African Americans from more fully approximating the ideal of their faith convictions and racial-ethnic solidarity. A nagging question that accompanies this kind of thinking is: "Can a complex notion of Diaspora as we have understood it in *nation language* and in *migratory patterns* of black religious and cultural practices serve as a foundation for a more radical proposal for national and global citizenship which embraces plurality of ethnic and racial identities?"[38]

Books on King's leadership—Jones's book included—and their relevance to this larger Diaspora vision are severely limited. I am suggesting that there be more experimentation with creative practical applications of King's notion of "the World House," as the democratic awakening of new movements of global consciousness like the Occupy movement and the current immigration debate gather diasporic tendencies that extend beyond national boundaries, race, and color, and include a consortium of "our inescapably plural identities."[39] Global citizenship asks a different set of questions related to the alienating forces of global capital as it influences the kinds of jobs that are available, who gets those jobs, and the role of public policy that is framed in relation to global economies.[40]

Clarence Jones's interpretation of King has no place for global citizenship, as we see, for example, in his perspective on immigration. Jones views current US immigration policy, especially as it relates to Mexicans and Latin

37. Martin Luther King Jr., *Where Do We Go From Here: Chaos or Community?* (Boston: Beacon, 1967), 167.

38. Albert J. Raboteau, *A Fire in the Bones: Reflections on African-American Religious History* (Boston: Beacon, 1995), 17–36; See Walter F. Pitts, *Old Ship of Zion: The Afro-Baptist Ritual in the African Diaspora*, Religion in America Series (New York: Oxford University Press, 1996), 130–31; Eddie S. Glaude Jr., *Exodus! Religion, Race, and Nation in Early Nineteenth-Century Black America* (Chicago: University of Chicago Press, 2000), 102–3. The terminology around global citizenship is highly problematic in respect to definitions of "globalized," "globalization," "citizenship," etc.

39. Amartya Sen, *Identity and Violence: The Illusion of Destiny* (New York: Norton, 2006), xiii (prologue).

40. See Fareed Zakaria, *The Post-American World* (New York: Norton, 2008).

Americans, as deplorable and unconscionable. He uses the term "slave labor" to describe the work of such immigrants and alleges that such labor is used to displace African American workers.[41] In addition, Jones identifies the current immigration situation as an affront to national sovereignty,[42] and most importantly, as showing disrespect for the law: "This is where Martin would throw up his hands . . . To him breaking the law meant paying the price for it. Willingly and gladly. Even voluntarily. Anything less was dishonest, ignoble and unworthy."[43] By placing the argument within the context of the civil rights movement's metaphors, symbols, and images, Jones legitimates his argument without connecting the larger questions of the impact of postindustrialism to the disappearance of jobs in black communities and the displacement of peoples below the US border. For African Americans, our collective condition prior to the advent of postmodernism, and perhaps more tragically expressed under current postindustrial conditions, has been and is characterized by continued displacement, profound alienation, and despair.

From Exodus to Exile: Theological-Ethical Contexts of Black Church Practices

From our earliest beginnings as a nation and a people, "exodus" has been the central paradigmatic theological and ethical statement of black church life and practices. The idea of exodus has served multiple functions in an ongoing cultural narrative "deeply anchored in themes of captivity, exile, enslavement and deliverance." Exodus has referred to the language of *nation* espoused by early nineteenth- and twentieth-century church leaders and activists; it marked the transition from slavery to freedom in the historical events of Emancipation and Reconstruction; it evolved into "the second exodus" during the Great Migration that began around the First World War when large numbers of African Americans left the South for the urban North; and in the modern civil rights movement, exodus language was a powerful symbol of the journey to the Promised Land of full citizenship and equal opportunity.[44]

---

41. Jones and Engel, *What Would Martin Say?*, 109–10.
42. Ibid., 120–21.
43. Ibid., 120.
44. Glaude, *Exodus! Religion, Race, and Nation in Early Nineteenth-Century Black America*; Wallace D. Best, *Passionately Human, No Less Divine: Religion and Culture in Black Chicago, 1915–1952* (Princeton: Princeton University Press, 2005); Anthony B. Pinn, *Understanding and Transforming the Black Church* (Eugene, OR: Cascade Books,

The African American attachment to the exodus motif has been both helpful and hurtful. No one can read the great orations of the African American past or listen to the spirituals without knowing that the exodus has played a prominent role in our thinking about liberation, God, and history. Martin Luther King Jr.'s "The Death of Evil on the Seashore" and his last public address, "I've Been to the Mountaintop," are excellent examples of the kind of sermonizing that utilizes the exodus as a symbol of the historical plight of African Americans. During the rise of Black Power, James Cone's theology took as its point of departure the exodus of God's oppressed peoples from the bondage of Pharaoh. Womanist theologians, on the other hand, have complicated the exodus metaphor by introducing the idea of "wilderness," placing emphasis more on Hagar's triple-based oppression (the intersectionality of gender, race, and class) than on Sarah and Abraham.[45] Senator Barack Obama effectively utilized the exodus metaphor as a political rhetorical device early in his presidential campaign, comparing the civil rights movement to "the Moses generation" and the new post-civil rights activism to "the Joshua generation."[46]

William R. Jones, in what was probably the most controversial book written during the nascent days of black theology, *Is God a White Racist?*, challenged the appropriateness of the exodus metaphor for the experiences of African American people. However historically situated, Jones argued,

---

2010); and Isabel Wilkerson, *The Warmth of Other Suns: The Epic Story of America's Great Migration* (New York: Vintage, 2010).

45. Delores S. Williams, *Sisters in the Wilderness: The Challenge Of Womanist God-Talk* (Maryknoll, NY: Orbis, 1993); Diana L. Hayes, *Hagar's Daughters: Womanist Ways of Being in the World*, Madeleva Lecture in Spirituality 1995 (New York: Paulist, 1995); Carolyn Rouse, *Engage Surrender: African-American Women and Islam* (Berkeley: University of California Press, 2004).

46. David Remnick, "The Joshua Generation," *The New Yorker* (17 November 2008), 69–70. "It was only on March 4, 2007, a few weeks after he announced his candidacy for President, that Obama explicitly inserted himself in the time line of American racial politics. At the Brown Chapel A.M.E. Church, in Selma, Alabama, he joined older civil-rights leaders and churchmen in commemorating the voting-rights marches a generation ago. From the pulpit, Obama paid tribute to 'the Moses generation'—to Martin Luther King and John Lewis, to Anna Cooper and the Reverend Joseph Lowery—the men and women of the movement, who marched and suffered but who, in many cases 'didn't cross over the river to see the Promised Land.' He thanked them, praised their courage, honored their martyrdom. But he spent much of his speech on his own generation, 'the Joshua generation,' and tried to answer the question, 'What's called of us?' Life had improved for African-Americans, but 'we shouldn't forget that better is not good enough.' Discrimination still existed. History was being forgotten. Schools were underfunded, citizens left uninsured, especially minorities. People were looking for 'that Oprah money' but had forgotten the need for service, for discipline, for political will.'"

exodus suggests that there has been or will be an actual, historically verifiable liberative act for black people by the Hand of God. Jones contended that we could not point to such an act in history.[47] I agree with Jones that the historical plight of African Americans cannot be equated with the biblical exodus of the Hebrews, nor can we point to an eschatological event of freedom with historical certainty. The eschatological event of the future is based on the claims of a liberative exodus event from the past. Since we cannot refer to an actual historically verifiable exodus of the past, we risk serious error in anticipating an eschaton in which God will deliver the oppressed. The exodus motif also prevents black church leaders from thinking deliberatively and historically about their present political and social predicament. One only has to walk the streets of any major urban center or witness the increasing phenomenon of black bodies in correctional facilities around the country and see the sheer carnage of black humanity to know that there has not been an exodus from Egypt or Mississippi or Chicago for African Americans.

The affinity for the exodus also has striking parallels for African American discourse in a global perspective. In respect to the global community, from what have we been liberated? From whom? Where? When? In a way similar to the dilemma motif, African Americans have tended to respond out of an antiquated notion of exodus that may be, at this point in our history, more hurtful than helpful when it comes to articulating a global vision of ministry.

I would like to suggest some experimentation with the biblical and cultural notion of "exile" as a more appropriate mode of discourse for the present socio-political situation that black religious leadership must negotiate.[48] "Exile" like "Diaspora" speaks to a more world-oriented, historical picture of African American oppression and allows the black church leadership to take seriously the relationship of its socio-historical location amongst other oppressed peoples and nations. The exilic predicament of African Americans provides fertile ground for theologizing about our relationship with other brothers and sisters in Diaspora; and it also confronts us with the question of our existential and aesthetic *estrangement*; and the question of the "stranger" may be our other sisters and brothers from whom we have been "estranged," especially those who struggle from the same empire domination of global capital. Martin Luther King Jr. understood all too well the exilic condition of African Americans and the larger pursuit of global

---

47. See William R. Jones, *Is God a White Racist?* (New York: Anchor 1973), 113-18.

48. Peter Paris makes this point in his discussion of "moral agency in conflict." See Paris, *The Social Teaching of the Black Churches* (Philadelphia: Fortress, 1985), 59.

citizenship as part of Diaspora. Early in his leadership of the Montgomery bus boycott until his tragic death in Memphis, he made the critical linkages between the struggle against American segregation and racism and the plight of African and other oppressed peoples throughout the diaspora, and their common goal to break the chains of colonialism and capitalistic exploitation.[49]

In doing so, King challenged the nation to take seriously the larger global context of which we are a part. In many respects, King's vision of the World House anticipates the recent activity and aspirations of the Occupy Movement.[50] At the time of his death, the struggle for civil and human rights had become international in scope and he had raised the interconnected problems of militarism, poverty, and racism as the major impediments to the actualization of human community.[51] His recommendation for creative change was a call for a "revolution of values and priorities" that would be both national and global in scope. He called upon the United States, because of its unique democratic heritage and its great resources of wealth and technology, to be the leader in this revolution. King stressed, however, that a true "revolution of values and priorities" would issue forth in structural changes within the American economic and political systems and in its foreign policy.

> I am convinced that if we are to get on the right side of the world revolution we as a nation must undergo a radical revolution of values. A true revolution of values will soon cause us to question the fairness and justice of many of our present and past policies. A true revolution of values will look uneasily on the glaring contrast between poverty and wealth. With righteous indignation, it will look across the seas and see individual capitalists of the West investing huge sums of money in Africa, Asia, and South America only to take the profits out with no concern for the social betterment of the countries, and say 'This is unjust.' It will look at our alliances with the landed gentry of Latin America and say: 'This is not just.' The Western arrogance of feeling that

---

49. See Lewis V. Baldwin's excellent discussion on King's relationship to African leadership in his chapter, "Ethiopia Shall Stretch forth Her Hands," in *To Make the Wounded Whole: The Cultural Legacy of Martin Luther King Jr.* (Minneapolis: Fortress, 1992), 163–244.

50. See Amy Goodman and Cornel West, "Cornel West on Occupy Wall Street: It's the Makings of a U.S. Autumn Responding to the Arab Spring." *Democracy Now!* September 29, 2011; online: http://www.democracynow.org/blog/2011/9/29/cornel_west_on_occupy_wall_street_its_the_makings_of_a_us_autumn_responding_to_the_arab_spring.

51. King, *Where Do We Go From Here*, 173–86.

it has everything to teach others and nothing to learn from them is not just.⁵²

King had also come to a place in his thinking in which he understood more clearly the dynamic tensions at work between poverty, racism, and war within the American society, and their relationship to the exploitation of the poor and powerless abroad.⁵³ Shortly before his death, in April of 1968, the SCLC had planned a "Poor People's Campaign" to converge upon Washington DC and to demonstrate nonviolently in massive civil disobedience until Congress acted to help alleviate the abject poverty across the nation. King felt that such a national confrontation with the federal government by an interracial coalition of 3,000 poor whites, Native Americans, Hispanic Americans, and blacks (who would comprise the majority) would symbolically demonstrate the class-based economic and social discrimination inherent in the national policy.⁵⁴ He also argued that the national policy of discrimination against the poor and ethnic minorities was but a microcosm of the nation's foreign policy that was most dramatically illustrated in the Vietnam War. In King's words, "The war in Vietnam is but a symptom of a far deeper malady within the American spirit."⁵⁵ It was King's position that the problems of poverty and race within the United States are global in scope and therefore "inseparable from an international emergency which involves the poor, the dispossessed, and the exploited of the whole world."⁵⁶

James Cone suggests that Martin Luther King Jr.'s perspective on "racism, black empowerment and war led to a shift in emphasis and meaning regarding the themes of love, justice, and hope,"⁵⁷ which were operative concepts in his articulation of the beloved community. The theme of hope, according to Cone, became "the shining center of Martin's thinking,

---

52. "Conscience and the Vietnam War," in James M. Washington, ed., *A Testament of Hope: The Essential Writings and Speeches of Martin Luther King Jr.* (New York: Harper & Row, 1990), 639–40.

53. "Discerning the Signs of History," sermon preached by King at Ebenezer Baptist Church, November 15, 1964, King Center Library and Archives; King, *Where Do We Go From Here?*, 135–66; King, "A Christmas Sermon on Peace (1967)," in Washington, ed., *A Testament of Hope*, 253–58.

54. Stephen B. Oates, *Let the Trumpet Sound* (New York: Harper Perennial, 1994), 449–52.

55. Martin Luther King, Jr., *The Trumpet of Conscience* (San Francisco: HarperCollins, 1989), 21–34; and Washington, ed., *A Testament of Hope*, 639.

56. Ibid., 652.

57. James H. Cone, *Martin & Malcolm & America: A Dream or a Nightmare* (Maryknoll, NY: Orbis, 1991), 235.

revealing new interpretations of love and justice."[58] This shifting emphasis had significant implications for King's theological and spiritual perspectives surrounding the theological constructs of "exodus" and "exile." No place in King is this hope more vividly portrayed than in his courageous denunciation of the Vietnam War and in his trials within the African American community around the political philosophy of Black Nationalism, articulated by Malcolm X.

There is evidence in the later King that there was a precipitous movement toward an "exilic" metaphor as a way of understanding the "shifting" epistemic grounds for liberative claims for African Americans. King's last speech is normally interpreted in light of the exodus paradigm. In that speech, King stands on the summit of the mountaintop and sees the "Promised Land." The "Promised Land" conjures up images of the conquest of Canaan by Joshua, but a "shift" in lenses would offer a different reading. A closer examination of the substantive discourse in the speech reveals several levels of meaning. One is that King speaks out of a diasporic perspective. He begins his speech as a type of journey on which he takes a panoramic view of Western history. He calls his listeners to remember with him the long journey of Western civilization. He then locates himself in the latter half of the twentieth century in which there is a worldwide struggle for freedom. The exodus event is included as one instance in the long march of humanity toward freedom. The civil rights movement is situated in the broader context of a world movement that is taking place in America. This is a recurring theme throughout King, beginning in his initial speech at Holt Street Baptist Church in 1955. The primary discursive note throughout the speech is the element of "hope." In the exile motif, the dominant existential category is "hope." What is the source and direction of this hope for King? A reading from within the exile paradigm favors the source of hope in the history of suffering peoples to create new meanings out of overwhelming oppression. The direction of the hope is toward a worldwide revolution guided by the ethic of suffering love. King viewed the boycott of the garbage workers in Memphis as part of a worldwide struggle for equality and freedom. This line of thinking points toward an exilic existence within the United States in the hope for a global eruption of freedom.

Before his tragic death, Martin Luther King Jr. reminded this nation that we no longer live in a small house, but, rather, we have inherited a world house of interrelatedness and interdependability. He asserted in clear and strident language that we must learn to live together as brothers and sisters or die apart as fools. During his later years, King was acutely aware

---

58. Ibid.

of the need for a broader interpretive framework for understanding what he perceived as a crucial passage in history. He wrote: "[T]he civil rights movement in the United States is a special American phenomenon which must be understood in the light of American history and dealt with in terms of the American situation. But on another and more important level, what is happening in the United States today is a significant part of a world development."[59]

He further suggested that the struggles of African Americans must be understood in light of a "shifting" of the West's basic outlooks and philosophical presuppositions about "power." Indeed, King argued: "However deeply American Negroes are caught in the struggle to be at last home in our homeland of the United States, we cannot ignore the larger world house in which we are also dwellers. Equality with whites will not solve the problems of either whites or Negroes if it means equality in a world society stricken by poverty and in a universe doomed to extinction by war."[60]

This dream of a "world house" has striking implications for the plight of "the stones that the builders rejected" as we prepare to meet the challenges of a new era. Dr. King's prophetic insight of a global community is not quite the same as the "I Have A Dream" speech of 1963, of which many are so fond. That was a speech directed to the issue of the civil rights that African Americans had been denied. But the notion of a "world house" places our struggle within the context of liberation movements throughout world. It implies that the freedom of African Americans—our human rights—is inextricably bound with the yearnings and hopes of oppressed people everywhere. King often reminded us that "injustice anywhere is a threat to justice everywhere."[61]

As we witness the shifting grounds of social and political change in the "democratic awakening" of "the U.S. fall, responding to the Arab Spring," African Americans and other marginalized groups must ask new questions about the nature and scope of our long, arduous journey on these shores. *We must ask what does this new season of worldwide struggle mean for us, for this nation, and for the world?* Dare we hope or must we conclude that we are at "the end of history"? King did not think we were at the end of history. King believed that what we are witnessing is a worldwide revolution that challenges the very foundations of hegemony. In his last public sentences, King said that he was pleased to live during this chaotic and precarious age

---

59. King, *Where Do We Go From Here*, 169.

60. Ibid., 167.

61. King, "Letter from Birmingham City Jail," in Washington, ed., *A Testament of Hope*, 290.

because beyond the despair and hopelessness that abounded, he believed that this was a great moment for the united struggles of people throughout the world. King said:

> But I know, somehow, that only when it is dark enough, can you see the stars. And I see God working in this period of the twentieth century in a way that men, in some strange way, are responding. Something is happening in our world. The masses of the people are rising up. And wherever they are assembled today, whether they are in Johannesburg, South Africa; Nairobi, Kenya; Accra, Ghana; New York City; Atlanta, Georgia; Jackson, Mississippi; or Memphis, Tennessee, the cry is always the same: 'We want to be free.'[62]

From the Frying Pan to the Fire: Existential and Aesthetic Contexts of Black Church Strivings

A number of scholars have begun to look more deeply into the existential and aesthetic contexts of black church life and strivings along the lines of the thinking presented here.[63] They invite us to carefully straddle the diverse worlds of religious meaning and tradition, leaving space for a sustained conversation between black church scholars and religious humanists which, in my opinion, may be the most difficult, yet most salient public conversation in a postracial and post-American world. Anthony Pinn's book, *Understanding and Transforming the Black Church*,[64] is a prolegomenon to a larger complicated set of questions that black churches will need to rethink in light of the nagging historical problems of racialized, sexualized, gendered politics of the church and the larger culture; but more importantly, he challenges scholars working in these traditions to reframe these *quest*(ions) in respect to the shifting grounds of political and social realities that *stretch*

---

62. Clayborne Carson and Kris Shepard, eds., *A Call to Conscience: The Landmark Speeches of Martin Luther King, Jr.* (New York: Warner, 2001), 209.

63. See Norm R. Allen Jr., ed., *African American Humanism: An Anthology* (Buffalo: Prometheus, 1991); Mike Featherstone, et al., eds., *The Body: Social Process and Cultural Theory*, Theory, Culture & Society Series (London: Sage, 2001); Norm R. Allen, *The Black Humanist Experience: An Alternative to Religion* (Buffalo: Prometheus 2002); Kelly Brown Douglas, *What's Faith Got to Do With It? Black Bodies/Christian Souls* (Maryknoll, NY: Orbis, 2005); Dwight N. Hopkins, *Being Human: Race, Culture, and Religion* (Minneapolis: Fortress, 2005); and Victor Anderson, *Creative Exchange: A Constructive Theology of African American Religious Experience* (Minneapolis: Fortress, 2008).

64. Anthony B. Pinn, *Understanding and Transforming the Black Church* (Eugene, OR: Cascade Books, 2009).

toward complex subjectivity, diversity, openness, and inclusiveness. A critical dimension of this *stretching* will involve a new aesthetic sensibility and appreciation of *the body*, the many colored and estranged bodies that are heirs to *Somebodyness*. In reflection on the "New Negro" involved in the Montgomery campaign, King wrote: "Once plagued with a tragic sense of inferiority resulting from the crippling effects of slavery and segregation, the Negro has now been driven to re-evaluate himself. He has come to feel that he is somebody. His religion reveals to him that God loves all His children and that the important thing about a man is not 'his specificity but his fundamentum'—not the texture of his hair or the color of his skin but his eternal worth to God."[65]

King's reference to "fundamentum" reflects the classic Enlightenment dualism of mind/body, permanence/change, and universality/particularity, and his philosophical allegiance to Boston Personalism,[66] which eludes the deep appreciation he demonstrated in an embodied struggle for justice. An example of his own sense of embodiment is reflected in the revealing personal testimony where he writes: "My personal trials have taught me the value of unmerited suffering . . . I have lived these past few years with the conviction that unearned suffering is redemptive. There are some who still find the cross a stumbling block, others consider it foolishness, but I am more convinced than ever before that it is the power of God unto social and individual salvation. So like the Apostle Paul I can now humbly say, 'I bear in my body the marks of the Lord Jesus.'" [67] This place in King provides an excellent site for scholars to engage the question of the "sacredness of the body" in King, in ways in which the captivity of liberal theological discourse of his time could not. It is also an excellent site to engage the questions of the shape-shifting character of race and the postmodernist interpretation of subjectivity.

Somebodyness places emphasis on the *body* as a critical source for the ethical life. One can hardly imagine living ethically or unethically without a body. Moreover, the body constitutes a critical frame of reference for the aesthetic life, apart from which ethics as a narrative quest is impossible. This

---

65. King, *Stride toward Freedom*, 167.

66. See Rufus Burrow Jr., "The Personalism of John Wesley Edward Bowen," *The Journal of Negro History* 82/2 (1997) 251. For a full discussion by Burrow, see his *Personalism: A Critical Introduction* (St. Louis: Chalice, 1999), especially 66–90; and his development of "Militant Personalism," as a strategy for overcoming dualism and disembodied theological discourse and praxis, 244–49. See also his *God and Human Dignity: The Personalism, Theology, and Ethics of Martin Luther King Jr.* (Notre Dame: University of Notre Dame Press, 2006).

67. Martin Luther King Jr., "Pilgrimage to Nonviolence," in *Strength to Love* (Minneapolis: Fortress, 1981), 154.

is especially important for ethical reflection in African American life and culture. Ethics, as a discipline, not only seeks answers to questions of right and wrong, but responses to beauty, balance, and symmetry that are equally significant for the moral development and deportment of leaders, in this case black church leaders.[68]

What about the body as an aesthetic site for pondering new and fresh approaches to dilemma/Diaspora and exodus/exile in rethinking African American leadership practices? What if we were to take this aesthetic approach seriously in respect to the shifting grounds of black church tradition and its leadership? What would our churches look like if we took reconstructed notions of Diaspora and exile seriously? What would be the content of our preaching and the form and shape of liturgy? Far from a more comfortable predicament, I am suggesting that we would be (to use an old saying borrowed from my mother) "jumping from the frying pan to the fire." The "fire" metaphor like "Diaspora" and "exile" takes us beyond the temptation to quietism embodied in the notions of "dilemma" (which suggests "standing still"; indecisiveness; or what Robert Michael Franklin calls "the strenuous self");[69] "exodus" (which suggests that the liberative event has already happened and conspires with the temptation to quietism); and the "frying pan"(a static notion in which African Americans are seen as passive objects subjected to present sociopolitical arrangements that act as a literal hell, "lake of fire").The frying pan seems the appropriate context in which to talk about the historic ways in which we have wrestled ambiguously in dilemma and hoped in exodus. Fire, on the other hand, takes the black church to a deeper dimension of a discourse and practice that is already present. Fire is far more terrifying than the frying pan, far more dangerous, far more costly—but fire is also purgative and stretches toward what Howard Thurman called "the search for common ground." Let us reimagine what it means to be bodily "baptized by fire and the Holy Ghost." "I indeed baptize you with water unto repentance: but he that cometh after me is mightier than I, whose shoes I am not worthy to bear: he shall baptize you with the Holy Ghost, and with fire" (Matt 3:11). Fire is universal and purgative. What I have in mind here is akin to Diana L. Eck's experimentation

---

68. Cornel West asserts, "the notion that black people are human beings is a relatively new discovery in the modern West. The idea of black equality in beauty, culture, and intellectual capacity remains problematic." West, *Prophesy Deliverance!*, 47. See also Richard Shusterman, "Somaesthetics: A Disciplinary Proposal," *Journal of Aesthetics and Art Criticism* 57 (1999) 299-313.

69. See Robert Michael Franklin's discussion on "strenuous life" in *Liberating Visions: Human Fulfillment and Social Justice in African-American Thought* (Minneapolis: Fortress, 1990), 7 and 43-44.

with cross-cultural and religious themes associated with the Spirit. One of the common themes that bind traditional religious cosmologies is the element of fire as denoting Spirit (also breath, wind). [70] African American religious discourse is anchored in practices that seek the fullness of baptism in the Spirit and "fire shut in our bones."[71]

Fire demands that our commitments to the nation be judged by a more inclusive and prophetic norm, not unlike the tongues of fire at Pentecost. Our commitments to the nation would be judged in the context of a greater loyalty to the world community, particularly to people of African descent and other oppressed peoples of the world: Haiti? Darfur? Tibet? Zimbabwe? Columbia? Ecuador? Palestine? When King made that fateful decision to talk about a World House in which the triplets of war, poverty, and racism had to be removed, he was prophesying in tongues of fire. This courageous vision of world community cost him dearly—some of us think with his life.

In many respects, Martin Luther King Jr.'s prophetic vision of the World House mirrors what we have in mind with the idea of "fire" or reverence that sees the interrelatedness and inherent value of all life. It was his sense of community that led him to identify the great new problem of humankind as the challenge of divided loyalties: loyalty to the particularized and local visions of race, ethnicity, and the state versus the demand for global community. For King, the remedy for this problem of loyalty was a "revolution of values and priorities." At the heart of such a revolution is the question of loyalty. "A genuine revolution of values means in the final analysis that our loyalties must become ecumenical rather than sectional," King wrote. "Every nation must now develop an overriding loyalty to mankind as a whole in order to preserve the best in our individual societies."[72] King suggested that this spiritual revolution would lift us beyond tribe, race, class, and nation to a worldwide fellowship of love.[73] At once, in this singular vision of reverence and possibility, King articulated the dream of the beloved community in which civility was inspired and supported within the context of global communion. Many believe that he was speaking in many languages as the Spirit gave utterance—languages that speak in loving and just ways to the agoniz-

---

70. See Diana L. Eck, *Encountering God: A Spiritual Journey from Bozeman to Banaras* (Boston: Beacon, 1993), chapter 5: "The Breath of God: the Fire and Freedom of the Spirit," 118–43.

71. See Harvey Cox, *Fire from Heaven: the Rise of Pentecostal Spirituality and the Reshaping of Religion in the Twenty-First Century* (Reading, MA: Addison-Wesley, 1995); Albert J. Raboteau, *Fire in the Bones: Reflections on African-American Religious History* (Boston: Beacon, 1995).

72. King, *Where Do We Go From Here*, 190.

73. Ibid.

ing, yet redemptive possibilities inherent in recognition, respectability, and reverence for a beloved community more grand than even the nation and the world can ever hope for—*a new heaven and a new earth.*

5

Drum Major for Justice or Dilettante of Dishonesty

Martin Luther King Jr., Moral Capital, and Hypocrisy of Embodied Messianic Myths

CHERYL A. KIRK-DUGGAN

A Nobel Peace Prize-winner, Martin Luther King Jr. went from birth in a Southern Baptist pulpit to a meteoric rise of global recognition. This preacher was a prophetic voice and could appreciate a joke by a colleague. His charisma was stellar, and his rhetoric helped move and motivate the 1960s civil rights movement. A Morehouse man, King completed his PhD degree in systematic theology and was called to pastor the Dexter Avenue Baptist Church in Montgomery, Alabama. A husband and father, he incorporated Mohandas K. Gandhi's principles of nonviolent direct action. In a moment of understandable fear, King had a kitchen table experience, which rejuvenated and forged his faith.[1] He espoused his dream at the foot of the Lincoln Memorial in 1963, and was assassinated when he went to Memphis to support oppressed sanitation workers. King had unique gifts; King was human. Like many leaders, he left powerful legacies and was a flawed person. People who live large, often have considerable flaws.

In dialog with Clarence B. Jones's chapter on leadership in his book, *What Would Martin Say?* (2008), this essay explores moral capital amidst plagiarism in the writings and adultery in the marriage of Martin Luther

---

1. Martin Luther King Jr., *Stride toward Freedom: The Montgomery Story* (New York: Harper & Row, 1958), 134–35.

King Jr. After presenting my methodology, the chapter (1) analyzes Jones's notion of King's thoughts about leadership; (2) provides an overview of plagiarism and adultery in King's life; (3) explores how moral capital, power, prestige, and vulnerability, shaped by a messianic complex, is problematic for African American leadership; and (4) engages some of Jones's projected concepts of King's leadership, with King's strengths and weaknesses, and offers an enhanced reading of the beloved community for healthy leadership and communal wellbeing.

Seeing through a Purple Lens: A Womanist Perspective

Womanist theory, an interdisciplinary analytical lens, can help us expose numerous oppressions in our world and face our own complicity in such injustice. The term *Womanist*, coined by Alice Walker[2] from the term "womanish," refers to women of African descent who are outrageous, audacious, in charge, serious, and responsible. The term refers to a Black feminist who challenges oppressions regarding gender, class, race, sexual orientation, ability, age, and ecology. Such a justice stance requires us, individually and communally, to uncover, name, and act to stop all acts of injustice, and of violence. Womanist thought provides a vibrant, expansive matrix and instructive framework for critical, creative analysis, where one seeks awareness, deals with the necessity of acceptance of those things we cannot change, then commit to appropriate personal and communal action, framed by gifts of resilience and humor, staying the course even when change seems impossible and uncertain.

Womanist sensibilities celebrates the gift and freedom to love all people, sexually and nonsexually, all parameters of difference and confidently embody a woman's culture and life. Womanist theory is aesthetic, physical, spiritual, emotional, and creative, and it evokes a palette of variegated reality, yielding imaginative passion, love, hope, and change. Such engagement invites, requires, that one live in present time, is a student of history, and participates in radical listening and discerning, to see, know, challenge, analyze, and make a difference. Significant to this work is the experience of those who are usually forgotten, who matter least, symbolized by poor Black women. A Womanist liberative theory engenders mutuality and community amid the responsibility and stewardship of freedom; honors the *Imago Dei* (the image of God), the essential goodness and divine beauty in all persons; and engages texts held as authoritative with a careful, critical,

---

2. Alice Walker, *In Search of Our Mothers' Gardens: Womanist Prose* (San Diego: Harcourt Brace Jovanovich, 1983), xi.

creative reading. Womanist liberatory theory invites mutuality, community, and stewardship of freedom amid responsibility. Womanist thought comprises, but is not limited to theology, sacred texts, ethics, and diverse contexts, which excavate questions about divine and human, faith, thought, power, language, values, praxis, history, behavior, culture, aesthetics, and community.

A Foot Soldier, Advisor, and Scholar Looks Back to Look Forward

Martin Luther King Jr. recruited Clarence B. Jones, now Scholar in Residence at the Martin Luther King Jr. Research and Educational Institute, Stanford University, to serve as an attorney and advisor during the 1960s Civil Rights campaigns. Thus, Jones has a unique vantage point from which to reflect on what King's thoughts would be today.

For Jones, King decided to be politically impartial to avoid alienating the opposing party. Today, many Black politicians move at the behest of the Democratic Party. That many politicians seek to patronize Blacks speaks to racism and infantilism, which ironically receives the support, perhaps the encouragement of Black leaders. Jones sees current Black leadership as being interested solely in self-aggrandizement, to such an extent that they have not used their clout and Black voting bloc to press the Republican Party regarding so called illegal immigration, which Jones argues has stolen jobs from Black people. While Jones makes a solid point on the loss of Black jobs, his reading seems too simplistic, and it signals another divide and conquer tactic that sees Hispanics as culprits, when the issue is much more complex. Michelle Alexander, in her ground breaking volume, *The New Jim Crow: Mass Incarceration in the Age of Color Blindness*,[3] makes it plain that the prison industrial complex has limited Black male presence in the workplace, and such a reality is a direct result of the so-called wars on crime and on drugs, when statistically acts of crime and drug activity were down. These wars intentionally set out to limit African American access to the outcomes of 1960s Civil Rights legislation. Documented in multiple places, many jobs have either become extinct because of modern technology and others have been shipped to South or East, to Mexico, India, Taiwan, and China. Second, Jones argues that King would always take the moral high ground over against oral exposition, out of a love for people and justice. Such commitment also meant a call to nurture new courageous, intelligent leadership.

---

3. See Michelle Alexander, *The New Jim Crow: Mass Incarceration in the Age of Color Blindness* (New York: New Press, 2012).

Jones posits that contemporary leadership ought to have to pass the "King test of integrity," because the former seem more impressed with publicity and economics over against justice. Such a comment begs the question, as to whether King could pass his own test of integrity, which we explore subsequently. Not to minimize the incredible work for justice to the point of martyrdom, one has to ask if integrity is so important socio-politically, how can it not be that important academically, particularly as King's profound, persuasive use of words are the hallmark of the Rubicon of his legacy?[4]

As a leader, Jones remarks that King's goal was to work for justice, framed by a call to serve God and humanity. King expressed his talent and commitment through ministry, and his academic training afforded him the opportunity to think clearly, critically. His fame and popularity made him a local and domestic target. Thus, the issues and energies that were sometimes a hindrance on the inside, were a help on the outside. While some of King's naysayers spoke of him as "De Lawd," Jones posits that no one doubted his commitment and integrity related to social justice. If King was alive today and asked about leadership, Jones believes King would talk about how far the movement has strayed from its ethos four decades ago, when marching for justice was the primary objective. King worked and ultimately gave his life because he advocated for a beloved community.[5]

If indeed King's academic experience provided him with the rigor to think critically, clearly, how could he not use these skills to critique his ethical violations of plagiarizing and adultery? Were people actually trying to knock King from off a pedestal, and further, should one ever be on a pedestal in the first place? Can one not lead in partnership, or must leadership always engage in hierarchical management? Was such a strategy an elitist tactic learned in observing how majority culture engaged leadership? When we place anyone on a pedestal, do we create a catalyst for bad boy behavior? There is also the question of whether Martin was an initiator of programs, or was he a spokesperson for the work of others, including many of the women in the Civil Rights movement like Septima Clark, Ella Baker, and JoAnne Robinson. King's commitment to justice, his courage and selfless leadership, are not in question. His charismatic gifts and persuasive rhetoric positioned him to lead Blacks and whites alike. Yet, Jones's deep admiration for King seems to hint of demagoguery. Are the days of needing messianic leadership ever over?[6]

---

4. Clarence B. Jones and Joel Engel, *What Would Martin Say?* (New York: Harper, 2008), 31–35.

5. Ibid., 42–49.

6. Ibid.

A Glimpse of "Bad Boy" Escapades of the Drum Major for Justice

One challenge to analyzing the life and contributions of King is that he has become mythic, heroic: larger than life. He was human and he himself recognized that reality. He fought against crippling fear, while his moral compass so demanded that he speak out against oppression, he critiqued the Vietnam War, ostensibly signing his death warrant.[7] Before his untimely death, several instances of inappropriate behavior has surfaced in recent scholarship that relate to issues of leadership, then and now; specifically acts of plagiarism and infidelity.[8]

Plagiarism is an intriguing dilemma, particularly in a world where downloading and sampling of the music of others, despite copyright, occurs in rap music. With technology and the Internet, many engage in plagiarism, see nothing wrong with it, and invariably are able to get away with this violation. Some people care and some do not. Many have dismissed King's plagiarism, and fail to see it as a blemish on his historical legacy. Conversely, can one really believe that a person, even a Martin Luther King Jr., can be justified in using the works of others without giving credit to the originator of the words or thoughts? Can one seriously think that using another's words even for the cause of dismantling injustice, evil, and hate, without crediting the originator is a righteous act? What would King's followers have said if the reverse had happened: if someone else had plagiarized King's words for some allegedly noble cause? History attests to a tradition of Black preachers studying and then using the mannerisms, rhetoric, and gestures of other preachers generally without the assumption of plagiarism, instead assuming a tribute of mimetic embodiment.[9] Does this mean then that the tradition needs to monitor itself? Is there and/or should there be a clearly articulated standard that when such practices are in print or recorded that the writer/speaker needs to at the very least indicate the originator of the ideas? Is it not injustice to take credit for the work of others?

Scholars know that King's papers are tragically flawed by copious examples of plagiarism. When comparing his scholarly indiscretions with his fame and martyrdom, some scholars often disregard the former, or see these

---

7. Bryan Massingale, "King and I," *U.S. Catholic* 72/2 (2007) 46–47.

8. For my earlier thoughts on King, particularly as relates to women, please see Cheryl A. Kirk-Duggan, *Refiner's Fire: A Religious Engagement with Violence* (Minneapolis: Fortress, 2001), 79–92.

9. Sam Fullwood III, "Plagiarism: Playing by the Rules. In the Academic World, in Music and Even in Church, What Constitutes Plagiarism Is under New Scrutiny after Journalism's Wake-up Call." *Black Issues Book Review* 5/5 (2003) 24–25.

indiscretions as not a break with rules of academia, but as evidence of his gift of combining his thoughts and words with others' words to articulate his beliefs in powerful ways and to create a persona with global appeal. In his *Stride toward Freedom*, King posited that his sociopolitical ideas derived from his readings of major theological texts, and toned down the impact of his lived, non-scholarly, and African American experiences on his writings. When speaking about his social justice commitments, he focused little on his abstract theological work. Clayborne Carson, along with other scholars, note that King frames his personal and public image in this work. These scholars are so committed to the King Project and legacy that they tend to assuage King's shortcomings and the approaches he took, by focusing on King's intent to provide the framework for his intellectual development, which afforded other interpreter's an excuse to foreground certain influences over other nonintellectual and historic inspirations. King's view of life and God grew, synthesized, and changed as his studies and life experiences increased. In school, King struggled to come up with a picture of the nature of God that is personal, emotional, and intellectually satisfying. He combined intellectual prowess, skilled oratory, Black Baptist tradition, to be an educated activist pastor. For many scholars, King's appropriation and use of other people's materials allowed him a public profile, enabled him to mobilize people across incredible differences, and to become a public figure of note to enhance his orality and writing, ultimately as preacher. King assumed his historical legacy was not about his gifts, but about how he used them.[10]

That King's professors did not check his plagiarism causes one to pause. Were they too busy, too lazy, and too impressed with his intellect and ambition? Alternatively, was it a form of racism that they did not expect any better, and decided to go along so King could get along? While students, congregants, and others can get caught up in the engagement of rhetoric and being wordsmiths honing persuasive orality, notably as homileticists, such desire in no way justifies the use of others words without giving due credit. How can one espouse justice, truth telling, and freedom in one venue and not engage the same moral imperative in written or oral scholarship? Most people, particularly in the academy, know what plagiarism is, but seem hesitant to call it for what it is, particularly when the culprit has the stature of Martin Luther King Jr. Is plagiarism tolerated out of a lack of responsibility by academic guilds, by a cynical attitude, by a sense of entitlement to use others' works? Alternatively, is it a sense of shame that somehow the system

---

10. Clayborne Carson et al., "Martin Luther King Jr. as Scholar: A Reexamination of His Theological Writings," *Journal of American History* 78/1 (1991) 92–105.

failed to help King and others when it could, and with his accomplishments and legacy, we do not want to be viewed as a naysayer?[11] Do we not want to equate charismatic greatness with clay feet? Have we romanticized this 39 year old, frozen him in time, and each year increased the height of his pedestal? Do we wonder that if we talk about his shortcomings, we might start to unravel the tightly woven garment known as the civil rights movement, and we fear it will all fall apart? A brief glance at today's economy, educational systems, and housing foreclosures indicate that the latter has already happened, particularly with governmental deregulation, cuts in social programming while providing welfare (dubbed tax cuts) to the rich and famous; bank bailouts, and misguided policy like "No Child Left Behind," which leaves many behind, stifles creativity and thwarts the capacity to think as teachers must teach to the test to keep the schools open and keep their jobs. Regardless as to how one spins it, King's lived oral experience of the Black church is not a valid argument for omitting documentation when he uses the words of others. Intellectual integrity cannot be compromised, regardless of the reputation of the plagiarist, or their place in history.

Historical documents and their assessment tell us that King plagiarized from his Morehouse days of carelessness around writing to his more intense plagiarism during his Boston University days. Sometimes he failed to include references in his bibliography; other times he failed to provide correct attribution. Was the fact that no one called him on his blatant disregard at Boston University a matter of racism, of victimization of King, or was King being ironic signifier, trickster, or kokopelli?[12] Whatever the motivation, socio-cultural and historical pressures and bigotries, or any personal duress that drove the plagiarism, King sometimes has equally high marks for breaking rules of his marriage contract, depending upon who you read.

King allegedly was having extramarital affairs during the Montgomery campaign, and had participated in liaisons within the company of Ralph Abernathy as well. Fall, 1958, J. Raymond Henderson, a leader in Baptist circles, recognized the precarious position their sexual escapades placed them in, and wrote them a letter naming the types of problems and violence that could arise from many portals. Significantly, Henderson pointed out that some women would aspire to sleep with prominent men, and King and Abernathy's enemies could use women to entice them into compromising positions. Henderson's letter focused on King's public reputation; however, without challenging King's ministerial ethics or the pain he could cause

11. John Higham, "Habits of the Cloth and Standards of the Academy," *Journal of American History* 78/1 (1991) 106–10.

12. Ralph E. Luker, "Plagiarism and Practice: Questions about Martin Luther King Jr.," *International Social Science Review* 68/4 (1993) 152–61.

his female liaisons. King confided his innermost personal secrets to an innermost circle and a small group of preachers, including Clarence Jones. This select group accepted, sometimes applauded his provocative exploits. Patriarchal, male privilege of men, complicitly observed by women, allowed this group to see King's immorality as a function of him being a man, as a ministerial vocational benefit, where socio-cultural pressures were catalysts for those obsessed by success or love or having to deal with the heinous constraints of the white world. If King David of biblical notoriety could have concubines and leave a legacy, could not Martin Luther King Jr. do the same?[13]

Between FBI tapes and general gossip, *The Pittsburg Courier*, a national Black newspaper, implied that King, a prominent southern Black preacher, was an adulterer. Allegedly, he had a liaison in a Northern hotel room with a woman other than Coretta. King would have rendezvous with women in places away from either of their home towns. He had formal, long-standing liaisons with particular women, and other brief encounters with various women. King knew his indiscretions were sinful, and said as much to his congregation at Ebenezer. He also felt unworthy of the many accolades people placed upon him and did not want to be put upon a pedestal; he felt guilty.[14] King's indiscretions weighed upon him, as his admitting matters of guilt indicate. Should a known adulterer be a leader in the worlds of religion and politics?

Dennis Prager, a religious conservative, says that a person committing adultery in no way indicates that person is unfit to hold political office. He justifies this deduction by agreeing with others that while King David's indiscretion with Bathsheba results in a child born out of David's adulterous acts, which included pre-meditated homicide against Uriah, with the audacity to have Uriah deliver his own death warrant, David still gets to be the "root of Jesse," an ancestor of Jesus Christ, the messiah. Prager argues that one's adultery should not mark a person as an ineffective or unethical political or religious leader. Some leaders with utmost fidelity have been horrible presidents. Prager says he is not defending adultery; rather argues the complexity of marriage and the spectrum of how people actually define adultery—from a lap dance and reading pornography to lust and actual physical liaisons. Barring those who are indiscreet and embarrass their families, Prager argues people's sexual lives are a private matter, and those

13. Taylor Branch, *Parting the Waters: America in the King Years, 1954-63* (New York: Simon & Schuster, 1988), 239, 242-43, 860-62 and 880-81.

14. David J. Garrow, *Bearing the Cross: Martin Luther King Jr., and the Southern Christian Leadership Conference*, Perennial Classics (New York: Morrow, 2004), 96 and 587-88.

news commentators who focus on such activity need to review their own ethical mores. He suggests that the only purpose such a fascination serves is to hinder capable, honest, brilliant, outstanding "men" from running for public office.[15] I wonder what Coretta would have to say?

In folk culture, people will often say hold on to your first impression of an individual, regardless of what others have to say or think. Coretta Scott King's initial impression of Martin Luther King Jr. was that he was a very short, spoiled playboy preacher, who was full of himself. Yet, she was always there for him, paid no attention to gossip, rumors, or FBI shenanigans.[16] King expected women, all wives to stay at home, presuming she was physically and aesthetically suitable. In her book, *My Life with Martin Luther King Jr.*, Coretta Scott King claims that King vaguely thought women were equal to men in capabilities and intelligence, yet her role was mother to his children and as homemaker.[17] Such a stance is not surprising. Not only is he a product of his times, but King rarely offered commendation and gratitude for the women in the Movement. Eventually, his sexism was not as rigid, but his awareness and action were never to the extent of Frederick Douglass and W. E. B. DuBois, who supported women's rights. He cared for Coretta King, but only spent about ten percent of his time at home. His troubles moved him toward passion, tenderness, and encouragement from other women. King was human; he could joke and tease, yet be hurt and sensitive. He was troubled and angry, and the power of his anger was simultaneously the power of his love. The gospel of love involved *agape* and the erotic admiration of countless numbers of desiring women.[18]

In sum, by engaging in plagiarism and adultery, King betrayed himself and subverted the rules of academic scholarship and Christian morality. The Martin Luther King Jr. Papers Project and several prominent biographers from Abernathy to David Garrow and Taylor Branch have documented his phenomenal contributions to the cause of freedom, his rise to global notoriety, his humble spirit, and his unethical behavior. King's lived faith and scholastic experience had to provide a personal awareness that King

---

15. Dennis Prager, "What Does Adultery Tell Us about Character?" *The Paragould Daily Press*, Wednesday, December 14, 2011. Online: http://townhall.com/columnists/dennisprager/2011/12/06/what_does_adultery_tell_us_about_character/page/full/.

16. Andrew Young, "The Untold Story of Martin Luther King Jr. & Coretta Scott King," *Ebony* 61/6 (2006) 172–80.

17. Coretta Scott King, *My Life with Martin Luther King Jr.* (New York: Holt, Rinehart & Winston, 1969), 91.

18. James H. Cone, *Martin & Malcolm & America: A Dream or a Nightmare?* (Maryknoll, NY: Orbis, 1991), 273–78; and Stephen B. Oates, *Let the Trumpet Sound: The Life of Martin Luther King Jr.* (New York: Harper & Row, 1982), 265 and 280–84.

had committed academic fraud and moral turpitude. Further, there were rumblings that most of his books were ghost written.[19] What were the foundational rubrics for King's life, and where did he go from there?

Ethics, Messianism, and Problematic Leadership

African American religious and socio-cultural, historical traditions, and experiences are critical to King's development, thought, strategies, and commitments. Nurtured in his parents' faith, he knew the history of oppression and witnessed his father's experience of blatant racism. King saw the import of focusing on the individual soul along with socio-economic matters that often systemically oppress people's lives. This reality satisfied his intellectual need to deal with social evil. King saw the church as the venue and power base for social change and empowerment, and inherited a sense of a personal God of immeasurable love and boundless power who works throughout history to save humanity. All humanity had value and dignity, framed in his concept of *beloved community*. King's beloved community embraces a prophetic visualization of freedom, equality, and justice steeped in an activist faith and hope that emerged out of the African American lived experience and traditions of antebellum enslavement, extolled in African American Spirituals. The Spirituals reflect beloved community, signaling one's level of responsibility for one's neighbor. For King, the 1960s Civil Rights Movement was the perfect venue for applied Christian ethics rooted in agape love, the import to forgive, and for oppressed and oppressor to experience reconciliation as foundational for embodying beloved community. Steeped in Black messianic hope, King believed in redemptive suffering of Blacks and other oppressed people, framed by spirituality, democracy, and optimism.[20] These tenets helped hone his theology, his understanding of God, God's children, and their experiences of evil.

Some scholars posit King as one who discerned theological anthropological problematic issues as steeped in evil social structures, not people who did evil; further King understood that Christian faith finds humanity trapped into social, ideological separation where rituals fomenting evil are inescapable. Framed by a personal theology, King rooted his beliefs in Jesus Christ as real, relevant, radical, righteous, redemptive, reconciling, agape

---

19. David Levering Lewis, "Failing to Know Martin Luther King Jr.," *Journal of American History* 78/1 (1991) 81–85.

20. Lewis V. Baldwin, "Martin Luther King Jr., the Black Church, and the Black Messianic Vision," *Journal of the Interdenominational Theological Center* 12/1–2 (1984–1985) 93–108.

love, born amidst his experience of the Black religious tradition. King's theology allowed him great concern for the disenfranchised, impoverished masses, those without socioeconomic and political capital. Thus, he saw and used the church as a vehicle for gaining human rights for the oppressed, and for gaining access via education.[21] Education, religious and academic, helps shape one's character.

Moral character critically informs King's understanding of nonviolence, and concerns how one's dedication to nonviolence connects social change and individual integrity. King's ethical, social vision emerges from his religious commitment where he views God as one who unfolds the need for justice, as creator of humanity, determining our true selves, the epitome of what it means to be human, and the shape of society as community. As part of the created universe, we are expected to respond ethically. Because the universal moral law is love, we are to resist evil as God reveals to us what it means to be human. When human beings engage in moral law, they connect with God. King wants oppressor and oppressed together to engage in moral law toward a beloved community. In this agape context, one can inspire dignity and self-respect in the oppressed, helping them overcome mental lethargy towards self-liberation, towards freedom. To be free or liberated requires personal and social change. King helped those in the movement overcome self-deception, and move toward reorientation steeped in nonviolent direct action.[22] King connects activism and access to power with love. His own words say it best: "What is needed is a realization that power without love is reckless and abusive, while love without power is sentimental and anemic. Power at its best is love implementing the demands of justice. Justice at its best is love correcting everything that stands against love."[23]

Unable to live out the balance of access to power and love in his marital and academic life, King committed adultery, as he was a womanizer; he plagiarized, appropriating the work of others continuously, without attribution. King biographer, David Garrow, notes that King had many extramarital affairs, one steady "girlfriend," and numerous incidental intimate couplings, engaging emotional energies outside his marriage. King espoused a type of sexual ethics of integrity that he did not live out, a source of much guilt. He plagiarized work in his dissertation. Rufus Burrow contends that the ordinary individual King did phenomenal things to empower human

---

21. Noel Leo Erskine, "King and the Black Church," *Journal of Religious Thought* 48/2 (Winter 1991/Spring 1992) 9–15.

22. Ron Large, "Martin Luther King Jr.: Ethics, Nonviolence, and Moral Character," *Journal of Religious Thought* 48/1 (Summer 1991/Fall 1991) 51–58.

23. Martin Luther King Jr., *Where Do We Go from Here: Chaos or Community?* (Boston: Beacon, 1968), 37.

beings and communities, domestically and globally, towards the beloved community. While the evidence is overwhelming as to King's clay feet as evidenced in his adultery and plagiarism, of significant import is that the God of scripture used one with such clay feet to empower others and to make such strides for social justice. He was faithful to the divine call upon his life.[24] Since God used a donkey to speak to Balaam (Numbers 22:28), God can use anyone God so chooses to do the work of justice and love. To begin to understand the complexity of achieving balance between love and justice and living a life of integrity one espouses, we must carefully articulate the textures and layers of the issue, the personal and societal impetus to act, and be willing to state and assess the wrong, as a righteous move. In assessing King's reality around promiscuity and plagiarism, framed by Clarence Jones's reading of King's leadership, it is essential to review the theological and cultural milieu of King's time, particularly from a perspective of gender.

Gendered politics in Christian theology and ecclesiastic traditions intersect with cultural productions, media depictions of issues of class and gender within African American communities, and the complexities of race and racism in a segregated Jim Crow milieu. To equate King as the singular metaphor for the 1960s Civil Rights movement, skews actual history and renders an androcentric, sexist interpretation, and drips of messianism. Forging King in this light equates leadership exclusively with maleness, allows for white liberal racism, and ultimately makes King a failure; as great as King was, he was no god, made plain with his adulterous relationships. Intriguingly, King supporters and detractors acknowledge that this is bad ethical behavior, but disconnect this behavior from his leadership.[25] From the time of antebellum enslavement, those under bondage wondered who would be their Moses. Harriet Tubman was one such figure. The Mosaic figure of the Hebrew Bible led God's people out of enslavement and the wilderness. In the New Testament, Jesus is Messiah, one to lead God's people out of all bondage and sin. King arrives at a pivotal moment in history, when the network was already in place to launch a movement. As the new kid on the block with rhetorical skills and charisma, he became the designated leader. King did not aspire to be a Messiah. He did not have a Messiah complex, a state of mind where he believed he was, or was destined to become a savior. Yet, placing a messianic mantle on King also meant supporting a bifurcated

---

24. Rufus Burrow Jr., "The Humanity of Martin Luther King Jr: Vigilance in Pursuing His Dream," *Encounter* 64/2 (2003), 141–47; and David J. Garrow, *Bearing the Cross: Martin Luther King Jr., and the Southern Christian Leadership Conference* (New York: Morrow, 1986), 375–76.

25. Traci West, "Gendered Legacies of Martin Luther King Jr.'s Leadership," *Theology Today* 65/1 (2008) 41–45.

life, which juxtaposed public/private experiences, privileging Black male heterosexism. White male racist privilege allowed J. Edgar Hoover, FBI chief, to stalk King and send surveillance tapes to Coretta Scott King, to push the preacher to suicide as a response prior to the public release of the tapes. King's extramarital sexual escapades demanded attention because of King's status as international social justice activist and religious leader. As leader, King was invested with the authority authenticated by his ordained Christian minister status. A bifurcated view of public vs. private ethical standards gave King permission to sleep with women other than his wife, thus devaluing his wife and women with whom he had sexual liaisons, a function of his heterosexist sexual practices. In the process, King dishonors God and devalues himself. Such practices, then and now, are part of the repertoire of charismatic, popular Black male preachers, where they envision such alliances as employment perks; some saw such sex as stress reducing strategies. This type of culture is so widespread that often when young Black male ministers come to town, the brothers invite him to lunch and then school him in the etiquette of where and how to have extramarital affairs discreetly, as an accoutrement and benefit of his appointment.[26] Sometimes the overture comes from women, like those who offered themselves to King or to his other male colleagues from the inner circle, asking to be with King sexually. While these acts reflect indifference to objectifying people via class, race, and gender, many saw King's private indiscretions as a private issue, irrelevant to his public persona, or to the reality of social injustice.[27]

Sexism pervades Western society, the church, and thus all civil rights organizations, the world into which King emerged as a leader. These institutions continue to relegate women to the margins. Ella Baker, for example, probably did more as a brilliant strategist and leader to help create SCLC (Southern Christian Leadership Conference) and SNCC (Student Nonviolent Coordinating Committee), yet she rarely received credit for her work, and was not allowed to rise in SCLC leadership. King had an uneasy relationship with her. King rarely challenged the patriarchal, sexist, masculinist practices of his day, and the socio-cultural ethos of the movement embodied this same sexist, oppressive spirit. The exclusive agenda was to restore manhood to African American men, and to control and hold women in their place. King also failed to make significant liaisons with women who had substantive insight and power, particularly on behalf of poor people. Men in the Movement had trouble envisioning women leadership. Perhaps

26. Alton Pollard III, "Teaching the Body: Sexuality and the Black Church," in *Loving the Body: Black Religious Studies and the Erotic*, ed. Anthony Pinn and Dwight Hopkins (New York: Palgrave Macmillan, 2004), 315–46.

27. West, "Gendered Legacies of Martin Luther King's Leadership," 45–52.

had he lived longer, and as he came to see the wrongs of classism, imperialism, and militarism, he may have come to see the diabolical nature of sexism.[28] Unfortunately, Jones, in his *What Would Martin Say?*, failed to help us imagine such a shift. Would King have come to see gross discrepancies of differences that exist in our world, and include race, gender, ability, age, and homophobia?

When one cannot live out their lives in balance as they negotiate matters of power and love, achieving justice in personal and societal life can become problematic. King's grasp of the power/love continuum has theological and ethical grounding that avoids excessive guilt and would help one have more levity around the demands of others to place them on a pedestal; would provide the fortitude, at the least, to think critically and hopefully abstain from engaging in the proclivities to use the work of others without attribution; and to commit adultery and have sexual liaisons with others when one has a spouse or partner. Unfortunately, many in positions of power do co-opt the words of others; some are married or in committed relationships and have sexual relationships with other people; the temptation is there and boundaries can get blurred quickly. The taste of power and privilege can be intoxicating and mesmerizing. Not all men with power steal the words of others or sleep with other people when they are in committed relationships. We have biblical, societal, and ethical rules that charge us to be more responsible. To be a faithful leader is to abide by those rules.

Invitation to an Activist Scholar

Thanks to Clarence B. Jones for rendering the volume, which has inspired this conversation. While he includes critical components of a leadership paradigm for the twenty-first century, there are vital components that are missing in light of what we know about the life and times of King. In the future revision of his work, I invite Jones to engage the issues of plagiarism and promiscuity, notably in light of how these issues have surfaced in society in the last two decades.

King scholars, biographers, and researchers connected with the King Papers Project concede that King plagiarized graduate school papers, his dissertation, and his autobiographical writings. With the unveiling of this truth, many focused more on how this revelation would taint King's mythic status instead of why and how such a gifted individual could use language as

---

28. Gwendolyn Zohara Simmons, "Martin Luther King Jr. Revisited: A Black Power Feminist Pays Homage to the King," *Journal of Feminist Studies in Religion* 24/2 (2008) 191 and 194–97.

he did, particularly without attribution. A review panel undertook the quest to find out how one who borrowed the words of others became so great. Some posit that King existed in a zone of borderlands, facing two different directions, where leaders were unsure of whose guiding principles were to govern, providing a kind of ethical limbo or purgatory, in a quest to find a voice that could address both worlds. The worlds of Black rhetorical traditions, where words were commonly used, and white academic theological traditions, where words had hierarchical significance and needed to be cited when using the work of others, often were more fluid, particularly in the class room where professors may not give attribution to their secondary sources. Such practices created confusion between original and derivative texts. Because King had to navigate bridging both worlds and pleasing his professors, he excelled and received approval for summarizing accurately, rather than positing originality. When one has not come to her/his voice, then they often internalize and imitate the voice of others: this happened to King.[29]

Whether one adores or demonizes King, King himself indicated that he had to wrestle with his demons, including the evils of promiscuity as a womanizer and his plagiarism. These matters are complex. For in a world of racist, white supremacist oppression, one could view King's sexual indiscretions as sometimes crude, pathetic, and ironically, as a move to garner privacy infiltrated by the FBI and live a life that lay captive to segregated, separate, and unequal. According to Ralph Abernathy, King's confidante and close associate, following King's monumental "I've Been to the Mountaintop" speech, hours before his assassination, King met with two women at different times and had a spat with a third female friend.[30] In Abernathy's autobiography, he reveals secrets about King, hitherto unknown, to paint a picture of the total King: he had greatness, was humorous, was afraid but fought anyway, and had particular personal weaknesses. Abernathy was not the first to write about the weaknesses. In dealing with these weaknesses, we come away with a greater sense of King's true, authentic humanity, his greatness, and his challenges in being a preacher-king, who positioned at the right time and place, at a critical time in history. To understand King, we have to remove him from our propensities toward demagoguery and take him off the pedestal. We need to view King's guilt, grief, and angst over his immoral acts in the context of an intense federally supported smear campaign to derail King's efforts and the impact of the Civil Rights movement.

29. John Thielen, "Becoming Martin Luther King Jr.—Plagiarism and Originality: A Round Table," *Journal of American History* 78/1 (1991) 11 and 14-22.

30. See Ralph David Abernathy, *And the Walls Came Tumbling Down: An Autobiography* (New York: Harper & Row, 1989), 434-36.

This campaign emerges out of a deep-seated fear of Black male sexual prowess, and a need to control them, an issue since the antebellum era. King's sexual behavior is a testament to social practices in churches and other religious traditions, in which mores exists where pastors/preachers/priests engage in sexual misconduct out of a sense of entitlement. King was both predator and prey, for many women across class and race desired to get into the center of attention with him, and into his embrace, his pants. King posited that the church too often has censured sexuality and that we need to appreciate and never abuse this sacred gift. King taught that the church should help people understand the causes behind the abuses and learn to honor the gift. He not only spoke about his infidelities in veiled language before the Ebenezer congregation, he also spiritualized his sensual lapses juxtaposed against the pressures to represent his race and be a respectable, an honorable Negro. Michael Dyson posits that one can deduce that King's foibles reflect a flaw in judgment, yet never a flaw in character, for as guilt plagued King, he struggled continuously against some of the same sins he indulged in, as he cared for the millions who had no voice, who suffered, who had been disenfranchised.[31] In the language of King, "where do we go from here?" First, let us cite the questions that King's experiences and this chapter suggest need to be reconciled.

Are scholarly guilds and sometimes the general public hesitant to pursue plagiarists because no one wants "to bail the cat," because of cynicism, or because in King's case, his life has become so synonymous with the civil rights movement that to criticize King is to discount and disavow the gains and truths garnered by the civil rights movement? Can one have such a commitment to an agape love and not understand sexual indiscretions and plagiarism as breaks with this ethical stance? Such a response seems disingenuous. Can we continue to posit claims that push us to honor the greater good of King's contribution while glossing over the breaking of the commandments against lying and adultery? At best, this scenario proposes a schizophrenic ethic, and a bifurcated reality. Clearly and historically, leaders, especially men in high places, have assumed access to women, regardless of their wants or needs. From bishops and priests and politicians and physicians to professors, many leaders, particularly those with senior status, have viewed having sex with women who are their parishioners, patients, employees, clients as a perk of the office. While this may have been accepted practice, how can we not hold accountable one who so worked against injustice, and worked for the beloved community and freedom? Are women not a part of the beloved community? To respond, I return to some of Clarence

---

31. Michael Eric Dyson, *I May Not Get There with You: The True Martin Luther King Jr.* (New York: Free Press, 2000), 136 and 154–67.

Jones's leadership concepts and expand their scope out of the categories of ethos, expectations, education, and ethics.

Ethos, Expectations, Education, Ethics

For Jones, King remained politically impartial to avoid alienating the opposite political party. The ethos of politics is complicated and often skewed based upon who carries the money, the influence. Institutionally, at a societal level, much oppression remains. Many of the legal gains of the Movement have been sidestepped in practice. Many schools are more separate than ever and definitely not equal. We now have laws against domestic violence and sexual assault, yet with a culture that allows one in four people to be victimized. Cyber bullying, identity theft, and Ponzi schemes along with smart bombs and assault weapons further complicate our reality. As leader, one would have to be careful about not being manipulated by politicians and not allowing one's constituents to be taken advantage of by any party. Jones is spot on wondering why Black folks are not insulted by the pandering reflecting a kind of racism amid political irony and sadness. This milieu can reflect several realities: (1) the Movement never radically changed the plight of the poor; (2) we do not live in a post-racial world and there is no such thing as color blindness, particularly when those in charge have skillfully learned to divide and conquer, to keep the power for themselves; (3) to avoid a malaise, a kind of pathological passivism, we need a paradigm shift in leadership. We cannot continue to look for "the one" to lead; rather we need to engage the insights of Paulo Freire in his *Pedagogy of the Oppressed* and bell hooks in her *Teaching to Transgress*, to empower people to think for themselves and live ethical, moral lives. We have to help people learn what are important values and that notoriety and excess bling ultimately does not make one whole, complete, or even happy. The capacity to achieve happiness often pertains to one's expectations.

In the 2006 film, *The Pursuit of Happyness*,[32] that chronicles the real life of Chris Garner, a motivated man who wants to be a stock broker against all odds, we can see short and long term goals for happiness. Short-term happiness comes moment by moment; long term happiness depends 60 percent upon what we inherited through our family tree and 40% upon what we do with our lives.[33] Garner had expectations of himself that he could succeed,

32. Gabriele Muccino, director; Steve Conrad, writer. *The Pursuit of Happyness*, Sony Pictures Home Entertainment, ASIN: B000OW77UU, 2006.

33. Josh Lipovetsky, "The Pursuit of Happyness—How Can We be Happy?," *Film Insight: Analyzing Movies since 2008*; http://filminsight.net/2008/09/24/the-pursuit-of-happyness-how-can-we-be-happy/.

and he had the audacity to be imaginative and stay the course. Recognizing that we really cannot do anything we want to do, that we can do what is in the realm of the possibility of our own gifts and graces, we need to do the work and trust God, in hope, without fear. We must balance out expectations of others and ourselves with love and a sense of shared responsibility. Following Jones, as leaders we cannot pimp our constituency for our good. To lead means to engage respectfully, and have a personal mission statement of what God calls us to accomplish and a personal vocational vision of what success looks like. What would a twenty-first century beloved community look like? How do we create such engagement?

If we work for justice and follow a call to serve God and humanity, as Jones rightly indicates was a galvanizing factor for King's life, we can begin by committing to educate as an ethical imperative. Emancipatory education requires that we listen to each other with respect and help each other experience liberation in the acquisition of knowledge. Such participatory education is ministry and allows us to express our talent and commitment, to think critically and clearly. While fame and popularity may make us a target, we learn how to focus on God and do the next right thing in a manner that respects boundaries and allows us to remain humble. We learn to keep situations and people in perspective so that they cannot coerce us to do bad behavior. We understand that the fabric of integrity needs to drape our being at all times, and that while we may desire something that is illegal or immoral, we do not have to act out on those desires, regardless of peer pressure. The fabric of integrity embraces love of God, neighbor, and self in creative ways, where every venue is a laboratory of learning. We instill ethical values from cradle to grave as central to what it means to be a person of faith. When we do make mistakes, we learn from them, so we do not have to repeat them. We have a community of accountability who will support us to do the right thing. They understand that they are not to control or judge us, yet can lovingly be a Nathan to our Davidic sense, so that we come to awareness regarding the error of our ways. In advocating for a beloved community, we must be wise as serpents and gentle as doves, for those persons and systems who lust after power will always try to make sure those without are left wanting. As a leader, it becomes an ethical and educational imperative that we provide an environment where all people have opportunities to gain access to their human needs: physiological wellbeing, safety, love/belonging, esteem, and self-actualization.[34] Such engagement allows us to embrace the best of King's notion of the beloved community, without need-

---

34. See Abraham Maslow, "A Theory of Human Motivation," *Psychological Review* 50/4 (1943) 370–96; Abraham Maslow, *Motivation and Personality*, 3rd ed. (New York: HarperCollins, 1987).

ing to accept his notions of redemptive suffering. Some find redemptive suffering problematic, because it makes the oppressed the scapegoat and savior, and ultimately does not redeem or empower the oppressor to experience transformation. Conversely, in his work on King, Rufus Burrow Jr. has tried to show that for King, suffering as such is never redemptive. Rather, the type of suffering he devoted his life to fighting against is *made* redemptive by relentlessly and nonviolently struggling against it, to eradicate it. The real redemption lies here.[35] Given the strong connections between suffering, blood sacrifice, and atonement, preached by many, the language could still be misleading to the general reader, and needs much more nuancing to avoid re-victimizing the victim, and providing a "get out of jail card" for the perpetrator. While beyond the scope of this chapter, it would be interesting to place King's notion of redemptive suffering in dialog with the theological ethics of South Africa's Truth and Reconciliation Commission.

Having revisited the life and experiences around leadership through the vantage point of Clarence B. Jones, the tapestry and message of Leonard Bernstein's song, "Make Our Garden Grow," from *Candide*,[36] provides a poignant message: "We'll do the best we know . . . And make our garden grow." Candide grows up as an outcast in his German uncle's home, yet is taught that he lives in the best of all possible worlds by his tutor, Pangloss. Through his life, with various friends, he experiences poverty, injustice, travel, multiple cultures, optimism, utopia, and violence. Despite all of the injustice Pangloss experiences, he remains optimistic. When Candide and friends finally settle down with family and friends, they become agitated and quarrelsome. An encounter with a farmer who lives simply, works hard, and avoids immorality and leisure, inspires Candide and his friends to cultivate a garden. They work tirelessly, no longer have time for philosophical speculation, and are fulfilled and happy. The garden can serve as a metaphor for self and community fulfillment.

While we live in a complicated, technologically sophisticated world, there remains room for us to create gardens of justice, for that which is simple in design, if not in execution. As justice, love, and respect become embodied in our lives, where we follow the edicts of Micah 6:8 CEB ("He has told you, human one, what is good and what the LORD requires from you: to do justice, embrace faithful love, and walk humbly with your God") and Luke 10:27 CEB ("He responded, 'You must love the Lord your God with all your heart, with all your being, with all your strength, and with all

---

35. Rufus Burrow Jr., "The Doctrine of Unearned Suffering," *Encounter* 63/1–2 (2002) 65–76.

36. See Lillian Hellman and Richard Wilbur, *Candide: A Comic Operetta Based on Voltaire's Satire* (New York: Schirmer, 1958), 196–98.

your mind, and love your neighbor as yourself'"), we will honor life as a gift. When we fall short, we will confess and make amends; and do all that we can to stay the throes of recidivism.

6

Ruminating about Martin Luther King Jr. and Sex

RUFUS BURROW JR.

Throughout the decade of the 1980s several scholars and writers on King, e.g., Stephen B. Oates, David J. Garrow, Taylor Branch, and Ralph D. Abernathy documented the rumors that he engaged in extra-marital relations.[1] The innuendoes and rumors had been cited in much earlier works on King, such as John A. Williams, *The King God Didn't Save* (1970).[2] It was too soon for Williams and others to gain access to FBI, State Department, and other files that would have verified the rumors.

This essay reflects some of my ruminations about King and sex. Some of these were prompted by what Clarence Jones says and fails to say about the subject. My reflections are also much influenced by King's sermon, "Unfulfilled Dreams," preached at Ebenezer Baptist Church on March 3, 1968, one month and a day before he was assassinated. Although I do not consider them here, there are sermons in which King was quite explicit about his stance on sex—a stance that was as different from his actual behavior as night is from day.[3] Although King does not name in "Unfulfilled Dreams"

---

1. See Stephen B. Oates, *Let the Trumpet Sound: The Life of Martin Luther King Jr.* (New York: Harper & Row, 1982); David J. Garrow, *Bearing the Cross: Martin Luther King Jr., and the Southern Christian Leadership Conference* (New York: Morrow, 1986); Taylor Branch, *Parting the Waters: America in the King Years, 1954–63* (New York: Simon & Schuster, 1988); and Ralph David Abernathy, *And the Walls Came Tumbling Down: An Autobiography* (New York: Harper & Row, 1989).

2. John A. Williams, *The King God Didn't Save* (New York: Coward-McCann, 1970), chapters 19–20.

3. See the following sermons by King: "Is the Universe Friendly?" Dec. 12, 1965; "New Wine in Old Bottles," Jan. 2, 1966; and "The Prodigal Son," Sept. 4, 1966 (Center

the specific thing that was troubling his soul, those closest to him, who carefully observed the last three years of his life, knew that it had to do with his extramarital sexual relations. Admittedly, my reflections only scratch the surface of what I consider to be a very complex and important issue.

I think there are things that are as bad as, indeed worse than pre- and extramarital sex between *consenting* adults that do not seem to disturb some of the most vocal critics of King's sexual ethic and behavior. Racism is one such thing. The racist critic of King, for example, does not easily acknowledge his own racism or his unearned privilege, if he acknowledges them at all. In his eyes, neither racism nor unearned privilege is problematic, but sex between consenting adults is in his mind altogether different and must be criticized at every juncture.

Although Ralph Abernathy was as much a womanizer as King, he was not wrong when he said, "Sexual sins are by no means the worst. Hatred and a cold disregard for others are the besetting sins of our time, but they don't sell books or tabloid newspapers—and that's the reason why people have talked about Martin's failings and left the flaws of some others alone."[4] Of course, Abernathy himself—whom King characterized as his best friend in the world—also wrote at length about his friend's sexual failings in his bestselling autobiography, *And the Walls Came Tumbling Down* (1989). Abernathy did not focus on his own long history of extramarital failings, however.[5]

Nevertheless, I feel compelled to muse about King and sex for two reasons. First, I have consistently argued in my teaching and writing on King that he was thoroughly human, and like all human beings he was flawed in one way or another. Moreover, he had no pretensions about sainthood—his own or anybody else's. Consequently it has always seemed reasonable to me that those who contribute to scholarship on King should be willing to expose and examine the limitations as well as the strengths of his life, thought, and practice. In this way, we get a truer, more realistic picture of the man who sacrificed and accomplished so much for humanity and the world over the course of a thirteen-year ministry. Not altogether certain about Ralph Abernathy's motives for writing about his friend's womanizing, Michael Eric Dyson offers an instructive commentary about the need to address King's weaknesses and limitations:

> But even if we doubt Abernathy's motives . . . we can still endorse his belief that the more honestly we confront King's moral

---

for Nonviolent Social Change, Atlanta, Georgia).

4. Abernathy, *And the Walls Came Tumbling Down*, 470–71.

5. Branch, *Parting the Waters*, 239.

lapses, the more we are able to extract from his failings a sense of his authentic humanity and a fuller grasp of his towering achievements. To avoid exploring King's weaknesses is to deny him the careful consideration that should be devoted to any historic figure. And to pretend King didn't sin is to subvert the healthy critical distance we should maintain on all personages, the lack of which leads to charges of uncritical black hero worship. As Abernathy suggests, King "will grow in the hearts of future Americans regardless of what I or other biographers have to say about him."[6]

A second reason I see the need to reflect on King and sex is that it seems to me that Clarence Jones says much too little and is much too soft in what he does say. Indeed, Jones does not even broach the subject of King's extramarital relations and how this might have affected him, his family, and his movement work. It almost seems that Jones pretends that the womanizing did not happen.

In light of the writings by Oates, Garrow, Branch, and Abernathy, I take it as a given that Martin Luther King Jr. engaged in extramarital affairs on a regular basis, and that he struggled long and hard to right his behavior, albeit unsuccessfully. It is not clear to me that he was at peace about the matter when he was assassinated. My sense is that he was not, and that had he lived longer the struggle around that issue would have continued.

It is strange indeed that Clarence Jones did not include a chapter in his book on what King might say about matters of sexuality, especially about his extramarital relations, homosexuality, and sexism. His virtual silence on the point is all the more surprising and telling since he mentions Bayard Rustin's homosexuality,[7] but without comment as to what King might say about sexual orientation were he alive today. In addition, the term *sexism* does not even appear in Jones's book. Moreover, as a member of King's inner circle Jones most certainly knew about his womanizing, and in fact said so in an interview for the *Johnson Tapes*,[8] just as he knew about King's sexism

---

6. Michael Eric Dyson, *I May Not Get There with You: The True Martin Luther King Jr.* (New York: Free Press, 2000), 157.

7. Clarence B. Jones and Joel Engel, *What Would Martin Say?* (New York: Harper & Row, 2008), 153.

8. In the documentary *The Johnson Tapes, Uncivil Liberties*, part 1, Jones stated unequivocally that King had sex with a woman at the Willard Hotel in 1963. Putting the morality of the matter aside, Jones, in an indignant tone, said that he blamed King "for falling into the trap of the FBI." Although they did not know the extraordinary extent of the FBI's surveillance, Jones said, they knew that King was being watched. In political terms, Jones said, King's behavior was dangerous and irresponsible. But in the moral sense, he said that what King did at the Willard was between him, his family,

towards women involved with SCLC, such as Ella Baker and Septima Clark, and yet there is total silence about these matters in his book.

Although the term "sexism" was not in vogue in Martin Luther King's day, he likely knew the term "male chauvinism" and its meaning. He also knew and understood the meaning of the term "headship," having seen it played out in the King household as he was growing up. It was modeled for him in many ways by his father, by other male relatives, as well as by men in his father's church, and it affected his thinking about marriage and family life, as well as the role of women outside the home.

Coretta Scott King reflected on their conversations about male and female roles in the home during their engagement. Although King was apparently more liberal than many men in his thinking about women, about marriage and what partners should expect, Mrs. King recalled that when it came to his own marriage and household, he expected to be the breadwinner and the head of the house, while his wife was to raise the children, keep the house, pay the bills, and be home to greet him when he returned from work.[9] Mrs. King wrote about a comical speech that King made to her about his role in the family, although she concluded that he was more serious about it than he was willing to let on. She remembered the conversation this way:

> After we were married he said, "I want my wife to respect me as the head of the family. I *am* the head of the family." We laughed together at that slightly pompous speech, and he backed down. "Of course, I don't really mean that," he said. "I think marriage should be a shared relationship." *But he really did mean it.* That was an adjustment I had to make, and I believe I made it very well. At the same time he encouraged me to express myself, he did not like the idea of my working.[10]

It appears that this conversation took place fairly early in their marriage. They married on June 18, 1953. Because Mrs. King was such an intelligent and strong woman, it is not far fetched to say that this was neither the first nor the last time they discussed this and related matters. Indeed, she and her fiancée had told Daddy King, who officiated at their wedding, that they

---

and his God. Taylor Branch documented Jones's awareness of King's extramarital affairs through interviews with him on November 22 and 25, 1983, and August 18, 1986. See Branch, *Parting the Waters*, 860, 898.

9. Coretta Scott King, *My Life with Martin Luther King Jr.* (New York: Holt, Rinehart & Winston, 1969), 60.

10. Ibid., 91 (my emphasis).

wanted the word *obey* deleted from their marriage vows. The request was honored.¹¹

In addition, as pastor of Dexter Avenue Baptist Church during this period, King had many well-educated, self-determined, professional, and strong women to contend with in the congregation. Many of these, e.g., Mary Fair Burks and JoAnn Robinson, both professors at Alabama State College, did not make a habit of deferring to or backing down to men. There is no question that they challenged their pastor on the matter of the role(s) of men and women in the home and the public sphere. King was without question aware of men's expectation that women should be submissive to them. Having been married for less than two full years, King preached a Mothers Day sermon at Dexter on May 8, 1955, in which he addressed the issue of roles in the marital relationship. He made it clear that he was against the idea and practice of male headship, and that he considered it an inappropriate practice in the home. He told the congregation:

> Men must accept the fact that the day has passed when the man can stand over the wife with an iron rod asserting his authority as 'boss.' . . . the day has passed when women will be trampled over and treated as some slave subject to the dictates of a despotic husband. One of the great contributions that Christianity has made to the world is that of lifting the status of womanhood from that of an insignificant child-bearer to a position of dignity and honor and respect. Women must be respected as human beings and not be treated as mere means. Strictly speaking, there is no boss in the home; it is no lord-servant relationship.¹²

---

11. Ibid., 73–74.

12. Martin Luther King Jr., "The Crisis in the Modern Family," in *The Papers of Martin Luther King Jr.*, ed. Clayborne Carson et al. (Berkeley: University of California Press, 2007), 6:212. I think that King went too far in applauding Christianity as such, for what he declared as its role in the uplift of women. This was a role played not by institutional Christianity or the Church but by small, courageous, dissenting factions within it. Both Frederick Douglass and Walter Rauschenbusch pointed to this truth. "One thing is certain," Douglass said at the Twentieth Annual Meeting of the New England Woman Suffrage Association in Boston on May 28, 1888, "when the chains of woman shall be broken, when she shall become the recognized equal of man, and is put into the full enjoyment of all the rights of an American citizen, as she will be, church and ministry will be the first to claim the honor of the victory, and to say, 'We did it!'" [Frederick Douglass, "Emancipation of Women," in *Frederick Douglass on Women's Rights*, ed. Philip S. Foner (New York: Da Capo, 1992), 119. Nearly twenty years later, Rauschenbusch wrote that "the most important effects of Christianity went out from it without the intention of the Church, or even against its will. For instance, the position of woman has doubtless been elevated through the influence of Christianity, but by its indirect and diffused influences rather than by any direct championship of the organized Church . . . It is this diffused spirit of Christianity rather than the conscious

The marriage that expects to last and to be a happy one cannot be based on the idea of male headship, with the woman as subordinate and without rights.[13]

From such statements, it seems clear that King was aware of the issue of male chauvinism. They also indicate awareness in the early part of his tenure as pastor of the need to articulate more progressive views about women. This did not mean, however, that he actually reflected this stance in his daily living. In fact, his own chauvinism was most apparent in his relations with women affiliated with leadership roles in the SCLC; e.g., Ella Baker and Septima Poinsette Clark.[14] Both Coretta Scott King and John Lewis pointed to King's chauvinism regarding Baker.[15] Lewis, however, attempted to deflect the brunt of the criticism from King, saying that it was mostly the chauvinism of Wyatt Walker and Ralph Abernathy that made things so difficult for Baker.[16]

Jones refers to the situational element in King's social ethics, claiming that for King "the context of an action determined its morals." He uses sex as an example (an interesting example indeed, considering King's extramarital sexual relations). In any event, Jones characterizes King's thinking on sex as follows: "This highest physical expression of love between people is blissful and righteous when consensual, or horrifying and repulsively evil when performed against the other's will. All actions must be judged by their context—even, he would insist, those that seem otherwise inexcusable."[17] Considering that Jones—a close confidant and advisor of King—was aware of his extramarital sexual activities, one wonders whether this is what he had in mind in the last words of the previous quotation. That is, is he implying that King applied this caveat about context to sexual activities even outside marriage, and that this somehow enabled him to feel at peace?

---

purpose of organized Christianity which has been the chief moral force in social changes." Walter Rauschenbusch, *Christianity and the Social Crisis* (New York: Macmillan, 1907), 150. Only many years later—after the fact—does the church proudly claim that it was she who liberated the enslaved blacks, she who liberated woman.

13. King, "Secrets of Married Happiness," in *The Papers of Martin Luther King Jr.*, 6:432.

14. See Barbara Ransby, *Ella Baker & the Black Freedom Movement: A Radical Democratic Vision* (Chapel Hill: The University of North Carolina Press, 2003), 172–89; and Septima Clark, *Ready from Within* ed. Cynthia Stokes Brown (Trenton, NJ: Africa World Press, 1990), 77–83.

15. See Coretta Scott King, *My Life with Martin Luther King Jr.*, rev. ed. (New York: Holt, 1993), 142; and John Lewis, *Walking with the Wind: A Memoir of the Movement*, with Michael D'Orso (New York: Simon & Schuster, 1998), 92, 212.

16. Lewis, *Walking with the Wind*, 212.

17. Jones and Engel, *What Would Martin Say?*, 151.

King's Struggle with His Conscience

It is known that as late as March 3, 1968, Martin Luther King grappled with how God judges the personal moral failures of human beings. In the sermon, "Unfulfilled Dreams," preached at Ebenezer Baptist Church on that date, he said: "In the final analysis, God does not judge us by the separate incidents or the separate mistakes that we make, but by the total bent of our lives. In the final analysis, God knows that his children are weak and they are frail. In the final analysis, what God requires is that your heart is right."[18] The point, King argued, was not to have actually reached the destination, but whether one was on the right path and doing his or her best to stay the course. King acknowledged that like all of God's children, he too was a sinner, although he was striving "to be a good man."[19] He was without question struggling with some of his own moral shortcomings in that sermon, and thus was not pointing fingers at any member of the congregation and others who came up short in the moral arena. Stewart Burns contends that "sexual guilt" ate at King throughout the 1960s, and contributed substantially to his bouts with deep depression.[20] King, according to Burns, brooded over his moral shortcomings, but he continued to seek "refuge in partying and sexual excess."[21]

In his excellent introduction to "Unfulfilled Dreams," historian Vincent Harding provides a full and accurate account of the heart of the sermon, such that the reader knows without doubt that in the last year of his life King was struggling with some very heavy issues of personal morality. However, apart from innuendo Harding never says explicitly what King was grappling with internally, although as one of King's close friends and speechwriters, he surely knew what it was. Indeed, we do not find explicit indication in the sermon itself as to the actual cause of King's internal struggle. Nevertheless, one gets the sense that King needed to tell somebody about it, and that he felt most comfortable telling the members at Ebenezer Baptist Church where he was known and loved by the people, some of whom were members long before he was born. However, he never actually named the issue he preached about that day. But this was his church family, and he believed they were at least willing to allow him to make the effort and would go on loving him even if he failed in his trying.

18. King, "Unfulfilled Dreams," in *A Knock at Midnight*, ed. Clayborne Carson and Peter Holloran (New York: Warner, 1998), 196.

19. Ibid., 198.

20. Stewart Burns, *To the Mountaintop: Martin Luther King Jr.'s Sacred Mission to Save America 1955–1968* (New York: HarperSanFrancisco, 2004), 260, 261, 287.

21. Ibid., 217.

Martin Luther King Jr. knew that some of his closest confidants and members of his inner circle were aware of his excursions with various women throughout his civil rights ministry. Taylor Branch offers some provocative comments on this matter in *Parting the Waters*, the first volume of his massive political biography-trilogy on King:

> By this time [around 1962], King had lowered his personal barriers to [Clarence] Jones, offering him the essential secrets of his private life. Unerringly, King chose to reveal himself to men and women who could absorb the news without developing blisters of uneasiness between themselves and him. They did not scorn him as a fallen preacher, nor lapse into paralyzing discomfort. These were people who tolerated or even applauded King's demon delights as a humanizing revelation that bonded them even closer to him and his public purpose. Often they accepted King more easily than he accepted himself. They saw sexual adventure as a natural condition of manhood, or of great preachers obsessed by love, or of success, *or of Negroes otherwise constrained by the white world*, and they objected to King's mistresses no more than to the scores of concubines who had soothed King David during the composition of his Psalms. Some of them grew tired of King's insistence that it was a sin, and of his endless cycles from hedonism to self-recrimination and back.[22]

But the fact that Jones knew, as did other members of King's inner circle, including Ralph Abernathy, Wyatt Walker, Andrew Young, Bernard Lee, and a few others, clearly was not enough to provide permanent relief to his conscience. For since King was so inclined to self-criticism and because of how he interpreted the Christian ethic, he believed deep within that his behavior was sinful. In "Unfulfilled Dreams" he seemed to *need* to try to make confession to his ecclesial community, his church family. Perhaps he felt that he owed them an explanation, for surely at least some of the members of the congregation had heard the rumors and were wondering whether there was veracity in them.

I think that King's real intention in "Unfulfilled Dreams" was to tell God about his inward struggles, with his church family listening in, for he knew that in the end all must answer to God for their behavior in this world. It was as if he was pleading for mercy and understanding from the God of his faith. The members at Ebenezer were the conduit, for King knew that God already knew, but he also knew that he needed to make the effort to

---

22. Branch, *Parting the Waters*, 282–84 and 860.

confess publicly before his community of faith, if he could only be explicit about what he was confessing.

Without actually naming what he was struggling with, King wanted God to know that his heart was right and that he had honestly tried to do the right thing, especially regarding his call to ministry. As it turned out, what he actually confessed was too general. He confessed to being a sinner like all human beings, and he made it unmistakably clear that he was not a saint. This was not news, since it applied to every human being. After all, had he not said that in the final analysis only God is good?[23] What King desired was noble enough, namely, "to be a good man." He said that he wanted to be faithful to God and the task to which he was called. Even when he had moral lapses, he wanted God to know that his heart was right, that he really wanted to do the right thing, and he certainly wanted to be what God would have him be.

Other than confessing that he was a sinner like all other human beings, and that he was not a saint, King was not specific in his confessions. And yet the hearer and reader of "Unfulfilled Dreams" can't help but sense that something was rubbing his soul raw; was so heavy and bothersome that he felt compelled to deliver this particular sermon when he did. What, specifically, had he done that caused such turmoil in his soul?

Vincent Harding was right about King and this sermon: "He needed to confess how deeply he had failed himself and his own best possibilities, *not only in the great public arena*, where everyone could see his magnificent efforts at building temples of righteousness, justice, and peace. Where everyone could see the implacable opposition and the shadow of death that seemed to envelop him."[24] His failure, said Harding, was "not only in the great public arena," implying that his spirit was being tormented by failure in the more personal or private sphere. What so ailed and tormented his soul?

FBI Telephone Surveillance

John Edgar Hoover, director of the FBI, had King under surveillance for a number of years prior to Attorney General Robert Kennedy's approval in 1963 to tap his telephones at home, work, and other places King went, including and especially motels. In October, Kennedy approved the taps for one month only. However, when President Kennedy was assassinated in

---

23. King, "Unfulfilled Dreams," in *Knock at Midnight*, 197.

24. Vincent Harding, Introduction to "Unfilled Dreams," in Carson and Holloran, eds., *Knock at Midnight*, 188 (italics added).

November, the Attorney General's limited approval for the telephone taps was lost sight of, and Hoover essentially took license to do what he wanted, going way beyond what Kennedy intended. To be sure, from the beginning Hoover interpreted much more broadly what the attorney general actually approved.[25] Not only did the FBI go beyond the approved period of one month, thus abusing their authority, but continued the illegal surveillance right up to the time of King's assassination. Hoover was determined to use his massive power and resources to destroy King in every way possible. Arthur Murtaugh, then of the Atlanta field office of the FBI, said that Hoover simply hated all blacks, believed that they had no integrity and character, and were in fact less than human. He said that Hoover's order to place King under surveillance had nothing to do with anything illegal that King had done. The highest law enforcement agent in the United States simply hated black people.[26]

There is evidence that Kennedy did not want to authorize the wiretaps, but his hand was forced inasmuch as he was aware that Hoover had secret files on numerous top government officials, including the attorney general and the president of the United States. Kennedy had no way of knowing what Hoover might leak about either him or his brother, the president.[27] From a political standpoint, then, King's privacy and constitutional rights were expendable. His private life was completely exposed to the surveillance tactics of the FBI, an instance of democracy at its worst.

It was not long before FBI agents discovered through the wiretaps and bugging of King's motel rooms that more went on in those rooms than strategizing for civil rights campaigns. Hoover, a diehard racist who despised King and embarked on a personal vendetta to destroy his public image and to destroy him psychologically and emotionally, had characterized him as "a 'tom cat' with obsessive degenerate sexual urges."[28] He also described King—deemed by many as the moral leader of the nation—as "the most notorious liar in the country." In December 1964, Hoover sent a box containing a reel of tape and a note to the SCLC headquarters in Atlanta. Thinking that the tape was of one of King's speeches, the staff set it aside to be sent to Mrs. King who collected them. When the tape was finally sent to Mrs. King in early January 1965, she discovered that it was anything but a tape of one of her husband's speeches or sermons. Although King's voice was on some

25. Michael Friedly and David Gallen, *Martin Luther King Jr.: The FBI File* (New York: Carroll & Graf, 1993), 39.

26. Murtaugh shared these ideas in *The Johnson Tapes, Uncivil Liberties*, part 1.

27. See Fred Powledge, *Free at Last?: The Civil Rights Movement and the People Who Made It* (New York: HarperPerennial, 1992), 558–59.

28. Quoted in Garrow, *Bearing the Cross*, 312.

of the tape, he was clearly not delivering a public speech. David Garrow contends that included on the tape were "dirty jokes and bawdy remarks King had made a year earlier at Washington's Willard Hotel, plus sounds of people engaging in sex."[29] The enclosed note admonished King to commit suicide. All of this had been done on the authorization of Hoover, and was carried out by assistant FBI director William C. Sullivan. Clarence Jones wrote about the taps on King's phones as well as his own.[30] Consequently, he most assuredly knew about King's womanizing, although he chose not to include a discussion on it in *What Would Martin Say?*

Striving to Be Faithful to God

There were other things that troubled Martin Luther King Jr. during the last two years of his life, but nothing was apparently as devastating and unsettling as the warring, "tension," or "schizophrenia" within him regarding extramarital sexual involvements that included both short-and long-term relationships. I think this is what King was hinting at in "Unfulfilled Dreams." And yet he was not able to come clean about it; to confess precisely what it was. He would come just to the brink of real confession, and then pull back. According to Harding, the closest that King came to a true confession in the sermon was when he told the congregation: "You don't need to go out this morning saying that Martin Luther King is a saint . . . I want you to know this morning that I'm a sinner like all of God's children. But I want to be a good man. And I want to hear a voice saying to me one day, 'I take you in and I bless you, because you try. It is well that it was within thine heart.'"[31]

But this was not the only time that King made such public remarks. On April 9, 1967, he preached at New Covenant Baptist Church in Chicago, where the Reverend John Thurston was the senior minister. He deviated from his sermon notes and said to Thurston and Bernard Lee: "I hope I can live so well that the preacher can get up and say 'He was faithful.' That's all, that's enough. That's the sermon I'd like to hear: 'Well done thy good and faithful servant. You've been faithful; you've been concerned about others.'"[32] My sense is that this too was about that internal warfare that was going on within him.

---

29. Garrow, *Bearing the Cross*, 373–74.
30. Jones and Engel, *What Would Martin Say?*, 72.
31. King, "Unfulfilled Dreams," in Carson and Holloran, eds., *Knock at Midnight*, 198–99.
32. King, "The Three Dimensions of a Complete Life," in ibid., 131.

Without question, Martin Luther King Jr. was much affected by the sex ethic of traditional Christianity and its emphasis on monogamous heterosexual relations. Why else would he have been at war with himself about his deviations from that ethic? Why would he want so desperately to confess before his home congregation, although he was not able to do more than simply allude to what was troubling him?

Although not intended as an excuse for King's behavior, it is reasonable to say that because he was away from home more and more doing civil rights work he found it increasingly difficult to comply with what he believed in his heart to be the right thing regarding extramarital sex. In "Unfulfilled Dreams," the matter brought to his mind the words of Paul: "The good that I would I do not: And the evil that I would not, that I do." But I also think that this was complicated for King because even as a young man in college and graduate school, it was well known that he loved women and was in fact known as a lady's man. Moreover, I think it did not help that once he became a pastor he was frequently surrounded by other pastors who, though married, apparently had no qualms about being involved with other women. In addition, while black Baptist churches did not advocate pre- and extramarital sex for their pastors, many church members often seemed fairly forgiving as long as the pastor did not openly philander, was a good preacher, kept the coffers full, and kept the church's ministry vibrant. Right or wrong, that's the way it was in many of those churches, and it might well be the case today. However, let us not be mistaken. This was not the case with black Baptists only. Without question, such activities occur within all denominations, regardless of racial-ethnic membership.

Everything that I have learned about Martin Luther King Jr. convinces me that he really did want to be a good man. In fact, he said so several times in "Unfulfilled Dreams." King was so torn up inside because he really believed in his heart and mind that the relationships with other women were morally wrong. His pangs of conscience were heightened because the FBI publicized his behavior. In addition, it did not help that his Ebenezer family knew about his behavior.

Notwithstanding his relations with other women, King was indeed a man of honor. He was generally a man of integrity. This is one of the reasons he struggled over the issue of womanizing as he did. He *wanted* to do the right thing in his private life, even when he was having difficulty doing so. To be sure, he rationalized his sexual involvements with other women as did many of the men close to him. Indeed, these men essentially served as a support group for each other, and this helped to make their extramarital involvements bearable. Then Hoover exposed King, effectively publicizing his deeds. It appears that this is when King really began to struggle internally with his behavior, even though he continued to see other women right up to the night before he was assassinated.

Former Kentucky state senator Georgia Davis Powers has written of her nearly two-year affair with King and their time together the night before the assassination.[33] If Stephen B. Oates is right, it can be said that King was grappling with his sexual conscience even from the Montgomery years. Oates detected in *Strength to Love*, King's book of sermons, what he saw as evidence that King was struggling with his sexual transgressions from the beginning of the civil rights movement.

> In *Strength to Love* . . . he betrayed something of his suffering when he wrote of how every man had good and evil warring inside and how we see evil expressed in "tragic lust and inordinate selfishness." He bemoaned "the evils of sensuality" and warned that "when we yield to the temptation of a world rife with sexual promiscuity and gone wild with a philosophy of self-expression, Jesus tells us that 'whosoever looketh on a woman to lust after her hath committed adultery with her already in his heart.'" But in moments of loneliness, beset with temptation, he would succumb again to his own human frailties.[34]

The sermons in *Strength to Love* were preached during and after the bus boycott. The book was published in 1963. King apparently brooded over his moral shortcomings, even though he continued to engage in extramarital sexual relations.[35]

That King was exposed by Hoover might well have contributed to his deep need to confess before his congregation. The general direction of his life was one of trying to be honorable and to do things with integrity. Every now and then, however, he strayed from the straight and narrow. But as he told the Ebenezer faithful, his aim was to be a good man and to be faithful to God. In addition, as a Christian King was more focused on social morality than personal morality. It seems that he was in good company in this regard.

Emphasis on Social Rather Than Private Morality

It is interesting to note that professed social ethicists such as King and Reinhold Niebuhr did not focus much in their sermons, speeches, and writings

---

33. See Georgia Davis Powers, *I Shared the Dream* (Far Hills, NJ: New Horizon, 1995).
34. Oates, *Let the Trumpet Sound*, 283.
35. Burns, *To the Mountaintop*, 217.

on issues of personal morality, such as forbidden sex and overconsumption of alcoholic beverages. Niebuhr illustrated this tendency when he criticized the liberal and orthodox religious views on sin. In the early 1930s, he criticized the liberal church for its failure to take sin seriously, whether in its individual or group forms. On the other hand, while the more conservative church focused much on sin, its failure, according to Niebuhr, was its emphasis on the sins of personal morality, such as drinking, smoking, gambling, illicit sex, etc., to the exclusion of social sins such as injustice. "The orthodox church," said Niebuhr, "still convicts people of sin, but the sins of which it makes people conscious are usually not those which are most significant in our society."[36] According to Niebuhr and King, those "most significant" moral issues that the church failed to address were those involving public morality, and most especially those of large complex groups such as corporations, races, states, and nations. This was also the view of the Hebrew prophets of the eighth century BCE, who stressed the sins of the nation. The church, in Niebuhr's view, should focus on the oppression and injustice committed by such groups.

In addition, Walter Rauschenbusch, whose book, *Christianity and the Social Crisis*, was said by King to have left an indelible imprint on his thinking, argues repeatedly that of all moral questions, the most pressing ones are those of public, not private, morality. Rauschenbusch, like Niebuhr and King, was much influenced by the Hebrew Prophets, whom Rauschenbusch himself characterized as "the beating heart of the Old Testament."[37] Indeed, Kenneth Smith and Ira Zepp Jr. are right in their claim that with the possible exception of the Sermon on the Mount, King was most influenced by the Hebrew prophets.[38]

The primary concern of the eighth-century prophets was not the pious morality of individuals but the social morality of the nation. According to Rauschenbusch, "the morality which the prophets had in mind in their strenuous insistence on righteousness was not merely the private morality of the home, but the public morality on which national life is founded. They said less about the pure heart for the individual than of just institutions for the nations." He went on to say: "The evils against which we contend in the churches are intemperance, unchastity [sic], the sins of the tongue.

---

36. Reinhold Niebuhr, "The Weakness of the Modern Church," in his *Essays in Applied Christianity*, selected and edited by D. B. Robertson (New York: Meridian, 1959), 71.

37. Walter Rauschenbusch, *Christianity and the Social Crisis* (New York: Macmillan, 1907), 3.

38. Kenneth Smith and Ira Zepp Jr., *Search for the Beloved Community: The Thinking of Martin Luther King, Jr.* (Valley Forge, PA: Judson, 1974), 39.

The twin-evils against which the prophets launched the condemnation of Jehovah was injustice and oppression."[39] Consequently, Rauschenbusch insisted that the most pressing moral problems of his day were those of social or public morality. These, he felt, were the problems that ministers of the Gospel and the churches should be focusing on. In Rauschenbusch's view, ministers had no right to back away from or fail to address social problems.[40] Similarly, when one reads Martin Luther King's sermons, speeches, and writings that focus on moral issues, as most of them do, one sees less emphasis on the moral practices of the individual, while most of the focus is on morality in the public sphere.

Nevertheless, it is true that during his pastorate at Dexter, King sometimes preached against issues of personal morality such as extramarital sex. But on occasion he also preached on such issues in the post-Dexter years. In addition, in his "Advice for Living" column in *Ebony* magazine, in November 1957, he advised against premarital sex, and in favor of "premarital virginity."[41] However, by all measures the general drift of his preaching and writing did not focus on issues of personal morality. Instead, King's was primarily social gospel preaching that focused on the need for individuals and the church to be maladjusted to social evils such as racism, militarism, and economic injustice.

In a 1954 sermon, preached during the early weeks of his pastorate at Dexter Avenue Baptist Church, King told the congregation that God was more concerned about moral behavior, by which he meant social morality, than the aesthetics of a church building or even how one carried out the liturgy. In an unacknowledged idea borrowed from Harry Emerson Fosdick, King admonished the members that "Christ is more concerned about our attitude towards racial prejudice and war than he is about our long processionals. He is more concerned with how we treat our neighbors than how we sing his praises. Christ is more concerned about our living a high ethical life than our most detailed knowledge of the creeds of Christendom."[42] The emphasis here is on social rather than personal or individual morality. In most cases this is what we find in King's sermons, speeches, and writings. I think that King knew almost instinctively that personal and social morality are interconnected; that what one does privately generally have social implications, and what one does in the public sphere impinges on the private

39. Rauschenbusch, *Christianity and the Social Crisis*, 8.

40. Ibid., 358.

41. King, "Advice for Living," in *The Papers of Martin Luther King Jr.*, ed. Clayborne Carson et al. (Berkeley: University of California Press, 2000), 4:306.

42. King, "A Religion of Doing," in *The Papers of Martin Luther King Jr.*, ed. by Clayborne Carson, et. al. (Berkeley: University of California Press, 2007), 6:173.

lives of individuals. In most cases, King tried hard to espouse and practice a consistent ethic of dignity in this regard, i.e., endeavoring to be moral in both his private and public behavior and practice. And yet, in the matters of sex and sexism he fell short.

Presently I am not quite certain what to make of the fact that the post-Montgomery King preached and wrote little on pre- and extramarital relations but focused instead on social issues. While he was most certainly influenced by the focus of Rauschenbusch and Niebuhr on social ethics, he was already committed to social gospel Christianity and the influence of the Hebrew prophets before he entered seminary and read their work. Therefore, one cannot easily say that King's emphasis on social morality was solely a result of the influence of Rauschenbusch and Niebuhr, though it was most certainly enhanced by their ideas.

And yet one can say that as a social gospel minister, King practiced consistently his ideas and what he actually preached, namely, social morality. This is what C. T. Vivian meant when he wrote: "Martin always practiced in public places what he preached in the pulpit. He demanded courage from churchmen, and he personally preached it. His courage caused him to actively challenge all systems—first the church, then political systems, and finally economic systems."[43] He preached primarily about the need for individuals and the church to address social, political, and economic issues, and he himself addressed these more than anything else. Vivian did not address the matter of whether King practiced in private what he preached publicly about sex.

I have said in my work on King that so much has been written on his philandering that I see no real need to focus on it myself. The truth is that I am conflicted about the matter. On the one hand, I think that a number of white men who have written on King and focused on his womanizing have written more than I want to read again. I take this stance because white men continue to be implicated in so much that demeans and crushes blacks, and there is little indication of their willingness to confess their own moral shortcomings and to do something about them. I personally want to read about or hear such white men confess their unearned privilege and their complicity in "the underdevelopment of black America" (as the late Manning Marable put it), what they intend to do about it, and when. So presently I am not as eager to hear white men pontificate about King's womanizing. On the other hand, King's extramarital excursions were a glaring contradiction of his own insistence on the need for trust, loyalty, and mutual respect

---

43. C. T. Vivian, Introduction to "Paul's Letter to American Christians," in Carson and Holloran, eds., *A Knock at Midnight*, 23.

in the marital relationship,[44] as well as the sacredness of marriage.[45] They were violations of his own principles and faith claims. Because King was one who sought to be a consistent and thoroughgoing Personalist—let alone Christian—I know deep within that he must be called out for this contradiction. In my judgment, members of King's own community—black people— are in the best position to critique his moral behavior, not white men who uncritically benefit from unearned white privilege.

We can be certain that Coretta Scott King had questions about her husband's practice regarding women in the public sphere, especially. Mrs. King made this point unequivocally clear in her comments at the symposium "We Shall Overcome: Martin Luther King Jr.—The Leader and the Legacy," in Washington DC in October 1986. There she said, "But we have yet to deal with how Martin Luther King Jr. saw women and how he dealt with women and women's roles."[46] But she also argued that her husband really wanted to do organizing work among women, but time ran out. Literary artist Alice Walker has written that Mrs. King told her as much during an interview in 1971. "She says that she and Martin used to talk a lot about trying to organize women and she regrets that he never had time to get around to addressing women as women."[47]

Mrs. King was no sideline cheerleader when it came to women and their potential contributions to establishing the beloved community. In a speech to supporters of the peace movement in Central Park in New York City, on April 27, 1968, barely three weeks after her husband was assassinated, she expressed her deep conviction that women can and must play a significant role in solving the most devastating social problems of the nation and the world. At one point in the speech, she told the crowd that she wanted to address herself specifically to women, saying,

> The woman power of this nation can be the power which makes us whole and heals the rotten community, now so shattered by war and poverty and racism [the trilogy of social problems that King addressed throughout his civil rights ministry]. I have great faith in the power of women who will dedicate themselves whole-heartedly to the task of remaking our society. I believe

---

44. Carson, et. al., eds., *The Papers of Martin Luther King Jr.*, 6:571.

45. Ibid., 6:433, 570.

46. Coretta Scott King, "Thoughts and Reflections," in *We Shall Overcome: Martin Luther King Jr. and the Black Freedom Struggle*, ed. Peter J. Albert and Ronald Hoffman (New York: Da Capo, 1993), 255.

47. Alice Walker, "Coretta King: Revisited," in *In Search of Our Mothers' Gardens* (New York: Harcourt Brace Jovanovich, 1983), 155.

that the women of this nation and of the world are the best and last hope for a world of peace and brotherhood.[48]

How wonderful and potentially fruitful it will be when the legal issues are settled regarding Mrs. King's papers and we are able to examine them. One cannot help wondering about how she felt about her husband's extra-marital relations and whether she ever penned thoughts about the matter. In a blog written for the *Minneapolis News*, dated February 3, 2006, Peter S. Scholtes quotes a 1993 *Atlanta Journal Constitution* article where Mrs. King reportedly said that she was not concerned about the claims in Ralph Abernathy's book that her husband engaged in extra-marital relations because she knew her husband. "I don't have any evidence of one instance of infidelity. Not one,"[49] she reportedly said. She was adamant that her husband's moral sensibility was such that he would have been "guilt-ridden" to the point that had he been with other women sexually he would have been compelled to tell her. "He couldn't have lived with himself because he was serious about his religion."[50] Moreover, she was his wife and he respected her.[51] Once Mrs. King's papers are available, it may be possible to examine more fully what she did and did not know about her husband's alleged philandering.

In any case, I think that black women in particular, and women generally, have some instructive things to say about this Christian, theologian, activist, husband and father who contributed so much to this nation and the world, and was also a participant in extramarital affairs. (I purposely use the term "participant" here, for King's decision to engage in this behavior was a shared decision with each partner.) In the mean time, I know at least three black women theologians who have begun to assess how King saw women as women: Cheryl Kirk-Duggan of Shaw Divinity School, Traci West of Drew Theological School, and Rosetta Ross of Spelman College (all contributors to this volume). Indicators are that this work will continue, and my hope is that others will join the conversation.

Conclusion

I frequently think of philosopher and Nobel laureate Lord Bertrand Russell when the subject of King's sexual excursions comes up. In another context,

---

48. Coretta Scott King, "10 Commandments on Vietnam." Online: http://www.americanrhetoric.com/speeches/corettascottkingvietnamcommandments.htm/.

49. Peter S. Scholtes, "You Can't Do It All By Yourself." Online: http//blogs.citypages.com/pscholtes/2006/02/coretta_scott_k.php/.

50. Ibid., 4.

51. Ibid.

Russell thought it curious that at a time when the Roman Empire was disintegrating from the inside out Church fathers such as Jerome and Augustine were, respectively, more concerned about whether women were retaining their virginity, and whether unbaptized infants were damned. Lord Russell put it this way:

> It is strange that the last men of intellectual eminence before the dark ages were concerned, not with saving civilization or expelling the barbarians or reforming the abuses of the administration, but with preaching the merit of virginity and the damnation of unbaptized infants. Seeing that these were the preoccupations that the Church handed on to the converted barbarians, it is no wonder that the succeeding age surpassed almost all other fully historical periods in cruelty and superstition.[52]

Jerome and Augustine wrote many letters through which they communicated their concerns about women retaining their virginity and the damnation of unbaptized infants. Interestingly, Ambrose wrote numerous letters as well, but his were frequently directed to emperors, "telling them in what respects they have fallen short of their duty, or, on occasion, congratulating them on having performed it."[53] The others were more worried about the sexual behavior of consenting adults.

Martin Luther King Jr. really did want to be faithful to God and especially to God's call. He wanted to be a good man. I have no doubt that he was both faithful to God, *and* a good man. Indeed, had he not been faithful to God, had he dropped out of civil rights ministry—which he occasionally mused about—he might well have lived to eat old age and longevity (as the Yoruba proverb says), rather than having the right side of his jaw torn away by a 30.06 slug at the age of thirty-nine. King was not a perfect man, nor was he a sinless man. But he was faithful to his call to the very end.

Wherever we stand on the subject of King and sex, we should remember the words of Dyson that King "was a great but flawed man . . . King's [moral] failures were significant, but they pale in comparison to the majestic good he did. . . . We need not idolize King to appreciate his worth; neither do we do honor to him by refusing to confront his weaknesses and his limitations."[54] Martin Luther King Jr. was a human being, with all the potential strengths and limitations, positive and negative attributes, thereto pertaining. Similar to Dyson, Michael G. Long adds an instructive word

---

52. Bertrand Russell, *A History of Western Philosophy* (New York: Simon & Schuster, 1945), 366; see also 336, 342.

53. Ibid., 336.

54. Dyson, *I May Not Get There with You*, 173–74.

that we do well to remember: "The whole King is greater, far greater than the man who . . . expressed interest in women other than his wife. In my estimation, the whole King included not only those actions, real or imagined, but also his willingness to suffer for the God-given dignity of his brothers and sisters, his courage to stand against a government that sought to degrade him, his abiding love for his family and friends, his deep faith in the Anchor—and, of course, his compelling vision of creative living. Like each of us, the whole King is both sinner and saint."[55]

We must not sidestep the fact that according to the more traditional interpretation of the Christian ethic, the only allowable sex is with one's heterosexual marriage partner. With all of the social problems tearing away at the fabric of this society, the church, even today, appears to be more concerned about what consenting adults do with each other sexually. To be sure, as an issue of personal morality it is one that the church has addressed from its inception. Indeed, King himself, as Christian minister, was aware of this and in principle viewed it as sin. King would not have disagreed with Ralph Abernathy's statement that the two of them, as well as all other ministers involved in movement work, "understood and believed in the biblical prohibition against sex outside marriage. It was just that he had a particularly difficult time with that temptation."[56] The sex ethic of traditional Christianity was part of his fundamentalist upbringing in the church, and he accepted it—at least in principle—as his own. At any rate, the church sees clearly the sin of what it considers to be illicit sex, but it often appears to be totally blind to sins in the public sphere that literally crush massive numbers of innocent people because of their race, gender, sexual orientation, age, class, and health. What causes the church, even today, to be so fixated on sex? If we could answer that question satisfactorily, I think we will have gone a long way toward solving some aspects of the race problem.

I have argued in my work on King that his philandering was a contradiction and violation of his personalism and his doctrine of human dignity. Even though I have some sympathy with the fact that King's sexual escapades involved choices made by consenting adults, the fact remains that as one who was married, he owed the obligation of fidelity to his wife. Among other things, his affairs violated Mrs. King's human right to be respected and treated with dignity. As one who sought to be more than a theoretical theistic personalist (i.e., one who grounded the dignity and sacredness of human beings in God), that King persisted in marital infidelity was a major

55. Quoted in Rufus Burrow Jr., *God and Human Dignity: The Personalism, Theology, and Ethics of Martin Luther King Jr.* (Notre Dame: University of Notre Dame Press, 2006), 12.

56. Abernathy, *And the Walls Came Tumbling Down*, 471.

contradiction to his personalism and doctrine of human dignity. Personalism is significant ethically precisely because it says something important about how human beings ought to behave and be treated by virtue of being human beings imbued with God's image. King's personalism required that he respect the dignity and worth of Mrs. King. Indeed, the King type of personalism is, by definition, a strong judgment against marital infidelity. For now, suffice to say that this is a point that begs for much fuller exploration in King studies.

7

Gay Rights and the Misuse of Martin[1]

TRACI C. WEST

In Miami-Dade Florida in 2002, a coalition of citizens groups that included the "African American Council of Christian Clergy" launched a campaign to rescind the addition of "sexual orientation" to an existing county statute. The statute banned discrimination in employment, housing, lending, and public accommodations. "Sexual orientation" had been added in 1998 alongside other protected categories, including race, color, religion, ancestry, national origin, gender, pregnancy, age, disability, marital status, and familial status. During the 2002 battles over the deletion of "sexual orientation" from the statute, a flier targeting local black voters was circulated by proponents of the repeal. It stated that "Martin Luther King, Jr. would be OUTRAGED! if he knew homosexualist extremists were abusing the civil rights movement to get special rights based on their sexual behavior."[2]

In response to the controversial fliers, a Miami newspaper sought a comment from Atlanta's Martin Luther King Jr. Center. Their spokesperson cited Coretta Scott King, widow of Martin Luther King Jr., as indicating that her husband had privately expressed concern about discrimination against gay men and lesbians. The King Center also issued a statement that quoted Coretta King's own view imploring "everybody who believes in Martin Luther King Jr.'s dream to make room at the table of brother and sisterhood for

---

1. I would like to thank Natalie Williams and Charon Hribar for their invaluable research assistance on this chapter.

2. Karl Ross, "Center Appalled by MLK Use in Flier," *The Miami Herald* (August 2, 2002) 1B.

lesbians and gay people."³ Reacting to the King Center statement, one of the leaders of the Miami-Dade repeal effort, Eladio José Armesto, reportedly stated: "Coretta Scott King is entitled to her opinion. She can't speak for her husband."⁴ This retort raises several questions about the political use of Martin Luther King Jr. Who *can* speak for him today? By what criteria would such a person be seen as appropriately authorized to do so? Should his widow's private access to King during his lifetime be considered sufficiently authoritative to speak for him? Does her personal history of having shared her life with him, as his spouse, secure her legitimacy to interpret his vision for social justice? Should the moral necessity for gay rights be vested in an authentic representation of King's views for or against them?

Speaking for King: Public Debates

The battle over the 2002 Miami-Dade referendum not only included dueling claims about King's views but also competing understandings of the criteria that could rightfully authorize a spokesperson representing his views. Issuing a challenge to "other people [who] might be trying to speak for him"⁵ (such as King's widow), one Miami minister, Nathaniel Wilcox, touted his shared ministerial vocation with King as most authoritative. Wilcox had helped to write the pro-repeal flier. In the same *Miami Herald* article mentioned above, he explained that Martin Luther King Jr. would be outraged because "as a minister, he believed in the word of God . . . And if Dr. Martin Luther King was the man of God I think he was, then he preached against all sorts of immorality—including lying, stealing and homosexuality."⁶ According to this circular logic, Wilcox could speak for King because they were both men of God. King would have supported the repeal of this antidiscrimination ordinance because, in Wilcox's view, that is what any man of God would do. If it were true that King would oppose the repeal, then King could not have legitimately been a man of God. When Wilcox speaks for King in this situation, he teaches the public that King's

---

3. Ibid. Former Chairperson of the US Commission on Civil Rights, Mary Frances Berry wrote in an opinion editorial, "But as Coretta Scott King said to me as she tried to imagine what position the Rev. Dr. Martin Luther King Jr. would take on 'don't ask, don't tell': 'What's the yardstick by which we should decide that gay rights are less important than other human rights we care about?'" Mary Frances Berry, "Gay But Equal?" *New York Times*, January 16, 2009, 29.

4. Ross, "Center Appalled by MLK Use in Flier," 1B.

5. Ibid.

6. Ibid.

civil rights leadership can only be considered authentic Christian ministry if King preached against "lying, stealing, and homosexuality."

In another instance, in Massachusetts in 2004, when King was used as a reference point in public conflict over gay rights, the wrangling over issues of authenticity took a slightly different form. Certain anti-gay rights arguments were made that expressed a racially based imperative for blacks to speak up in behalf of an accurate understanding of Martin Luther King. During a 2004 statewide battle over equal marriage rights for same-gender couples in Massachusetts, an anonymous voice message was distributed to home answering machines in black communities in the Boston area. It claimed that Martin Luther King's dream was being violated.[7] The taped message attempted to persuade its hearers that "if Dr. King were alive today" he would not permit the same-gender marriage movement to be compared to the civil rights movement.[8] According to this organized political effort, since the slain leader could not speak for himself, those receiving the message needed to defend Martin Luther King and his "dream," ostensibly by expressing their disapproval for "gay marriage." The expression of their disapproval was made to seem like a kind of racial duty; an indicator of black racial loyalty encoded in the idea of allegiance owed to King.

Within this same 2004 battle over marriage equality in Massachusetts, a Boston black clergy group issued a strongly worded statement denouncing marriage equality and any comparisons of the 1950s and 1960s civil rights struggle to the "gay marriage" movement. One response to the clergy statement quoted in the Boston press was from a pro-marriage equality black state legislator, Byron Rushing, an active Episcopal layperson. Rushing asserted the responsibility of one oppressed group to struggle for the civil rights of other oppressed groups. In a direct response to the black clergy group, he added: "Martin Luther King [Jr.] is rolling over in his grave at a statement like this."[9] Rushing's reference to King expressed his own disgust with the way in which King's name and the movement that King helped to lead was being used by opponents of marriage equality. In this remark about King, Rushing can be seen as representing King's view on marriage equality as the same as his own support for it. Or, at a minimum, Rushing speaks for King by complaining that the blatantly opportunistic use of his name by anti-equality activists prevented King from resting in peace in his grave.

---

7. Adrian Walker, "Misusing King's Legacy," *Boston Globe* (April 29, 2004) B1.

8. Ibid.

9. Michael Paulson, "Black Clergy Rejection Stirs Gay Marriage Backers," *Boston Globe* (February 10, 2004) B1.

A 2009 *Washington Post* letter to the editor written by local black Baptist co-pastors, Reverends Christine and Dennis Wiley, offered a perspective similar to Rushing's. Their letter was published immediately after the Washington DC city council voted to legalize same-sex marriage. It analyzed the meaning of the vote for diverse members of the District's black community and invoked Martin Luther King in support of their pro–marriage equality position:

> A final piece that shapes black attitudes toward same-sex marriage is the preoccupation with racism in the black community. This obsession, although justifiable, has led to a failure to appreciate how racism is inextricably connected to all other forms of oppression. Those who fail to see this connection may resent the comparison of gay rights with civil rights. But as Martin Luther King Jr. once said, "Injustice anywhere is a threat to justice everywhere."[10]

For these Baptist pastors, King is regarded as a teaching resource. His name is attached to specific ideas that he espoused, and then those ideas are deployed to illustrate the kind of attitude blacks should have about injustice.

A 2011 conflict over access to marriage in Iowa provides an example where an opponent of gay rights specifically addressed the use of King's quotations to support marriage equality, decrying it as misappropriation. One speech at a Des Moines rally employed the rhetorical tactic of refocusing attention from the substance of King's recorded ideas to what King would supposedly say about same-gender marriage. The speech was given by a black Baptist minister, Rev. Keith Ratliff Sr., before a crowd gathered at the state capitol to call for a statewide referendum to constitutionally ban same-gender marriages. Ratliff declared that there was nothing in Martin Luther King's speeches or writings to suggest that he would support gay and lesbian marriages "even though some people try to take certain quotes out of context to prove he would have" done so.[11] For Ratliff, King's public silence on political struggles for gay rights substantiated Ratliff's claim about King's opposition to them. But I am not sure how it would even be possible for King, who died in 1968, to have commented on twenty-first-century state initiatives regulating marriage. King's supposed support of "traditional marriage" and rejection of same-gender marriage, Ratliff continued, is also proven by the fact that King was a "Bible-believing Baptist preacher" raised

---

10. Dennis W. Wiley and Christine Y. Wiley, "Gay Marriage and Our Black Church," *Washington Post* (December 20, 2009) B01.

11. "Keith Ratliff at LUV Rally in Iowa," YouTube Video, 8:31, posted by CaffThoughts, March 16, 2011, Online: http://www.youtube.com/watch?v=piTxH2JL__I/.

by a father who also was one.¹² This claim seems less credible, however, when one recalls that King frequently differed with his father's politics and theology as well as that of his Baptist denomination.¹³ Additionally, if Ratliff includes monogamy as part of his definition of "traditional marriage," King's practices clearly did not indicate strong support for it because he repeatedly engaged in extramarital sexual relationships.¹⁴

As this sampling of public battles attests to, there have been few, if any, heated, political disputes in recent decades in the United States, in which the viewpoint of Martin Luther King Jr. is more frequently invoked than when the civil rights of gay and lesbian citizens are contested. In these debates, speculation on the content of what King would say has often included polar opposite representations. Embattled leaders have referenced King on public policy issues that include hate crimes against gay, lesbian, and transgender persons, employment discrimination against them, "don't ask, don't tell" rules barring them from openly serving in the military, as well as their entitlement to the pursuit of happiness through state sanctioned marriage. Why, however, must Martin Luther King have a position on every current struggle being waged to end discrimination based on sexual orientation and gender expression? Didn't King fight hard enough during his life and made more sacrifices for equal rights and ending war than any social movement leader should ever be asked to make?

Christians usually reserve their expectations for ongoing moral guidance across historical time periods for their God. But there is a kind of deification of King in the continuous attempts to decipher what he would say about gay rights or about any other contemporary political debate. The parsing of King's views about events occurring thirty to forty years after his death by Christian leaders relies upon an overly inflated image of King that encourages their audiences to conflate the moral culture the leaders want to create with their selective depictions of King. Clarence Jones, who became one of King's attorneys and advisers in 1960, epitomizes this kind of

---

12. William Petroski, "Gay Marriage Debate Gets Double Dose of Activism at Iowa Capitol Today," DesMoinesRegister.com, March 15, 2011; online: http://blogs.desmoinesregister.com/dmr/index.php/2011/03/15/gay-marriage-debate-gets-a-double-dose-at-iowa-capitol-today/.

13. For discussions of disagreements between King and his own National Baptist denomination, see David L. Lewis, *King: A Biography* (Urbana: University of Illinois Press, 1978), 157-58; Taylor Branch, *Parting the Waters: America in the King Years, 1954-1963* (New York: Simon & Schuster, 1988), 504-7.

14. For a candid analysis of King's extramarital sexual relationships, see Michael Eric Dyson, *I May Not Get There with You: The True Martin Luther King Jr.* (New York: Free Press, 2000), 155-74.

appropriation of King in his book, *What Would Martin Say?*[15] In a formulation more extreme than some of the leaders quoted above, Jones creates a definitive, albeit fictional, voice of King on current events. Whether constructed by community leaders commenting on gay rights or by Jones on a range of other issues, statements about King's supposed current political positions reveal a disturbing, masculinist pattern.[16] Their depictions expose combined assumptions about god-like status and maleness deeply embedded in the quest to resurrect King's role on the public stage of US politics in perpetuity.

Speculation by community leaders about King's views on gay rights does, however, open a window of opportunity for a closer examination of the 1950s and 1960s civil rights movement and the role of Bayard Rustin in it. In twenty-first-century disputes over the relevance of that history to gay civil rights initiatives, Rustin's leadership role has occasionally been invoked by proponents of gay rights.[17] Rustin helped to lead the Fellowship of Reconciliation (FOR) and was an adviser to King and also the person who taught King the techniques of Gandhian nonviolent direct action. Rustin was a gay man. King knew Rustin was gay, as did certain opponents who tried to use that information to discredit the movement. Attention to some of the historical details of Rustin's leadership in the 1950s and 1960s civil rights movement can be a resource for debunking current references to King in popular culture that attempt to foster a view of him as a solitary font of truth, either then or now.

Instead, King should be seen as a pivotal leader within a movement that relied upon an array of interdependent, courageous, and thoughtful leaders, including several women. We ought to be inspired by their persevering struggle and apply lessons learned from studying them to contemporary social justice struggles. But the choices about what we learn from

15. Clarence B. Jones and Joel Engel, *What Would Martin Say?* (New York: Harper, 2008).

16. Some black Christian political commentators speculate about what Martin Luther King's contemporary views would be, including his position on gay rights. These offer a more nuanced appropriation of King than I assert here. For example, see Bernice Powell Jackson, "What Would Martin Luther King Jr. Do?" *Philadelphia Tribune* (January 18, 2005) 9A; Herb Boyd, "A Question for King: Whose Side Are You On?" *New York Amsterdam News* (January 13, 2005) 1; Bayard Rustin, "Martin Luther King's Views on Gay People" [1987] Interview by Redvers Jeanmarie, in Devon W. Carbado and Donald Weise, eds., *Time on Two Crosses: The Collected Writings of Bayard Rustin*, San Francisco: Cleis, 2003), 292–94.

17. Norman Hill, "Commentary: Bayard Rustin and the Civil Rights Movement," *New Pittsburg Courier* (April 8, 2000) A7; Derrick Z. Jackson, "Blacks, Gay Rights Linked in History," *Boston Globe* (February 13, 2004) A19; Marc H. Morial, "Hate Crimes Prevention Act Signed into Law," *The Louisiana Weekly* (Nov. 16–Nov. 22, 2009) 5.

studying them and how that is relevant to current justice issues must be explicitly acknowledged as our choices. The same choices could not possibly be made by those who negotiated the sociopolitical realities of a bygone era. With regard to Martin Luther King Jr. the kind of approach I am suggesting here will not satisfy those with certain targeted political aims. Some Christian political leaders want to use this slain Christian civil rights crusader as moral currency in making racial and religious claims they hope will sway public opinion against legalized protections for gay, lesbian, and transgendered people from discrimination. The racial claims of those leaders are often predicated upon distorted, heteronormative assumptions about black people that deny the reality of diverse sexual orientations among blacks. Nevertheless, the resulting, racially charged, public discourse can have significance that stretches beyond haggling over what constitutes truthful, iconic, descriptors of this one male figure, King. The discourse opens up possibilities for exploring the role of race and gender in constructing a communal moral vision for just social change.

Clarence B. Jones and Exclusionary Visions of Justice

In *What Would Martin Say?*, Clarence Jones creates a range of assessments that he imagines Martin Luther King Jr. would make about various twenty-first-century US public policy issues such as race-based affirmative action, Latino/a immigrant rights, and the legitimacy of the US war in Iraq. Jones does not mention gay rights. He does craft political stances he believes King would take against affirmative action policies and in support of stemming the "illegal immigration" of Latinos/as. I must admit that I find Jones's political positioning of King to be a thinly veiled ploy for articulating his own rather conservative opinions. But his selective account of King during the civil rights movement and problematic assertions of imaginary King viewpoints can still provide the chance for critical reflection on social movement building questions germane to race-related conflicts over gay rights.

Jones's socioeconomic analysis of affirmative action and immigration issues coalesce around the task of sorting out which oppressed groups should be included under the umbrella of King's moral vision for social change, and which groups should be rejected from it. Jones situates his affirmative action discussion within a description of King's politically fraught deliberations about the most effective method of calling for some form of government compensation for the nation's historic "exploitation and humiliation of blacks."[18] According to Jones, King comes to the realization that this idea

18. Jones and Engel, *What Would Martin Say?*, 72.

of government compensation needs to be broadened. Jones explains that "Martin began wondering about what might happen if Negroes weren't the only beneficiaries of these proposed compensatory damages. What would happen if poor whites, too, benefited?"[19] But to Jones, if King were here today, he would realize the error of this attempt to include poor whites.[20] In his admonishing tone about this supposed error in judgment, Jones notes that King was not the only civil rights leader guilty of "opening a door that allowed more people through than should have been for this *specific purpose*" of economic justice.[21] Jones claims that "Martin" would now recognize that arguments for some kind of government compensation would have been better confined exclusively to blacks.[22]

Jones's argument about Latino/a immigrants who supposedly take jobs from blacks, robbing them of "their hard-won livelihoods,"[23] displays an aggressive bid for the uniqueness of black victim status. Unless they come to the United States seeking sanctuary from unjust laws, Jones argues via King's persona, immigrants who enter this country should obey the immigration laws or willingly accept the penalty for breaking them, including deportations that separate parents from their children. Jones assumes King's first person voice as if speaking directly to Latino/a immigrants who live in the United States. He writes, "I find it offensive and insulting when you wave Mexican and Salvadoran flags and compare yourself to civil rights demonstrators—black American citizens—who were denied their inalienable rights as Americans . . . entirely because of their skin color."[24] There is a hierarchical ranking of deserving societal victims of discrimination suggested by this male, moral arbiter to whom Jones assigns King's name and voice. The ranking places black American citizens (do black African immigrants share this entitlement?) at the top, on the basis of "their skin color," which is reductively seen as the sole reason for discrimination against them. If included at all, Mexican Americans and Salvadoran Americans appear to be placed at the bottom.

Jones's fictitious representation of King as a neoconservative, anti-Latino/a racist deserves a disdainful and dismissive response. At the same time, there are broader questions about the goals of social justice activism inferred here that deserve attention because vulnerable people's dignity and

19. Ibid., 75.
20. Ibid., 77.
21. Ibid.
22. Ibid.
23. Ibid., 109.
24. Ibid., 121.

lives are at stake. How can a social justice movement primarily concerned with systemic forms of anti-black white racism in the United States incorporate injustices that victimize other peoples besides African Americans? Said differently, how can other forms of injustice besides racism productively combine with an antiracism social change agenda? Should they be combined together? For Lesbian, Gay, Bisexual, Transgender, Queer (LGBTQ) people in the US, who are Afro-Latinos/as from Colombia, Brazil, or Dominican Republic, for example, the monolithic assumptions about racial/ethnic identity and injustice embedded in such questions erase their multiple positioned marginal status. Imagine what it might be like for an Afro-Latina to sit in a US Immigration and Customs Enforcement (ICE) detention center, for instance, after being rounded up by officials on mere suspicion of being an unauthorized immigrant, which some state laws now allow. It may not be possible to telephone her spouse both because telephone access is routinely blocked by ICE authorities,[25] and because one's same-gender covenantal relationship does not have state (in most states) or federal government recognition. She may also be sexually assaulted by a male guard.[26] Anti-black white racism is undoubtedly operative in these multiple forms of discriminatory treatment that an Afro-Latina lesbian in such a situation might experience but impossible to isolate, as Jones's approach requires. The racialized formula Jones proposes, which privileges systemic oppression due to one's African ancestry over other forms of oppression, would be ineffectual and absurd to even consider for addressing the plurality of social identities inhabited by such immigrants who face discriminatory public policies.

The same kind of argument offered by Jones about the unique victim status of blacks has also been made by opponents of gay rights. In these arguments, a unique racial victim group must be distinguished from those who fall into categories of oppressed peoples who are not black (for Jones) or who are not black heterosexuals (for black anti–gay rights advocates). For oppressed persons outside of the unique black victim group, comparison of their victim status claims to those made by 1950s and 1960s civil rights movement leaders about the racist victimization of blacks is strictly

---

25. Karen Tumlin et al., "A Broken System: Confidential Reports Reveal Failures in US Immigration Detention Centers," National Immigration Law Center, 2009. Online: http://www.nilc.org/immlawpolicy/arrestdet/A-Broken-System-2009-07.pdf.

26. See discussion of allegations (note that these allegations are unproven) retrieved by the American Civil Liberties Union by Freedom of Information Act request from US Department of Homeland Security. Online: http://www.aclu.org/sexual-abuse-immigration-detention/; and online: http://www.aclu.org/maps/sexual-abuse-immigration-detention-facilities/.

forbidden. The history of black (heterosexual?) suffering due to white racist discrimination, violence, and humiliation is to be understood as *sui generis*. Ironically, Jones creates a narrative that resembles the perspectives of black leaders he criticizes for marketing "black victimhood."[27]

The temerity of this claim about suffering is compounded by the justifying links to Martin Luther King Jr. that are attached by Jones as well as some gay rights opponents. King becomes the ultimate moral filter for determining which social struggles may be seen as comparable to 1950s and 1960s civil rights movement history and what constitutes an authentic, present-day civil rights concern. Criteria for a social justice agenda composed of a hermeneutic of what one man did, said, thought, wrote, or might determine to be right (postmortem) is too narrow, too male centered, and too fantastical.

Suppose that a 1962 secret letter was suddenly discovered wherein Martin Luther King Jr. unequivocally stated that he opposed any form of civil rights protections for gays and lesbians. Why should King's perspective be granted the moral authority to determine that such protections should, therefore, never be included in US law? Couldn't King be wrong? Or, what if, right now, someone was able to communicate with King's living spirit and he clearly articulated support for the harshest anti–immigrant rights laws that could be enacted. Are not the realities that immigrants experience a more urgent focus than speculation about what King's current views about them might possibly be?

A man-god-King focal point sabotages the justice-oriented goals of social justice movement building. It distracts from the arduous work of nurturing compassionate, routinized, communal responses to the socioeconomic marginalization of specific peoples. Certain moments in the movement in which King actually participated illustrate the difficulty, for its leaders, of steadfastly maintaining their economic and racial justice goals without being deterred by controversy over the identities of individual movement leaders, such as homosexual identity and/or communist party political identity.

Bayard Rustin: Learning from Social Movement History

Popular interpretations of Martin Luther King Jr. as the singular, ultimate authority for strategic decision making during the civil rights movement of the 1950s and 1960s represent distorted recollections of the nature and dynamics of the movement's leadership. The planning process for the August

27. Jones and Engel, *What Would Martin Say?*, 64–65.

28, 1963 March on Washington, for example, included a broad group of leaders. Both the involvement of several leaders and their collaborative process of checking in with one another—sometimes agreeably, sometimes competitively clashing—were typical of that movement. A. Philip Randolph, president of the Negro American Labor Committee, was the architect of the 1963 March and had first envisioned it as a mass demonstration focusing on unemployment and unfair labor practices. As the leader of Southern Christian Leadership Conference (SCLC), King wanted to utilize the March to pressure the Kennedy administration to fight for passage of civil rights legislation then pending in Congress. With decades of experience as a nonviolent protest organizer with the Fellowship of Reconciliation (FOR), the War Resisters League (WRL), Congress of Racial Equality (CORE), and MIA during the Montgomery bus boycott, Rustin hoped that the March would be accompanied by sit-ins at the offices of key congressional legislators.[28] As director of the NAACP, the largest and oldest civil rights organization, Roy Wilkins was undoubtedly one of the most influential members of the planning committee. He argued against the inclusion of civil disobedience at the March, fearing that it would jeopardize the passage of the civil rights bill. In the end, the event was called the "March on Washington for Jobs and Freedom" and civil disobedience was excluded from the plans. Decades later, when asked to reflect on the King centered popular accounts of the March, Rustin commented: "Now, it's called Dr. King's March. Well, Randolph, who conceived it, and Roy Wilkins, who helped to pay for it [raising over $10,000 for it], are almost never mentioned."[29]

Gay rights issues were certainly not part of the conceptualization of the goals of the 1950s and 1960s civil rights movement. Yet, it would be untrue to claim that the subject of discriminatory treatment of gays had nothing to do with that freedom struggle. On a few occasions, debates about the role of a gay male leader (Rustin) were an explicit focus of movement leaders and their opponents. The planning of the March on Washington illustrates one such moment.[30] A. Philip Randolph selected Rustin as the lead organizer for

28. An initial memo Rustin prepared had elaborate plans for a sit-in, see Charles Euchner, *Nobody Turn Me Around: A People's History of the March on Washington* (Boston: Beacon, 2010), 18.

29. "Bayard Rustin on the Civil Rights Movement: An Unpublished Interview," in Leonard R. Sussman, *A Passion for Freedom: My Encounters with Extraordinary People* (Amherst, NY: Prometheus, 2004), 415.

30. A 1960 discussion concerning Rustin's sexuality and movement strategy revolved around Adam Clayton Powell's threat to spread a false rumor linking King and Rustin in an illicit sexual affair if King did not heed Powell's demands. See John D'Emilio, *Lost Prophet: The Life and Times of Bayard Rustin*, (New York: Free Press, 2003), 297–301. Also see Rustin's own account of difficulties that surfaced related to his

the March. Randolph had a thirty-year record of historic victories for black workers in national labor organizing. At the initial meetings when concerns were expressed by Wilkins and others about Rustin's homosexuality being a liability that could be used to torpedo the efficacy of the March, Randolph's insistence on having Rustin as his deputy director prevailed.[31] Throughout this intense period of civil rights organizing, Randolph, in his seventies, was a devoted mentor to and supporter of Rustin.

Rustin managed the details of planning for a demonstration of a historically unprecedented size in the capital. His work ranged from the training of volunteers in nonviolence[32] to finding adequate parking and toilets. According to one biographer, John D'Emilio, Rustin had eight weeks to "build an organization out of nothing . . . to craft a coalition that would hang together despite organizational competition, personal animosities, and often antagonistic politics. He had to maneuver through a minefield of an opposition that ranged from liberals who were counseling moderation to segregationists out to sabotage the event."[33] Some of the opposition to the March by white segregationists specifically targeted Rustin and his homosexuality.

In the weeks preceding the March, Senator Strom Thurmond led a public campaign to discredit it. On August 2, 1963, he read into the *Congressional Record* "material showing Communist connections with the [race] riots" that he alleged the "Negro demonstrations" were spawning.[34] Along with accusations against many other Negro leaders, including Martin Luther King, Thurmond's material cited Rustin as a leader of the upcoming August 28th Washington, D.C. demonstration who had communist ties. On August 7, Thurmond again stood in the Senate chamber to place additional materials in the *Congressional Record*, supposedly establishing Communist Party connections to Negro demonstrations, and ominously asserting that such demonstrations had repeatedly turned into race riots across the

---

sexuality in "Martin Luther King's Views on Gay People" [1987] Interview by Redvers Jeanmarie, in Carbado and Weise, eds., *Time on Two Crosses*, 292–94.

31. Branch, *Parting the Waters*, 846–48; D'Emilio, *Lost Prophet*, 339; Daniel Levine, *Bayard Rustin and the Civil Rights Movement* (New Brunswick, NJ: Rutgers University Press, 2000), 134–35.

32. Rustin "used the same kind of training that CORE and SNCC used to train new recruits. Some volunteers pretended to be marchers, and others pretended to be racist thugs—yelling and taunting, throwing things and kicking." Euchner, *Nobody Turn Me Around*, 102–3.

33. D'Emilio, *Lost Prophet*, 340.

34. *Congressional Record*—Senate, August 2, 1963, 13968.

country.[35] Once more, the allegations linked Rustin to the Communist Party and to Martin Luther King's inner circle.[36] On August 13, Rustin became the major focus of Thurmond's attack as he read into the Senate record "articles and materials" about "Mr. Rustin's criminal record."[37] Thurmond stressed Rustin's conviction on "sex perversion" in 1953, when Rustin was found with two other men in a parked automobile. Thurmond explained the necessity to call attention to Rustin's background "because of the position of prominence which Mr. Rustin commands in the Negro march on Washington, D.C. on August 28."[38] Thurmond even entered the booking slip into the Congressional Record from the Los Angeles County Jail where Rustin was arrested for sex perversion in 1953.[39] Thurmond's strategy in the Senate on these three occasions in August of 1963 was to generate a disreputable image of those who were leading this demonstration and had access to John F. Kennedy's White House to make civil rights demands, such as Martin Luther King.[40]

Additional efforts by government officials to undermine Rustin continued behind the scenes after the March took place. FBI director J. Edgar Hoover reported to attorney general Robert Kennedy a comment about Rustin's sexuality by King that was obtained by secret wiretapping. The FBI version of the conversation reported to Kennedy could easily be interpreted as a disparaging comment by King about how Rustin's drinking could lead to predatory behavior with young males.[41] The FBI also circulated material to government insiders with scandalous details about how Rustin's 1953 Los

35. *Congressional Record*—Senate, August 7, 1963, 14454–63.
36. Ibid., 14458.
37. *Congressional Record*—Senate, August 13, 1963, 14837.
38. Ibid., 14839.
39. Decades later, Rustin reflects on the pressure he experienced as a gay man: "After my arrest (in California in '53), I tried to get the black community to face up to the fact that one of the reasons that some homosexuals went to places where they might well be arrested was that they were not welcome elsewhere." See Carbado and Weise, eds., *Time on Two Crosses*, 286.
40. Earlier that summer, on June 22, 1963, for instance, several civil rights leaders had met with President Kennedy and Vice President Johnson in a highly publicized meeting on civil rights at the White House. Among other topics, plans for the March on Washington were discussed at that meeting, as reported in Branch, *Parting the Waters*, 833–41.
41. Ibid., 861. D'Emilio reports a similar conversation about Rustin between King and Clarence Jones. See D'Emilio, *Lost Prophet*, 372. However, in my view, quotations from private conversations that were secretly wiretapped and edited by Hoover's FBI must not be understood or utilized as credible representations of King's view of Rustin or of homosexuality. They are evidence of the abusive use of state power.

Angeles county arrest involved two white men, oral sodomy, and Rustin's "active" role in it.[42] In short, several US government officials utilized the tactic of attaching shame to March leaders with hopes of generating suspicion of the March as a nefarious endeavor. In particular, in order to disgrace Rustin, the combined stigma of homosexuality, interracial sex, and illicit sexual encounter were added to the commonly used tool of that period of anticommunist fearmongering.

This homophobic strategy set a precedent long before the 2002 flyers warning that Martin Luther King Jr. would be outraged that "homosexualist extremists were abusing the civil rights movement to get special rights based on their sexual behavior." Almost half a century before those flyers were distributed to black church voters in Florida to help repeal their County's inclusion of gay rights within its antidiscrimination laws, Strom Thurmond, J. Edgar Hoover, and other racists stirred up public homophobic outrage in an attempt to stop federal civil rights antidiscrimination law from being enacted.

Yet back in 1963, black civil rights leaders planning the March on Washington were unified in their public support for Rustin. A. Philip Randolph took the lead as spokesperson to the press. As Rustin recounted many years later, Randolph told reporters that the black leaders of the civil rights movement had "absolute confidence in Bayard Rustin's ability, his integrity, and his commitment to nonviolence as the best way to bring about social change. He will continue to organize the March with our full and undivided support."[43] Rustin also related Randolph's response to a direct, hostile question about how Randolph could tolerate having a homosexual working with him. According to Rustin, the veteran labor and civil rights leader replied: "Well, well, if Bayard, a homosexual, is that talented—and I know the work he does for me—maybe I should be looking for somebody else homosexual who could be useful" in our movement work.[44] Even Roy Wilkins was supportive after Thurmond's speech focusing on Rustin. Instead of gloating about how his fears about Rustin's homosexuality being a liability were now being realized, Rustin recalled that "Roy's attitude was, 'We're not going to let him get away with this kind of attack.'"[45] Earlier in the movement when his sexuality had surfaced as a controversial issue, there were hurtful and disappointing moments for Rustin in his relationship with movement

---

42. Branch, *Parting the Waters*, 862.

43. Bayard Rustin, "Black and Gay in the Civil Rights Movement: An Interview with Open Hands (1987)," in Carbado and Weise, eds., *Time on Two Crosses*, 286.

44. As quoted in ibid.

45. As quoted in D'Emilio, *Lost Prophet*, 349.

leaders.⁴⁶ But on this occasion in the summer of 1963, all of the major heterosexual black male leaders stood together with a black gay male leader against white racist attempts to derail the cause of legislatively prohibiting societal discrimination against historically marginalized groups, "on the basis of race, color, religion, sex and national origin," as the final version of the Act would read.

Some of the gendered lessons from these 1960s events are especially relevant to contemporary gay rights battles. In an aggressive defense against antigay, sexual shaming of one of their own, the leaders displayed strong black male solidarity. Their solidarity was generated by a common, intense political commitment to the expansion of civil rights and socioeconomic equality. If anyone concerned about current gay rights issues wanted to know what a prominent 1960s civil rights leader actually said about the slandering of the sexuality of gay people during that movement, Randolph's words at the August 12, 1963 press conference would be an apt example. In defense of Rustin, Randolph said: "I am dismayed that there are in this country, men who, wrapping themselves in the mantle of Christian morality, would mutilate the most elementary conceptions of human decency, privacy and humility in order to persecute other men."⁴⁷

This historical moment included another, less praiseworthy, but no less instructive form of gendered solidarity by the same group of black male leaders. The men on the committee stood together in dismissing the objections expressed by black women civil rights leaders about the exclusion of women from the roster of major speakers at the March.⁴⁸ Because of the prominent movement role that Daisy Bates had played in organizing the Little Rock campaign, or that Diane Nash had contributed as coordinator of the Nashville student protests, the prohibition of women speakers was reprehensible. In a letter to A. Philip Randolph about this decision, Pauli Murray complained: "'Tokenism' is just as offensive when applied to women as when applied to 'Negroes.'"⁴⁹ The men refused to include women as

---

46. See note 29 above.

47. As quoted in D'Emilio, *Lost Prophet*, 349.

48. See the account by Anna Hedgeman, the only woman among nineteen March on Washington planning committee members. She wrote an August 16, 1963, memo to Randolph complaining about the exclusion of women. See Anna Arnold Hedgeman, *The Trumpet Sounds: A Memoir of Negro Leadership* (New York, Holt, Rinehart & Winston, 1964), 179-80. Also, I discuss sexism, the women leaders, and the March on Washington in "Gendered Legacies of Martin Luther King Jr.'s Leadership," *Theology Today* 65 (2008) 41-65.

49. As quoted in D'Emilio, *Lost Prophet*, 352.

speakers but decided to list representative women under the heading "Tribute to Negro Women Fighters for Freedom" in the program.

In their sexist disregard for women activist leaders, Randolph, Rustin, and the other men planning the March failed to live out their movement's goals of increasing the society's recognition of equal human dignity and worth. The marginalization of the women leaders demonstrates that the struggle to be free of subjugating practices and logics even took place within the internal dynamics among movement leaders. They sometimes succeeded in courageously exhibiting countercultural norms of equality (the defense of Rustin). At other times, they upheld the same type of social exclusion and hierarchy that they were protesting.

Historical reflection on the goals and perseverance of the women and men who participated in this movement offer multifaceted, complex, lessons about social justice movement building. These lessons should be discovered and explored rather than the invention of historical narratives that exclusively revere Martin Luther King Jr. Sadly, in popular public discourse, manipulative political rhetoric that supports varying forms of discrimination is better served by a distorted, monolithic historical narrative of civil rights, than a complicated one that requires serious study. Whether it justifies racialized denunciations of contemporary gay rights activists or Clarence Jones's anti-Latino/a immigrant rights agenda, the contemporary misuse of King's name and reputation for furthering discriminatory political goals is fueled by idolatrous androcentrism and contempt for human rights and equality. This kind of misuse of King treats him as a man-god who confers moral authority and political currency in order to increase the marginal status of people who are already vulnerable to social identity based discrimination and violence.

8

What's Race Got to Do with It?
Anti-Semitism, Affirmative Action, and Illegal Immigration

LEWIS V. BALDWIN

Martin Luther King Jr. viewed race as an ideology and strongly discredited the fallacy that there are superior and inferior races. He also lamented the fact that notions of race in America had long been "surrounded by the halo of academic respectability," thus lending "intellectual credence" to slavery, segregation, white privilege, and violence and discrimination against people of color.[1] Moreover, King, in a moment of sheer prophecy, held that moral and spiritual death would be the fate of America if she failed to respond in creative and constructive ways to the challenges posed by the problem of race.[2] Although the problem has become increasingly complex, and has shifted in subtle but significant ways, the color bar still occupies a prominent place on the nation's political and social landscape, impacting virtually every other aspect of life and culture.

In his *What Would Martin Say?* (2008), Clarence B. Jones maintains that King remains an authority and inspiration for addressing the enduring realities of race in our times. But Jones's assessment of what King *would say* today about issues such as anti-Semitism, affirmative action, and illegal

---

1. See Martin Luther King Jr., *Where Do We Go from Here: Chaos or Community?* (Boston: Beacon, 1967), 73–75; and James M. Washington, ed., *A Testament of Hope: The Essential Writings and Speeches of Martin Luther King Jr.* (San Francisco: HarperCollins, 1991), 211–12.

2. King, *Where Do We Go from Here*, 176.

immigration is heavily marred by a limited and distorted view of race, and by the suggestion, at least at points in his writings, that we now live in a post-racial society. Also, Jones's consciousness is steeped primarily in the racial concepts and roles of the civil rights era of the 1960s, which further diminishes any possibility of a serious and credible analysis of King's relevance for the contemporary age. To be sure, an intense study of King's own words actually calls into question both Jones's logic about race and his tendency to use race as the lens through which to determine how the civil rights leader would address the current issues of anti-Semitism, affirmative action, and illegal immigration.

Beyond Anti-Semitism: Unpacking Jones's Thoughts on King and Racism

At points in his *What Would Martin Say?*, Clarence Jones discusses the King legacy in relation to the vexing problem of anti-Semitism in contemporary America. As a prelude to his discussion of the subject, Jones reminds us of the long history of black-Jewish partnerships in the quest for equal rights and social justice, and of how "blacks and Jews marched arm in arm" in the 1950s and '60s, "and together sang the civil rights anthem 'We Shall Overcome.'"[3] Jones makes specific references to the close friendship and working relationship between King and the Jewish Rabbi Abraham Joshua Heschel, who marched together for voting rights in Selma in 1965. King viewed Heschel as a real friend of "our struggle," and Heschel likened King's voice to "the voice of the prophets of Israel."[4] The relationship between the two men, as Jones suggests, was clearly indicative of how certain kinds of social and ethical values move across different faith traditions. Jones's recollection of this vital piece of history is commendable, but problems arise when he appeals to King in order to promote his own perspective on contemporary black-Jewish relations, and on who should be regarded as the chief sources of anti-Semitic thought and behavior in our society.

Jones gives the impression that anti-Semitism has a long history in the African American community, and that it remains a monumental problem. He points to Elijah Muhammad's Nation of Islam and other "black nationalist demagogues" who, in his estimation, epitomize anti-Semitism with their misguided critiques of "Zionists" and their persistent diatribes about "Jew

---

3. Clarence B. Jones and Joel Engel, *What Would Martin Say?* (New York: HarperCollins, 2008), 126.

4. Ibid., 125–28; and Washington, ed., *A Testament of Hope*, 657.

slave traders," "Jew landlords," and "Jew interlopers."⁵ Jones singles out Jesse Jackson, the Nation of Islam leader Louis Farrakhan, and Al Sharpton for exclusive attention, highlighting those instances in which they either made statements or engaged in activities that he feels reflected anti-Semitism.⁶ Jones would have us believe that King would see the problem as he himself sees it, and that King would be the first to verbally chastise these current black leaders. Jones is right in declaring that King would vehemently denounce anti-Semitism in all shades, but there are many points at which Jones's sense of the problem does not square with King's.

Although King was as mindful as Jones of those sporadic episodes of anti-Semitic behavior among his people, King denied that there was a history of anti-Semitism in the black community, and he downplayed the severity of the problem. In an interview with the Jewish rabbi Everett Gendler in March 1968, only days before his assassination, King insisted that "there is absolutely no anti-Semitism in the black community in the historic sense of anti-Semitism." King went on to assert:

> Anti-Semitism historically has been based on two false, sick, evil assumptions. One was unfortunately perpetuated even by many Christians, all too many as a matter of fact, and that is the notion that the religion of Judaism is anathema. That was the first basis for anti-Semitism in the historic sense. Second, a notion was perpetrated by a sick man like Hitler and others that the Jew is innately inferior. Now in these two senses, there is virtually no anti-Semitism in the black community. There is no philosophical anti-Semitism or anti-Semitism in the sense of the historic evils of anti-Semitism that have been with us all too long.⁷

King went on to further clarify his point, noting that "the anti-Semitism which we find in the black community is almost completely an urban Northern ghetto phenomenon," and is "virtually non-existent in the South." King attributed this to the fact that "the Negro in the ghetto confronts the Jew in two dissimilar roles"; namely, as both "his landlord" and "his most consistent and trusted ally in the struggle." By charging blacks excessively for rent and material goods, King held, the Jewish landlords and storekeepers had often failed to operate "on the basis of Jewish ethics," thereby creating an antagonistic relationship between themselves and the Negro ghetto dweller. King concluded nonetheless that anti-Semitism is "a very irrational

5. Jones and Engel, *What Would Martin Say?*, 129–34.
6. Ibid.
7. Washington, ed., *A Testament of Hope*, 668.

course" and "a very immoral course," and that "we have condemned it with all of our might."[8] There is obviously some conflict between what King said and what one reads in Jones's *What Would Martin Say?*, despite their agreement about the irrationality and immorality of anti-Semitism, and about the need to completely eliminate the problem. Indeed, one easily gets the sense that these are two different voices addressing the problem.

King suggested that economics, not race, figured prominently in the bitter feelings that some blacks occasionally evinced toward Jews. His belief that anti-Semitism had never been a major problem among blacks actually conflicts with Jones's suggestion that it has long been the paramount problem of nationalistically inclined African Americans when it comes to race.[9] King's thoughts also constitute a serious challenge to Jones' decision to use black leaders and activists like Elijah Muhammad, Jackson, Farrakhan, and Sharpton as the prototype anti-Semites, especially when the Ku Klux Klan, the Aryan Nations, neo-Nazis, and other white extremist groups have long been known to physically assault and even kill Jews, and are still far more vocal and persistent than any major black leader has ever been in their verbal attacks against Jews and their faith. King was quick to challenge any Negro who expressed a dislike for Jews,[10] but he knew that the most adamant and virulent purveyors of anti-Semitic thought and practice in the United States came not from the black community, as Jones would have us believe, but, rather, from the ranks of diehard white supremacists.[11] Jones's tendency to target Muhammad, Jackson, Farrakhan, Sharpton, and other "self-proclaimed black leaders,"[12] while ignoring Glenn Beck's offensive remarks against Jews,[13] the anti-Semitic rants and activities of the neo-Nazi

---

8. Ibid., 668–70. "There has never been an instance of articulated Negro anti-Semitism that was not swiftly condemned by virtually all Negro leaders with the support of the overwhelming majority," King wrote in 1967. "I have myself directly attacked it within the Negro community, because it is wrong. " King also called anti-Semitism "immoral and self-destructive." See King, *Where Do We Go from Here*, 92–93.

9. Jones and Engel, *What Would Martin Say?*, 129–41; and Washington, ed., *A Testament of Hope*, 212, 295, and 369–70.

10. King held that any Negro who disliked Jews had a problem "no different from the attitude that many whites have toward the whole Negro race." See King's response to "a Negro" who declared, "I don't like Jews," in Clayborne Carson, et al., eds., *The Papers of Martin Luther King Jr.* (Berkeley: University of California Press, 2000), 4:460.

11. Washington, ed., *A Testament of Hope*, 212, 295, and 370; and Rabbi Marc Schneier, *Shared Dreams: Martin Luther King Jr. and the Jewish Community* (Woodstock, VT: Jewish Lights, 1999), 172. King asserted in 1958 that the recent bombing of Jewish Temples by white bigots was no different from "the bombings of Negro churches in Montgomery." See Carson, et. al., eds., *The Papers of Martin Luther King Jr.*, 4:541.

12. Jones and Engel, *What Would Martin Say?*, 42 and 129–41.

13. The Southern Poverty Law Center, "Fox News Personalities Reaching for New

leader Tom Metzger, the Holocaust-denying Jew-hater Willis Carto, and the Aryan founder Richard Butler,[14] is virtually impossible to understand, particularly in light of his association with King and his involvement in the civil rights movement.

While maintaining that racism in all forms constitutes a colossal evil, King almost always had white supremacy in mind when addressing the issue. "I think we have to honestly admit that the problems in the world today, as they relate to the question of race," said he in early 1968, "must be blamed on the whole doctrine of white supremacy, the whole doctrine of racism, and these doctrines came into being through the white race and the exploitation of the colored peoples of the world." King went on to predict that "if the white world does not recognize this and does not adjust to what has to be, then we can end up in the world with a kind of race war." King felt that avoiding such a large-scale human catastrophe depended ultimately on "the spirit" and "the readjusting qualities of the white peoples of the world."[15] In sharp contrast to King, whom he claims to speak for in *What Would Martin Say?*, Jones trivializes and even ignores the lingering problem of white supremacy as an ideology and structure of institutions, and he actually suggests at points that America is a post-racial society—that we no longer live and function in a racialized culture. This is one of the most glaring examples of how Jones has embraced the politics of denial so typical of the conservative right in its dealings with race, and especially white supremacy.

Jones has a message for today's blacks about the evils of anti-Semitism, but he has nothing to say to Jews and other white Americans about the pervasive and enduring problems of white supremacy and white privilege. Jones denounces black anti-Semitism and hatred for Jews among Arabs but essentially ignores instances of Jewish racism against blacks and the Palestinians.[16] The suggestion is that all Jews are victims and people of color

---

Lows," *Intelligence Report* 139 (Fall 2010) 7.

14. The Southern Poverty Law Center, "Tom Metzger," *Intelligence Report* 141 (Spring 2011) 26; and Sonia Scherr, "Rooting Out Racism: In the Latest Attempt by Christians to Right the Past, Presbyterian Denomination Takes Action against Racist Activism in Its Ranks," *Intelligence Report* 138 (Summer 2010) 38; and The Southern Poverty Law Center, "Neo-Nazi Murderer Dies before Trial," *Intelligence Report* 137 (Spring 2010) 4–5.

15. Martin Luther King Jr., "Interview: Doubts and Certainties Link," unpublished version, London, England (aired 4 April 1968), The Library and Archives of the Martin Luther King Jr. Center for Nonviolent Social Change Inc., Atlanta, Georgia, 1. King rarely if ever used the term "black racism," even when discussing "black separatism." See King, *Where Do We Go from Here*, 48.

16. Jones and Engel, *What Would Martin Say?*, 129–41. Here Jones's work echoes much of the perspective of Rabbi Marc Schneier, who discusses black anti-Semitism

victimizers. Needless to say, King was far more perceptive, objective, and insightful in his own assessment of these problems, and was far less hesitant to attack racism wherever he found it. Having witnessed the gradual erosion of Jewish support for King when he turned increasingly to the intersecting evils of racism, capitalism, and economic injustice in the late 1960s, and having experienced firsthand the evils of white supremacy himself, Jones really defies logic when he employs black anti-Semitism as the critical factor in underlining the powerful potential of King and his ideas for addressing the issue of race today.

King not only provides a more perceptive and objective analysis of race and racism than Jones, the civil rights leader also put forth potential solutions to these problems that Jones completely ignores. Convinced that there was more than "one approach to the solution of the race problem," including anti-Semitism, King, during his first attempt at organized social protest in Montgomery, Alabama, in 1955–1956, called for a multifaceted approach involving religion, education, legislation and court orders, and nonviolent direct action. Through religion and education, he declared, "we seek to change attitudes" and "internal feelings (prejudice, hate, etc.)," and "to break down spiritual barriers to integration." Through "legislation and court orders," he added, "we seek to regulate behavior," to "control the external effects of those feelings," and "to break down the physical barriers to integration." Nonviolent direct action, for King, was a necessary supplement to all of the other approaches, especially since it afforded possibilities for eliminating both internal and external barriers to community. For King, one approach was "not a substitute for the other, but a meaningful and necessary supplement."[17] This must be seriously considered in any responsible retrieval of King as an authoritative voice that still affords much of the answer to anti-Semitism and the larger problem of racism.

Strangely, there are no significant references to religion in Jones's reflections on what King *would say* about anti-Semitism. King was obviously a man of the church, and he consistently stressed the centrality of spiritual values in any constructive approach to the issues surrounding race and racism. Knowing that the Christian church had too often been "an active participant" in shaping and crystallizing patterns of bigotry and intolerance toward Jews and people of color, King urged that institution to

---

at length while saying little or nothing about Jewish racism and participation in the preservation of the structures of white supremacy. Clearly, a more objective perspective is needed. Schneier's is an otherwise good and groundbreaking book on a number of levels. See Schneier, *Shared Dreams*, 29, 36, and 159-70.

17. Martin Luther King Jr., *Stride toward Freedom: The Montgomery Story* (New York: Harper & Row, 1958), 33-34.

work through its "channels of religious education" to get at "the ideational roots of race prejudice," and to effectively promote "the idea of a superior and inferior race" as "a myth that has been completely refuted by anthropological evidence." King went on to recommend other actions on the part of churches, such as uplifting "the dignity and worth of all human personality," "keeping men's minds and visions centered on God," "instilling within their worshipers the spirit of love, penitence, and forgiveness," "mitigating the prevailing and irrational fears concerning intermarriage," encouraging "their constituents to develop a world perspective," "urging all followers to go into this new age with understanding goodwill," and taking "the lead in social reform" and in creating "a moral balance within society so that all men can live together as brothers."[18] Here King had in mind the church as the chief symbol of the beloved community, or that institution that exemplifies and advances an egalitarian and communitarian vision of God and human relations. Jones's failure to seriously discuss King's vision for the church (and synagogue) in relation to anti-Semitism and the broader question of racism is unforgivable, and it helps explain why he is quite inept in so many of his judgments about what King *would say* about current social, political, and economic matters.

In churches and in other settings around the world, King issued a clarion call for a renewed collective effort to combat racism as a world problem. Convinced that "the powerful unity" of humans of goodwill everywhere "is stronger than the most potent and entrenched racism," King insisted, in 1965, that "the time" had indeed "come for an international

18. Martin Luther King Jr., *Strength to Love* (Philadelphia: Fortress, 1981; originally published in 1963), 61–63; Martin Luther King Jr., "A Challenge to the Churches and Synagogues," unpublished version of paper, delivered at the Conference on Religion and Race, Chicago, Illinois (7 January 1963), The Library and Archives of the Martin Luther King Jr. Center for Nonviolent Social Change Inc., 10; Martin Luther King Jr., "Crisis and the Church," *Council Quarterly* (October 1961) 1–4; Jack Gilbert, "King Urges Youth to Join in New Order," *Athens Messenger* (30 December 1959) 1; Martin Luther King Jr., "Beyond Discovery, Love," unpublished version of an address, delivered at The International Convention of Christian Churches (Disciples of Christ), Dallas, Texas (25 September 1966), King Center Library and Archives, 5; Martin Luther King Jr., "The Church on the Frontier of Racial Tension," unpublished version of The Gay Lectures, delivered at Southern Baptist Theological Seminary, Louisville, Kentucky (19 April 1961), King Center Library and Archives, 7; Martin Luther King Jr., "Address at a Dinner Sponsored by the Episcopal Society for Cultural and Racial Unity," delivered at The 61st General Convention, St. Louis, Missouri (12 October 1964), King Center Library and Archives, 2; Martin Luther King Jr., "Segregation and the Church," *New York Amsterdam News* (2 February 1963), 8; Martin Luther King Jr., "The Church and the Race Crisis," *Christian Century* 75/41 (8 October 1958), 1140–41; Martin Luther King Jr., "The Role of the Church," *New York Amsterdam News* (15 September 1962) 11 and 14; "Dr. King Urges Church," *St. Louis Post-Dispatch* (13 October 1964).

alliance of peoples of all nations against racism."[19] King was clearly putting forth a vision that has some meaning and relevance for today, and Clarence Jones should have felt compelled to move beyond sweeping claims about black anti-Semitism to explore what King said about engaging and eliminating racism as an international phenomenon. Such an approach would be more timely and compelling, especially in this age of "the globalization of racism."[20] We need to know how King's ideas might be meaningful and useful in addressing not only anti-Semitism and white supremacy in America, but also the "new" globalized racism, which finds tragic expression in ethnic cleansing, culture wars, terrorism, anti-immigration fears and paranoia, and intensified xenophobia.[21]

It is very difficult to find important resonances and affinities between Jones and King when it comes to anti-Semitism and the larger problem of racism. Apparently, Jones, unlike King, lacks a coherent and insightful concept of these problems. By targeting the African American community, and especially certain black leaders, to lend credence to his claims and conclusions about virulent anti-Semitism, Jones actually misplaces the problems. The most deeply entrenched and insidious form of racism in America and the world today is not black supremacy, but, as King himself said, white supremacy.[22] Clearly this suggests other points at which Jones's energetic championing of King's ideas should be carefully analyzed and called into question.

At a time when black-Jewish relations seem to be at their lowest point in generations, due in part to what is perceived by some Jews as President Barack Obama's "anti-Israel policies,"[23] we could benefit from ethical and theological dialogue with King around this issue. King's relations to and dealings with Jews in the 1950s and '60s yield important insights into how

---

19. Martin Luther King Jr., "Let My People Go," South Africa Benefit Speech, Hunter College, New York, New York (10 December 1965), 1 and 4–5; and Lewis V. Baldwin, *Toward the Beloved Community: Martin Luther King Jr. and South Africa* (Cleveland: Pilgrim, 1995), 49–50.

20. Donaldo Macedo and Panayota Gounari, eds., *The Globalization of Racism* (Boulder: Paradigm, 2006), 3–33.

21. Ibid.

22. This is not to suggest that racist ideology does not exist among African Americans, for King felt otherwise, occasionally noting that "Black supremacy "can be as "dangerous as white supremacy." At the same time, King understood the power of white society to more effectively practice and implement racist ideology through structures and institutions. See Washington, ed., *A Testament of Hope*, 215; and King, "Interview: Doubts and Certainties Link," 1–2.

23. Dan Senor, "Why Obama is Losing the Jewish Vote," *The Wall Street Journal* (14 September 2011) A17.

a seemingly growing rift might be ultimately healed.[24] Jones offers little or nothing that is useful in this regard.

Is Affirmative Action Necessary?: The Conflicting Voices of Jones and King

The issue of affirmative action as a form of redress for injustices committed over the centuries against blacks in the United States has long been controversial and greeted with dissenting voices. One side of the argument behind affirmative action is that America is morally obligated to not only atone for the abuse and victimization of black people through racism, slavery, and segregation, but also to provide compensation in the form of material resources, increased opportunities, or some other means. The contention on the other side is that African Americans have made great socio-economic progress since the civil rights movement and are no longer victims, and that black leaders who call for affirmative action today are merely seeking to "empower themselves" by capitalizing on "free-floating white guilt."[25] By raising and addressing the question, what Martin Would Say about Affirmative Action," Clarence B. Jones brings Martin Luther King Jr. into the center of this debate, and makes sweeping and questionable claims about where the late civil rights leader would stand today on the issue.

Jones's knowledge of how affirmative action has developed over time, as both an idea and a set of public policy initiatives, is exceptional, and this is not surprising, considering his standing as a lawyer. Jones reminds us that the term "affirmative action" was first introduced by President John F. Kennedy in the early 1960s, when he, King, and other black leaders were steeped in the struggle for racial and economic justice. According to Jones, King clearly understood at that time that the struggle was not simply about freedom but opportunity as well, and that King was committed to "the concept of fairness" or achieving "a level playing field" as both a public policy issue and a moral imperative.[26] Knowing that black people had been "deprived, robbed, enslaved," and even "denied the right to make a living," continues Jones, King was highly concerned about the kind of government action that would best address these historical injustices, "whose ramifications were

---

24. Martin Luther King Jr., "My Jewish Brother," *New York Amsterdam News* (26 February 1966), 1; and Israel Goldstein, "Martin Luther King's Jewish Associations," *Jerusalem Post* (22 October 1964) 3.

25. See Raymond A. Winbush, ed., *Should America Pay?: Slavery and the Raging Debate on Reparations* (New York: HarperCollins, 2003), xix, 3–21, and 165–71.

26. Jones and Engel, *What Would Martin Say?*, 69–70, 72, and 78–79.

still being felt across black America." Jones goes on to claim that the words of King's famous "I Have a Dream" speech, delivered in Washington DC on August 28, 1963, were echoed in President Kennedy's creation of the Committee on Equal Employment Opportunity, which prohibited "racial discrimination on projects funded by federal monies," and in President Lyndon B. Johnson's signing of the Civil Rights Act (1964) and the Voting Rights Act (1965), both of which "raised the bar on tolerable discrimination even higher."[27]

Jones's claims about King's support for reparations is clearly borne out in King's book, *Why We Can't Wait* (1963), in which the civil rights leader argued that "special" or "compensatory measures" had always been an acceptable principle in the United States, especially in cases where citizens had been "deprived of certain advantages and opportunities." To illustrate his point, King observed that the nation found "nothing strange" about a "Marshall Plan and technical assistance to handicapped peoples around the world." He also noted that this principle was "behind land grants to farmers who fought" in the American Revolution, the "GI Bill of rights" extended to World War II veterans, and "the establishment of child labor laws, social security, unemployment compensation, manpower retraining programs and countless other measures that the nation considered logical and moral."[28] The same principle, King held, was easily justifiable in the situation of "the Negro," who had been "enslaved for two centuries" and "robbed of the wages of his toil." At the same time, King reasoned that "not all the wealth of this affluent society" could justly compensate black people, but he conceded that a price could "be placed on unpaid wages," and that "payment should be in the form of a massive program by the government of special, compensatory measures that could be regarded as a settlement in accordance with the accepted practice of common law." For King, "such measures" would have certainly been "less expensive than any computation based on two centuries of unpaid wages and accumulated interest."[29]

While lauding King's stand on reparations in the 1960s, Jones contends that King made a serious error in "packaging a black reparations argument with what he called 'a Bill of Rights for the Disadvantaged.'"[30] Driven by a need to garner wide support from the masses of voters, labor unions, and other national organizations, King, Jones concludes, called for "a program

27. Ibid., 72–75.

28. Martin Luther King Jr., *Why We Can't Wait* (New York: New American Library, 1963), 136–37; and Jones and Engel, *What Would Martin Say?*, 73–75.

29. King, *Why We Can't Wait*, 137.

30. Jones and Engel, *What Would Martin Say?*, 75.

of economic aid" that would "benefit the disadvantaged of *all* races," thereby undermining "the eloquent justice of reparations for black America." Jones feels that the other races, and especially poor whites, should have been excluded from King's strategy because the circumstances that accounted for "whites' destitution" were not "strictly comparable with the Negro's."[31]

Strangely enough, Jones seems oblivious to the fact that any call for "black reparations," or an exclusively race-based "compensatory measures," would have been antithetical to King's most basic values, and especially his vision of the beloved community, or a truly integrated society. King was concerned not only about the plight of the black poor, but the poor in general. This was consistent with both his reading of the gospels and his social personalism, which affirmed the dignity and worth of *all* humans, the communitarian nature of persons, and also God's concern for all. Moreover, convinced that America was a land in which black power and white power inevitably intersected, there was no way for King to treat the uplift and empowerment of the races through affirmative action as separate issues.[32] Contrary to what Jones says, there is no reason to believe that if King were with us today, "he'd look back and see that his moral arguments for reparations of some kind would have been better confined" to his own race. Jones' suggestion that King should have pushed for "black reparations"[33] in the sixties is to some degree ironic, especially in view of his own tendency to ignore race, and particularly the lingering realities of white supremacy and white privilege, as a serious consideration in determining the need for and usefulness of affirmative action today.

Jones holds that King "would not understand affirmative action" as it is viewed and employed today, and would be compelled by his own "intellectual honesty" and moral vision "to consider the totality of what affirmative action has wrought."[34] Jones is probably right here. King often said, as in his famous "Letter from the Birmingham City Jail" (1963), that the first step in any direct action campaign is the "collection of facts to determine whether injustices exist," and, if so, how they might be addressed in some positive

---

31. Ibid., 75–77.

32. Martin Luther King Jr., "Address at a Mass Meeting," unpublished version, Clarksdale, Mississippi (19 March 1968), King Center Library and Archives, 7–10; Martin Luther King Jr., "Address at a Mass Meeting," unpublished version, Eutaw, Alabama 20 March 1968), King Center Library and Archives, 3-4; and Lewis V. Baldwin, *There Is a Balm in Gilead: The Cultural Roots of Martin Luther King Jr.* (Minneapolis: Fortress, 1991), 73.

33. Jones and Engel, *What Would Martin Say?*, 75 and 77.

34. Ibid., 69 and 79.

and constructive manner.³⁵ This was King's modus operandi, so to speak, and he never really deviated from it. But Jones goes a bit too far when he imagines King "waking up like Rip Van Winkle, from a long sleep," only to realize that the need for affirmative action is called into question by the "astonishing" progress made by his people. The "real question," Jones argues, is not what King favored almost a half century ago, for "the record is clear," but what King *would say* about reparations in these early years of the twenty-first century.³⁶ For those who feel that the King legacy affords answers for today, this is indeed the "real question," but the greater question is whether Jones or anyone else can answer it.

Jones feels that King would be literally astounded at the progress African Americans have made since his death. According to Jones, King would marvel at the "colossal number" of school board directors, mayors, and congresspersons, especially in the South; at the "robust and rising black middle class"; at black athletes who make millions while serving as heroes for whites and spokespersons for major corporations; at Oprah Winfrey, who is exercising enormous influence in American popular culture; at the many black actors and actresses producing and starring in movies and television shows; and at the scores of blacks currently holding chairmanships in companies, figuring prominently in police departments and as entrepreneurs, owning their own homes, and even occupying major positions in the federal government. "Being fair-minded," says Jones, King would declare that "we'd done it, we'd won, we'd made it, hallelujah, we'd reached" the mountaintop, and "'Thank God almighty, we're free at last.'"³⁷ King would see, Jones continues, that blacks who "come of age in the twenty-first century" can enjoy and "participate fully in the American dream" without being hampered by racism. "And then, after applauding the programs, quotas, set-asides, and preferences" that helped make this great progress possible, Jones adds, King would "end them all."³⁸

But Jones seems to undermine these claims by pointing to another side of black life, defined largely by astounding levels of intracommunity violence and homicide, low educational standards and expectations, high incarceration rates, countless numbers of teenage pregnancies and unwed mothers, and a host of other problems. Jones is right in saying that King would be "dismayed" by this more dismal side of black America, but one might raise serious questions about Jones's sense of how King would

---

35. King, *Why We Can't Wait*, 78.
36. Jones and Engel, *What Would Martin Say?*, 79.
37. Ibid., 79–81.
38. Ibid., 81.

respond. Jones suggests, for example, that King would make a sharp distinction between young black men who die at the hands of each other and the four little black girls who were murdered in Birmingham's Sixteenth Street Baptist Church in September 1963. The suggestion is that while King rightly blamed racism for the death of the four girls, he would determine that the root causes of the current high black homicide rate rests squarely on the shoulders of those young African American men who succumb to "the pathologies too common in his own race," and who become trapped in "the gangsta subculture." How could King believe anything else, Jones concludes, when we live in a country that has "become as colorblind as any society of human beings ever could be"?[39]

Again, Jones displays not only a stunning insensitivity to the plight of the masses of people of color in America today, but also a lack of knowledge of and appreciation for King's personalism, which affirms every human life as sacred in the sight of God. If every human being is a reflection of the divine image, as King held, then lives lost due to the poor judgment of misguided young black males are no less precious than lives taken by the bombs of vicious Klansmen. Also, King lamented the loss of black lives in Saturday night brawls and gang executions, and he, quite unlike Jones today, placed much of the blame on a larger, racist society in which black perpetrators turned their hostility and frustration with that society inwardly.[40] Also in contrast to Jones, who actually misplaces the problem when discussing crime and other maladies in the black community, King held that "criminality and delinquency are not racial; poverty and ignorance breed crime whatever the racial group may be."[41] It is highly likely that King, if present among us today, would make the same assessment regarding a range of problems in the African American community, even as he would attribute some of the blame to a lack of personal responsibility. As stated earlier, there was a level of objectivity in King's analysis of the problems black people faced that is missing in Jones's rhetoric today. In short, King was much more of a dialectical thinker than Jones, as evidenced by his propensity to take a both/and rather than an either/or approach to reasoning when it came to matters of both a personal and social nature.

In a disturbing conclusion, Jones insists that King would oppose both affirmative action and reparations today because we live in "a culture that no longer sanctions open racism." "The world we live in now," Jones declares, is not "inherently unfriendly to the thoughts of a young black." There

---

39. Ibid., 81–91.
40. King, *Where Do We Go from Here*, 64 and 125.
41. Washington, ed., *A Testament of Hope*, 179, 192, 470, and 489.

will always be "haters," he adds, but racial prejudice is not as obvious as it used to be, which means that it does not have the same powerful effect on the quality of black life.[42] Jones's image of contemporary America as "a colorblind society"[43] is strange in light of the reaction of most whites to the recent murder of Trayvon Martin and to high black incarceration rates, and it is yet another example of the extent to which he has capitulated to the thinking of right-wing conservatives, who have routinely used this image in their attacks on affirmative action. Like Newt Gingrich, Dick Armey, Clint Bolick, and so many others on the right, Jones identifies affirmative action exclusively with African Americans. He suggests that affirmative-action programs as administered today constitute "reverse racism," for they "discriminate against one racial group for the benefit of another."[44] The term "reverse racism" was really coined and first used by neoconservative analysts, and Jones's use of it says more about him than about King.[45]

Apparently, it has never occurred to Jones that vast numbers of white women are beneficiaries of affirmative action. In other words, affirmative action is not an exclusively *race-based* policy. To suggest that King would view affirmative action as the reason for "a loss of white amity"[46] in our times is very unfortunate, for it offers a flimsy explanation for white prejudice against blacks and other minorities of color, and it also encourages

---

42. Jones and Engel, *What Would Martin Say?*, 92–93.

43. Ibid., 81.

44. Ibid., 93.

45. Sociologists Joe and Clairece Feagin agree with this contention. The Feagins are certain that while studies show that some antiwhite discrimination exists, it is negligible when "compared with discrimination against people of color. With a modest number of exceptions, members of racially subordinate groups do not have the power or institutional position to express the prejudices they may hold about whites in the form of everyday discrimination." Moreover, the Feagins are instructive when they consider what would be the *reverse* of the centuries on institutional racism and discrimination experienced by blacks. The reverse of this would mean "reversing the power and resource inequalities for several hundred years. In the past and today, most organizations in major institutional areas such as housing, education, and employment would be run at the top and middle-levels by a disproportionate number of powerful black managers and officials. These powerful black officials would have aimed much racial discrimination at whites, including years of slavery and legal segregation. As a result, millions of whites would have suffered—and would still suffer—trillions of dollars in economic losses and lower wages, as well as high rates of unemployment, political disenfranchisement for long periods, widespread housing segregation, inferior school facilities, and violent lynchings. That social condition would be something one could reasonably call a condition that 'reversed the discrimination' against African Americans. It does not now exist, nor has it ever existed." See Joe R. Feagin and Clairece B. Feagin, *Racial and Ethnic Relations*, 5th ed. (Upper Saddle River, NJ: Prentice Hall, 1996), 24–25.

46. Jones and Engel, *What Would Martin Say?*, 93–94.

voices on the right which are determined to use King in defense of their claims against affirmative action and reparations. After all, Jones was one of King's closest associates and aides in the 1960s, and this alone could suggest, in the minds of many, that there is some credence to what he says about the civil rights leader in relation to contemporary issues and problems.

Jones's spirited defense of black Republicans in his chapter on King and affirmative action seems to provide further evidence of his political leanings, and especially his sympathy with the conservative right. Jones scoffs at blacks who call black conservatives, and particularly black Republicans, "Uncle Toms," "sell-outs," and "inauthentic."[47] At the same time, he is not beyond using words like "pimp," "self-serving," and "appallingly disingenuous" to describe black leaders on the so-called left, who happen to also be Democrats and staunch supporters of affirmative action.[48] This is clearly not in the spirit of King, who simply refused to resort to the indignities of name-calling, even when he vehemently disagreed with other black leaders. Such behavior was antithetical to King's call for "group unity," to the goals of the freedom movement, and to King's vision of the beloved community.[49]

Jones tells us in so many words that King's message to the black community today would be to forget quotas, set-asides, and preferences while pursuing excellence. For Jones, black uplift and empowerment rest not in government aid or handouts, but in the will to "pursue excellence." Jones drives this point home in several chapters in his *What Would Martin Say?*, and he indeed has a point. King constantly challenged his people with an ethic of personal responsibility and self-determination, urging them "to achieve excellence in their field of endeavor." King pointed to George Washington Carver, Mahalia Jackson, W. E. B. DuBois, Jesse Owens, and countless other blacks in history who, through sheer determination, broke "through the shackles of circumstance" and achieved excellence in various spheres of life.[50] There is no reason to doubt that King would offer the same message to his people today. But he would also be apt to say that government-based affirmative action has a place in this enduring effort to uplift and empower those who still suffer due to skin color and economics. We do not live in a post-racial society, and the Occupy Wall Street movement, which has often evoked the memory of King, stands as proof of a mounting frustration with a nation in which the gap between rich and poor gets wider daily.[51]

47. Ibid., 82.
48. Ibid., 30–34, 42, 44–45, 49, 55–57, 63–64, and 67.
49. King, *Where Do We Go from Here*, 123–25.
50. Ibid., 126–27.
51. Kit Schackner, "Main Street Wants Accountability from Wall Street," *The*

These are times during which cycles of poverty and the economic recession are actually reversing the black economic gains made in the sixties.[52] The employment rates and annual incomes for African Americans, Latinos, and other minorities remain significantly less than those of whites. Racial preferences in college admissions are under attack, and the controversy over affirmative action in government and public education seem headed for "a return engagement before the Supreme Court."[53] Furthermore, Republican-controlled state legislatures are setting up a showdown with civil rights groups by attempting black voter suppression through redistricting guidelines, the reduction of early voting, and voter ID requirements; the diversity programs of companies are still coming up with all-white slates of candidates; racial profiling is victimizing more people of color, and hate groups have escalated their efforts in spreading racist propaganda. This is no time for African Americans like Jones to be joining right-wing conservatives in the anti–affirmative action cause, especially since they have little or no credibility on issues like race and affirmative action.[54]

Jones's assessment of what King *would say* about affirmative action suggests that Jones does not live in the same world as the masses of blacks and other people of color, too many of whom are a paycheck from the homeless shelters and the bread and soup lines. Jones's inability to identify with this kind of existence actually grounds his insistence that affirmative action has outlived its usefulness or raison d'etre. This could also explain why Jones did not devote a chapter to how King would address poverty in the context of the current waves of economic distress and stagnation, an omission that is really inexplicable in view of the serious attention King gave this problem as both a thinker and activist.[55]

Tennessean (December 19, 2011) 8A.

52. Jesse Washington, "Great Recession Reverses Black Economic Gains: High Job Loss Sends Many Back to Poverty," *The Tennessean* (July 10, 2011) 4A.

53. George Will, "Court Should Revisit Racial Preferences in Admissions: National Opinion," *The Tennessean* (December 2, 2011) 14A; and David Ashenfelter, et al., "Affirmative Action Battle Likely to Return before Supreme Court," *The Tennessean* (July 2, 2011) 4A.

54. Fredreka Schouten, "Laws Limiting Early Voting Rile Democrats, Rights Groups," *The Tennessean* (December 12, 2011) 8A; Patrick McGeehan, "Told to Diversify, Dock Union Offers a Nearly All-White Retort," *The New York Times* (December 1, 2011) A28; Dwight Lewis, "Hate Groups Are Spreading Racist Propaganda," *The Tennessean* (February 26, 2009) 13A; and Leonard Pitts, "Conservatives Have Zero Credibility on Race Issues," *The Tennessean* (November 6, 2011) 17A.

55. King, *Where Do We Go from Here*, 176–81.

The Stigma of Color and Illegal immigration: What King Might Say?

Martin Luther King Jr. viewed America as a nation of immigrants, referring to her as "the mother of exiles." He was thoroughly mindful of the histories of the various racial and ethnic groups who had come to this country over time, and of their different experiences based on skin color. King gave powerful expression to this in his writings, mass meeting speeches, and sermons. In a telling remark, he noted how

> the situation of other immigrant groups a hundred years ago and the situation of the Negro today cannot be usefully compared. Negroes were brought here in chains long before the Irish decided *voluntarily* to leave Ireland or the Italians thought of leaving Italy. Some Jews may have left their homes in Europe involuntarily, but they were not in chains when they arrived on these shores. Other immigrant groups came to America with language and economic handicaps, but not with the stigma of color. Above all, no other ethnic group has been a slave on American soil, and no other group has had its family structure deliberately torn apart.[56]

As if to further drive home the point, King declared that "it does not take us long to realize that America has been the mother of its white exiles from Europe." This country, he reasoned, had never "evinced the same maternal care and concern" for its immigrants of color. King continued: "it is no wonder that our slave foreparents could think about it and start singing, in a beautiful soul song—'Sometimes I feel like a motherless child'. It was this sense of estrangement and rejection that caused our forebears to use such a metaphor."[57] Evidently, King's own experiences with persecution and rejection in the Jim Crow South helped make it possible for him to speak with vigor and clarity about the alien status of Africans in the evil world of slavery, highlighting their sense of being strangers in a strange land, of living as sojourners in Babylon, of existing on the margins or the periphery of

---

56. Ibid., 103; and Baldwin, *There Is a Balm in Gilead*, 42–43 and 46–47.

57. Martin Luther King Jr., "The Crisis of Civil Rights," unpublished version of an address, Operation Breadbasket Meeting, Chicago, Illinois (10–12 October 1967), King Center Library and Archives, 10; Martin Luther King Jr., "Transforming a Neighborhood," unpublished version of a speech at the NATRA Convention, RCA Dinner, Atlanta, Georgia (11 August 1967), King Center Library and Archives, 7–8; Martin Luther King Jr., "A Knock at Midnight," unpublished version of a sermon, All Saints Community Church, Los Angeles, California (25 June 1967), King Center Library and Archives, 14–16; and Lewis V. Baldwin, *The Voice of Conscience: The Church in the Mind of Martin Luther King Jr.* (New York: Oxford University Press, 2010), 105–6.

American life.⁵⁸ Clarence B. Jones would have done well to point this out in his discussion of what King *would say* about illegal immigration, especially since Jones makes race central to his claims and conclusions.

The debate over illegal or undocumented immigrants has reached fever pitch in the last decade, due largely to the thousands of Mexicans who have made their way to America as part of Guest Workers Programs. Supporters of these immigrants include corporations that profit from cheap foreign labor, civil and human rights groups who operate out of moral or ethical considerations, and ethnic advocacy groups interested in advancing their own political base and clout. Opponents include nativists who view foreigners as a grave threat to the culture and safety of Americans, environmentalists who dread trends toward overpopulation, labor advocates who feel that immigrants take away jobs that rightly belong to American citizens, and racial extremists who are driven by fears of the further erosion of white power and supremacy. The clash between the supporters and opponents is evident in American institutions and across the public square, leading states like Arizona, South Carolina, and Alabama to adopt the strictest immigration laws in American history. Jones obviously sides with the opponents of illegal immigration, and he uses King as the moral voice through which he conveys his own thoughts on the subject.⁵⁹

Jones has King raising a question that lies at the very core of the immigration debate; namely, should people of every country have the right to live in every other country? Jones suggests that King's answer would be *no*, and that the civil rights leader would feel that targeting America "as a special case would be both unfair and immoral."⁶⁰ But these points are questionable, particularly in view of King's oft-repeated conviction that no child of God is an "outsider" anywhere on this earth.⁶¹ Quoting Psalms 24:1, King believed that "the earth is the Lord's and the fullness thereof, the world, and they that dwell therein."⁶² This is why King never really used terms like "outsiders" or "illegal aliens," for these would conflict with his communitarian ideal, which was poignantly expressed in his concept of "the interrelated structure of all reality." Moreover, King's idea that humans everywhere are "caught in an inescapable network of mutuality" and "tied in a single garment of

---

58. Baldwin, *There Is a Balm in Gilead*, 42–43; and Baldwin, *The Voice of Conscience*, 105–6.

59. Jones and Engel, *What Would Martin Say?*, 101–24.

60. Ibid., 117.

61. King, *Why We Can't Wait*, 77.

62. Martin Luther King Jr., "The Meaning of Hope," unpublished version of sermon, Dexter Avenue Baptist Church, Montgomery, Alabama (10 December 1967), King Center Library and Archives, 11.

destiny"⁶³ would also seem to undermine any tendency to categorize certain human beings as "illegal immigrants." For King, the fact that humans are stewards of God's earth is no confirmation that they should control any part of it, let alone determine who should live and function here or there.

Jones holds that King would be very sympathetic to illegal immigrants who come to America for work because they have no other option for taking care of their families, and he surmises that King himself would do likewise if confronted with the same circumstances.⁶⁴ Considering King's capacity for empathy, there is no reason to doubt this. But Jones goes on to assert that King's position on illegal immigration "would not be what his supporters might hope—and indeed, what they've falsely credited him with." First, says Jones, King "would be outraged by the greater immorality" of bringing "a slave class" into this nation, "especially one that has robbed" so many black citizens of "their hard-won livelihoods" as construction and sanitation workers.⁶⁵

Jones uses the case of Elvira Arellano, a twenty-two-year-old woman from the Mexican state of Michoacan, to make his point. Including Elvira among what he calls "undocumented workers," Jones attacks her for not only taking custodian jobs that could have gone to some American citizen, but also for using motherhood "as an instrument of immigration policy," for possessing "a stolen Social Security number," for enlisting the assistance of church leaders, politicians, and immigration rights advocates, for forming "an illegal-alien activist group," for taking "sanctuary in a Methodist church," and for labeling her own plight and the plight of other illegals "a civil rights issue."⁶⁶ Jones feels that King, who "was no anarchist," would be greatly disturbed by all these actions, and particularly by the audacity of Elvira and other illegal immigrants to "wave Mexican and Salvadoran flags" while comparing themselves "to civil rights demonstrators."⁶⁷ Instead of treating Elvira like a decorated soldier or a fighter for constitutional rights, King would, in Jones's estimation, say that she has essentially no rights because she broke federal law. Moreover, King, Jones contends, would question Elvira's reason for being in America, the extent of her patriotism in comparison with that of Europeans who came to this country generations earlier, her "litany of complaints" against the nation for its treatment of ille-

63. King, *Why We Can't Wait*, 77; and Martin Luther King Jr., *The Trumpet of Conscience* (New York: Harper & Row, 1987; originally published in 1967), 69–70.
64. Jones and Engel, *What Would Martin Say?*, 109.
65. Ibid., 109 and 114.
66. Ibid., 110–15.
67. Ibid., 114 and 121.

gal aliens, and her lack of gratitude for the benefits she received here despite her undocumented status.[68]

It is hard to imagine a more distorted picture of King, who had enormous respect for basic human rights. Jones virtually dehumanizes Elvira because of her illegal actions, and he expresses his own frustration with her and other "undocumented workers" through the voice of King. This is obviously at odds with King's principle of the sacredness of all human personality. Elvira, due to her station in life, clearly ranks among what King labeled "the least of these,"[69] and it is hard to imagine him not affirming her personhood and her right to work to take care of her son, Saul. The same might be said of her efforts to seek whatever protection she needed.

There are other points at which one might question Jones against the background of what King said and did in his own time. Contrary to Jones's claims, it is doubtful that King would be annoyed with Elvira's tendency to identify her struggle with civil rights, for King believed that all forms of bigotry and intolerance are equally problematic, and that his own people had no exclusive claim to the language of "civil rights." Moreover, King would likely detect the racist implications of Jones's suggestion that illegal immigrants are somehow not as patriotic as "white Europeans." Jones's use of white immigrants, and not blacks who were forcibly brought to this country, as the standard for what it means to be truly patriotic, is really incomprehensible, and so is his critique of Elvira for complaining about the nation's mistreatment of illegals. As a prophet who boldly critiqued this nation for its mistreatment of the poor and outcast,[70] King would be most prone to think, feel, and act differently.

The issue of race apparently figures prominently in Jones's assessment of what King *would say* and *do* about illegal immigration. Although Latinos have been verbally and physically abused and occasionally killed by American immigration officials and members of hate groups, Jones would have us believe that King would determine that the nation's immigration policies are not *immoral, unjust,* and *racist.* King would be apt to judge such policies in these terms, Jones suggests, only if they benefit the illegals themselves, or those who break the law.[71] Jones appears to be oblivious to the fact that King

---

68. Ibid., 115, 120, and 122–23.

69. Martin Luther King Jr., "A Cry of Hate or a Cry for Help?," unpublished version of a statement (August, 1965), King Center Library and archives, 4; Martin Luther King Jr., "Revolution and Redemption," unpublished version of an address, the European Baptist Assembly, Amsterdam, Holland (16 August 1964), King Center Library and Archives, 9; and Baldwin, *The Voice of Conscience*, 92–93.

70. Baldwin, *There Is a Balm in Gilead*, 322–30.

71. Jones and Engel, *What Would Martin Say?*, 116–17.

always considered that which is moral to be ultimately more compelling than that which is defined as legal, and he judged his own actions in some cases to be supralegal. In any event, after making his observations about the morality, fairness, and nonracist character of the nation's immigration policies, Jones highlights the 9/11 attacks on America as justification for action against immigrants of color, some of whom, in his view, might actually be terrorists. He points to the several teenagers from Central America who, along with a Peruvian national, assaulted and robbed four black youngsters in an elementary school playground in Newark, New Jersey, and actually ended up killing three.[72] The tragedy is seemingly used to suggest something strange and quite unfavorable about illegal or undocumented immigrants of color in general. Jones's perspective is further complicated by his suggestion that deporting such persons, some of whom work very hard and are productive in the society, would hardly be a violation of human rights, let alone civil rights.[73]

Instead of calling upon African Americans to stand with illegal immigrants of color whose basic human rights are commonly violated, Jones urges his people to develop an action plan to stop those "who have no legal right to be here" from taking their jobs and gunning down young black men. Jones even raises the possibility of blacks organizing and protesting against the "sanctuary status" of illegals in major cities, while insisting that the mayors and city councils rescind them.[74] With the cities of this country becoming increasingly colored but not black, such actions could only lead to the spread of anti-immigrant fears and biases in black communities, and also new trends in the polarization and tension that exist between the growing ethnic populations in the central cities of America's metropolitan areas. The Southern Poverty Law Center in Montgomery, Alabama, which monitors hate groups in this country, is already reporting a rise in anti-immigrant propaganda among African Americans.[75] There is literally no credible way to associate King's legacy of ideas and activism with such insane and disturbing developments.

States like Arizona, South Carolina, and Alabama have recently passed some of the most restrictive laws in this country against illegal immigration. Some of these laws require immigrants to carry their papers at all times, evoking memories of similar requirements imposed on African American

72. Ibid., 118–19.
73. Ibid., 122–23.
74. Ibid., 124.
75. See Brentin Mock, "Smokescreen: Activists Say a Black Anti-Immigration Movement is Gathering Steam," *Intelligence Report of the Southern Poverty Law Center* 123 (Fall 2006) 18–24; and Baldwin, *The Voice of Conscience*, 239.

slaves and blacks under the South African apartheid regime. Schools are required to find out if students are in the country legally, and it is deemed illegal for undocumented workers to secure employment in public places. Warrantless arrests of suspected illegal immigrants are being encouraged, thus heightening the incidences of racial profiling to epidemic proportions.[76] This is largely the handiwork of right-wing conservatism, and it appears that Jones has uncritically embraced many of its ideas and much of its anti-immigration agenda. The true bearers of King's legacy are not the immigrant bashers, or conservative Supreme Court justices who uphold laws that encourages racial profiling in the case of immigrants. To the contrary, they are courageous men and women from every walk of life who take a stand against this nonsense. Some churches have already begun to make their voices heard, seeing this as a way to avoid repeating mistakes they made in the past when it came to people's basic human rights.[77] This is most certainly a hopeful sign, and yet another indication that King's dream still resonates in the hearts and minds of those determined to make America *be* America for all of her inhabitants.

---

76. Bob Johnson, "Ala. Law One-Ups Ariz. in Severity: Immigration Crackdown Requires Student Check," *The Tennessean* (June 10, 2011) 1A and 8A; Jay Reeves, "Hispanic Students Leave Ala. Schools, Fearing Law," *The Tennessean* (October 1, 2011) 4A; State Senator Jim Tracy, "Law to Punish Illegal Immigrants," *The Tennessean* (June 10, 2011) 12A; and Rachel Zoll, "Immigration Activist Focuses on Evangelicals," *The Tennessean* (August 14, 2011) 3B.

77. See Jay Reeves, "Ala. Churches Ready to Fight Immigration Law: Civil Rights Movement Was Call to Action," *The Tennessean* (July 14, 2011) 3A.

9

Nonviolence and a Moral Universe
What Martin Might Say about War and Terrorism

RUFUS BURROW JR.

Clarence B. Jones suggests that had Martin Luther King Jr. lived to witness the terrorist attacks on the United States on September 11, 2001, he would have softened his stance on nonviolence and counseled officials to go after the terrorists and destroy them. Moreover, he believes that King would be supportive of the war in Iraq, and that September 11, 2001, was a day of extreme emergencies and thus would have dictated a softening of King's stance on nonviolence. According to Jones, King was committed to a pragmatic nonviolence, not the absolute nonviolence to which King himself claimed to adhere.[1]

Was King's doctrine of nonviolence the pragmatic type that Jones writes about, (i.e., the type that one engages in only for as long as it works or achieves one's ends)? Or, was King's nonviolence a philosophy, creed, or way of life? This essay supports the latter position. In addition, the argument is made that although King began his civil rights career believing in a more pragmatic type of nonviolence and also abided by an ethic of self-defense, his position evolved through the guidance and counsel of Bayard Rustin and Glenn Smiley, as well as from day-to-day practice, to the much deeper conviction of nonviolence as a way of living and behaving in the world. By the time he reached this stance three or four months into the Montgomery bus boycott, King was no longer concerned about the workability or success

---

1. See Clarence B. Jones and Joel Engel, *What Would Martin Say?* (New York: HarperCollins, 2008), ch. 6.

of nonviolence. His conviction that the universe is fundamentally moral, along with his faith in the centrality of *agape*, led him to the firm belief that in a moral universe nonviolence is the only way. This basic point in King's philosophy seems to have eluded Clarence B. Jones.

In order to make his point that King's commitment was to a pragmatic nonviolence, Jones recalls overhearing a passionate conversation between two people at a cocktail party. The discussants included one who was not committed to nonviolence who wanted to know what the other, who was committed in an absolute sense, would do if he were present in a crowded mall and witnessed a madman with automatic weapons and a seemingly unlimited supply of ammunition randomly shooting children. If the only way to stop the man was to kill him, the questioner asks, would he suspend his commitment to nonviolence and take him out? When the man responded that he would not, and that he has no power to decide who lives and who dies, the inquisitor became furious and insisted that the right thing, the moral thing, to do in such a situation would be to kill the madman if one were able to do so. Although this too would involve the taking of life, it is seen as the lesser of the two evils, and this, Jones further contends, is what King would have concluded.

In one of a number of utterly fantastic claims in the book, Jones writes, "Faced with doing nothing or putting a bullet through the brain of Adolf Hitler in order to prevent the deaths of 50 million people, Martin might say to God, 'If not me, then who? If not now, then when?' To which God, seeing Martin pray for forgiveness, might answer, 'Martin, why do you think I gave you prescience and put you there with that gun?'"[2] He goes on to say parenthetically that when confronted with a scenario like this, King would have made an exception to "his otherwise unwavering commitment to nonviolence" and opted for the lesser of the two evils; namely, the elimination of Hitler.

It is true that as a seminary student, this option made enough sense to King that he supported it for a brief period. Had his ideas not changed since that time, it would be reasonable to agree with Jones's conclusion. However, we know that by 1958, King's commitment to nonviolence, whether on an individual or collective level, was absolute. Indeed, he was close to this position by the time of the Supreme Court ruling against Alabama's segregation codes in late 1956. Convinced of a moral obligation to resist evil, King would most assuredly have resisted Hitler and his henchmen, but he would have done so nonviolently, sacrificing his own life if necessary. Of course,

---

2. Jones and Engel, *What Would Martin Say?*, 165–66.

a real problem here is that giving up his life nonviolently would have left Hitler to continue the mass murders of human beings.

As for the discussion about the madman shooting children, and what the morally responsible person should be willing to do, Jones claims that had King been present he would have done all in his power to place himself between the gunman and the children. He would willingly have given his life in that situation. But Jones is not satisfied with this, and wonders what would have happened if King was not able to get close enough to make himself a human shield to protect the children. Would he have shot the man had he a gun, rather than merely pleading—unsuccessfully—that he drop his weapons and surrender? Jones wonders whether King would "have fired a righteous bullet—then prayed for the murderer's soul."[3] He contends further that in such a situation King would have concluded that it was indeed within his power to decide who lives and who dies. Jones then claims that King would add, "When you do nothing in the face of evil, you are indeed deciding who lives and dies."[4] But one wonders whether Jones is saying that King would have concluded that any nonviolent act, even presenting himself as a human shield for the children, would be the equivalent to doing nothing. For King's stance was not that of passive resistance, but nonviolent resistance to evil, which requires that one assert one's whole self against injustice. Therefore, to have intentionally made himself a human shield cannot be equated with doing nothing. But under the circumstances would that have been enough?

Indeed, I can even *imagine* King, if faced with a Hitler or the mad gunman, actually choosing to take them out if nonviolent measures failed, and deadly force was at his immediate disposal. But because of his conviction about the morality of the universe and his commitment to nonviolence as a way of life, such a decision would have been devastating for him, much like it was for Dietrich Bonhoeffer, when he participated in the failed plot to assassinate Hitler. Like Bonhoeffer, King was a staunch believer that all persons, including the Adolf Hitlers of the world, belong to the One God of the universe.

There is evidence that Bonhoeffer grieved long and hard over what he did all the way to the gallows, not certain that God had forgiven him, even though the attempt on Hitler's life had failed. This is a crucial point that Jones fails to consider when he suggests that under certain circumstances King would not only relax his commitment to nonviolence as a way of life, but would even take another life. For even in such a case, King would have

3. Ibid., 166.
4. Ibid.

grieved every bit as much as Bonhoeffer did, and possibly more. I therefore find it to be a major omission that Jones makes no reference to the Christian teaching that to kill a human being, for whatever reason, is a sin before God. This point takes on even more significance for King since he believed in nonviolence as a way of life, which meant that under no circumstance would he take a human life. It would be a sin against God to do so.

As noted previously, King would not be afraid to resist, but he would do so in nonviolent ways. He would not engage in violence, nor would he take a life. What he would do, however, is to give his own life to protect innocents. Of course, he could give his life for the innocents and they might be killed anyway, but he would have died living the nonviolent faith. The far deeper point about nonviolent campaigns for King was not to win or be successful, but to be obedient and faithful to this way of life. Nonviolence of this type is at bottom a faith act. Even if a specific nonviolent campaign fails to achieve its immediate goal, the proponents will have made the effort and remained committed to the nonviolent faith.

Jones imagines leaving his family in King's care. He imagines further that were the family attacked by gunmen, he would not return to his home to find his wife and children all dead and King alive proclaiming that his nonviolent stance forbade him to take deadly action against the attackers. Jones seems to be convinced that King would have retaliated even to the point of using violence to try to save the family. The issue here is not whether King would have resisted. He would have! But contrary to the claim of Jones, his resistance would have been of the nonviolent variety. And more so, under the imagined circumstances of whether he resisted violently or nonviolently, what Jones would have likely discovered on his return was dead family members and a dead Martin Luther King Jr. Jones does not come close to making his case that King was not committed absolutely to nonviolence.

Jones is grossly mistaken in this and related claims about King and the use of violence under special circumstances. For by the time the two men met, King had already been consistently rejecting violence of any kind, whether by the demonstrators advocating for social change, by oppressors trying to prevent it, or even for self-defense. In fact, we will see that this was one of the most significant ways in which King's view of non-cooperation campaigns against social injustice differed from Henry David Thoreau, whose commitment to nonviolence in such campaigns was not absolute. At least this is the sense that one gets from Thoreau's speech, "A Plea for Captain John Brown," after Brown's assault on the federal weapons arsenal at

Harper's Ferry in Virginia in 1859.[5] At any rate, King wrote that during his student days at Morehouse College, he was much influenced by Thoreau's "Essay on Civil Disobedience," especially by his emphasis on the *obligation to noncooperate with evil* and his focus on the *idea of a "creative minority"* contributing substantially to the achievement of social justice, which quite likely is how King thought of the black church at its best—a creative minority making for good and contributing to the establishment of the beloved community.

Claims such as those made by Clarence Jones can be made and sustained only by one who fails to understand King's doctrine of nonviolence as a philosophy or way of life, and the fact that throughout his ministry he was not merely a Christian social activist, but a man of deep theological, ethical, and philosophical ideas. Often people seem to forget that King was the recipient of the PhD degree in systematic theology and was an excellent thinker. Consequently, there was from the beginning an ongoing interplay and dialectical relation between King's best thinking and his sense of what needed to be done to achieve the beloved community. King was never *only* a social activist. He was in the best sense a theologian and thinker who persistently sought to put into practice his best ideas of what the God of his faith required of him in the world.

In order to support my stance that Jones did not have an adequate understanding of either basic theological-philosophical ideas that grounded King's thought and social activism, or even his ethic of nonviolent resistance to evil, I briefly address the following themes: 1) Heritage of Resistance against Social Injustice; 2) The Universe Hinges on a Moral Foundation; 3) From Just War Theory and Self-Defense to Nonviolence; 4) Nonviolence as a Way of Life; and 5) The Sixth Commandment: "You shall not kill" or "You shall not murder." Consideration of these themes will also provide a strong argument against Jones's insinuation that King would support the United States' violent tactics against the 911 terrorists, and that he would be a supporter of the war in Afghanistan and the ongoing conflict in Iraq.

From the time he was a boy, King spoke of wanting to do what he could to help his father address and eradicate racial injustice. This spirit of resistance to social injustice was deeply rooted in his family lineage. His formal theological study helped to ground an already bourgeoning social conscience.

---

5. Henry David Thoreau, "A Plea for Captain John Brown." Online: http://www.africa.upenn.edu/articles_Gen/Plea_Captain_Brown.html/.

Familial Heritage of Resistance to Social Injustice

From both the maternal and paternal sides of his family, King inherited a tradition of resistance against racial injustice. However, *nonviolent resistance* to injustice can be equated only with the maternal side. King's paternal grandparents, James Albert King and Delia Lindsay King, were not predisposed to nonviolence. Like many poor black men in the Deep South of his day, James King knew that lashing out against the system that dehumanized him and his family could have deadly consequences for himself and/or family members. He therefore internalized his anger and frustrations, turned to heavy alcoholic consumption, and too often engaged in the verbal and physical abuse of his wife. However, although James King did not retaliate against the system of racial injustice as such, he did not hesitate to confront white men who threatened to harm his children.[6] Although devoutly religious and dependent on prayer to help her through (unlike her husband), Delia King was no less hesitant to physically attack white people who caused harm to her children.[7] Although it cannot be said that Martin Luther King Jr. inherited the spirit of nonviolence from his paternal grandparents, they unquestionably passed on to him the spirit of protest and resistance.

King's maternal grandparents, Adam D. Williams and Jennie C. Parks Williams, not only passed on to him a legacy of resistance to injustice, but resistance of the nonviolent type. Since he was a little over a year old when A. D. Williams died, King had no recollection of him and his contributions to blacks' struggle in the South. King learned about his grandfather through his grandmother and mother. Since his grandmother lived with them before dying when he was about twelve, King had easy access to stories about his grandfather's contributions as a highly respected social gospel minister and civil rights leader.

A charter member of the local NAACP and its president, Williams was both courageous and determined to speak out for blacks' rights and even led a nonviolent organized boycott of businesses in Atlanta that supported the racist newspaper, *The Georgian*. This effort led to the demise of the newspaper. He also provided leadership against a proposal for a tax increase that made no provision for the construction of a high school for black children. Lewis V. Baldwin has written that throughout his tenure as

---

6. Daddy King writes of one such instance in *Daddy King: An Autobiography* with Clayton Riley (New York: Morrow, 1980), 35–36. See also Rufus Burrow Jr., *Martin Luther King Jr. for Armchair Theologians* (Louisville: Westminster John Knox, 2009), 27–28.

7. See *Daddy King*, 32–35. See also Rufus Burrow Jr., *Martin Luther King Jr. for Armchair Theologians*, 29–30.

pastor of Ebenezer Baptist Church, Williams "vigorously pursued his vision of a better day for his people, and in doing so provided broad shoulders on which later generations in his family could stand."[8] Young King therefore learned from his parents and grandmother about a clear legacy of an outstanding courageous protest tradition in his family lineage that dated back to the time of his maternal great-grandfather, the Reverend Willis Williams, an enslaved preacher on a Georgia plantation.

Young King learned much from his maternal grandmother and his mother about the importance of being a good listener and of exhibiting Christian love and compassion toward others, including one's enemy. Such values proved to be of inestimable worth in his relations with people in every aspect of his civil rights work. These also aided in helping him to avoid hating those who sought in various ways to crush the humanity and dignity of his people.

Whereas he only heard about the protest tradition inherited from his paternal and maternal grandparents, King had firsthand knowledge and experience of his father's resistance against both personal injustices as well as attempts to protest large-scale injustices. King wrote of his father's resistance against the insults of a white police officer, and of his refusal to go to the back of a shoe store to be served by a salesman. He recalled his father stating passionately that he would never passively accept such treatment and the system that spawned and supported it.[9] In addition, Daddy King led the fight for equal pay for teachers in Atlanta, and was in the forefront of the fight to eliminate segregated elevators in the courthouse there.

When circuit judge William A. Jenkins issued a court injunction the day before Good Friday in 1963, enjoining King and the SCLC to march in Birmingham, he decided that just as he was morally obligated to disobey unjust laws, so too was he obligated to disobey the unjust use of the courts, a habitual practice of the judicial system in the Deep South. The judicial system was in violation of the 1954 landmark ruling in *Brown v. Board of Education of Topeka, Kansas*, and thus in violation of the Constitution. When King decided to disobey the injunction and to march anyway, Daddy King urged him to comply. Interestingly, upon King's refusal, Daddy King reportedly responded: "Well, you didn't get this nonviolence from me. You must have got it from your Mama."[10] It is difficult to know whether

8. Lewis V. Baldwin, *There Is a Balm in Gilead: The Cultural Roots of Martin Luther King Jr.* (Minneapolis: Fortress, 1991), 95.

9. Martin Luther King Jr., *Stride toward Freedom* (New York: Harper & Row, 1958), 19–20.

10. Quoted in Taylor Branch, *Parting the Waters: America in the King Years 1954–63* (New York: Simon & Schuster, 1988), 730.

this was anything more than an emotional outburst by a concerned parent, especially since he had never used violence (nor would he) as a method of protesting injustice. However, it is fair to say that Daddy King was not among the small number of people in this country who were committed to nonviolence as a way of life. Nevertheless, it was to Daddy King that King Jr. attributed his own strong determination to work unrelentingly for justice and the eradication of racism.[11]

For King, the highest moral law is *agape* love, which for him is at the core of the universe. Thus, King's doctrine of nonviolence is motivated by and grounded in Christian *agape*, the spontaneous, unmotivated, unselfish, overflowing, and unceasing love of God. Consequently, the love given by the Christian is that which she has received from God. Such a love has no place for violence. As King's own understanding of *agape* matured, he came to understand this, which is why he placed it at the center of his philosophy of nonviolence. Unfortunately, Clarence Jones fails to grasp this point, which is also a reason that he makes misleading and false statements about King's nonviolence and what he would and would not support.

Space limitations prevent addressing the significance of more than one of the most fundamental ideas on which King grounded his theology, social ethics, and philosophy of nonviolence. Here I want to briefly address his staunch and oft repeated conviction that the universe itself is essentially moral, which implies that life—particularly human life—functions best when lived in conjunction with moral law, or the law of love.

The Conviction that the Universe Hinges on a Moral Foundation

King was a man of ideas and ideals, and this was one of King's most basic and important convictions. One must understand this idea if she wishes to grasp the true significance of King's theological social ethics generally, and his doctrine of nonviolence as a way of life in particular. Only when one understands his conviction that the universe is essentially moral is it possible to understand why he would not suspend nonviolence under any circumstance, regardless of what Clarence Jones says. For what was important to King was that human beings comply with God's expectation that justice be done. But the means to this end was also of utmost importance to him. More than anything else, this was dictated by how he understood God as Love, and how he understood God's way of working in the world.

---

11. Clayborne Carson, ed., *The Autobiography of Martin Luther King Jr.* (New York: Warner, 1998), 3.

As the source, enhancer, and sustainer of love and value, God expects that human actions will be characterized not by violence and the destruction of life—most especially human life—but by love and nonviolence. One does not exhibit respect for the humanity and dignity of the other by perpetrating violence against him. Rather, Love necessarily implies a policy of no harm, or what Gandhi called *Ahimsa*, toward either self or the other. If, as King liked to say, love makes the world go round, is at the center of the universe, and is "the most durable power in the world,"[12] then violence has no place in the world.

Only nonviolence and making the most of self and the other is consistent with the faith that the universe hinges on a moral foundation. One who lives by such a deep faith and who understands, as the prophets Ezekiel, Malachi, and Martin Luther King did, that all life belongs to God who is the Creator-Parent of all persons (Ezekiel 18:4, Malachi 2:10), *might* succumb to participating in a scheme to violently eliminate another human being who is known to brutally destroy human life on a massive scale. *However*, such a one would do so confessionally and with extreme heaviness of conscience and heart. Indeed, she would, like Bonhoeffer, live the remainder of her life wondering whether God would forgive her. Even though the plot against Hitler failed, Bonhoeffer knew that because all life belongs to God, it is a sin to abuse or destroy human life—or want to—even Adolf Hitler. Bonhoeffer could reason, as many did, that under the horrific circumstance of the Jewish Holocaust, such an action was necessary; was a wrong that was intended to prevent even graver wrongs; was the *right* thing to do, even if it could not be said that it was the *good* thing to do. And yet, who among we humans is morally positioned to determine the social uselessness of another human being? Surely human life consists of more than its instrumentality to society, Bonhoeffer believed. Accordingly, he declared that, "life, created and preserved by God, possesses an inherent right which is wholly independent of its social utility." Bonhoeffer went on to say: "The right to live is a matter of the essence and not of any values. In the sight of God there is no life that is not worth living; for life itself is valued by God. The fact that God is the Creator, Preserver, and Redeemer of life makes even the most wretched life worth living before God."[13]

Eliminating Hitler was without question the lesser of two evils. And yet the radical nature of the Christian love ethic and the idea that the universe is grounded on morality is such that the believer is required in

12. King, "Paul's Letter to American Christians," in *Strength to Love* (New York: Harper & Row, 1963), 133.

13. Dietrich Bonhoeffer, "The Value of a Life," in *The Martyred Christian* selected and edited by Joan Winmill Brown (New York: Macmillan, 1983), 118.

every situation not to do the lesser of two evils but to comply with God's expectations. When one acts contrary to this, one must be willing to bear the responsibility, guilt, and cost of his actions. Refusing to do so lands one in contradiction to his responsibility. "Here again it is precisely in the responsible acceptance of guilt that a conscience which is bound solely to Christ will best prove its innocence."[14] So Bonhoeffer himself admitted that his action was a sin before God, and thus threw himself on the mercy of God. He sought not to defend his actions in the conspiracy but only to take responsibility for them.[15] As individuals and nations we may—indeed often do—fail to behave nonviolently. When we do fail, we should admit our sin and failure before God, rather than try to justify or excuse our actions.

To say that the universe hinges on a moral foundation means not only that it rotates on such a foundation. It means also that the universe depends on that foundation for its continuation. So King insisted on the need to "believe in the ultimate morality of the universe ... and that all reality hinges on moral foundations."[16] This came to mean for him that in such a universe means and ends must cohere, i.e., that the means must be consistent and coherent with the end(s) sought, because the end is preexistent in the means. King was adamant that at the end of the day destructive means cannot bring about enduring constructive ends. If the end sought is justice, the means must cohere with it. Indeed, for King the doctrine of nonviolent resistance to evil is "the philosophy which says that the means must be as pure as the end, that in the long run of history, immoral and destructive means cannot bring about moral and constructive ends."[17] While violence seeks to destroy the other, nonviolence seeks to redeem or reconcile her. Violence may bring about temporary, but not lasting justice. According to King, only nonviolence can do that, a point to which we return subsequently.

To say that the universe is grounded in morality is to suggest that good and justice will have the last say in the world. This fosters a sense of optimism about what is possible, and it also assures the nonviolent resister to evil that she is not alone but has cosmic companionship in the struggle. Nonviolence as a policy "is based on the conviction that the universe is on

---

14. Bonhoeffer, *Ethics*, ed. Eberhard Bethge (New York: Macmillan, 1955), 214.

15. Eberhard Bethge, *Dietrich Bonhoeffer: A Biography*, rev. ed. (Minneapolis: Fortress, 2000), 829–30.

16. King, "A Christmas Sermon on Peace," in *A Testament of Hope: The Essential Writings of Martin Luther King Jr.* ed. James M. Washington (New York: Harper & Row, 1986), 257.

17. King, "Love, Law, and Civil Disobedience," in ibid., 45.

the side of justice,"[18] and that it favors love over hate, nonviolence over violence, optimism over pessimism, etc.

From Just War Theory and Self-Defense to Nonviolence

As noted earlier, Martin Luther King Jr. did not begin his civil rights ministry as one who was committed to absolute nonviolence. Even though he read Thoreau's famous essay at Morehouse College and was first introduced to Gandhian ideas there, he was not able at that time to see their true value for the social struggle in the United States. This would not happen until he met Bayard Rustin and Glenn Smiley approximately two months into the Montgomery bus boycott, early in 1956.

During his seminary days, King rejected the absolute pacifist position and essentially accepted the just-war stance of a number of his professors. During the second semester of the 1950–51 schoolyear, King took Kenneth L. Smith's course in Christianity and Society. In an unsigned essay, "War and Pacifism," often attributed to King, there is a staunch declaration against absolute pacifism because the author believed that it logically leads to anarchy. Furthermore, the author said it does not allow for a police force, nor does it take seriously enough the fact of sin, which he believed to be "the most serious criticism" of the absolute pacifist position.[19] King acknowledged that while in seminary he adopted the just-war stance for a period of time.[20] King came to reject this stance over time, a fact that seems to elude

18. King, "Nonviolence and Racial Justice," in ibid., 9.

19. In their note regarding the authorship of the essay in question the editors of the first volume of *The Papers of Martin Luther King Jr.* write, "Whether or not King was the author of this essay, the views presented herein are consistent with those he expressed in *Stride toward Freedom*. The author of "War and Pacifism" criticizes "absolute pacifism" on the grounds that it ignores the essentially sinful side of human nature and the need for coercion to avoid anarchy. The author questions the applicability of Gandhi's example to the world: 'That Gandhi was successful against the British is no reason that the Russians would react the same way.' This argument reflects both King's class notes on Smith's lectures and the assigned readings of Reinhold Niebuhr's works" [Clayborne Carson et al., ed., *The Papers of Martin Luther King Jr.* (Berkeley: University of California Press, 1992) 1:433)]. Although the author of the essay did not mention Reinhold Niebuhr and his Christian realism, his emphasis on the prevalence of sin among individuals and nations and the need for coercion to keep them in check is quite evident (and it is known that King was much influenced by Niebuhr while in seminary). In one passage the author writes: "It seems to me that we must recognize the presence of sin in man and that it can be done without [sic] seeing that there is also good. Since man is so often sinful there must be some coercion to keep one man from injuring his fellows. This is just as true between nations as it is between individuals." See ibid., 1:435.

20. King, *Stride toward Freedom*, 95.

Jones, who claims that given the scenario of the madman indiscriminately shooting children in a crowded mall, King "would have to choose between the most moral of the two actions."[21]

By the time King was voted president of the Montgomery Improvement Association (MIA) to lead the bus boycott, he had not worked out a systematic stance on the violence vs. nonviolence question. There is no evidence of Gandhian language during the early weeks of the boycott, only of the language and spirit of the love ethic of the Sermon on the Mount. But in addition, King did not initially see the contradiction between this ethic and the ethic of self-defense that appealed to so many in the Deep South. Constitutionally, one had a right to bear arms, and it was taken for granted that people have a right to self-defense and the defense—even through use of deadly force—of their families and homes.

In addition, blacks in the South had even more reason to adhere to an ethic of self-defense. Their well-being and safety were often threatened by members of the Ku Klux Klan and other racist individuals and groups. Moreover, they could not depend on the local police force for protection, nor could they depend on the courts to prosecute such violent racists. Therefore, as a matter of course, many blacks adhered to an ethic of self-defense. Upon returning to the South, King was no different. The turn the other cheek ethic of the Sermon on the Mount was fine as the regulating principle of the organized boycotters. However, when it came to the defense of one's self, family, and home, that was an altogether different matter, requiring a different regulating principle. This is why early in the boycott King himself saw no problem with having armed guards around his house. Indeed, Bayard Rustin even reported seeing a pistol on a chair in King's house not long after they met.[22]

Shortly after meeting Rustin and Glenn Smiley, King fairly quickly rejected the ethic of self-defense in favor of Gandhian principles. Rustin spent many hours in conversation with him about Gandhian principles and techniques. Smiley provided him with a number of books by and about Gandhi. Not long thereafter, sometime in 1956, King was finished with self-defense of any kind that was predicated on a violent response. He also made it clear that he was finished with the war business, on both moral and practical grounds. He was convinced that the destruction of human life on any scale was both sinful and a denial of the fundamental sacredness of persons. In addition, he believed that the destructive capability of bombs and missiles

---

21. Jones and Engel, *What Would Martin Say?*, 165.
22. Bayard Rustin, *The Reminiscences of Bayard Rustin* (New York: Columbia University Oral History Research Office, 1988), 139.

was such that no nation could win a war. In addition, King recognized that we humans now possess the military capability to destroy all life as we know it. By 1958, he had advanced to the conviction that the choice is no longer between violence and nonviolence, but between nonviolence and nonexistence.[23]

King knew that ordinarily people will instinctively protect home and family, but this alone, he held, fails to "provide any positive approach to the fears and conditions which produce violence."[24] Rather than engage in self-defense during nonviolent demonstrations, as members of the Congress of Racial Equality (CORE) were wont to do,[25] King insisted on the Gandhian principle that it is far better for the nonviolent demonstrator to accept blows without retaliating. "When violence is tolerated even as a means of self-defense," he said, "there is grave danger that in the fervor of emotion the main fight will be lost over the question of self-defense."[26] In the end, King concluded that violence, even of the self-defensive type, creates many more problems than it solves.[27] Thus he sought to be a consistent proponent of absolute nonviolence.

Nonviolence as a Way of Life

By the end of the Montgomery bus boycott, King's thinking about violence and nonviolence had evolved substantially. When he began as leader of the bus boycott, he was committed to nonviolence as a strategy or technique for social change. By the time the boycott ended, he was committed to the idea of pure nonviolence or nonviolence as a way of life. He was by this time moving toward the conviction of nonviolence as an absolute in all situations. King was convinced that the aim of this type of nonviolence is the establishment of the beloved community,[28] that community in which the humanity and dignity of every person is respected and honored as a matter

---

23. King, *Stride toward Freedom*, 224.

24. King, "Nonviolence: The Only Road to Freedom," in Washington, ed., *A Testament of Hope*, 56.

25. See Floyd McKissick's response to panel member Lawrence E. Spivak in *Meet the Press* television news interview, in Washington, ed., *A Testament of Hope*, 389. Here McKissick made it clear that CORE demonstrators are nonviolent as long as onlookers are, but if the demonstrators are attacked they will defend themselves.

26. King, "Nonviolence: The Only Road to Freedom," in Washington, ed., *A Testament of Hope*, 57.

27. Ibid., 58.

28. King, *Stride toward Freedom*, 102.

of course, and where every person shares equitably in the bounties of God's creation.

King declared after his trip to India in 1959 that he was even more convinced that nonviolent resistance is the most potent weapon available to an oppressed people struggling against racial and other forms of social injustice.[29] The fact is that by the end of the bus boycott, he was convinced that nonviolence had won a special place in the hearts of black participants.[30] This did not mean, however, that the majority of such persons were committed to the type of nonviolence to which King adhered.

Kingian and Gandhian nonviolence is not dependent on either the attitude or moral sensibility of the opponent, nor is it dependent upon the success of specific nonviolent resistance campaigns. What matters is the relentless effort to live the nonviolent faith, and the conviction that the nature of the universe itself sides with those who adhere to such an approach. In this regard, no nonviolent campaign can be said to actually fail. In addition, nonviolence does not work miracles overnight, nor does it easily lead to changes in the hearts of opponents. But, said King, it does do something to the hearts and souls of proponents, giving them a new sense of purpose, self-worth, and self-respect.[31]

In an interview on *Front Page Challenge*, dated April 28, 1959, King acknowledged that he had gotten his ideas about nonviolence from Jesus and Gandhi. On this point he said: "My whole Christian background had a great deal to do with my coming to this conclusion that love and nonviolence should be the regulating ideals in any struggle for human dignity." He went on to say: "And along with this, I read Mahatma Gandhi in my student days and got a great deal from him."[32] But this statement is misleading. It is known that while in seminary, King drove to Philadelphia to hear Mordecai Johnson, then president of Howard University, speak on Gandhi at Philadelphia's Fellowship House during the spring quarter of his junior year, and afterward claimed to have hurriedly gone out and purchased about a half dozen books by and about Gandhi. King implies that he read these voraciously. The truth, however, is that it is not known just how much he actually read and retained about Gandhi throughout the remainder of his formal theological and philosophical studies. The problem with what King said is that during the term that he went to hear Johnson speak, he was

---

29. King, "My Trip to the Land of Gandhi," in Washington, ed., *A Testament of Hope*, 25.

30. King, *Stride toward Freedom*, 161.

31. Ibid., 219.

32. Carson, et al., eds., *The Papers of Martin Luther King Jr.*, 5:193.

enrolled in five courses, one as an Audit. This was a heavy academic load. My own experience as a seminary and graduate student, as well as my experience teaching in a seminary for nearly thirty years, suggests to me that it is unlikely that King read (let alone retained!) much about Gandhi when he purchased those books. My judgment might be different had he pursued a systematic study of Gandhi as a doctoral student at Boston University. Instead, we find that although a seminar on Gandhi was offered during King's doctoral studies at Boston, he failed to enroll in it.[33] It is true that systematic theology was the focus of his doctoral program, and it might be argued that generally a student in such a program would not take many courses in social ethics. This sounds reasonable until it is remembered that King, beginning in seminary, essentially wanted to gain two things from formal theological studies: 1) a *formal* theological rationale for his already well-developed social conscience, and 2) a method for addressing and eradicating racism and other forms of social injustice.[34] King's reading and study of Walter Rauschenbusch and other white social gospelers provided the formal theological rationale. His brief introduction to Gandhi's doctrine of nonviolent resistance provided the method, although he would not know this in the deepest sense until eight weeks into the Montgomery bus boycott. My point here is that it is difficult to believe that King was no longer interested in such things during his doctoral studies. Because of his ongoing desire to address the race question after his formal studies, it would not have been unusual for him to enroll in the seminar on Gandhi. And yet he did not.

It is difficult to pinpoint with accuracy the precise incident, occasion, or period when King had a turning point experience with nonviolence that suggested that it was the moment that he evidenced a commitment to pure nonviolence. He surely believed that Gandhi, unlike the Indian ruler

---

33. See editors' note in Carson et al., eds., *The Papers of Martin Luther King Jr.*, 2:8 n30, where we find that King not only passed over the opportunity to take a course on Gandhi, but also on Social Christianity, Methods of Changing Social Attitudes, and Christianity and Race Relations.

34. I emphasize "formal" because King was already committed to the social gospel by the time he arrived at Crozer Theological Seminary, a point that is consistent with his claim during his first term when he proclaimed that he was a staunch advocate of the social gospel (Carson et al. eds., *The Papers of Martin Luther King*, 6:72). This must mean that King already possessed some semblance of a theological rationale for his stance, for he had not yet studied the social gospel at Crozer. In any case, what might have been lacking before he arrived at Crozer was a formal theological language to express his social gospelism. This was provided by his study of Rauschenbusch and other social gospelers.

Jawaharlal Nehru, was a proponent of absolute nonviolence.[35] But when did King actually arrive at this deepest form of nonviolence?

Taylor Branch writes of the incident in which King was physically attacked on stage by a member of the American Nazi Party during an integrated SCLC convention in Birmingham, Alabama, in September 1962. This might be the incident, or the one that comes closest to King's watershed experience regarding nonviolence. King was on stage giving some final announcements when Roy James, a white man in the audience, walked up and struck him flush on the left cheek with his fist. The force of the blow caused him to stagger and nearly lose his balance. Before others figured out that this was not a "sociodrama" or staged demonstration from the nonviolent workshops that were so popular, the man had struck King several more times. Taylor Branch reports that,

> After being knocked backward by one of the last blows, King turned to face him while dropping his hands. It was the look on his face that many would not forget. Septima Clark, who nursed many private complaints about the strutting ways of the SCLC preachers and would not have been shocked to see the unloosed rage of an exalted leader, marveled instead at King's transcendent calm. King dropped his hands 'like a newborn baby,' she said, and from then on she never doubted that his nonviolence was more than the heat of his oratory or the result of his slow calculation. It was the response of his quickest instincts. This impression struck a number of others, including perhaps the assailant himself, who stared at King long enough for Wyatt Walker and some of the others to jump between them.[36]

King would allow no one to "touch" or harm the man, insisting instead that they should pray for him. In addition, he refused to press charges when the police arrived. I do not know whether Jones was present that day. Had he been, I wonder whether his reaction would have been similar to that of Septima Clark's.

From this point forward it was clear to all who really knew King that he was absolutely committed to nonviolence, and that he would permit no suspension of this, either by himself or by his closest followers. Indeed in 1966 he declared: "Occasionally in life one develops a conviction so precious and meaningful that he will stand on it till the end. This is what I have found in nonviolence."[37] He was certain that nonviolence was a power greater than

---

35. Carson, et al., eds., *The Papers of Martin Luther King Jr.*, 5:194.
36. Branch, *Parting the Waters*, 654.
37. Carson, ed., *The Autobiography of Martin Luther King Jr.*, 331.

any form of violence. While planning for the Poor People's Campaign in 1967, King met with SCLC staffers and black militants Stokely Carmichael, H. Rap Brown, and others to work out a peace agreement. When executive director William Rutherford seemed to accommodate the militants' stance against nonviolence, King went ballistic. He felt that Rutherford and other staffers were actually flirting "with separatist black liberation, itself a violation of nonviolence as unifying and all-inclusive, as breaking down walls."[38] King particularly went after Rutherford after the meeting.[39] He knew that if his staffers questioned nonviolent principles and practice, there would be little reason to expect that others would follow the nonviolent path.

Like Gandhi, King was never naïve enough to believe that more than a "creative minority" (Henry David Thoreau's term) would subscribe to nonviolence as a way of life. The vast majority of people devoted to struggling against injustice adhere to the doctrine of pragmatic nonviolence, the type that Clarence Jones erroneously attributes to King. In any event, when it becomes apparent to pragmatic nonviolent resisters that nonviolence is not delivering the expected results, they are ready to turn to another method. However, the advocate of pure nonviolence does not, under any circumstance, deviate from the path. This is what King himself modeled, and this is what he expected, and indeed demanded, from his staff.

One for whom nonviolence is the philosophy of life will not embrace violence even to save the United States from (either external or internal) terrorists. We have already seen that for such a one, nonviolence reflects the very nature of the universe and vice versa. Since God is the Creator, it is also appropriate to say that nonviolence reflects the very nature of God; namely, God as *Agape*, as suggested by the Second Testament (cf. 1 John 4:16).

Rather than participate in, or contribute to, violence, the proponent of absolute nonviolence will, like King did on that Birmingham stage, simply submit, or, as he did in Memphis nearly six years later, simply give his life while struggling to overcome injustice. Such a one will *always* resist evil or injustice, but *only* nonviolently, preferring to receive, rather than inflict blows. This, in part, is what King meant when he characterized himself as "militantly nonviolent,"[40] and insisted in the last weeks of his life on the need to retain "a spirit of unshakable nonviolence."[41]

---

38. See Stewart Burns, *To the Mountaintop: Martin Luther King Jr.'s Sacred Mission to Save America 1955–1968* (New York: HarperSanFrancisco, 2004), 416.

39. Ibid., 395.

40. See *Playboy* Interview: Martin Luther King Jr., in Washington, ed., *A Testament of Hope*, 348.

41. King, "A Testament of Hope," in Ibid., 328.

King was a realist, and therefore he understood perfectly that governments will always have to grapple with the option of violence, whether war, capital punishment, or the use of deadly police force. But as a man of deep religious faith and conviction, he was even more certain that the stance of the believer and the church must be clear and understandable to both young and old; namely, that they must oppose any and all violence. It is this to which the Christian must ever be faithful, and few people understood and were more committed to it than King, who would agree wholeheartedly with Walter Wink's insistence on the need for the church to be unequivocally clear about its stance on violence, no matter what governments, theologians, ethicists, and others may say and do: "Governments will still wrestle with the option of war, and ethicists can perhaps assist them with their decisions. But the church's own witness should be understandable by the smallest child: *we oppose violence in all its forms*. And we do so because we reject domination."[42] The only option for Christians is what Wink characterizes as "Jesus' Third Way," i.e., the way of absolute nonviolence.[43] *This was the stance of Martin Luther King Jr.*

The Sixth Commandment

Despite the foregoing discussion, Jones looks to the Hebrew Bible to find support for his claim that, depending on the situation, King would suspend his commitment to nonviolence as a way of life. Aware that King was a strong student of the Bible, Jones insists that he rejected the "You shall not kill" translation of the Sixth Commandment (Exodus 20:13) for the "You shall not murder" translation. This is a strange statement since King, on more than one occasion, quoted the "Thou shall not kill" translation of the text. Indeed, filling in for her recently slain husband before a crowd of peace supporters in New York City's Central Park, Coretta Scott King said that on scribbled notes on scraps of paper pulled from her dead husband's pockets was found his "10 Commandments on Vietnam." She surmised that these might have been notes for the speech he was to deliver to them. The tenth Commandment said: "Thou shall not kill."[44] King was not willing to leave a moral opening for killing, whether by individuals or the state. For him all

---

42. Walter Wink, *Engaging the Powers: Discernment and Resistance in a World of Domination* (Minneapolis: Fortress, 1992), 229 (italics added).

43. Ibid., chapter 9, "Jesus' Third Way: Nonviolent Engagement."

44. Coretta Scott King, "10 Commandments on Vietnam," http://www.americanrhetoric.com/speeches/corettascottkingvietnamcommandments.htm/.

human life belongs to and is precious to God, including the Adolf Hitlers of times past and present in every nation of the world.

Consistent with his personalism and doctrine of human dignity, King reiterated the "Thou shall not kill" theme in "A Christmas Sermon on Peace" in December 1967, saying: "And when we say 'Thou shalt not kill,' we're really saying that human life is too sacred to be taken on the battlefields of the world . . . And when we truly believe in the sacredness of human personality, we won't exploit people, we won't trample over people with iron feet of oppression, we won't kill anybody."[45] If we truly believe in the inviolable sacredness of human beings; if we live by the commandment: "Thou shall not Kill," we will not kill human beings under any circumstance. But if we ever do, we will quickly confess our sin before God, and with extreme heaviness of heart beg God's mercy and forgiveness.

Nevertheless, Clarence Jones contends that the Commandment in question forbids murder, not killing as such. "As written in Hebrew, not the mistranslation codified by the King James Bible," Jones writes, "*lo tirtzach* refers to the act of murder, defined as unlawful and unjustified killing. Had the commandment been written to avoid all killings, it would have said *lo taharog*."[46] Furthermore, Jones maintains that having studied under expert scholars on the Bible, King would not use this or any of the Commandments "or God himself as an argument against fighting in general," as this "would be as intellectually dishonest as quoting Jesus to bolster a prohibition on wine."[47]

If Clarence Jones fully understood King as a man of ideas and as an excellent thinker committed to the personalist idea of coherence as the chief test of truth, he would know that what he claims about the civil rights leader is flawed. King was, by his own admission, unequivocally committed to the philosophy of personalism, including its method and criterion of truth—*growing empirical coherence*. He believed that in the quest for truth one begins and ends with self-experience. But in the process of seeking truth or knowledge, one must be open and committed to examining all of the relevant and available evidence. Having collected and examined such evidence, one is then bound to analyze the individual pieces of evidence, as well as to seek to organize or orchestrate the most relevant and important of these into a symphonic whole. One's ultimate criterion in the search for truth about anything is coherence, which literally means "a sticking together

---

45. King, "A Christmas Sermon on Peace," in Washington, ed., *A Testament of Hope*, 255.

46. Jones and Engel, *What Would Martin Say?*, 152.

47. Ibid.

whole." Upon arriving at "truth" one cannot be totally satisfied, since she knows that human beings are not omniscient, and the facts of experience are never all in. Consequently, one who adheres to personalist method, as King did, knows that in the quest for truth and knowledge the best we humans can hope to achieve are most reasonable hypotheses based on the best evidence available at the time. With the advent of new evidence and facts, it will be necessary to alter one's hypothesis. The search for truth and knowledge, then, always has a dynamic quality about it.

There is no question that while in seminary, King was exposed to some of the top biblical scholars of the day. He learned much about exegetical method and how best to interpret Scripture. However, Jones fails to see that King would have also learned that one cannot interpret Scripture or anything else in a vacuum; that whether one admits it or not, her theological and philosophical presuppositions, as well as her social context and politics, have bearing on how she interprets Scripture.

A major difficulty with Jones's claim that King would reject the "You shall not kill" translation for "You shall not murder" is that it does not square with two of King's fundamental theological convictions: 1) that of the ultimate morality of the universe and the idea that all of reality is fused with value; and 2) the idea that nonviolence is more than a strategy, more than that which one subscribes to only as long as one can get the expected results. More specifically, nonviolence is not a pragmatic option, and its relevance does not depend on the "success" of individual noncooperation campaigns. Nonviolence for King was, pure and simple, a way of life and the only option available to those who believe in the fundamental morality of the universe. In addition, he lived by the conviction that violence is contrary to what is required by the Christian gospel. We have already seen that by the end of the Montgomery bus boycott, King had moved from the idea of nonviolence as a mere strategy for social change to the tougher, more mature view that it is what reality itself requires. By the publication of *Stride toward Freedom* (1958), there is no question about King's conviction about nonviolence as a way of being and living in the world, even though he knew that only a few people, regardless of racial-ethnic background, were "unswervingly committed to the nonviolent way."[48] Indeed, although he was briefly a proponent of the just war theory while in seminary, he came to reject that view and war altogether.

There is no question that King had a deep appreciation for the state and its responsibility to protect and defend its citizens from enemies from within and without. Because he was against anarchy, he understood that

---

48. King, *Stride toward Freedom*, 218.

the state had the responsibility to control the criminal element in society, as well as respond to threats against the state by external enemies. In addition, he believed that the state is obligated to use its police force to protect innocent nonviolent demonstrators, as well as to prevent anarchy. Reflecting on the Little Rock, Arkansas debacle in 1957, when black children were under protection of federal troops, King made it clear that he believed "in the intelligent use of police force."[49] And yet he was very clear about his deep regret that force would ever have to be used, regardless of the reason. This was apparent as he thought about the role that Mississippi Governor Ross Barnett played in trying to deny the admission of James Meredith to the University of Mississippi in 1962. Because the state was violating federal law and seeming to instigate anarchy, King did not see as problematic the use of federalized troops to effect Meredith's admission and the state's compliance with the law. Instead he said:

> Though I regret the use of force in the Mississippi situation, nevertheless, in my humble judgment, it was necessary and justifiable. Whereas I abhor the use of arms and the thought of war, I do believe in the intelligent use of police power. Though a pacifist, I am not an anarchist. Mississippi's breakdown of law and order demanded the utilization of a police action to quell the disorder and enforce the law of the land. Armed force that intelligently exercises police power, making civil arrests in which full due process is observed, is not functioning as an army in military engagement, so I feel the presence of troops in Oxford, Mississippi, is a police force seeking to preserve law and order rather than an army engaging in destructive warfare.[50]

King was not a situationalist regarding his doctrine of nonviolence. We have seen that by the late 1950s he made it clear to critics that he rejected war and violence, considering both impractical and immoral. He was convinced that war is immoral because by its very nature it has no respect for human and other life forms. Therefore, war is a final judgment against the sacredness of persons.

To be sure, Clarence Jones is not—and does not claim to be—a Hebrew Bible scholar. I do not find his discussion on the wording of the Sixth Commandment to be compelling since he does not examine enough of the best scholarship on the translation. In addition, he does not consider the place and importance of the assumptions and theological claims brought to bear on the text by those who interpret it to mean "you shall not murder."

49. Carson, ed., *The Autobiography of Martin Luther King Jr.*, 109.
50. King, "Who Is Their God?," *The Nation* (October 13, 1962) 210.

Wilma Ann Bailey, a very careful Hebrew Bible scholar, published an excellent little book on this very topic: *"You Shall Not Kill" or "You Shall Not Murder"?: The Assault on a Biblical Text* (2005). Bailey examines the best scholarship on the wording of the Commandment and concludes that the most reasonable and accurate translation is the tougher "You shall not Kill" translation. Mindful that we all bring a variety of assumptions (e.g., social, political, religious, theological, etc.) to our reading and interpretation of the Bible, Bailey contends, among other things, that many of those who support killing traditions such as war and capital punishment are already predisposed to the "You shall not murder" translation, because they already accept the viability of killing even before they read the Bible. In addition, Bailey admits that there is evidence in the Bible of killing *and* nonkilling theologies, but she finds no compelling evidence that killing theologies necessarily trump nonkilling ones. Bailey goes on to say:

> Even where a penalty of death is stated in the Bible, often the question of who, if anyone, is to carry out the penalty is vague. Many modern commentators place that authority in the hands of the state or the nation even though such entities did not exist in ancient times and would not have been in the mind of the biblical author. Moreover, biblically speaking, if God reserves the right to kill, this does not mean that humans have the same right.[51]

This is not the place to go into detail about Bailey's argument and supporting data, but I do think that Jones would have benefited much from reading and pondering her book, rather than resorting solely to a laymen's interpretation. Had he read Bailey's book and also given thoughtful consideration to King's fundamental theological presuppositions and his commitment to nonviolence as a way of life, I cannot see how Jones could have reasonably drawn the conclusion that King would have privileged the "You shall not murder" translation, which seems to give the state biblical sanction to kill, by way of capital punishment and war.

For the reasons given, it must now be clear why I have taken issue with the claim of Clarence Jones that Martin Luther King Jr. would be supportive of the wars in Iraq and Afghanistan, or that he would take the life of a madman on a murderous shooting rampage. And yet Jones is absolutely right when he implies that in the face of the 911 terrorist attacks and the aftermath, no voice of protest would have been louder and more persistent than

---

51. Wilma Ann Bailey, *"You Shall Not Kill" or "You Shall Not Murder"?: The Assault on a Biblical Text* (Collegeville, MN: Liturgical, 2005), 22. See entirety of chapter 1, "You Shall Not Kill."

King's. But Jones is most certainly wrong in his claim that depending on the context, King would suspend nonviolence and inflict or advise violence. For it is known that to the very end King was convinced that nonviolence, adapted to the conditions of the location—South or North—was still the best solution to social injustice. Moreover, he persistently advocated the need to internationalize nonviolence.[52] He never advocated the suspension of nonviolence as a way of life. Rather, to the end he staunchly advocated the idea that "the church has a vocation for nonviolence" (as Walter Wink put it).[53] The church is called to be nonviolent not in order to preserve or protect its purity, but because that is what God expects.[54] Indeed, in his "The State of the Movement" address at the SCLC staff retreat in Frogmore, South Carolina on November 28, 1967, King vowed to be married to nonviolence no matter what. "I have taken a vow," he said. "I, Martin Luther King, take thee, nonviolence, to be my wedded wife, for better or for worse, for richer or for poorer, in sickness and in health, till death do us part."[55] And for one like King, who lived by the conviction that the universe hinges on a moral foundation with God as its source, it follows that nonviolence reflects the very essence of the divine nature and what God expects in the world and for humanity.

Like many, Clarence Jones fails to take seriously enough the fact that Martin Luther King was fundamentally a man of faith and a man of ideas and idealism. That he was the quintessential man of social action is indisputable. And yet, it is just as indisputable that he consistently applied his faith, his sense of what God requires, and the best of his religious, theological, and philosophical ideas, in his quest to achieve the beloved community. All of King's social and political perspectives were solidly grounded in his theology and deepest faith claims. What people often lose sight of is the fact that what was fundamental to Martin Luther King was *God's perspective* on what was happening in the world and what God expected, namely, that we do justice, love mercy, and walk humbly with God. Believing as strongly as he did that the universe is value fused King could not, under any circumstance, advocate violence.

---

52. See King, "Impasse in Race Relations" and "A Christian Sermon on Peace," in his *The Trumpet of Conscience* (New York: Harper & Row, 1968), 14, 68.
53. Wink, *Engaging the Powers*, 216.
54. Ibid., 217.
55. Quoted in Burns, *To the Mountaintop*, 371.

10

What Martin Might Say about Intracommunity Violence and Homicide among Young African American Males

An Extreme Emergency

RUFUS BURROW JR.

One of the most tragic social issues that Clarence B. Jones does not devote a chapter to, and only briefly calls attention to in several places, is black-against-black violence and homicide among young black males, especially in the inner cities of the United States. Jones contends that were he alive today, Martin Luther King would be devastated by the frequency and the massive number of young black male homicides committed by other young black males every week in the urban centers of this nation. Jones puts it this way:

> Martin would be inconsolable at the thought and sight of dead young men piling up in the streets and morgues like cordwood every weekend—killed not by Klansmen or freelance racists or even the cops, but by someone who looks just like them, talks like them, acts like them. This would rip Martin's heart out, I think, because these are literally senseless killings in that they're inspired by senselessness. In war, after all, you hate the reality but you accept that the enemy, hailing from another country or ideology, intends to kill as many good guys as possible. But when the enemy is Damian from across the street, and he either

covets your sneakers or doesn't like your friends, then it's not war; it's suicide, fratricide, genocide.[1]

Indeed, the senseless killings and piling up of young black male bodies do not happen solely or even primarily on the weekend. It happens throughout the week, and virtually every week in many inner city black communities, not least Indianapolis, Indiana, where I live and teach.

Although Jones rightly observes that Martin Luther King would be heartbroken about this tragic intracommunity phenomenon, he seems also to imply that King was not aware of the existence of this problem during the civil rights movement. This, however, is totally incorrect. Consequently, this essay seeks to do several things. First, to show that not only was King aware of the alarmingly high incidence of young black males' violence against each other and other members of the black community, but that he also responded to the problem a number of times, making it unequivocally clear that black lives were too sacred to be so easily violated and killed, whether in bar fights or as a result of gang executions. Second, since the doctrine of nonviolent resistance to evil was such a central part of King's philosophy and practice, this essay examines the extent to which it may be a viable response to the tragic issue before us. Third, since I have argued elsewhere that this particular social evil is a textbook example of a *borderline situation*, (i.e., an extreme emergency situation in which no traditional or "acceptable" response either is adequate or seems to make sense as a viable "solution"[2]), this essay also ponders the question of the relevance of King's philosophy of nonviolence as a solution to the borderline situation under discussion. I begin with brief reflections on this tragedy in the city of Indianapolis.

Even the Funeral Director Was Grief Stricken

I will never forget watching the evening news a few years ago and seeing an elderly black funeral director literally crying during an interview with a reporter as he appealed to his people to stop the senseless killings of young black boys and periodically girls in Indianapolis. This man was crying uncontrollably. He was clearly overwhelmed, devastated by the sheer numbers and frequency of young black bodies showing up on his embalming table.

---

1. Clarence B. Jones and Joel Engel, *What Would Martin Say?* (New York: Harper, 2008), 84.

2. See my essay "Borderline Ethics and Intra-Community Violence and Murder among Young African American Males," in *Theology in Global Context: Essays in Honor of Robert Cummings Neville*, ed. Amos Yong and Peter G. Heltzel (New York: T. & T. Clark, 2004), ch. 5.

I knew that on that particular day, at least, it was not about the money to be made by that mortician. That man saw huge numbers of the sons and grandsons of the black community in his funeral parlor. Most were victims of merely a wrong word or a misunderstood look. Too many were engaged in disputes over their "manhood" and their sense that they had been disrespected. Imagine! Young teenage *boys*—many well under the age of twenty—making claims to manhood! Too many were in the wrong place at the wrong time. Some were innocent bystanders in drive-by shootings. Some were in what was thought to be the safety of their own homes, playing video games, and in some instances actually doing homework when they were mortally wounded by stray bullets that missed their out-of-doors target.

Because he was having to embalm so many of these lifeless young black male bodies, the funeral director was simply grief stricken, recognizing that virtually all of them died for little or no reason. But he could also see that the black community was faced with what could only be described as an extreme state of emergency, and that only the residents of that community could effectively address and put an end to it. He and other local black funeral directors did not know how to stop the violence, but a few years later the homicide rate escalated to the point that they got together and organized a motorcade of hearses carrying empty caskets. They drove the hearses through some of the most violence-prone black neighborhoods in Indianapolis. They thought that at the very least their procession would provide a substantial shock effect that might slow or even deter the violent behavior. The very next day a young black male under age twenty-four was felled by bullets from the gun of a young black male.

I cannot imagine Martin Luther King Jr. not declaring a state of emergency regarding the tragic phenomenon of intracommunity violence and homicide among young black males. He would surely be concerned about the lack of attention given this tragedy by celebrity leaders not only of his era but the next generation of leaders who, according to Clarence Jones, have been more concerned about career development, grandstanding in front of reporters' cameras, and being considered the expert, rather than about putting this tragedy at the forefront of all that they do, and never allowing any of us to rest as long as the life of young black males is considered insignificant in these United States of America.

Observing that black leaders such as Jesse Jackson and Al Sharpton have not directed enough energy, attention, and resources to this ongoing tragedy, Jones is convinced that King would be deeply distressed and saddened by their failure.[3] Many of these homicide victims had barely entered

---

3. Jones and Engel, *What Would Martin Say?*, 49.

their teen years. Many of them really are boys, although most—the boys themselves as well as too many black adults—will find my use of the term *boy* when referring to them to be offensive. After all, many of these have either killed or been killed ostensibly for defending their manhood. Often these are teens or barely teens, junior-high or high school dropouts, unemployed, and whose only fulltime job seems to be hanging out and terrorizing their respective neighborhoods. In addition, too often these fellows fail to exhibit a willingness to accept responsibility for virtually anything they do, including impregnating ostensibly willing young black girls. In any case, even this phenomenon—babies having babies—is a problem of first-magnitude proportions that does not receive adequate attention from today's black leaders.

One dare not challenge or question the manhood of these young boys unless one is willing to severely wound or be wounded, kill or be killed. I know from personal experience how easily even mature, professional, otherwise respectful and well-meaning black males can find themselves in senseless confrontations with some of these young boys; how easy it is for such men to lose their cool with black boys who lack any semblance of respect for their elders, and who seem completely devoid of even a modicum of civility or any sense of what it means to take responsibility for their actions and the consequences thereof. Indeed, many seem to care nothing whatever about such things.

Frequently such boys exhibit what Cornel West characterizes as "*a life of horrifying meaninglessness, hopelessness, and [most important] lovelessness*."[4] They are mean spirited and exhibit a complete disregard, disrespect, and lack of love either for self or for others, including property, in the neighborhoods they terrorize. West hits the nail dead-center when he writes: "The frightening result is a numbing detachment from others and a self-destructive disposition toward the world. Life without meaning, hope, and love breeds a coldhearted, mean-spirited outlook that destroys both the individual and others."[5] This is an excellent description of the personality at the center of the tragic phenomenon of black-against-black violence and homicide. From the time of the enslavement of blacks in this part of the world, whites have disrespected and disregarded black life, which must have some connection to how many young black males think of themselves today. What is more important today, however, is not whites' disregard and disrespect for blacks, although in the wider scheme of things this too is important. What is even more important is blacks' disregard and disrespect for

---

4. Cornel West, *Race Matters* (Boston: Beacon, 1993), 14.
5. Ibid., 14–15.

themselves and their community. Clearly, persons who exhibit such disregard and disrespect for themselves and the people in their community are devoid of love of and respect for self.

King's Awareness of Intracommunity Violence

The problem of intracommunity violence and murder among young black males was not quite as severe in King's day, but there is no question that he, like Malcolm X, was aware of this tragic phenomenon.[6] It was not a new phenomenon or one that escaped King's attention, as Jones wrongly implies.[7] One of the first places that King became acquainted with this tragedy on a personal level was during the Chicago movement in 1966, when he and his wife rented a dilapidated slum apartment in Lawndale and lived among some of the poorest blacks in the city, including gang members. By the time King and the SCLC arrived in Chicago, gangs there "had grown in size, organization, and ferocity."[8] A major consequence was almost daily out-of-control intracommunity violence.

Looking back, King said that on occasion they had witnessed riots in Chicago, but "much more frequently and consistently, brutal acts and crimes by Negroes against Negroes. In many a week in Chicago, as many or more Negro youngsters have been killed in gang fights as were killed in the riots there last summer."[9] He was deeply hurt and troubled by this, knowing that some of the very conditions he and the SCLC were in Chicago to address were a significant part of the causal equation. In a closed-door meeting with Mayor Richard J. Daley, King tried desperately and unsuccessfully to get him to hear and respond positively to the concerns of gang members. Refusing to embrace them, Daley saw the young people as uncivil, unproductive members of society.[10] His stance was little different from that of most urban

---

6. See Malcolm X, "See for Yourself, Listen for Yourself, Think for Yourself," in *Malcolm X Talks to Young People*, ed. Steve Clark (New York: Pathfinder, 1991), 50. Here Malcolm talks about how blacks in Harlem often talk about being nonviolent with the white man, but every weekend they engage in violence against each other that lands them in the emergency room at Harlem Hospital in record numbers.

7. Jones and Engel, *What Would Martin Say?*, 88.

8. James R. Ralph Jr., *Northern Protest: Martin Luther King Jr., Chicago, and the Civil Rights Movement* (Cambridge: Harvard University Press, 1993), 94.

9. Martin Luther King Jr., "A Gift of Love," in *A Testament of Hope: The Essential Writings of Martin Luther King Jr.*, ed. James M. Washington (New York: Harper & Row, 1986), 63.

10. Eric Gerard Pearman, "Martin Luther King Jr. and Chicago's Gangs," *The Sphinx* (Spring 1997) 31.

mayors. King knew, as did Coretta Scott King, that these were basically "decent young men with aspirations, but the system had forced them in the direction of hate and violence."[11] Then, much like Daley in Chicago, the powers that be refused to hear and acknowledge their legitimate grievances, which only fueled the riots and other disturbances that followed. King reflected that many of these teenage boys had only "known life as a madhouse of violence and degradation." They had never known real family life and what it means to be loved and responsibly cared for by parents; many had "dropped out of incredibly bad slum schools."[12]

Unlike Clarence Jones, King was quick to point to the systemic causes of the violence and homicides. He saw that it was also largely a result of blacks turning their disgust and hatred of the system and the larger society on themselves, and too often the result was violence against other blacks. But in addition, we will see that King was just as quick to point to the role of individual decision making and responsibility among blacks regarding the violence and homicides.

In *Where Do We Go from Here?*, King lamented the fact that a visit to hospital emergency rooms in predominantly black areas of inner cities was proof positive of the seriousness of black-against-black violence and homicide.[13] Calling for group unity, King pointed to the need for black women to be respected, as well as the recognition that the lives of blacks generally are too sacred and "precious to be destroyed in a Saturday night brawl, or a gang execution."[14] Citing environmental and other causes of this phenomenon, King also stressed the need for governmental assistance to aid black men in getting on their economic feet. In addition, he cited the need for blacks themselves to do all in their power—including but not limited to better parenting—to solve this problem. King was not one to blame the victim, as Jones seems to do in his discussion of the black youth involved in the "Jena Six" controversy. Nor did King ever preach a "fire-and-brimstone" sermon of damnation to gang members when he had occasion to meet with them. Rather, his approach to dealing with them "was one of compassion, understanding, warmth, honesty, openness, and direct accessibility in listening and talking with them,"[15] writes Eric Gerard Pearman. However, King

11. Coretta Scott King, *My Life with Martin Luther King Jr.*, rev. ed. (New York: Holt, 1993 [1969]), 262.

12. Clayborne Carson, ed., *The Autobiography of Martin Luther King Jr.* (New York: Warner, 1998), 312.

13. Martin Luther King, Jr., *Where Do We Go from Here: Chaos or Community?* (Boston: Beacon, 1967), 64.

14. Ibid., 125.

15. Pearman, "Martin Luther King Jr. and Chicago's Gangs," 30.

believed without question that to the extent that human beings are moral agents they are always at least responsible for *how they respond* to what is done to them. This is no less true of gang members.

In light of the more recent occurrence and the seeming unending proliferation of this tragedy, King would be much more than grief stricken, heart-broken, and simply overwhelmed by the sheer numbers and frequency of these deaths. He would, as Jones rightly says, shed "tears of anger at killings more pointless than those caused by any war in history."[16] His anger would be directed not only at the senseless killings, but at the conditions that have created the openings for this tragedy. This means that his anger would also be directed at those socioeconomic and political forces that contribute to these death-inducing conditions. But it also means that some of his anger would be directed toward those African American adults who have failed miserably at parenting and raising children to be civilized and responsible citizens who strive to live together in community.

Martin Luther King realized that his people were facing an extreme situation, an emergency of the first magnitude. He was convinced that such situations require extreme remedies, a point that he made not long after the bombing of the Sixteenth Street Baptist Church in Birmingham, Alabama in 1963. "We were faced with *an extreme situation*," King said, "and our remedies had to be extreme."[17] The phenomenon of black-against-black violence and homicide is no less an extreme situation today. It is a state of emergency that requires unprecedented measures if there is to be hope for a solution.

No compassionate and thinking person can deny that the problem before us is among the most extreme of emergency situations. I liken this to what Helmut Thielicke, in another time and context, characterized as the *borderline situation*. The remainder of this essay examines the general meaning of the borderline situation, and what may be required to responsibly and adequately address it. Attention will also be given to what King, the chief proponent of nonviolence, might say about remedying this tragic phenomenon. Last, I briefly consider whether Kingian nonviolence can be adapted to responsibly and adequately address it.

The Borderline Situation

From the time I was a boy growing up in the projects on the Westside of Pontiac, Michigan, I was aware of the tendency of inner-city young black males to engage each other and others in the community violently, and

---

16. Jones and Engel, *What Would Martin Say?*, 87.
17. Carson, ed., *The Autobiography of Martin Luther King Jr.*, 234 (italics added).

seemingly without remorse. This phenomenon seemed to escalate from my high school years onward, so much so that I remember periods when virtually every week there were reports of such violence, not only in the projects, but in other black communities throughout the city. Indeed, I wrote early drafts of my doctoral dissertation during the summer of 1979 amid the horrific sound of frequent gunfire in the projects. In every instance, both perpetrator and victim were young, black, and male. Although I lived during this time in the same apartment unit in which I grew up, I felt my life and that of others around me were under constant threat of harm and death. I found it almost impossible to get a sound sleep, as I was frequently awakened by vociferous arguments, fights, or gunfire. Talk about a dissertation written under fire!

It was unclear to me at the time how widespread this phenomenon was across the state and nationally, although I knew it was not isolated to the city of Pontiac. I had a strong hunch that urban centers throughout the country experienced this tragedy, especially in Detroit, twenty-five miles to the south. This was confirmed when I, a few years later, read the anthology edited by Jewelle Taylor Gibbs, et al., *Young, Black, and Male in America: An Endangered Species* (1988). It was here that I read for the first time that data analyzed by the Center for Disease Control (CDC) led to the conclusion that the number-one cause of death for black males 15–24 years of age was homicide committed by another black male;[18] here I read for the first time the characterization of this group as "an endangered species."[19]

By this time, I had been teaching at Christian Theological Seminary in Indianapolis for about five years. Devastated by my discovery, I began immediately paying attention to what was happening in black communities throughout Indianapolis, only to find that I was right smack in the middle of this tragic phenomenon. From that point, I knew that nothing I teach would have meaning if I could not find ways to also address the ongoing escalating tragedy of intracommunity violence and homicide among young black males. At the very least, I had to keep this issue before my students, as well as my colleagues. I could not allow anybody to pretend that this tragedy was not occurring right under their noses each day and that it had nothing to do with them. If I knew nothing else at that time, I knew that this tragic phenomenon did not have to exist, and that the fact that it did implicated us all, regardless of race, ethnicity, and class.

18. Richard Dembo, "Delinquency among Black Male Youth," in *Young, Black, and Male in America: An Endangered Species*, ed. Jewelle Taylor Gibbs (New York: Auburn House, 1988), 138.

19. Gibbs, "Young Black Males in America: Endangered, Embittered, and Embattled," in *Young, Black, and Male in America*, 1.

When I began thinking about types of theological and philosophical ethics that might be relevant to addressing this phenomenon, I could identify nothing that was really adequate to the task. Like King, I knew that an extreme emergency situation existed and that a radical ethic would be required to address it. It was around this time that I began reading Helmut Thielicke's massive three-volume text, *Theological Ethics*. It was in the first two volumes, *Foundations* and *Politics*, respectively, that I discovered the concept of the *borderline situation*. From this I began thinking and talking about *borderline ethics* as a type that might be adequate to the task of effectively addressing the tragedy of black-against-black violence and homicide.[20] According to Thielicke, the borderline situation—what Dietrich Bonhoeffer characterized as "the extraordinary situation or ultimate necessities that are beyond any possible regulation by law"[21]—is likened to the extreme or emergency ethical situation, thus requiring extreme or radical measures. The extreme emergency situation is one in which the conflict is overwhelming and from which victims cannot seem to extricate themselves by normal or acceptable means.

According to Thielicke, the borderline situation has four essential marks, all of which are relevant to addressing the tragic phenomenon before us. Together these traits point to the idea of being willing to do wrong in order to eradicate or prevent a graver wrong. First, the struggle against those perpetrating injustice or engaging in massive destructive behavior should not be directed against individuals as such. Rather the struggle should be against the injustice and destructive behavior. This is quite similar to King's oft repeated mantra that the struggle is not against the white man, but against injustice. "In the end," King said, "it is not a struggle between people at all, but a tension between justice and injustice. Nonviolent resistance is not aimed against oppressors but against oppression."[22] Any victory at all in the struggle is a victory for all people, "a victory for justice and the forces of light," King said while reflecting on the Montgomery bus boycott. "We are out to defeat injustice and not white persons who may be unjust,"[23] he said. The aim is not to humiliate or defeat the white man but to win his friendship and understanding.[24]

20. Thielicke does not use the term *borderline ethics* but develops the concept of *the borderline situation*.

21. Dietrich Bonhoeffer, *Ethics*, ed. Clifford J. Green, Dietrich Bonhoeffer Works 6 (Minneapolis: Fortress, 2005), 273.

22. Martin Luther King, Jr., *Stride toward Freedom: The Montgomery Story* (New York; Harper & Row, 1958), 214.

23. Ibid., 103.

24. Clayborne Carson, et al., ed., *The Papers of Martin Luther King Jr.* (Berkeley:

Second, the struggle in the borderline situation can be waged only if proponents are willing—to some extent—to adopt the means or methods of those engaging in extreme and unacceptable behavior, which also means being willing "to incur a measure of guilt."[25] For to adopt such measures or an adaptation of them means that activists will invariably end up with dirty, and quite possibly bloody, hands. Such ones, therefore, will no more be able to declare their innocence than those engaging in massive destructive behavior.

Third, because of the nature of the extreme measures to which activists may be forced to adopt in the borderline situation, all such measures must be seen as standing under judgment of the gospel and in need of forgiveness. As noted above, this also means that all parties are complicit in a measure of guilt; the perpetrators for committing the crime or extreme wrong, and the activists for adopting their measures in order to resolve the matter.

The fourth mark of the borderline situation is that Christian activists must be able to act without hatred against their opponent. This is implied in the first trait, where the emphasis should be on the evil deed rather than the person committing it. Consequently, one is to hate the deed, but not the person, a point often made by King. The opponent is never just an agent of dirty-handed methods. Such a one is also "a child of God who has been bound by the chains of evil and thus gone astray"[26] Both the just and the unjust, the oppressed and the oppressor, the enslaved and the enslaver, the Jews and Adolf Hitler belong to the one God of the universe, another point with which King would wholeheartedly agree.

Implied in Thielicke's four marks of the borderline situation is the need for all parties to seek forgiveness from each other and from God. Because forgiveness is so important in the Christian tradition, I think it should be acknowledged as a fifth mark of the *borderline situation*. The activists will need to repent and seek forgiveness not only from God and the victims who continue to live, but from the perpetrators as well. The reason for needing to seek forgiveness from the latter is that the activists will have adopted and implemented their methods. The perpetrators were also children of God, and activists must always be cognizant of this fact.

Although Clarence Jones appears to be open to the borderline ethic, since he believes that given the means King would kill the madman who indiscriminately shoots and kills people in an imagined crowded mall, I

University of California Press, 2005), 5:504.

25. Helmut Thielicke, *Theological Ethics*, 3 vols., ed. William H. Lazareth (Philadelphia: Fortress, 1966), 1:587.

26. Ibid.

have found no evidence that King would adopt such measures were he alive today. He surely would ponder how to make nonviolence more militant, but it would be too much for him to suspend nonviolence for even a moment. King's was a consistent ethic of nonviolent resistance.

Can We Solve the Borderline Situation?

I am not at all optimistic that the extreme emergency that haunts and violently tears at the fabric of the black community will be adequately addressed in my lifetime. Clarence Jones rightly observes that the tragic incidences of black-on-black violence and homicide get far too little attention from black leaders today. This is true, but it is also true that a problem of this magnitude is not that of a few black leaders only. It is a problem for the entire black community, which suggests the need for a more communal leadership model (See chapter 3, the essay by Ross and Geiger, in this volume).

Not only do the choices in the borderline situation make no sense, the victims are often forced to adopt and adapt the methods of oppressors. These methods are generally not those of nonviolent resistance, but rather potential life-destroying ones. These are the methods that those in the borderline situation may be forced to adopt. Without question, this would be unacceptable to King.

Granted that Martin Luther King insisted on the primacy of nonviolent resistance to social evil, we must remember that during his time organized nonviolence campaigns were directed toward social evils inflicted on black communities from the outside. The aim, then, was to organize the black community to resist, and where possible, eradicate such evils and injustices imposed from the outside. But throughout this discussion, I have implied that something quite different is going on within the context of the black community that now requires internal resistance to an intra-community tragedy perpetrated by black male youth. This is not to say in the least that the external threats to the community no longer exist. Indeed, such ongoing threats are intricately linked to the tragic internal phenomenon under discussion.

What I am really proposing here is that the black community needs to turn resistance methods upon itself, even as it continues to work at breaking the stranglehold of negative outside forces. Because our focus is on King, the method of choice is nonviolent resistance. I know of no prolonged organized nonviolent campaign that King led against a social ill perpetrated by the black community on itself. Although King was aware of the existence of youth gangs and their too-easy tendency to commit violent acts and homicides against other gangs and innocent people in the black community in places like Chicago, he did not devote time and energy to devising and executing nonviolent resistance campaigns against them. And yet it seems to me that this is precisely the issue before us today. Therefore, the question becomes, what is the relevance of nonviolent resistance to the issue of intracommunity violence and homicide among young black males? To what extent is it possible to adapt King's doctrine of nonviolence to addressing this borderline problem? Can we imagine mass nonviolent demonstrations against the violence and homicides in local black communities? Can we imagine such demonstrations against young black males who perpetrate these intra-community tragedies with painful regularity? To what extent may the demonstrators, or a representative group of demonstrators, need to adopt the methods of the perpetrators of violence and homicide in black communities before they even stand a reasonable chance of being able to implement the methods of nonviolence, let alone to launch a successful campaign?

A Kingian Response

No matter what else Martin Luther King Jr. might say about the internal tragedy devastating the black community, he would demand that the violence and homicides cease immediately. Were King alive and called upon to eulogize many of the dozens of victims across the country, he would find it impossible to praise them as he did the four young black girls who were murdered in the bombing of the Sixteenth Street Baptist Church in Birmingham in 1963; or Jimmy Lee Jackson, who was killed by a racist policeman in Marion, Alabama, during the Selma campaign in 1965. These were martyrs in the struggle for justice, for civil and human rights; theirs was a righteous and noble cause. But this cannot be said of most of the victims of intracommunity violence and homicide in the black community today. Surely there is nothing noble and righteous in these deaths and their causes. King could only say that it is time to cease and desist from such horrendous behavior, and that every resource at the disposal of the black community should be marshaled and directed toward ending this tragedy.

I cannot imagine Martin Luther King Jr. not also insisting that in the deepest sense the black community is *responsible for how it responds* to black-on-black violence and homicides. Although he would acknowledge the need to determine and address the root causes of the nihilistic threat in the black community, King would see just as clearly the need to get the violence and homicides stopped forthwith, and that the community needs to do this from within.

In his "Advice for Living" column in *Ebony* magazine in 1958, King responded to the question of how to reduce the crime wave in the black community and whether the church had a role to play in this. He addressed both the systemic and the self-determination aspects of the question:

> The Negro is not criminal by nature. Indeed criminality is environmental, not racial. Poverty and ignorance breed crime whatever the racial group may be. So we must work to remove the system of segregation, discrimination and the existence of economic injustice if we are to solve the problem of crime in the Negro community. For these external factors are causally responsible for crime. On the other hand, the Negro must work within the community to solve the problem while the external cause factors are being removed . . . The church must extend its evangelistic program into all of the poverty-stricken and slum areas of the big cities, therefore touching the individuals who are more susceptible to criminal traits.[27]

We can be certain of one thing. If we do not get the violence and homicides stopped, there is the very real possibility of losing virtually an entire generation of young black males to this intra-communal tragedy.

Martin Luther King would remind residents of the black community that no response to this problem is in fact a response. He would therefore insist on the need to be intentional about the types of responses given. Just here King was likely influenced by Jean Paul Sartre, whom he studied during his formal academic training.[28] Sartre taught that human beings are "condemned forever to be free."[29] Therefore, even when we choose not to decide, not to act, we have in fact made a decision, have in fact acted. Human beings cannot, not choose, for "what is not possible is not to choose," said Sartre. "I can always choose, but I ought to know that if I do not choose, I am still choosing."[30] This essentially means that nobody gets off the moral hook, neither oppressor or oppressed. None understood this better than Martin Luther King. All persons are responsible for how they respond to whatever is done to them. King would be the first to say that the black community is not responsible for the socio-economic and political causes of

---

27. Carson, et al., eds., *The Papers of Martin Luther King Jr.*, 4:471. King also addressed this matter in *Stride toward Freedom*, 222–23.

28. King, "Pilgrimage to Nonviolence," in Washington, ed., *A Testament of Hope*, 36.

29. Jean Paul Sartre, *The Age of Reason*, trans. Eric Sutton (New York: Bantam, 1959), 76.

30. Jean Paul Sartre, *Existentialism and Human Emotions*, trans. Bernard Frechtman and Hazel E. Barnes (New York: Philosophical Library, 1957), 41.

intra-community violence and homicide, but he would also be the first to say that it is responsible for how it responds to this tragedy.

Where Do We Go from Here?

From Montgomery onwards, Martin Luther King Jr. realized, as did Mahatma Gandhi in South Africa and India, that it would be necessary to adapt the method and principles of nonviolence to each community where the SCLC intended to engage in mass demonstrations in its bid to "save the soul of America." In part this is why, before he would accept an invitation by local black leaders to lead mass demonstrations, King would send a fact-finding group to essentially gather intelligence and to get a sense of the nature of the community, its leaders, the people, information regarding the powers that be, etc. King considered fact-finding to be one of the four basic steps in every nonviolent campaign.[31] The information gathered from such investigation helped King and others to determine whether a problem actually existed and what they might need to do different than in previous campaigns. King believed the method of nonviolence to be adaptable in most contexts. Each community and its people are different, and thus must be given careful consideration before launching a nonviolent campaign.

It would be no different when considering launching mass demonstrations against the extreme emergency condition of black-against-black violence and homicide. Because so many young black males in urban battle zones seem to possess little to no sense of civility and no sense of their own humanity and dignity, it is crucial that the proponents and planners of such demonstrations do their homework. Their intelligence and fact-finding must be impeccable. In addition, before a decision is made to actually launch demonstrations, it will be important to know that most of the instigators of black-against-black violence and homicide have no respect for themselves or others in their community. This is why during drive-by shootings they do not hesitate to fire automatic weapons indiscriminately into crowds of people or in the direction of surrounding houses, sometimes mortally wounding innocent children and others. Since they take no thought of their own and the lives of others in the community, they essentially behave like suicide bombers in Iraq, Afghanistan, and other places in the world. Consequently, rather than talk about the nuts and bolts of how nonviolence may need to be adapted to address the problem under consideration, I want to suggest the

---

31. King, *Why We Can't Wait* (New York: Harper & Row, 1964), 79. The other three steps are negotiation, self-purification, and direct action.

need to first consider taking the extreme step of removing the most violent perpetrators in order to prepare the way for the mass nonviolent campaign.

Although King understood the need to adapt nonviolence to the specific community, my sense is that unlike what *I* think the present state of affairs requires, he would insist on thoroughly nonviolent means. Remember, Martin Luther King Jr. believed fundamentally that the universe is constructed such that the world works best when human beings appeal to nonviolent means of addressing social problems. Although I believe this in principle, I am not at all certain of its reasonableness in every concrete situation. We humans are too greedy, selfish, and proud; these traits manifest themselves exponentially in our group relations. Such facts make it difficult for me to understand how nonviolence is necessarily the most realistic approach in every situation, especially the borderline situation. Nevertheless, we can be sure that because nonviolence was more than a method or strategy for King, there is no circumstance in which he would advocate violence. And yet, although he would be repulsed by any suggestion that young black males who perpetrate wanton violence be subjected to violence as a means of removing them from the scene, more and more it seems to me that if the black community is to ever get the violence and homicides stopped, it may be necessary to temporarily invoke violence against the perpetrators before it will be possible to introduce nonviolent methods. Such violence must be invoked only confessionally, however. That is, it must be confessed outright that the use of violence to maim or destroy human life—whatever the reason may be—is a sin before God, and thus those involved in such schemes must know that they will have to answer to God. This is the situation that some Germans, not least Dietrich Bonhoeffer, found themselves in when they participated in plots to kill Adolf Hitler in order to prevent the further mass murders of Jews. They felt compelled to commit a wrong in order to prevent an even graver wrong, but those like Bonhoeffer did so confessionally.

What I am really suggesting here is that even before organized nonviolent campaigns can be effectively directed against the black-on-black violence and homicides in the black community, it may be necessary to acknowledge that the only way to get the attention of the most violent of the perpetrators is to first get their attention by making an example of some of them. I think of Malcolm X when I say that the only way to do this is to engage them in language (and behavior!) that they understand; language and behavior that they have been exposed to all their lives through the media and day-to-day experiences on the streets. They learn early, for example, that as much as the powers that be talk about the need for civility and nonviolence in human relations, they are the supreme culprits when it comes to instigating and perpetrating anything but civilized behavior and nonviolence. To be sure, not even Malcolm suggested the prospect of blacks subjecting other blacks to violence (even temporarily and in a controlled way) as a means to stopping the violence in black communities. But somehow the message must be sent that no matter what it takes, clearer heads in the black community will no longer permit the indiscriminate violence and homicides that wreck and take the precious lives of so many before they have really had a chance to live. The way must first be cleared if nonviolent campaigns are to stand a chance of eradicating the borderline situation under discussion.

Planners and organizers will need to know whether efforts have already been made to address the violence and homicides in the area. What were the results? Why did the violence and homicides continue? Did leaders at any time try at least to do what King did in Chicago to communicate with and relate to gang members and others who contributed to the intracommunity violence and homicide rate?

In an intriguing essay, Eric Pearman said that King used three methods of communication with Chicago gang members: 1) He identified with the poorest blacks, many of whom were gang members, by renting and living in a dilapidated slum apartment; 2) he held private meetings with gang members in his apartment to listen to their concerns, and held public forums for them to share their grievances with city officials; and 3) he put his own life on the line by trying to stop a riot.[32] In the end, gang members trusted and respected King, but the violence and homicides continued. However, it seems to me that the better part of wisdom demands that methods such as those used by King be adapted and tried before considering the possibility of implementing extreme borderline measures that will surely lead to dirty, even bloody, hands. Indeed, everything short of such measures should be exhausted before taking that awful step.

Other questions should be considered: What should be the role(s) of churches and other religious and civic organizations? What will be the best use of the local police, if any? This latter is particularly important since law enforcement and the element of racism are implicated in inner city violence. Nevertheless, because King had a fairly positive outlook regarding the state generally, he also believed in "the intelligent use of police force,"[33] and that the police have the responsibility of enforcing the law of the land and protecting demonstrators and innocent bystanders from the violence of white racist onlookers.

---

32. Pearman, "Martin Luther King Jr. and Chicago's Gangs," 30–32.
33. Carson, ed., *The Autobiography of Martin Luther King Jr.*, 109.

One thing is clear about what I propose. It is the responsibility of black people to put a stop to the violence and homicides in black communities. Furthermore, those causing this tragedy are, whether we like it or not, sons of the black community. They are essentially *our* children, and we—not those outside the community—must decide the best means to get the violence and homicides stopped. This is in the best interest of humanity in general. It is most particularly in the best interest of the black community.

I have no doubt that Martin Luther King Jr. would disagree with and reject the temporary means I propose in order to create the space or opening for nonviolent change to take place regarding intracommunity violence and homicide among young black males. Were King alive today, I could only say to him that I do not by any means suggest such a thing with an easy conscience, believing as I do—as any personalist theological social ethicist must!—that at the end of the day all life is precious to and belongs to God. And yet, this is in part the very reason I feel compelled to make the aforementioned deadly proposal—that in the end more black lives will be saved.

11

Transforming Death
Life's Ultimate Tragedy and Hope for the Dawn

MICHAEL G. LONG

Clarence B. Jones, for many years legal counselor to Martin Luther King Jr., has sought to answer the question of what King would say about who killed him on April 4, 1968.[1] Although Jones's work is provocative and fascinating, and offers insights that only he could know, any prediction about what King *would* say about death or anything else is historically untenable, mere conjecture, and ultimately groundless. Whether King would say that James Earl Ray acted alone or with accomplices, or that the US government played a direct role in his death, or that black militants secretly plotted to kill him, is entirely unknowable.

Because such claims about King's thoughts are merely speculative, it is far more productive to answer the question of what he *did* say about death, including the certainty of his own. The purpose of this chapter will thus be to sketch the major points of King's theological understanding of death and immortality. Doing so, the chapter will seek to fill a significant gap in the apparently unending literature about King's assassination.[2] For the most part,

---

1. See Clarence B. Jones and Joel Engel, *What Would Martin Say?* (New York: HarperCollins, 2008), 179–212. Chapter 7 is titled, "What Would Martin Say about Who Killed Him?"

2. See, for example, Hampton Sides, *Hellhound on His Trail: The Electrifying Account of the Largest Manhunt in American History* (New York: Anchor, 2011); William F. Pepper, *An Act of State: The Execution of Martin Luther King* (London: Verso, 2003); Dexter Scott King, with Ralph Wiley, *Growing Up King: An Intimate Memoir* (New York: Warner, 2003), 273–90; William F. Pepper, *Orders to Kill: The Truth behind the Murder of*

this material, often salacious and conspiratorial in tone, has focused on the identity of the assassin(s) to the exclusion of King's own death theology—especially his stated belief that identifying racist assassins is never sufficient for advancing civil rights.

Desiring Longevity

On September 15, 1963, not even one month after King delivered his famous "I Have a Dream" speech from the Lincoln Memorial, four young girls—Addie Mae Collins, Denise McNair, Carole Robertson, and Cynthia Wesley—were killed when white racists dynamited their home church, Sixteenth Street Baptist, in Birmingham, Alabama. King was crushed when he heard the terrible news, and a few days later he delivered a somber message to those gathered to memorialize three of the girls. "Death comes to every individual," he stated. "There is an amazing democracy about death. It is not an aristocracy for some of the people, but a democracy for all of the people."[3]

Martin Luther King Jr. (New York: Warner, 1998); John Larry Ray and Lyndon Barsten, *Truth at Last: The Untold Story behind James Earl Ray and the Assassination of Martin Luther King Jr.* (Guilford, CT: Lyons, 2008); Mark Lane and Dick Gregory, *Murder in Memphis: The FBI and the Assassination of Martin Luther King* (New York: Thunder's Mouth, 1993); Harold Weisberg, *Martin Luther King: The Assassination* (New York: Carroll & Graf, 1993); Gerald Posner, *Killing the Dream: James Earl Ray and the Assassination of Martin Luther King Jr.* (New York: Random House, 1998); James Earl Ray, *Who Killed Martin Luther King Jr.? The True Story by the Alleged Assassin* (New York: De Capo, 1997); Phillip H. Melanson, *The Murkin Conspiracy: An Investigation into the Assassination of Dr. Martin Luther King Jr.* (New York: Praeger, 1989); George McMillan, *The Making of an Assassin: The Life of James Earl Ray* (New York: Little, Brown, 1976); Gerold Frank, *An American Death: The True Story of the Assassination of Martin Luther King Jr. and the Greatest Manhunt of Our Time* (New York: Doubleday, 1972); and William Bradford Huie, *He Slew the Dreamer: My Search, with James Earl Ray, for the Truth about the Murder of Martin Luther King Jr.* (New York: Delacorte, 1970). A wide-ranging book that does explore King's comments on death in light of his assassination is Michael Eric Dyson, *April 4, 1968: Martin Luther King Jr.'s Death and How It Changed America* (New York: Basic Civitas, 2008). Numerous articles also address King's assassination. For the best among these, see David J. Garrow, "The Assassin's Name Is James Earl Ray," *The New York Times* (April 2, 1997). For a countervoice to Garrow, see Vincent Harding, "Martin Luther King and the Future of America," *Cross Currents* 46/3 (1996); online: http://www.crosscurrents.org/king/. See too the numerous news reports of the trial of Loyd Jowers (e.g., Emily Yellin, "Memphis Jury Sees Conspiracy in Martin Luther King's Killing," *The New York Times* [December 9, 1999]).

3. Martin Luther King Jr., "Eulogy for the Young Victims of the Sixteenth Street Baptist Church Bombing," in *A Call to Conscience: The Landmark Speeches of Dr. Martin Luther King Jr.*, ed. Clayborne Carson and Kris Shepard (New York: Warner, 2001), 97.

By the time he delivered these words, King himself had faced countless death threats. They started with his leadership of the Montgomery Improvement Association (MIA)—he received thirty to forty threats a day within a month of the beginning of the famous Montgomery boycott—and they continued until the time of his assassination. Death was always in the air, as omnipresent as King's God, and its ashen hue marked him wherever he went. Unable to escape it, King faced death with at least a double attitude. On the one hand, he sought to hold onto the life he found sacred. On the other, he surrendered to its inevitability, trusting that God could and would overcome the oppressive power of death.

King did not want to die. He openly expressed this sentiment throughout his public career, even while noting his willingness to die for the civil rights movement. In 1957, shortly after the bombing of Ralph Abernathy's home in Montgomery, King offered a public prayer that spoke in part to his desire to live: "Lord, I hope no one will have to die as a result of our struggle for freedom in Montgomery. Certainly I don't want to die."[4] During the Chicago campaign, when the movement seemed to be faltering in the face of Mayor Daley's uncompromising politics, King expressed anew his desire to avoid an early death: "I am tired of the threat of death. I want to live. I don't want to be a martyr."[5] And he stated basically the same point on the night before he died in Memphis in 1968. "Like anybody," he said, "I would like to live a long life—longevity has its place."[6]

King's desire to live a long life was rooted in the immense value he attributed to each and every human life—a value he grounded in the religious and philosophical principle of human personality.[7] This principle—

---

4. *The Autobiography of Martin Luther King Jr.*, ed. Clayborne Carson (New York: Warner, 1998), 102. Because of the accessibility of this volume—which is a compilation of many important primary sources deposited in the King Papers Project—I will sometimes cite this source. For a list of the primary sources used in this volume, as well as their location, see the document titled "Source Notes" in the back of the book (371–90).

5. Quoted in David J. Garrow, *Bearing the Cross: Martin Luther King Jr., and the Southern Christian Leadership Conference* (New York: Random House, 1986), 512–13.

6. King, "I've Been to the Mountaintop," in Carson and Shepard, eds., *A Call to Conscience*, 222.

7. For expert analyses of this principle in King's thought, Rufus Burrow Jr., *God and Human Dignity: The Personalism, Theology, and Ethics of Martin Luther King Jr.* (Notre Dame: University of Notre Dame Press, 2006); Rufus Burrow Jr., "Personalism, the Objective Moral Order, and Moral Law in the Work of Martin Luther King Jr.," in Lewis V. Baldwin et al., *The Legacy of Martin Luther King Jr.: The Boundaries of Law, Politics, and Religion* (Notre Dame: University of Notre Dame Press, 2002), 213–52; Rufus Burrow, Jr., "Personal-Communitarianism and the Beloved Community," *Encounter* 61/1 (2000) 23–43; Rufus Burrow Jr., *Personalism: A Critical Introduction* (St. Louis: Chalice,

informed by America's founding documents, the legacy of black churches since the time of slavery, and a school of philosophy and theology known as personalism—has three interrelated dimensions in King's thought.

First, it holds that the individual person—each person in every time and place—is *sacred* and *equal* in value to all other persons. Precious dignity inheres in each individual just by virtue of his or her existence; it is not determined by anything human that exists outside or beyond the individual, especially governments. Theologically speaking, King understood the sacred worth of the individual to be the handiwork of a personal God who shows love for each person by creating him or her in the divine image. Because we are all made in the image of God, each of us has sacred worth conferred by the Creator, a worth that is shared equally by all of God's people.[8]

Second, King's principle of personality maintains that the essence of the human individual is *freedom*. It is freedom that makes each of us uniquely human—not just freedom of the human will but freedom of the entire person. King understood freedom to be the human capacity to weigh alternatives, to decide among them, and to answer for the choices one makes. Although this may seem abstract at points in his writings, he also depicted it in the most practical of terms. Freedom is about having the everyday capacity to choose where to learn, work, play, and love. Again, this was a theological point for King: God creates each person to be sovereign of his or her own life choices, and thus not to be enslaved by anyone else's thoughts or actions.[9]

Third, the principle of personality sees each person as part of a *community* of people. Each person is in solidarity with others, bound together by similar characteristics, needs, and desires. And because all human life is interrelated, no one person can become wholly fulfilled while others are oppressed. Whatever affects one, affects all. When expressing this point theologically, King stated that God created the universe with an interrelated structure of reality, and that God continues to form all people as equal, and precious, members of the human family. In his explicitly Christian

---

1999); and Douglas Sturm, "Crisis in the American Republic: The Legal and Political Significance of Martin Luther King's 'Letter from a Birmingham Jail,'" *Journal of Law and Religion* 2/2 (1984) 309–24.

8. See, for example, King, "The Ethical Demands for Integration," in *A Testament of Hope: The Essential Writings and Speeches of Martin Luther King Jr.*, ed. James M. Washington (New York: HarperCollins, 1986), 118–19. This is perhaps the best article for a brief and clear statement of King's doctrine of humanity. For a secondary source on this doctrine, see Noel Leo Erskine, *King among the Theologians* (Cleveland: Pilgrim, 1994), 147–54.

9. See King, "The Ethical Demands for Integration," in Washington, ed., *A Testament of Hope*, 119–21.

moments, King also claimed that we are all sisters and brothers in Christ—alike not in appearances but in the reality that God in Christ loves us equally as part of one family.[10]

This tripartite principle is the key to understanding King's affirmation of life and his aversion to death. Simply stated, King wanted to live a long life because he considered human life, including his own, to be deeply precious.[11] Death is so troubling to King exactly because it kills a person who is made in the image of God, free and equal, and bound in community with others. Death destroys something precious. Just as troubling is its permanent elimination of an individual's opportunity to bear witness to God's creation of the human personality; the deceased, after all, cannot be equal with others, free to deliberate and decide, and in communion with other members of the human family. Death destroys possibilities to witness to God's priceless creation.

On a more concrete level, King's desire to live a long life was also rooted in his passionate feelings about civil rights work. These feelings came to public expression especially when he recounted a letter he had received from a young girl shortly after his nearly fatal stabbing by a mentally challenged woman in Harlem in 1958. The girl was inspired to write after she heard a news report that, given the blade's proximity to the main aorta of his heart, King would have died had he sneezed while the blade was still in him. She reacted to this news by writing King that she was so happy that he did not sneeze.

King agreed. And in his last public speech, as in many others before it, he stated that if he had sneezed, he would have missed the student sit-ins, the Freedom Rides, and the chance to see blacks straightening their backs in Albany and Birmingham. He would have missed the opportunity to tell America about his dream, to lead the March from Montgomery to Selma, and to join his brothers and sisters in Memphis. "I'm so happy that I didn't sneeze," he said.[12]

King also had a deeply personal reason for saying no to death, and he publicly expressed this reason many times too, especially when recounting the "kitchen experience."[13] The kitchen experience grew out of a frightening

---

10. See ibid., 121–22.

11. See too King, "Advice for Living," *The Papers of Martin Luther King Jr.*, ed. Clayborne Carson et al. (Berkeley: University of California Press, 2000), 4:306: Each and every person is "a being of spirit, born for the stars and created for eternity."

12. King, "I've Been to the Mountaintop," Carson and Shepard, eds., *Call to Conscience*, 222.

13. For more on this experience, see Lewis V. Baldwin, *Never to Leave Us Alone: The Prayer Life of Martin Luther King Jr.* (Minneapolis: Fortress, 2010), 69–70.

moment of despair on a January night in 1956. It had been a long day of dealing with the never-ending demands of the famous bus boycott in Montgomery, and the end of this particularly stressful day stretched on, almost unbearably, when the phone rang just as King was beginning to doze in the comfort of his bed. On the other end was a voice of rage: "Listen, nigger, we've taken all we want from you; before next week you'll be sorry you ever came to Montgomery." It was not a new message—King had heard similar death threats so many times before—but this time he had finally reached his saturation point. Unable to sleep, he went to the kitchen to make a cup of coffee and think of ways to pull out of his leadership position. As he later remembered the moment, "I sat there and thought about a beautiful little daughter who had just been born. I'd come in night after night and see that little gentle smile. I started thinking about a dedicated and loyal wife, who was over there asleep. And she could be taken from me, or I could be taken from her. And I got to the point that I couldn't take it any longer."[14] King's kitchen experience did not stop there, as we will see below, but the important point to note here is that his love for his family gave him yet another reason, perhaps the most important one, to desire a long life.

Life's Ultimate Tragedy

King said no to death not just because he saw human life as precious and cherished his civil rights work and his family, but also because he was deeply familiar with the raw pain of death. One of his earliest formative experiences was the death of his grandmother, Jennie Williams. By his own account, Mama Williams held a special place in her heart for young King, and when she died, he was devastated. That intense feeling was a foretaste of an awful feast to come—one painful death after another in the civil rights movement. King's eulogies for the victims of the movement were not happy celebrations of life, as contemporary funerals tend to be, but lamentations of the soul, plaintive sighs, and echoes of the sad psalms of the Hebrew Bible. Consider his words at the funeral for the four Birmingham girls: "Now the curtain falls; they move through the exit; the drama of their earthly life comes to a close. They are now committed back to the eternity from which they came."[15]

King was not inclined to downplay the agony and finality of death. Even when death did not come prematurely, he still depicted it in the

14. Carson, ed., *Autobiography of Martin Luther King*, 77.

15. King, "Eulogy for the Young Victims of the Sixteenth Street Baptist Church Bombing," in Carson and Shepard, eds., *A Call to Conscience*, 95.

starkest of terms. Preaching to his home congregation in 1966, and without any premature death in mind, he stated: "And then there comes life's ultimate tragedy, that *something* that always makes for a broken heart."[16] For King, that is what death is in its core—the ultimate tragedy that breaks hearts.

The evidence of King's affirmation of human life, and of his desire to live a long life, lies not only in what he said but also in what he did. He took concrete steps throughout his public career to ensure his own personal safety. He used bodyguards early in his career, for example, and he later asked the federal government to provide him with personal protection. On occasion, he also skipped events when death threats were too credible and numerous for him to ignore. King also sought to ensure the safety of those who marched with him and even the safety of his enemies. His whole philosophy of nonviolence, coupled with his pleas for federal troops and marshals at various points in his career, was designed to safeguard the lives of not only his fellow activists but also those who sought to do harm to the civil rights movement. Clearly, King did not want to die a premature death; neither did he want anyone else, even his worst enemies, to experience the same.

Divine Presence and Immortality

Partly because he envisioned death as one of life's *inescapable* tragedies, King also cautioned against resisting it in excess. More positively stated, he envisioned death as a fact of life that we would do well to transform into a positive benefit for humanity. As he put it in the 1966 sermon noted above, "Don't try to escape when you come to that experience. Don't try to repress it." Don't become cynical or bitter, but rather "take your grief and look at it, don't run from it. Say this is my grief (*Yes, sir*) and I must bear it. (*Yes*) Look at it hard enough and say, 'How can I transform this liability into an asset?'"[17]

After 1955 King never really had the chance even to try to escape from death. In addition to the constant threats he faced, one of the lasting impressions of the 1958 stabbing was a scar at the point where the blade had entered his chest—a scar that he saw as a precious reminder of the threat of

---

16. Martin Luther King Jr., "Guidelines for a Constructive Church," in *A Knock at Midnight: Inspiration from the Great Sermons of Reverend Martin Luther King Jr.*, ed. Clayborne Carson and Peter Holloran (New York: Grand Central, 1998), 107–8.

17. King, "Guidelines for a Constructive Church," in Carson and Holloran, eds., *A Knock at Midnight*, 109.

death. Andrew Young reports that King would sometimes say to his followers: "'Each morning as I brush my teeth and wash my face, I am reminded by the cross-shaped scar on my chest that each and any day could be my last day on this earth.' Then he'd smile and say we'd better make sure that what we were doing was worth dying for."[18] Therein lies the meaning of transforming death—using the inevitability of death as inspiration for devoting one's life to a precious cause.

King never systematized his thought about transforming death, but it is possible to identify various parts of his notion of this life-affirming practice. Most fundamentally, it requires conquering one's fear of death. King himself found it difficult not to be concerned about the daily death threats that came his way, and his friends and colleagues believed that the threats clearly took their toll on his emotional state, even driving him into depression at times. But as he wrestled with his concerns in private, King publicly claimed throughout his career that he had moved beyond a paralyzing fear of death.

In King's telling, he was able to do so partly because of his kitchen experience in 1956. After expressing his fears in prayer on that lonely January night, King began to sense the presence of God—and to hear God promising him to remain by his side forever, and calling him to remain resolute in the face of death. As King remembered the event, "It seemed as though I could hear the quiet assurance of an inner voice saying, 'Martin Luther, stand up for righteousness. Stand up for justice. Stand up for truth. And lo, I will be with you. Even until the end of the world.'" The personal experience of hearing that voice—and trusting in it—was life-changing for King. "At that moment," he recounted, "I experienced the presence of the Divine as I had never experienced him before. Almost at once my fears began to go. My uncertainty disappeared. I was ready to face anything."[19]

From the kitchen experience until the time of his death, King publicly claimed that he had conquered the fear of death. When asked about the death threats he constantly faced, he stated: "I have learned now to take them rather philosophically . . . One has to conquer the fear of death if he is going to do anything constructive in life and take a stand against evil."[20] Even on the day before his death, when death itself was just around the corner, King stood before the gathered throng of his followers and announced:

---

18. Andrew Young, "Introduction: I've Been to the Mountaintop," Carson and Shepard, eds., *A Call to Conscience*, 202.

19. Carson, ed., *Autobiography of Martin Luther King Jr.*, 78.

20. Quoted in Garrow, *Bearing the Cross*, 393.

"I'm not worried about anything; I'm not fearing any man. Mine eyes have seen the glory of the coming of the Lord."[21]

On the one hand, conquering the fear of death requires trusting in the *abiding* presence of a God who, right here and now, can make a way out of no way.[22] But on the other, it means trusting that God can make a way out of no way even *after* death.

King did not believe in a heaven bordered by pearly gates and paved with gold (or, for that matter, in a hell overseen by the devil). As a student, he had argued that the traditional belief that Jesus and his followers physically resided in heaven made no sense in a Copernican understanding of the universe. But throughout his life King did believe in personal immortality—a belief that he had stated in seminary: "The Christian sees reality in immortality because he sees reality in God." For King, death is a gateway to life eternal because of who God is: "God is a God that will conserve all values of the universe."[23]

In life eternal, as King understood it, God will conserve values, including human life, and bring earthly virtue to fulfillment. "Would this not be a strangely irrational universe," he wrote in 1963, "if God did not ultimately join virtue and fulfillment, and an absurdly meaningless universe if death were a blind alley leading the human race into a state of nothingness?"[24] But the conservation of values and the fulfillment of virtue will not be physical; heaven is not a physical place, and life after death is not physical, either. "For us," King wrote as a student, "immortality will mean a spiritual existence."[25] Trusting in personal immortality was part of King's method for overcoming the fear of death. He could face death because of his belief that God would conserve him and bring virtue to fulfillment in life after death. Such trust was also the path he commended for survivors of deceased loved ones. Consider his comments to the parents of the murdered Birmingham girls:

21. King, "I've Been to the Mountaintop," in Carson and Shepard, eds., *A Call to Conscience*, 223.

22. For more on King's trust in the presence of God, see Thomas Mikelson, "Cosmic Companionship: The Place of God in the Moral Reasoning of Martin Luther King Jr.," *Journal of Religious Ethics* 18 (Fall 1990) 1–14. Mikelson argues that as King's thought grew more radical in the last three years of his life, his doctrine of God (and his trust in God as "cosmic companion") remained constant.

23. King, "The Christian Pertinence of Eschatological Hope," in *The Papers of Martin Luther King Jr.*, , ed. Clayborne Carson et al. (Berkeley: University of California Press, 1992), 1:271.

24. "Shattered Dreams," in Martin Luther King Jr., *Strength to Love* (New York: Harper & Row, 1963), 86.

25. King, "The Christian Pertinence of Eschatological Hope," in Carson et al., eds., *The Papers of Martin Luther King Jr.*, 1: 272.

> I hope you can find some consolation from Christianity's affirmation that death is not the end. Death is not a period that ends the great sentence of life, but a comma that punctuates it to more lofty significance. Death is not a blind alley that leads the human race into a state of nothingness, but an open door which leads man into life eternal.[26]

King did not dare to explain how all this would happen; he never offered a developed theory of atonement, for example. Rather, he seemed content enough simply to announce that "God through Christ has taken the sting from death by freeing us from its dominion."[27] Although trying to explain exactly how God did that was not in his theological repertoire, King nevertheless gave consistent expression to his unwavering belief that God would indeed take us by the hand not only here on earth but also in that transition from physical life to spiritual existence.

The Politics of Salvation

While embracing heaven, King's death theology maintained that it is wholly insufficient, even unfaithful, to focus merely on the immortality to come. "It's all right to talk about heaven," he said. "I talk about it because I believe firmly in immortality. But you've got to talk about the earth. It's all right to talk about white robes over yonder, but I want a suit and shoes to wear down here."[28] As one who preached a social gospel, King resisted the traditional practice of depicting heaven as the "pie in the sky" that we will one day get to enjoy. Instead, he consistently preached that life eternal should give shape to everyday life on earth. With this advice, King held to a fluid notion of salvation: Life eternal is a place of rest, but salvation itself is a process that begins on earth.[29]

Transforming death thus requires not only conquering fear but also using the image of heaven—where God conserves and fulfills each and every person—to form earth into a place where everyone respects the dignity and worth of human personality. Practically, this means that salvation, as a process that begins on earth, is at least partly political—it is about working

---

26. King, "Eulogy for the Young Victims of the Sixteenth Street Baptist Church Bombing," in Carson and Shepard, eds., *A Call to Conscience*, 98.

27. "Shattered Dreams," in King, *Strength to Love*, 95.

28. King, "Why Jesus Called a Man a Fool," in Carson and Holloran, eds., *A Knock at Midnight*, 147.

29. King, "Unfulfilled Dreams," in Carson and Holloran, eds., *A Knock at Midnight*, 196.

for civil rights right here and right now. The reason for this is eminently clear: for King, respect for the human personality requires the establishment of civil and human rights for everyone.

King argued time and again that the principle of human personality is best expressed, politically, in the most famous words of the Declaration of Independence: "All men are created equal. They are endowed by their Creator with certain inalienable rights, among these are life, liberty, and the pursuit of happiness." These inalienable rights, in King's thought, are *political* expressions of the *theological* reality that God created all people to be free, equal, and bound together in community.[30] Moreover, King believed the same about all the rights identified in the US Constitution, as well as what he called human rights, like the right to a livable wage—all of them are essential and necessary expressions of the principle of personality.[31]

Further, as a political liberal, King maintained that the purpose of civil rights is not to maximize the independence of the individual but, rather, to act as claims on social and political systems in order to provide a context for the flourishing of our life together, all of us. The struggle for civil rights, as he conceived it, is thus a positive movement to establish justice within a community that gives individuals—all individuals—the space and resources required for realizing their God-given dignity, equality, and freedom in a spirit of cooperation with all other individuals. To build this "beloved community" is not only to encounter salvation, in King's thought, but also to undertake a mission worth dying for, even at the hands of vicious racists.

The Dangerous Road of Salvation

King quickly came to realize that the road of salvation, as he defined it, was lined with would-be murderers lying in wait—individuals and organizations fully prepared to kill anyone who called for a beloved community marked by racial reconciliation, economic justice, and nonviolence. In the last three years of his life alone, these folks included the Christian Nationalist State Army, the Ku Klux Klan, racist loners, and even some black militants. King fully knew that there was no shortage of people who wanted him dead—they were everywhere.

---

30. See "The American Dream," in Washington, ed., *A Testament of Hope*, 208–9; and King, "The Ethical Demands for Integration," in ibid., 119. King began drawing connections between his Christian doctrine of humanity and the US Constitution as far back as his high school years (See "The Negro and the Constitution," in Carson, et al., eds., *The Papers of Martin Luther King Jr*, 1:361).

31. "I Have a Dream," Washington, ed., *A Testament of Hope*, 217.

In 1964 as he was plotting his campaign to secure the right to vote for African Americans, King also realized that his would-be killers included the US government. In November, agents of J. Edgar Hoover's FBI sent King a tape recording of his sexual indiscretions in hotel rooms. Included with the recording was a note, signed by "us Negroes," with the following message: "King, like all frauds, your end is approaching. You could have been our greatest leader.... But you are done.... King, there is only one thing left for you to do. You know what it is.... There is but one way out for you."[32] The message from the FBI was clear: Kill yourself, or we will let the world know about your indiscretions.

With their focus on keeping order in the Cold War era, Hoover and his agents had identified King as an "enemy of the state" and devoted extraordinary resources to silencing him.[33] In addition to making the direct threat in November 1964, Hoover and his team also refused to inform King of numerous death threats against him at various points. There is little doubt, as Clarence B. Jones rightly suggests, that the US government, in the form of Hoover and his agency, helped to create the culture of violence that led to King's death.

The threats against King, delivered by multiple sources, many of them still unknown, never stopped from 1955 until the day of his assassination, and they weighed heavily on him, especially on the night before he died in Memphis, when he mentioned "what would happen to me from our sick white brothers."[34] King did not want to die that night in 1968, but he also made sure to tell his rapt audience that the threats did not really matter to him—what mattered was doing the will of God. It was a familiar message. Throughout his public career King had openly expressed a willingness to die for the sake of civil rights. In the 1956 Montgomery speech in which he had claimed that he did not want to die, for example, he had also stated: "But if anyone has to die, let it be me."[35]

Being willing to die was another essential requirement in the practice of transforming death into a life benefit. For King, there comes a time

---

32. US Congress, Senate, Select Committee to Study Governmental Operations with Respect to Intelligence Activities, *Supplementary Detailed Staff Reports on Intelligence Activities and the Rights of Americans, Book III, Final Report*, April 23, 1976 (Washington DC: GPO, 1976); as quoted in Jones and Engel, *What Would Martin Say?* 199–200.

33. Jones uses the expression "enemy of the state" in Jones and Engel, *What Would Martin Say?*, 201.

34. King, "I've Been to the Mountaintop," in Carson and Shepard, eds., *A Call to Conscience*, 222.

35. Carson, ed., *The Autobiography of Martin Luther King Jr.*, 102.

when we must place our whole body—our very life—into the protest against wrong and the struggle for right. His clearest statement of this belief—an unmistakable echo of the kitchen experience—can be found in his November 5, 1967, sermon at Ebenezer Baptist Church in Atlanta. "I say to you . . . that if you have never found something so dear and so precious that you will die for it, then you aren't fit to live," King preached. If you refuse to place your body on the line because of fear, he added, or because you want to live a long life, you are already dead. "And the cessation of breathing in your life is but the belated announcement of an earlier death of the spirit. You died when you refused to stand up for right. You died when you refused to stand up for truth. You died when you refused to stand up for justice."[36] The willingness to die is so necessary because the road of salvation is such a dangerous place, full of murderous thugs. Salvation is not only a political thing—it is a deadly thing.

As he called upon his followers to offer their very lives for the sake of right, including civil rights, King often extolled the many victims who had been murdered on the road of salvation. Doing so, he refused to give the murderers more attention than they deserved. Focusing on the killers, whoever they were, would have detracted from King's concerted efforts to extract meaning from the martyrs' deaths—morally noble deaths—for those yet to die on the road. Consider, once again, his moving eulogy for the Birmingham girls:

> And yet they died nobly. They are the martyred heroines of a holy crusade for freedom and human dignity. And so this afternoon in a real sense they have something to say to each of us in their death. They have something to say to every minister of the gospel who has remained silent behind the safe security of stained-glass windows. They have something to say to every politician (*Yeah*) who has fed his constituents with the stale bread of hatred and the spoiled meat of racism. They have something to say to a federal government that has compromised with the undemocratic practices of southern Dixiecrats (*Yeah*) and the blatant hypocrisy of right-wing northern Republicans. (*Speak*) They have something to say to every Negro (*Yeah*) who has passively accepted the evil system of segregation and who has stood on the sidelines in a mighty struggle for justice. They say to each of us, black and white alike, that we must substitute courage for caution. *They say to us that we must be concerned not merely about who murdered them, but about the system, the way of life, the philosophy which produced the murderers. Their death*

---

36. Ibid., 344.

says to us that we must work passionately and unrelentingly for the realization of the American dream.[37]

King did not want survivors to focus exclusively on those who killed the martyrs, but to see their deaths as part of a much wider culture of violence and as a source of inspiration for advancing respect for the human personality on earth. In effect, King transforms the death of martyrs into a call to action—a call to place our own bodies on the dangerous road of salvation in pursuit of the beloved community. Identifying the assassins of the martyrs is important, to be sure, but never as important as transforming the liability of their deaths into an asset for the beloved community—the primary reason for placing our own bodies in service of the will of God.

Dreams Killed

King was a realist about the possibilities of transforming death into an asset for peace and justice. After all, so many good people had already died in the civil rights movement, and his own life seemed just minutes away from being snuffed out at various points. He thus fully conceded that the act of transforming death may not be completed in short order, either for an individual or for society. To be sure, he remained hopeful that transformation could take place. As he put it in his eulogy for the Birmingham girls:

> The innocent blood of these little girls may well serve as a redemptive force (*Yeah*) that will bring new light to this dark city. (*Yeah*) The holy Scripture says, "A little child shall lead them." (*Oh yeah*) The death of these little children may lead our whole Southland (*Yeah*) from the low road of man's inhumanity to man to the high road of peace and brotherhood. (*Yeah, Yes*) These tragic deaths may lead our nation to substitute an aristocracy of character for an aristocracy of color. The spilled blood of these innocent girls may cause the whole citizenry of Birmingham (*Yeah*) to transform the negative extremes of a dark past into the positive extremes of a bright future. Indeed this tragic event may cause the white South to come to terms with its conscience.[38]

But King's use of the word "may" was significant; it revealed his realistic understanding that there was no guarantee that the death of the girls would *in fact* transform their killers and the culture of death that fueled the killings.

37. "Eulogy for the Young Victims of the Sixteenth Street Baptist Church Bombing," in Carson and Shepard, eds., *A Call to Conscience*, 96 (italics added).

38. "Eulogy for the Young Victims of the Sixteenth Street Baptist Church Bombing," in ibid., 96–97.

Although he did not give direct voice to his realism in his eulogy, his use of "may" nevertheless indicated his belief that the death of the girls *may not* transform the South, especially in light of the deadly resistance that the beloved community faced there.

King was no rosy idealist when assessing the ability of death to transform the broken community into the beloved community, and near the end of his life he certainly gave loud voice to his realism. "So many of us in life," he preached in March 1968, "start out building temples: temples of character, temples of justice, temples of peace. And so often we don't finish them." We don't finish them because we cannot. "And I guess one of the great agonies of life is that we are constantly trying to finish *that which is unfinishable*. We are commanded to do that." King had in mind the Vietnam War. "We speak out against war, we protest, but it seems that your head is going against a concrete wall," he added. "It seems to mean nothing. And so often as you are set out to build the temple of peace you are left lonesome; you are left discouraged; you are left bewildered. Well, that is the story of life."[39]

For King, the story of life is that death often wins. Perhaps the most compelling indication of his realistic sense about the power of death, though, is that famous seven-word sentence he delivered near the end of the "mountaintop speech": "I may not get there with you."[40] Although he did not know that James Earl Ray would assassinate him the next day, on the last evening of his life King recognized that his dream of transforming death into the beloved community might not come to fulfillment in his lifetime: Death was just too strong, too powerful, too resistant to life.

Death Defied

But it is wholly insufficient to characterize King merely as a realist in the face of the power of death. In the final analysis, he was a tempered realist—one relentlessly driven by Christian duty and hope. Despite shattered dreams, King's final advice was unwavering: Stay on the road of salvation, especially when the would-be murderers seem to be gaining the upper hand. What matters most in life, he claimed, is not that we *succeed* in transforming death but that we consistently *try*, even in the face of abject failure, to serve others.[41]

39. "Unfulfilled Dreams," in Carson and Holloran, eds., *A Knock at Midnight*, 192.

40. King, "I've Been to the Mountaintop," in Carson and Shepard, eds., *A Call to Conscience*, 223.

41. King, "The Drum Major Instinct," in Carson and Holloran, eds., *A Knock at Midnight*, 184–86.

King expressed two primary reasons for counseling against despair. One reason is self-evident and driven by duty: If we stop trying, death will win every battle. King made this point in his last speech, albeit rhetorically, by referring to the parable of the Good Samaritan. Unlike the priest and the Levite, according to King, the Good Samaritan asked, "'If I do not stop to help this man, what will happen to him?' That's the question before you tonight. Not, 'If I stop to help the sanitation workers, what will happen to my job?' . . . The question is not, 'If I stop to help this man, what will happen to me?' The question is, 'If I do not stop to help the sanitation workers, what will happen to them?'"[42] King's point was unmistakably clear: If we stop trying, lots of people, all of them made in the image of God, will suffer—or even die—and we will fail miserably in our Christian duty to respect the human personality. Hence, we need to exercise "a kind of dangerous unselfishness."[43]

A second reason for counseling against despair emerged out of traditional Christian faith. King was a realist full of Christian hope. Even when death threats came his way, and when the movement suffered its worse defeats, he kept faith that death would lose.[44] King did not surrender—he defined hope as "a final refusal to give up . . . It means going on *anyhow*"[45]—because he believed that the character of God was morally trustworthy. "Faith in the dawn," he proclaimed, "arises from the faith that God is good and just."[46] Exactly because God is good forever, "The dawn will come. Disappointment, sorrow, and despair are born at midnight, but morning follows."[47]

King thus never surrendered his hope that the power of death would be defeated on earth. So when he confessed his belief that the beloved community was not just around the corner in 1965, one year after the murder of the Birmingham girls, he also made it a point to say: "But [that day] is certainly my hope and dream. Indeed, it is the keystone of my faith in the

42. King, "I've Been to the Mountaintop," in Carson and Shepard, eds., *A Call to Conscience*, 219.

43. Ibid., 217.

44. See James H. Cone, "Martin Luther King Jr., and the Third World," *Journal of American History* 74/2 (1987) 467: "No matter how difficult the struggle for justice became, no matter how powerful were the opponents of justice, no matter how many people turned against him, King refused absolutely to lose hope, because he believed that ultimately right will triumph over wrong."

45. Quoted in Robert Michael Franklin, "An Ethic of Hope: The Moral Thought of Martin Luther King Jr.," *Union Seminary Quarterly Review* 40 (January 1986) 49.

46. King, "A Knock at Midnight," in Carson and Holloran, eds., *A Knock at Midnight*, 76.

47. Ibid., 78. King turns here to the witness of Psalm 30:5.

future that we will someday be a thoroughly integrated society."[48] Shortly before his death, he announced that he would "not yield to a politic of despair."[49] Instead, he claimed that because of the trustworthy promises of God, "however dark it is, however deep the angry feelings are, and however violent explosions are, I can still sing 'We Shall Overcome.'"[50] And in his last speech, his hope continued to soar: "I may not get there with you. (*Go ahead*) But I want you to know tonight (*Yes*), that we, as a people, will get to the Promised Land. [*Applause*] (*Go ahead, Go ahead*) And so I'm happy tonight; I'm not worried about anything; I'm not fearing any man. Mine eyes have seen the glory of the coming of the Lord."[51] This speech was the final curtain, and with death calling all around him, King bowed in hope.

As we are left standing, and the depressing but occasionally helpful literature about King's assassination continues to build, it is necessary to remember, if only to keep his legacy straight, that King himself called for all of humanity to transform the power of death, not by focusing on those who kill or assassinate, but by overcoming the fear they seek to instill, working for the civil rights they vigorously oppose, standing ready to die by their blood-stained hands, and trusting all the while that God will one day defeat death and fulfill all of life, including the lives of the assassins. King did not dare to suggest that these practices would lead to the Promised Land anytime soon; he was far too realistic to make such wild predictions. But, as a Christian, he never surrendered his hope that God, working in concert with dangerously unselfish individuals, would one day lead the living into the Promised Land and thereby take away the sting of death on earth. Nor did King ever surrender his trust that death was but a gateway to life eternal. To the bitter end, he believed that God, on earth and in eternity, would conserve and fulfill the human personality in all its glory. In the final analysis, Martin Luther King Jr. died believing that he, and all of us, will live.

48. King, "*Playboy* Interview 1965," in Washington, ed., *A Testament of Hope*, 375.

49. King, "Remaining Awake through a Great Revolution," in Carson and Holloran, eds., *A Knock at Midnight*, 222.

50. Ibid., 223. I disagree with Richard Lischer's sense that King's hope dissipated in the last part of his life. "[King's] sermons of this period," Lischer writes, "do not dispense with metaphorical language, but the soaring images of hope have disappeared" (*The Preacher King: Martin Luther King Jr. and the Word That Moved America* [New York: Oxford University Press, 1997], 160).

51. King, "I've Been to the Mountaintop," in Carson and Shepard, eds., *A Call to Conscience*, 223.

12

A Prophet with Honor?
The Martin Luther King Jr. Holiday and the Making of a National Icon

G. RUSSELL SEAY JR.

The irony of a person's legacy is that it is shaped by others after his or her death. This begins at the very moment that funeral arrangements are being made. The obituary, bulletin photo, and the eulogy are the first attempts at crafting the person's public image and legacy. While one's life and relationships provide the material for one's legacy, these must be fashioned and created into a comprehensible narrative that gives meaning to the person's life. This process of shaping and interpretation is left to persons who may or may not honor or properly appreciate that legacy. A funeral story on the circuit tells of a wife and mother who, after listening to laudatory comments about her deceased husband, instructed her young son to go look into the casket to make sure that they were at the right funeral. This humorous tale illustrates the human tendency to be generous in talking about the dead, and also how communities so often conspire to transform those who were hardened sinners in life into saints in death.

The public legacy of Martin Luther King Jr. has been the subject of constant debate for over forty years. Some persons and groups insist it is their exclusive prerogative to forge and interpret King's legacy. Some claim ownership of King's legacy, on the one hand, because of their personal relationship to him or their participation in the cultural community of which he was a part (i.e., the African American ethnicity, the black church, the civil rights movement, the American citizenry, the liberal political tradition, and so forth). On the other hand, some claim that their lack of a close relationship with either King or the culture in which he participated makes them more objective observers, thus providing the best vantage point from which to assess King's legacy. Michael Eric Dyson discusses these conflicting claims at great length, with some attention to the question of who owns King's intellectual legacy as contained in his papers. With this in mind, Dyson artfully navigates the thorny issues raised by legal versus moral claims with respect to the rights of King's biological family. He concludes that the family members of the slain civil rights leader clearly have the right to harness the King legacy to generate the necessary resources to sustain their existence, but that they should not claim to do so in King's name, especially when this violates the spirit and ethical standards of their dead husband and father.[1]

The battle for control of the legacy of Martin Luther King Jr. began in earnest with the initial push for a national holiday in his honor only four days after his assassination.[2] It continues to the present day and has assumed a special aura with Clarence B. Jones's claim that he, as one of King's closest advisors and confidants, put words in the civil rights leader's mouth, and is therefore the most authoritative interpreter of what King would say about today's social issues.[3] But what Jones claims King would say about issues such as affirmative action, the war in Iraq, and illegal immigration, seems so inconsistent with King's public and well-documented positions that it is difficult to imagine they were as close as Jones claims. Glenn Beck, the conservative television cultural critic, provided another example of using King's legacy. Beck staged a national event on the forty-seventh anniversary of the March on Washington in the place where King gave his "I Have a Dream" speech. Beck invoked King as his inspiration and insisted that he was merely continuing King's work. When King's niece, Alveda King, was challenged because of her participation in Beck's rally, she responded in an opinion piece in the *Christian Science Monitor*. In her 753-word statement she invoked Uncle Martin seven times, and defended Beck's insistence that "Martin Luther King didn't speak only for African-Americans. He spoke for all Americans."[4] While Clarence Jones and Alveda King established their right to define King's legacy on the basis of their personal relationships with

---

1. See Michael Eric Dyson, *I May Not Get There with You: The True Martin Luther King Jr.* (New York: Free Press, 2000), 249–81.

2. John Conyers (D-MI) introduced legislation on April 8, 1968.

3. Clarence B. Jones and Joel Engel, *What Would Martin Say?* (New York: Harper, 2008), xv–xvi.

4. Alveda King, "Glenn Beck 8/28 Rally: It's a Matter of Honor," *The Christian Science Monitor* (August 26, 2010).

him, Glenn Beck highlighted what he sees as his shared convictions with King, noting that they both wanted the best for America.

The National Martin Luther King Jr. holiday and the King monument on the National Mall give Beck and any American citizen, regardless of race, ethnic origin, political persuasion, gender, age, class, or sexual orientation, the right to claim the benefits of the King legacy. As beneficiaries of this legacy, they have a legitimate right to interpret that legacy. Those who desire to honor King's legacy through a national holiday and monument have, in effect, de facto resigned their rights to an exclusive claim to the guardianship of his legacy. They have made a contract with the United States government, having forgotten to read the fine print. Martin Luther King Jr. is no longer exclusively the symbol of the civil rights movement or of the African American community; he is now a national symbol or icon. His words are part of the canon of American sacred texts, and his image is resident in the pantheon of national heroes. As such, King has taken on a larger-than-life image, and is part of the public discourse when it comes to defining and redefining the meaning of America.

This chapter will make the case that the Martin Luther King Jr. national holiday and monument invite an expanded, inclusive community of interpreters of his legacy, not an inclusive, vetted cadre of guardians of his legacy. Clarence B. Jones, Glenn Beck, Alveda King, and the right-wing conservative ideologues have as much right to interpret King as those who are confirmed card-carrying civil right activists. The political processes that created the permanent time and space in the national consciousness necessarily transformed the King image to serve the nation's interest and not the concerns of those who lobbied for it. In other words, the Martin Luther King that the King family and the larger African American community have honored over time is not necessarily the King that is being honored today. This chapter will also argue that King is more specifically elevated to iconic status to serve the interest of American civil religion. It is around this religious dimension of the national life that the continuing impact of King's life and words is being most profoundly felt. The chapter concludes with some assessment of the problems and the potential of the iconic King for the future of the American nation and its citizens of color.

The Politics of the Martin Luther King Jr. National Holiday

Needless to say, the establishment of the Martin Luther King Jr. national holiday in 1983, like the completion of the King monument on the National Mall in 2011, stands as an unparalleled accomplishment. These were accomplished in the short spans of fifteen and forty-three years, respectively, after King's death. Civil rights historian Taylor Branch puts the King holiday in historical perspective, observing that President George Washington's national birthday holiday came eighty years after his death, and that the Columbus Day holiday was 176 years in the making.[5] The Washington Monument was completed eighty-five years after Washington's death.[6] William H. Wiggins frames the historical development of the national King holiday as a three-act drama. The prologue of the drama began with Michigan's Democratic Congressman John Conyers's introduction of a bill in the US House of Representatives on April 8, 1968, to make King's birthday a national holiday. The first act occurred in the streets with marches and demonstrations in favor of a national holiday. The second act unfolded in the halls of Congress through political debates and hearings. The third and final act culminated in the Rose Garden of the White House, where President Ronald Reagan begrudgingly signed into law the Martin Luther King Jr. national holiday.[7]

Wiggins assigns the leading actors' parts in this unfolding drama to Representative John Conyers and King's widow, Mrs. Coretta Scott King. Conyers introduced the bill initially in 1968 and reintroduced it each year until its passage. Mrs. King lobbied for the bill from its beginning until it was signed into law. There were a number of supporting actors. Among those singled out for special mention were Walter Fauntroy and Andrew Young, both of whom were close associates of King in the civil rights movement, and both of whom later served as US congressmen.[8] It is important to note that these individuals, all African Americans, were either involved in the movement or had a close relationship with King. They had their own ideas of what the King holiday should mean. Mrs. King framed the day around the idea of nonviolence. After her husband's birthday was made a federal holiday, she stated, "For me the overriding importance of the holiday is that it can help America focus on forging a new commitment to nonviolence ... The efficacy of the philosophy of nonviolence is the most important lesson we can draw from the life and work of Martin Luther King, Jr."[9] However, in

---

5. Taylor Branch, "Uneasy Holiday: How Should We Honor a Man We Still Don't Know?," *The New Republic* (February 3, 1986) 22.

6. Online: http://www.nps.gov/nr/travel/wash/dc72.htm/.

7. William H. Wiggins, *O Freedom! Afro-American Emancipation Celebrations* (Knoxville: University of Tennessee Press, 1987), 134–35.

8. Ibid., 150–51. It is significant that in 1983 singer Stevie Wonder funded a lobbying office in Washington, DC that ultimately led to obtaining more than 6 million signatures on petitions to Congress in support of a King national holiday. See Clayborne Carson et al. eds., *The Martin Luther King Jr. Encyclopedia* (Westport, CT: Greenwood, 2008), 184.

9. Quoted in Wiggins, *O Freedom!*, 151

the context of what it took for King's birthday to become a federal holiday, Mrs. King's observation should be understood as deriving not merely from her capacity as his wife or the guardian of her husband's legacy but largely from her role as a private citizen.

It is not the first or the second act of Wiggin's drama that holds the key to understanding the transfer of the guardianship of King's legacy from the private to the public realm. To be sure, both the demonstrations and the signing of the bill by Reagan were important, but the demonstrations could only influence, not make the decisions. President Reagan could have vetoed the bill, but at what cost to his own legacy, the nation's tranquility, and his political party's detriment? As it turned out, Reagan's decision to sign the bill was motivated by political expediency rather than moral considerations, for his view of King's meaning for the nation was just as distorted as that of others on the right side of the political spectrum.

It was in the halls of Congress that the issues would be resolved as to whether the holiday would become a reality. Four hundred thirty-five congresspersons and one hundred senators ultimately decided the fate of the Martin Luther King Jr. Birthday Act. This also made the decision essentially a political one, for the persons making the decision confronted enormous pressure from their constituencies. As with all political decisions, compromises shaped the final outcome. It was in the context of a national political debate over fourteen years that the Congress eventually passed the King Holiday bill. For the bill to become a reality, the image of King had to transcend race and civil rights. The Congressional Black Caucus had only forty-three of the 535 representatives and senators, and, under such conditions, it would have been impossible to motivate the Congress to pass such a bill on the basis of race or racial interests alone. It was in the sphere of the national debate that a number of issues had to be addressed with respect to Martin Luther King Jr. the man, in order for the nation to confer such an honor.

The primary obstacles to the efforts to enshrine King in the national consciousness through a federal holiday involved issues that related to the timing of the honor, the suitability of King for a national honor, and the appropriateness of the honor itself.[10] To be sure, there were many more side issues, but in order to overcome these obstacles, King necessarily had to be transformed into a symbolic figure that transcended race, class, and gender. Out of political necessity, government officials were forced into creating an iconic figure to gain support for the legislation for the Martin Luther King Jr. national holiday.

10. For a summary of the arguments surrounding these issues see ibid., 139–50.

On the Timing, Suitability, and Nature of the King Honors

The issue of the timing of such an honor was valid. King had not been funeralized when the first effort at a national holiday occurred. During the joint congressional hearings, the issue of timing was raised, as testimony was given before Congress by Clifford J. White III, the national director of Young Americans for Freedom, North Carolina's Republican senator Jesse Helms, and Georgia's Democratic congressman Larry McDonald. Wiggins notes that the testimony of White echoed concerns entertained by Helms, McDonald, and "a host of other bit players," especially when he said:

> National holidays are important occasions for all Americans. When an individual is recognized—or rather almost canonized—through a national holiday in his honor, it is understood that the individual had a unique and indispensible impact on this nation's history. So great a recognition is this that only Christopher Columbus and George Washington have in this way been honored. To recognize Martin Luther King, a patriotic American to be sure, would classify him along with Washington—and above Lincoln, Jefferson, and Adams. We would do this without the benefit of being able to put his memory under the test of time.[11]

While White's argument made an important concession, particularly in reference to Martin Luther King's patriotism, he, at the same time, raised a twofold question regarding timing and suitability. First, had enough time passed to assess King's legacy; and, second, would King's legacy in the light of the long view of history match that of Christopher Columbus and George Washington in terms of its impact on the nation? The persuasiveness of these questions was steeped in White's assertion that such an honor canonized the person. The idea was that a national icon should have sacred meaning for all citizens.

Joseph Lowery, a minister and lieutenant of King's in the Southern Christian Leadership Conference (SCLC), while sidestepping the first part of the question, addressed the second part in his testimony before the Congress. Lowery countered Clifford White's suggestion that a national King holiday would only have significance for African Americans. Lowery then addressed the concerns raised with respect to King's historical stature. He argued:

---

11. US Congress, Senate, Committee on the Judiciary, and House, Committee on Post Office and Civil Service, *Martin Luther King, Jr., Holiday Bill*, 96th Congress, 1st Session, Senate 25 (Washington, DC: GPO, 1979), 31. Quoted in ibid., 144–45.

> While it is regrettably true that in our more than 200-year history, we have not so honored a black American, the designation of Dr. King's birthday as a national holiday would transcend the issue of race and color . . . If Columbus discovered America, Martin helped America discover itself . . . If Washington established a Nation, Martin led the Nation to understand that there can be no nationhood without brotherhood.[12]

Lowery's argument essentially conceded that the rationale for a King holiday had to be grounded in the civil rights leader's transcendent value to the national identity, and not in what he did for a specific demographic within the nation. In other words, King, as symbol of the nation, had to be essentially stripped of his racial and regional identity as well as his civil rights mantle. These classifications were to be judged as secondary to his American identification.

Wiggins contends that another obstacle to the King holiday was whether or not King was the most suitable African American for such an honor. Persons such as Booker T. Washington, George Washington Carver, and General Daniel "Chappie" James were offered as possible alternatives to Martin Luther King Jr. for such an honor.[13] Coretta Scott King conceded that there were other African Americans deserving of such an honor. However, she insisted that her husband met the essential qualifications raised by White, stressing the essential universality of King as an American symbol. She observed,

> It may be argued that throughout American history, there have been many black historical figures other than Martin who deserve to be honored with a holiday in their name—Crispus Attucks to Harriett Tubman to Booker T. Washington—to name just a few. But it should be remembered that previous black leaders necessarily addressed issues that tended to concern blacks exclusively, while Martin Luther King, Jr., spoke to us all.[14]

Mrs. King's response followed the same logic and strategy used by Lowery (i.e., to distance King from his racial and ethnic identity, and quite indirectly from his southern identity, while emphasizing his significance to all Americans). The irony is that King's final and most controversial years were the most universal in scope, as he challenged America on the issues of class

---

12. US Congress, Senate, Committee on the Judiciary, and House, Committee on Post Office and Civil Service, 27–28. Quoted in ibid., 145.

13. Ibid., 146.

14. Quoted in Ibid., 147.

and the Vietnam War. However, these years were virtually ignored in the shaping of King's persona and image as a national symbol.

Another obstacle that had to be overcome was the nature of the King honor. The most compelling compromise came with the suggestion that instead of a paid holiday, there could be a National Day of Remembrance similar to Mother's Day or Father's Day. Anything more substantial, according to this line of thinking, would imply that King was more significant than even the nation's founders. Massachusetts Democratic senator Edward M. Kennedy responded emphatically to these points, arguing that while the founding fathers did a magnificent job in framing the Constitution and establishing the nation, they failed to live up to their own ideals and courage in the Revolutionary War by not addressing the race issue and denying self-determination to African slaves. Furthermore, the issue of race was at the center of the Civil War, but even that war left the race business unfinished. Kennedy continued: "We have one person that has done more than our Founding Fathers to push back the walls of discrimination and prejudice in this country. And that was Martin Luther King, Jr."[15] Kennedy argued for King's place in the pantheon of national heroes because his work was consistent with that of the founding of the nation and the establishment of its basic and most cherished values.

Wiggins observes that the second act of drama surrounding the King Holiday closed with at least three dimensions of the symbolism of the Martin Luther King Jr. national holiday bill. The day would commemorate the greatness of the man, the resilience of the African American people, and the enduring power of the nation's democratic values and identity.[16] King had been effectively transformed into the self-reflecting icon of the American ideal. Wiggins underscores Senator Kennedy's words as capturing the essence of the tripartite transcendent and symbolic nature of the holiday:

> it is long time past for our Nation to observe not only the birthday of one of the greatest men in our history, but the contributions of an entire race brought here not in hope but in chains, who built so much of this land, and who in their own liberation have lifted the shadow of prejudice from so many of our fellow citizens. Martin Luther King's day *must be a day for all*

---

15. US Congress, House, Subcommittee on Census and Statistics of the Committee on Post Office and Civil Service, *Designate the Birthday of Martin Luther King, Jr., as a Legal Public Holiday Bill*, 94th Congress. 1st Session, HR1810 (Washington DC: GPO, 1975), 23–24. Quoted in ibid., 135.

16. Ibid., 149.

Americans, because Martin Luther King's dream is the American dream.[17]

In the halls of Congress, in which the will of the nation could be officially expressed, the national Martin Luther King Jr. holiday was enacted. By emphasizing King's meaning to all Americans, this body could commit the nation to honoring him. By transcending the particularity of King the person, a universal symbol could emerge. Those who were the closest to King, such as his widow and fellow civil rights leaders, decided to give up their exclusive claim to his legacy, thus making him more available to all citizens under the banner of the American dream.

On October 19, 1983, the United States Senate voted overwhelmingly to designate the third Monday in January, beginning in 1986, a federal holiday in honor of King. While Congress found the rationale for passing the bill officializing the Martin Luther King Jr. national holiday, the public shaping of the meaning of the holiday began with President Ronald Reagan's "Speech on the Creation of the Martin Luther King, Jr., National Holiday," delivered when the bill was signed into law. President Reagan's speech located King's permanent legacy for America in King's "I Have Dream" speech. Reagan declared: "If American history grows from two centuries to twenty, his words that day will never be forgotten. 'I have a dream that one day on the red hills of Georgia, the sons of former slaves and the sons of former slave owners will be able sit down at the table of brotherhood.'"[18] Reagan then talked about the nation's progress toward the realization of that dream, while acknowledging that the dream had not yet been fully realized. This is what Chris Matthews, a national political analyst, calls *the spin*. The spin, according to Matthews, happens when a politician gains credibility by admitting his failures or indiscretions.[19] Reagan's message in essence was, "we have a long way to go as a nation to realize King's dream, but we are making progress." From the very beginning, it was the King who talked about a dream of brotherhood and the integration of buses, schools, and lunch counters; this King would be memorialized. The King who attacked capitalism, talked about the redistribution of the nation's resources in the interest of the poor, and challenged the nation for its escalation of the war in Vietnam, however, would be ignored.

Beginning in 1994 with President William J. Clinton, a presidential proclamation would be issued annually in honor of the Martin Luther King

---

17. Quoted in ibid. (italics added).
18. Online: http://millercenter.org/president/speeches/detail/5455/.
19. A word commonly used by Chris Matthews on *Hardball* on the MSNBC Television Network.

Jr. national holiday. Clinton's successor, George W. Bush, continued to issue King holiday proclamations, as does the current president, Barack Obama. President Clinton and his successors would also follow Reagan's pattern in his "Speech on the Creation of the Martin Luther King, Jr., National Holiday" by making use of King's "Dream" language and by challenging the nation on the unfinished business of realizing the dream. Each of President Clinton's King proclamations, except his last one in office, would make a direct or indirect reference to Martin Luther King Jr.'s "I Have a Dream" speech. In the first proclamation he declared:

> Three decades ago, Dr. King described his goals most eloquently in his famous "I Have a Dream" speech at the historic Civil Rights March on Washington. The impassioned plea that rose from the steps of the Lincoln Memorial that summer day stirred the entire Nation, awakening people everywhere to turn from the scourge of racism to embrace the promise of opportunity and democracy for all. He prophetically described a future in which our children are judged "not by the color of their skin, but by the content of their character." His unparalleled commitment to justice and nonviolence challenged us to look deeply within ourselves to find the roots of racism.[20]

President Clinton then issued a profound challenge: "Today, we live in a nation that is stronger because of Dr. King's work. Unfortunately, there is still much division in this great land. Even though the signs that once segregated our communities have been removed, we are still far from achieving the world for which Dr. King struggled, toiled, and bled."[21] While the particular issue to which the dream is applied varied, the pattern remained consistent.

In all eight of his Martin Luther King Jr. federal holiday proclamations, President George W. Bush made either a direct or indirect reference to the "I Have a Dream" speech. His first such proclamation, in 2002, came on the heels of the September 11, 2001, terrorist attack on the World Trade Towers in New York and of the Pentagon in Washington DC. Bush used the speech to call for national unity in the name of King's dream. He asserted:

> We enter this New Year and this annual celebration with a revived national spirit. The events of September 11, 2001, have drawn us closer as a nation and increased our resolve to protect the life and liberty we cherish. And while our patriotism and neighborly affections run high, these circumstances have given

20. Presidential Proclamation, "Martin Luther King Jr., Federal Holiday, 1994, Proclamation 6645," *Federal Register* 59/11 (January 18, 1994) 1.

21. Ibid.

us renewed purpose in rededicating ourselves to Dr. King's 'dream.' As he said on the steps of the Lincoln Memorial on August 28, 1963: "I have a dream my four little children will one day live in a nation where they will not be judged by the color of their skin but by content of their character."[22]

Bush, much like President Clinton, used the proclamation to connect various issues. In proclamations about the 9/11 tragedy, the No Child Left Behind law,[23] and the Voter Rights Act's reauthorization,[24] President Bush alluded to the relevance of King's dream.

In his first two presidential proclamations in celebration of the King holiday, President Barack Obama departed from the use of the "dream" language. Rather, Obama grounded his proclamations in the imagery in King's final speech, given the night before his assassination, in which King talked about reaching the mountaintop and seeing the Promised Land. King uttered these words in Memphis, Tennessee, on April 3, 1968. The civil rights leader told the audience that night that he may not get to the Promised Land with them, but "we, as a people, will get to the Promise Land."[25] In his 2010 proclamation, President Obama challenged the nation in the areas of social and economic justice, invoking words from King's "Mountaintop" speech: "We have an opportunity to make America a better Nation. I may not get there with you. But I want you to know tonight that we, as a people, will get to the promise land."[26] In his second proclamation, President Obama, using the "mountaintop" and "promise land" metaphors, urged the nation to continue to make sacrifices so that all of its citizens are able to participate in the opportunities that America provides.[27]

The presidential proclamations routinely pick up on the theme established by President Ronald Reagan, framing the King legacy via the national holiday in terms of King's dream of equality around the table of brotherhood,

---

22. Presidential Proclamation, "Martin Luther King Jr. Federal Holiday, 2002, Proclamation 7518," *Federal Register* 67/16 (January 17, 2002) 3575.

23. Presidential Proclamation, "Martin Luther King Jr., Federal Holiday, 2003, Proclamation 7642," *Federal Register* 68/15 (January 17, 2003) 3169.

24. Presidential Proclamation, "Martin Luther King Jr., Federal Holiday, 2007, Proclamation 8099," *Federal Register* 72/9 (January 11, 2007) 1907.

25. Martin Luther King Jr., "I've Been to the Mountaintop" in *A Call to Conscience: The Landmark Speeches of Martin Luther King Jr.* ed. Clayborne Carson and Kris Shepard. (New York: Warner, 2001), 222–23.

26. Presidential Proclamation, "Martin Luther King Jr. Federal Holiday, 2010, Proclamation 8473," *Federal Register* 75/14 (January 22, 2010) 3575.

27. Presidential Proclamation, "Martin Luther King Jr., Federal Holiday, 2002, Proclamation 8624," *Federal Register* 76/13 (January 14, 2011) 3819.

but without committing the resources of the nation to guaranteeing that equality. Conspicuously absent in the proclamations, except in the case of President Obama's, is any recognition of the later struggles of King with the nation's economic exploitation, classism, and militarism. In order to secure the holiday, King's family and fellow companions in the struggle for full social and economic justice participated, perhaps unconsciously, in stripping the slain civil rights leader of some of the particularities that gave power and impact to his personality. Obviously, this was done to create the kind of universal transcendent symbol that would be acceptable in the halls of government and in the larger public square.

This process was continued through the annual presidential proclamations and their calls for the nation to celebrate the dreamer, but not the radical prophet and activist. The Martin Luther King Jr. national holiday, from its inception in the halls of Congress to its celebration by the chief executives of the nation, became a means of ensuring that a sanitized and domesticated Martin Luther King Jr. would be presented to the nation for veneration. This is evident in the repetition of certain selected passages from King's "I Have a Dream" speech each January, and in the widespread tendency to cast King in the image of the gentle, harmless preacher who located love and nonviolence, not a revolution of values and priorities, at the core of the Christian faith.

On the King Celebrations and American Civil Religion

Robert Bellah's 1967 article, "Civil Religion in America," appeared almost a year prior to Martin Luther King Jr.'s assassination.[28] This article would create a flurry of conversation and activity around the theme of American civil religion. Phillip Hammond notes that Bellah, using presidential inaugural addresses as a source, provided a "systematic method for observing the rhetoric of American civil religion."[29] The point of Bellah's essay was to make explicit the reality of an American civil religion and to differentiate it from other institutionalized religious expressions found in Christianity and Judaism. While there has long been a fundamental commitment in American culture to the separation of church and state, such separation does not deny

---

28. Robert Bellah, "Civil Religion in America," *Daedalus*, 96/1 (1967) 1–21.

29. Philip E. Hammond, "The Sociology of American Civil Religion: A Bibliographic Essay," *Sociological Analysis* 37/2 (1976) 169. cf. James A. Mathisen "Twenty Years after Bellah: Whatever Happened to American Civil Religion?" *Sociological Analysis* 50/2 (1989) 129–46.

that there is in "the political realm a religious dimension."[30] The religious dimension of the American political and civil society is captured in its set of beliefs, symbols, rituals, sacred texts, and holidays, and is what Bellah refers to as American civil religion.[31] The sociologist Meredith McGuire provides an additional dimension to this definition with respect to the purpose and use of civil religious ritual. She asserts that, "civil religion is the expression of the cohesion of the nation . . . It includes rituals by which members commemorate significant national events and renew their commitment to the society."[32] As shown later, these reflections are essential for viewing the King Holiday in the context of the American civil religious ethos.[33]

Bellah traces the development of the character of American civil religion through what he calls three times of trials: the American Revolution, the American Civil War, and the Vietnam War. The first two events drew on Jewish and Christian imagery found in the Hebrew and Christian sacred texts. The Revolutionary era and the founding of the nation are viewed as parallel to the tradition of the exodus event of the Hebrew sacred text. The essential claim is that the nation's founders were the new Israel establishing a new community of faith, not based on denominations or church affiliations, but on humanity's ability to self-govern. Thus, no limits would be placed on an individual's ability to pursue his or her dreams. The first trial centered on the "question of independence, or whether we should or could run our own affairs in our own way."[34] The nation canonized the Declaration of Independence and the Constitution, the founding documents to which King so often appealed, as the sacred texts which contained its transcendent national values. American self-governance would be ritualized through annual July Fourth celebrations marking the signing of the Declaration of Independence. The national anthem, in which the lyrics memorialize the nation's victorious revolution, would be sung at public gatherings. George Washington emerges from this period as the iconic figure, symbolizing the ideals of the new nation; and while eschewing the title of king, Washington was dubbed the Father of the Nation. Washington's uniqueness and

30. Bellah, "Civil Religion in America," 3.

31. Ibid., 4; cf. 8, 11.

32. Meredith B. McGuire. *Religion, the Social Context.* (Belmont, CA: Wadsworth, 1997), 191, quoted in "Introducing Civil Religion, Nationalism and Globalisation," in Annika Hvithamar and Margit Warburg, eds., *Holy Nations and Global Identities: Introducing Civil Religion, Nationalism and Globalisation*, International Studies in Religion and Society 10 (Leiden: Brill, 2009), 4.

33. See Robert N. Bellah and Phillip E. Hammond, *Varieties of Civil Religion* (San Francisco: Harper & Row, 1980), 15, 171–72, and 194–95; and Lewis V. Baldwin, "The Perversion of Public Religion," *Orbis*, 5/7 (2006), 12.

34. Bellah, "Civil Religion in America," 16.

greatness would later be used by some on the political right in a feeble attempt to deny King a similar niche in the pantheon of the nation's heroes.[35]

Bellah's second time of trial for the nation came during the American Civil War, a period to which King also referred frequently. The issue at stake was whether the nation would extend to all people that same opportunity to participate in the American experience. Slavery prevented the nation from fully institutionalizing the democratic values of the revolution within the country,[36] as both Bellah and King so often said. According to Bellah, the issues surrounding the Civil War required expressions of civil religion. Abraham Lincoln embodied this civil-religious dimension in both his words and his life.[37] Lincoln's Gettysburg Address, delivered at the dedication of the National Cemetery for those who had given their lives for the cause of the preservation of the nation at the Battle of Gettysburg, has been added to the canon of American sacred texts. Bellah points out, "with the Civil War through Lincoln, a new theme of death, sacrifice, and rebirth enters civil religion."[38] The Civil War would give rise to one of the holidays of the national calendar, Memorial Day, to honor those who "gave the last full measure of devotion" in war.[39] Bellah offers little or nothing about how King drew on this kind of Civil War symbolism in his own civil-religious speech, and especially the "I Have a Dream" speech.

Bellah does hint at the fact that the civil rights movement provides some glimpse of the religious dimensions of society, and he and Phillip Hammond conclude that King is "destined to go down in history as a true interpreter and prophet of the American civil religion."[40] However, Bellah sees the third trial of the American civil religion dramatized in the Vietnam War. For him, the issues raised in the civil rights movements were a continuation of the crisis provoked by the Civil War. He observes: "The second time of trial was over the issue of slavery, which in turn was only the most salient aspect of the more general problem of full institutionalization of democracy within our country. Clearly, we are still far from solving this second problem, though we have some notable successes to our credit."[41]

While Bellah points to the assassinated President John F. Kennedy's funeral as an example of the vitality of American civil religion, he misses the

35. See Patrick Buchannan, "A Rascal's Bedroom Escapades Diminish His Status as a Saint," *The Tennessean* (October 22, 1989) 5G.
36. Bellah, "Civil Religion in America," 16.
37. Ibid., 9.
38. Ibid., 10.
39. Ibid, 11.
40. Bellah and Hammond, *Varieties of Civil Religion*, 194.
41. Bellah, "Civil Religion in America," 16.

powerful appeal to American civil religion in the civil rights movement as reflected in the speeches of Martin Luther King Jr. As suggested previously, the most notable example was his "I Have a Dream" speech. Bellah's failure to capture the civil-religious dimension of the civil rights movement in its wholeness was perhaps due to his exclusive focus on the political and presidential speeches. Thus, he picked up on President Lyndon Johnson's appeal to the American civil religion in his speech to Congress regarding the critical need for a voting-rights bill, while missing a similar element in King's "I Have a Dream" oration.[42] Apparently, Bellah did not foresee the concretization of the American civil religion as expressed in the civil rights movement and by the national holiday in honor of its chief spokesman, Martin Luther King Jr. At the same time, Bellah was not completely oblivious to King's significance as an American civil-religious figure.

In spite of the limitations of his perspective, Bellah provides ways to understand the Martin Luther King Jr. federal holiday and the King monument on the national mall as symbols or iconic markers of American civil religion. It is doubtful that those who advocated for the King holiday and participated in the construction of the King monument had in mind the national civil religion. In any case, the best way to understand how the King holiday and monument function in the life of the nation is through the lenses of American civil religion. As discussed earlier, during the Congressional debates around the question of a national holiday in King's honor, some of those involved placed him on a par with the Founding Fathers and Abraham Lincoln. King's significance in the life of the nation was captured in Senator Edward Kennedy's characterization of him as one who helped the nation finish the business that the Founders and Lincoln had left undone. King's words and life became the embodiment of the ideals of America—liberty, freedom, democracy, and justice.

King's death and the manner in which he died are essential elements of the religious nature of his iconic being. Congressman Larry McDonald's expressed opposition to the King holiday because King presumably caused violence in the name of nonviolence may have an element of validity, depending on how one views the situation.[43] While it may be true that King-led demonstrations resulted in violence at times, he did not create the violence. King's actions actually brought to the surface the inherently violent nature of the segregated system and its most vicious white supporters. Convinced that it is always moral and rational to expose the evils of a social order, King, along with those who adhered to his ethic of nonviolence, willingly

---

42. Ibid., 13–14.
43. Wiggins, *O Freedom!*, 141.

absorbed the violence of their opponents with their own bodies. King believed that unearned suffering is redemptive. In this regard, he maintained: "I realize that this approach [nonviolence] means a willingness to suffer and sacrifice. It may mean going to jail. If such is the case the resister must be willing to fill the jail houses of the South. It may even mean physical death. But if physical death is the price that a man must pay to free his children and his white brethren from a permanent death of spirit, then nothing could be more redemptive."[44] It is this notion of redemptive suffering[45]—problematic as it is for some—that allowed King to give his life for what was in the end a human rights cause. To be sure, King not only represented the best in the American tradition of creative protest and dissent but also reintroduced the themes of redemptive suffering, freedom, sacrifice, hope, and deliverance into the nation's public faith.[46]

While Lincoln, according to Bellah, added the concepts of death, sacrifice, and rebirth, King contributed the idea of a nation redeemed through service and suffering. Lincoln's sacrifice has a sense of national atonement for its sin, especially that of slavery. King's redemptive suffering carries the idea of service, self-sacrifice, and hope for the redemption of the other. The impact of the assassination of Martin Luther King Jr. on the national psyche was encapsulated in Pennsylvania's Republican congressman Robert Nix's stirring acknowledgement that "for the first time since the days of Lincoln, America was forced to examine its national guilt, its betrayal of Christian teachings, and its violation of the democratic ethic."[47] The King holiday and the King monument provide an opportunity for the nation to ameliorate its guilt because of slavery and de-facto slavery in the form of Jim Crowism. King, as a symbol of the African American's quest for equality throughout American history, became the scapegoat by which America's guilt is ab-

---

44. Martin Luther King Jr., "The Rising Tide of Racial Consciousness," in James M. Washington, ed., *A Testament of Hope: The Essential Writings of Martin Luther King Jr.* (New York: Harper & Row, 1986), 149.

45. See Joanne Carlson Brown and Rebecca Parker, "For God So Loved the World?" in *Christianity, Patriarchy, and Abuse: A Feminist Critique*, ed. Joanne Carlson Brown and Carole R. Bohn (Cleveland: Pilgrim, 1989), ch. 1; Delores Williams, *Sisters in the Wilderness: The Challenge of Womanist God-Talk* (Maryknoll, NY: Orbis, 1993), 161–70, 199–201; and M. Shawn Copeland, "Wading through Many Sorrows: Toward a Theology of Suffering in Womanist Perspective" in *A Troubling in My Soul: Womanist Perspectives on Evil & Suffering*, ed. by Emilie M. Townes (Maryknoll, NY: Orbis, 1993), ch. 7.

46. See John D. Elder, "Martin Luther King and American Civil Religion," *Harvard Divinity Bulletin*, new ser. 1/3 (Spring 1968) 17–18; Baldwin, "The Perversion of Public Religion," 12; and Andrew M. Manis, *Southern Civil Religions in Conflict: Civil Rights and the Culture Wars* (Macon, GA: Mercer University Press, 2002), 4.

47. Wiggins, *O Freedom!*, 135.

solved. Mrs. Coretta King, lobbying before Congress for the King holiday, observed, "No amount of money can compensate for the brutal injustice of slavery in the United States. But given the hundreds of years of economic sacrifice and involuntary servitude of American Blacks, is it too much to ask that one paid holiday per year be set aside to honor the contributions of a black man who gave his life in an historic struggle for social decency?"[48] The same logic might be applied in the case of the recently dedicated King National Monument.

Mrs. King's argument appeals to the national guilt of slavery and provides a means by which that guilt can be mitigated. Honoring the death of one man becomes one way of paying the nation's debt to its citizens of color, whose involuntary servitude contributed greatly to the nation's economic foundation. The King holiday and the King monument also stand as living symbols to this nation's determination to live out the true meaning of its democratic and Jewish and Christian creeds.

The examination of the presidential proclamations in honor of the Martin Luther King Jr. federal holiday since 1994, like the words inscribed on the King monument, suggests that the "I Have a Dream" speech is now a part of the nation's canon of sacred texts. Of the eighteen proclamations, only two of them did not make direct or indirect reference to the speech.[49] The occasion of the Martin Luther King Jr. federal holiday and the ideas and words of the "I Have a Dream" speech have been used to address a variety of issues directed at advancing some ideal of America. For instance, President George W. Bush used these to call the nation to continued unity in the face of the 9/11 terrorist attacks, while President Barack Obama used them to encourage support for the victims of a devastating earthquake on the island nation of Haiti.[50] What is common to all of the proclamations is that they have an essential element that McGuire believes all civil religions have, namely, "rituals by which members commemorate significant national events and renew their commitment to the society."[51] In all eighteen proclamations, the presidents call the nation to a renewed commitment to

48. Ibid., 143.

49. Only President Clinton's eighth King Holiday proclamation and President Obama's first King holiday proclamation had no direct or indirect reference to the "I Have a Dream" speech. See Presidential Proclamation, "Martin Luther King, Jr. Federal Holiday, 2002, Proclamation 7390," *Federal Register* 66/12 (January 12, 2001) 5417; and Presidential Proclamation, "Martin Luther King Jr. Federal Holiday, 2010, Proclamation 8473," *Federal Register* 75/14 (January 15, 2010) 3841.

50. Presidential Proclamation, "Martin Luther King Jr. Federal Holiday, 2011, Proclamation 8624," *Federal Register* 76/13 (January 14, 2011) 3819.

51. McGuire, 191, quoted in Hvithamar and Warburg, "Introducing Civil Religion," 4.

some ideal that they see as indispensable to America. As a recent addition to American material culture, the King monument is a more tangible testimony to this enduring and pressing need.

Having established the holiday in 1983, the Congress passed the *King Holiday and Service Act of 1994*, which President Bill Clinton signed into law on August 23, 1994.[52] This Act ritualized and further defined the core value of the King legacy as one of service. The Act was promoted through King holiday presidential proclamations. In his second King holiday proclamation, President Clinton declared:

> This year, the Martin Luther King, Jr., holiday is celebrated with a national day of service, a call to join together in purpose and care for one another. On this occasion, I urge the citizens of this great country to reflect upon Dr. King's teachings and to take positive and life-affirming action in his memory. Give back to your community, help the homeless, feed the hungry, attend to the sick, give to the needy. In whatever way you choose to serve the public good, do something to make life better for the people around you. As Dr. King said on many occasions, "Life's most persistent and urgent question is, 'What are you doing for others?'"[53]

Each of President Clinton's successors embraced this theme in their proclamations for the King holiday, in part because the holiday name change also changed the nature and official significance of the day. Additionally, the change brought it national funding to insure that it would be ritualized as a day of service.[54] According to Robert N. Bellah, George Washington represents the value of independence and Abraham Lincoln the value of sacrifice. In addition to these same values, King contributes the value of service to the American civil religion. To be sure, a host of other values are associated with King's legacy that could have been chosen, e.g., justice, equality, dignity, and community. However the nation, through its legislative and executive branches, chose the theme of service.

The national holiday in honor of the life of one who made the ultimate sacrifice in challenging the nation to live up to its high ideals of liberty, justice, and equality provides the elements for redemption and healing.

---

52. King Holiday and Service Act of 1994, Public Law 103-304, 103rd Congress, 2nd session (August 23, 1994).

53. Presidential Proclamation, "Martin Luther King Jr. Federal Holiday, 1995, Proclamation 6765," *Federal Register* 60/9 (January 11, 1995) 3333.

54. The *King Holiday and Service Act* of 1994 provided for the funding of community service projects under the Corporation for National and Community Services. It provided $300,000 for 1995 with a scheduled $50,000 increase each year through 1999.

The power and impact of the King holiday celebration is in its service to American civil religion. It provides an opportunity for a national celebration through its collective remembrance and rituals. Through these celebrations, the nation is called to recommit itself to the pursuit of its transcendent values and ideals. Implied in its recommitments is its recognition that it has not always lived up to its values and ideals.

Honoring Martin Luther King Jr.: A Hindrance or a Challenge?

Taylor Branch raised the question with respect to the first celebration of the national King holiday: "How should we honor a man we still don't know?"[55] A quarter of a century later the question is still valid. The holiday has not provided insights into the man or his message. The repetition of the Dream speech without any illumination of the dream grounded in historical fact has only served to shroud King and his goals in mystery. King has been domesticated to serve the nation's need for cohesion and common commitments in the midst of an ever expanding diversity in political ideology, economic status, cultural pluralism, and religious outlooks. Thus, it is necessary to raise questions as to whether both the King holiday and the King monument are a hindrance or a challenge to moving the nation closer toward the realization of the African American community's quest for full equality and opportunity. In other words, how do we prevent the domestication of King through the national honors bestowed upon him? How might we prevent these honors from undermining or weakening the African American community's drive towards self-determination, empowerment, and uplift? Such questions must be repeatedly asked and seriously addressed, especially in light of the glaring efforts to Americanize King's image so it can be less challenging and threatening.

The first and most important step in seeing the national King holiday for what it is could be the opportunity for the nation as a whole to remember how far we have come in dealing with citizens of African descent. To be sure, the King that is celebrated is only a partial image of the true Martin Luther King. It is the part of King that mainstream America can celebrate without much controversy. In King, the nation has created an iconic figure for the furtherance of the goals of its civil religion. The political processes of icon making have of necessity removed the most uncomfortable particularities of the historical personage of Martin Luther King Jr. The result is a

---

55. Branch, "Uneasy Holiday," 22.

vacuous, nonoffensive personality that can easily be accepted, venerated, and celebrated, even by society's most conservative elements.

The debate over the epithet on the King monument, which reads, "I am a drum major," further highlights this reality. Those who knew King object to what they perceive as the truncating of the words of his sermon. Critics contend that this abbreviated form of what King said gives a false impression of King, the man. In his sermon, King said, "if you want to say that I was a drum major, say that I was a drum major for justice. Say that I was a drum major for peace. I was a drum major for righteousness."[56] It is highly unlikely that the creator of the monument was attempting to project an image of an arrogant King claiming to be a drum major, but this is most certainly suggested. It is more likely that he and others simply missed the nuance of the wording. It appears to have been a matter of utility and space on the stone rather than a conscious effort to project a certain image of King.

While both the holiday and the monument celebrate the iconic King, the African American community should not devote an inordinate amount of time, energy, and resources to insisting that the nation celebrate the historical King. Moreover, African Americans should constantly remind the nation that celebrating King does not mean that we have reached the Promised Land in race relations, or that we now live in a postracial society. The King one chooses to celebrate is likely to determine whether the celebration will hinder or challenge the continuing push for equality and social justice. The iconic King created by the powers that be tends toward complacency and even conformity, while the historical King challenges us to push towards the fulfillment of our most far-reaching dreams and possibilities. The iconic King allows the nation to celebrate without taking actual steps toward radical social and economic change. The King fossilized in 1963 at the Lincoln Memorial allows the nation to remain in the dream state, forever pursuing integration without a sharing of power, and never reaching the goal of full equality. President Reagan could sign the King holiday bill even though he was ambiguous about King's loyalty to the country. He signed it because it was a prop for the national political interest.[57] Similarly, after the 9/11 terrorist attacks, President Bush unhesitatingly and seamlessly weaved the elements of King's dream speech together with patriotism and veiled threats of violent retaliation for the attacks.[58] Such actions suggest an abuse

56. "The Drum Major Instinct," in Clayborne Carson and Peter Holloran, eds., *A Knock at Midnight: Inspirations from the Great Sermons of Reverend Martin Luther King Jr.* (New York: Warner, 1998), 185.

57. Branch, "Uneasy Holiday," 24.

58. Presidential Proclamation, "Martin Luther King Jr. Federal Holiday, 2002,

of the King legacy that no sincere and well-meaning advocate for peace and freedom can casually accept.

The celebration of the iconic King encourages rituals and rhetoric without righteousness, and expressions of concern and goodwill without the pursuit of justice and the actualization of the beloved community. The King monument draws visitors from across the nation and abroad, but it means little in a nation that neglects the poor and helpless. The *King Holiday and Service Act of 1994* encourages individual acts of charity and righteousness, but collective action is eminently more effective and productive. President Clinton emphasized joint acts of service in five of his eight King holiday proclamations. Words typical of his admonition are found in his 2000 proclamation:

> Each year since 1994, when I signed into law the *King Holiday and Service Act*, Americans have marked this observance by devoting the day to service projects in their communities. By renovating schools, cleaning up neighborhoods, tutoring children, donating blood, organizing food drives, or reaching out in some other way to those in need, our citizens can work together to make this a day on, not a day off, and to make their own contributions to Dr. King's legacy of service. [59]

Without question, such acts are important and necessary in a civil society. However, it is easy for anyone to give a day of service to someone less fortunate than himself or herself, and to feel that for the other 364 days he or she has done his or her part. This can become a ritual without becoming a serious part of one's life's commitment and work. More importantly, such individual service alone leaves in tact and unchallenged the structures that keep people in a state of need and dependence. While King would agree with such acts of individual service, the major focus of his efforts was to dismantle the structures of oppression through collective action and coalition politics.

A growing middle class within the African American community is widening the gap between the haves and have-nots within that community. Such ritual celebrations as the King holiday allow middle-class blacks to declare their solidarity with their African American brothers and sisters trapped in poverty and all of its attending woes, and then to return to their comfortable and safe neighborhoods until the next such event. Black institutions such as historically black colleges and universities and the black

---

Proclamation 7518," *Federal Register* 67/16 (January 17, 2002), 3575.

59. Presidential Proclamation, "Martin Luther King Jr. Federal Holiday, 2000, Proclamation 7268," *Federal Register* 65/12 (January 14, 2000), 2837.

church can participate in the ritual celebrations of King without disturbing the social structures that continue to exploit the black underclass. King talked about the black churches that contained their religion within their own consecrated walls, unaffected by the plight of millions of African Americans in their communities.[60]

The celebration of the iconic King provides a mild national sedative that does not put the nation to sleep, but according to Michael Eric Dyson, it does give the nation amnesia. This amnesia is designed to "spare our nation the prospect of reliving the agony that made the King Holiday necessary."[61] While Dyson describes various types of amnesia at work in the nation's collective memory with respect to King,[62] one aspect of amnesia "makes it easier for Americans to believe that racial progress was an inevitable feature of American history."[63] Such amnesia allows the celebrants of the King legacy to avoid any personal commitments to continue the struggle for social and economic justice. The nation is making progress and needs the efforts of both individuals and groups. King is therefore seen as an agent of historical progress and not as a real person who exercised his freedom to effect change in the world. The symbol of the iconic King obscures the fact that he is far more than a symbol, and that he was part of a movement and not the movement itself. Therefore, King is not the totality of those involved in moving this nation toward the ideals of its founding documents. There were numerous nameless persons involved in the struggle. King was not the only, and certainly not the first person, to die in the struggle for African Americans' full citizenship.

Celebrating the iconic King should never mean that the historical Martin Luther King, Jr., with all of his particularities and limitations, should be dismissed. The historical King actually provides a model for the continuation of the struggles against the various -isms—racism, classism, sexism, heterosexism, ageism, militarism, and the like—that divide humanity. King continued to evolve as a person and a leader. The King who led the bus boycott in Montgomery, Alabama, was not the same King who was assassinated in Memphis, Tennessee. King kept pushing back the horizon of human potential and confronted each barrier that stood in the way with courage,

60. "A Knock at Midnight" in Martin Luther King, Jr., *Strength to Love* (Minneapolis: Fortress, 1981), 60–65.

61. Dyson. *I May Not Get There with You*, 290. Vincent Harding was actually the first to call our attention to this problem of "national amnesia" in the celebrations of King. See Vincent Harding, *Martin Luther King Jr.: The Inconvenient Hero* (Maryknoll: Orbis, 2008; originally published in 1996), ix (introduction).

62. Dyson, *I May Not Get There with You*, 290–94.

63. Ibid, 294.

determination, and perseverance. The transformation that took place during the Montgomery bus boycott is an example of the wider transformation that would take place in the civil rights movement under his leadership. Initially, the bus boycott's goals were to accommodate a milder form of segregation by simply insisting that Negro passengers be allowed to sit in any open seat in the Negro section. King and others quickly discovered that the bus authorities resisted this, and they then decided to work toward the complete elimination of Jim Crow laws and practices, which allowed Negro passengers to sit in any vacant seat on the bus. The significance of this is that the quest for freedom and dignity is a never ending struggle. When one issue is effectively addressed, it exposes the next issue. It was only after the buses had been desegregated and the laws limiting where blacks could shop or live were removed that the issue of economics came into sharper focus.

The historical King underscores the fact that perfection is not a requirement for heroic efforts. While much is made of King's education, intellectual capacity, and his oratorical gifts, there is also much to be said about his failures in the areas of strategy, tactics, and organization. It is important to celebrate his victories in Montgomery, Selma, and Birmingham, Alabama, but it is equally necessary to remember and learn from his defeats in Albany, Georgia, and in Chicago, Illinois. Moreover, we are compelled to cherish the best of King's virtues and ethical claims while also taking into account his moral failings. Only a month and a day before his assassination, King preached a sermon titled, "Unfulfilled Dreams," in which he admitted, "You don't need to go out this morning saying that Martin Luther King is a saint . . . I'm a sinner like all of God's children."[64] King was keenly aware of his human frailties, but he drew strength from his awareness that he did not struggle alone. He had a Cosmic Companion that provided the internal resources to press on in spite of his fears, doubts, and weaknesses.[65] The celebration of the historical King affirms that the task is to ultimately be on the right side of the issues that plague humanity, and to dedicate our efforts to do all we can to make a difference, while leaving the rest to God.

The historical King also reminds us that to fight for just causes does not require that we live to realize the fulfillment of our dreams. It requires that we be faithful and vigilant in the struggles against the enemies of human progress. In the closing days of his life, King's sermons and public addresses had a recurring theme: that his task was to be faithful to the struggle for human dignity and equality even though he was not likely to live to

---

64. King, "Unfulfilled Dreams" in Carson and Holloran, eds., *A Knock a Midnight*, 198.

65. "Pilgrimage to Nonviolence" in King, *Strength to Love*, 153.

see the final victory. On February 4, 1968, King in effect preached his own eulogy, saying in part:

> I'd like somebody to mention that day that Martin Luther King, Jr., tried to give his life serving others. I'd like for somebody to say that day that Martin Luther King, Jr., tried to love somebody. I want you to say that day that I tried to be right on the war question. I want you to be able to say that day that I did try to feed the hungry. And I want you to be able to say that day that I did try in my life to clothe those who were naked. I want you to say on that day that I did try in my life to visit those who were in prison. I want you to say that I tried to love and serve humanity. Yes, if you want to say that I was a drum major, say that I was a drum major for justice. Say that I was a drum major for peace. I was a drum major for righteousness. And all of the other shallow things will not matter. I won't have any money to leave behind. I won't have the fine and luxurious things of life to leave behind. But I just want to leave a committed life behind. And that's all I want to say.[66]

In the sermon, "Unfulfilled Dreams," preached March 3, 1968, King, in equally compelling terms, lamented:

> So many of us in life start out building temples: temples of character, temples of justice, temples of peace. And so often we don't finish them. Because life is like Schubert's 'Unfinished Symphony.' At so many points we start, we try, we set out to build our various temples. And I guess one of the great agonies of life is that we are constantly trying to finish that which is unfinishable. We are commanded to do that. And so we, like David, find ourselves in so many instances having to face the fact that our dreams are not fulfilled.[67]

The night before his death, King told those assembled at Mason Temple in Memphis to press on even if he did not live to see the realization of the promised land of equality, freedom, and justice. But in a powerful climax he assured them that they would get to the Promised Land:

> Well, I don't know what will happen now; we've got some difficult days ahead. But it really doesn't matter with me now, because I've been to the mountaintop. And I don't mind. Like anybody, I would like to live a long life—longevity has its place. But I'm

---

66. "The Drum Major Instinct," in Carson and Holloran, eds., *A Knock at Midnight*, 185–86.

67. King, "Unfulfilled Dreams," in ibid., 192.

not concerned about that now. I just want to do God's will. And He's allowed me to go up to the mountain. And I've looked over, and I've seen the Promised Land. I may not get there with you. But I want you to know tonight, that we, as a people, will get to the Promised Land. And I'm so happy, tonight; I'm not worried about anything; I'm not fearing any man. Mine eyes have seen the glory of the coming of the Lord.[68]

These passages reveal a human being who was reconciled to his own mortality, while affirming the transcendent nature of reality. It is the commitment to expending one's life in pursuit of the values expressed in the transcendent that gives life its fulfillment. No iconic figure can give real meaning to real people in the midst of real struggles. This can come only from God, a point that should never get lost in our annual celebrations of King.

The domestication of Martin Luther King Jr. through the process of creating a national icon is not the ultimate tragedy. Neither is it the fact that those who were close to King unwittingly participated in the fabrication of this inane symbol. The ultimate tragedy is that the very community that produced Martin Luther King Jr. has largely ceased to challenge itself and the nation to continue to understand the historical King and to translate the insights and lessons of his life into purposeful action. The tragedy mushrooms to even greater proportions if we allow the historical King to become so inaccessible to future generations that it makes it impossible to produce others with the same commitment and dedication to the transcendent ideals that make this nation great.

---

68. Martin Luther King, Jr., "I've Been to the Mountaintop," in Clayborne Carson and Kris Shepard, eds., *A Call to Conscience: The Landmark Speeches of Martin Luther King, Jr.* (New York: Warner, 2001), 222–23.

Index

A

Abernathy, Ralph D., xiv, xxvii, 106, 108, 114, 120–22, 125, 127, 137, 139, 221
Adams, John, 241
Alexander, Michelle, 102
American Civil Liberties Union (ACLU), 22n74
American Nazi Party, 194
Anderson, Marian, 67
Anderson, Victor, 86
Angelou, Maya, xxii
Antony, Mark, xiv
Apostle Paul, 96
Appiah, Kwame A., 81
Arellano, Elvira, 45, 175–76
Armesto, Eladio Jose, 142
Armey, Dick, xxii, 16, 41, 170
Arps, Christopher, 18
Attucks, Chrispus, 242

B

Bailey, Wilma A., 200
Baker, Ella J., xxvi, 65, 68, 71, 103, 112, 123, 125
Baldwin, James, 83
Baldwin, Lewis V., 184–85
Barnett, Ross, 199
Barnette, Henlee, 4
Bates, Daisy, 155
Bates, L. C., 68
Bauer, Gary, 47
Beck, Glenn, xx, xxii–xxiii, 21–27, 42n51, 160, 237–38

Belafonte, Harry, 31–32
Bell, Mychal, 76n7
Bellah, Robert N., 247–51 and 253
Bennett, Lerone, Jr., xx
Billingsley, Orzell, 32
Bin Laden, Osama, 49–50
Bob Jones University, Greenville, SC, 8
Bolick, Clint, xxii, 16, 41, 170
Bonhoeffer, Dietrich, 181–82, 187–88, 210, 216
borderline ethics, 210
borderline situation, xxix, 208, 210–11
Branch, Taylor, 108, 120, 122, 123n8, 194, 239, 254
Brown, H. Rap, 195
Brown, Jim, 80n17
Brown, John, 182–83
Brown, Stefanie, 23–24
Brown v. Board of Education (1954), 185
Bryant, C. L., 53n89
Buchanan, Patrick, 14
Burks, Mary Fair, 124
Burns, Stewart, 126
Burrow, Rufus, Jr., 110, 118
Bush, George W., 17, 20, 48, 245–46, 252, 255
Butler, Richard, 161

C

Caine, Curtis, 14
Canada, Geoffrey, 62

Candide, 118
Carmichael, Stokely, 195
Carto, Willis, 161
Carver, George Washington, 171, 242
Center for Disease Control (CDC), xxix, 209
Children's Defense Fund (CDF), 62
Christian Coalition, 15
Christian Nationalist State Army (CNSA), 229
Christian Zionists, 47
Churchill, Winston, xiv
Citizens United v. Federal Elections Commission (2010), 55–57, 59, 62
civil religion, 247–54
Civil Rights Act (1964), 166
Clark, Septima P., xxvi, 68, 103, 123, 125, 194
Clarke, John H., xx–xxi
Clinton, William Jefferson (Bill), 244–46, 252n49, 253, 256
CNN *Crosfire*, 18
Collins, Addie Mae, 220
Columbus, Christopher, 239, 241–42
Committee on Equal Employment Opportunity (CEEO), 166
Communist Party, 152–53
Cone, James H., 89, 92–93
Congress of Racial Equality (CORE), 151, 152n32, 191
Congressional Black Caucus (CBC), xxiv, 56–59, 240
Congressional Black Caucus Foundation (CBCF), 57–59
Congressional Black Caucus Institute (CBCI), 59
Congressional Black Caucus Political Action Committee (CBCPAC), 59
Conyers, John, 239
Cooper, Anna J., 86, 89n46
Cosby, Bill, 43
Crenshaw, Cornelia, 66
Curry, George E., 43–44

D

Daley, Richard J., 206–7, 221
Delany, Martin, 86
D'Emilio, John, 152, 153n41
Dilling, Elizabeth, 23n75
Dollar, Creflo, 37
Douglass, Frederick, 108, 124n12
DuBois, William E. B., 82, 86, 108, 171
Duckett, Al, 34n19
Dyson, Michael Eric, 21, 29n1, 74, 80n17, 115, 121–22, 138, 237, 257

E

Eastland, James O., 3
Eck, Diana L., 97–98
Edelman, Marian Wright, 62
eliminativist philosophers, 81
Equal Rights Amendment (ERA), 11, 13
Evers, Medgar, 67–68
Exxon Valdez, 62

F

Fackre, Gabriel, 15
Falwell, Jerry, xxii, 5–6, 11–13, 18–19, 24, 48, 54
Farrakhan, Louis, 47, 159–60
Faubus, Orval, 3
Fauntroy, Walter, 239
Federal Bureau of Investigation (FBI), 35n21, 50, 107–8, 112, 114, 120, 128–31, 153–54, 230
Fellowship of Reconciliation (FOR), 146, 151
Fluker, Walter Earl, 64–66, 71
Fosdick, Harry Emerson, 134
Franklin, Robert M., 97
Frazier, E, Stanley, 2
Friere, Paulo, 116

G

Gandhi, Mohandas K., 9, 35, 38, 100, 187, 189–95, 215
Gandhi Society, 35n21
Gardner, John, 64–65, 71
Garner, Chris, 116–17
Garnet, Henry Highland, 86
Garris, Carolyn, 17–18
Garrow, David, 108, 110, 120, 122, 130
Garvey, Marcus, 86
Gendler, Rabbi Everett, 47, 159
Gibbs, Jewelle Taylor, 209
Gingrich, Newt, xxii, 16, 24, 41, 170
Goldwater, Barry, 6
Graham, William Franklin (Billy), 3–5, 9
Gray, Fred, 32
Greenberg, Jack, 35n21

H

Hagar, 89
Hagee, John, 47
Hairston, Loyle, xx
Hamilton, Charles V., xx
Hammond, Phillip, 247, 249
Harding, Vincent, xx, 27, 30, 126, 128, 130, 257n61
Harlem Children's Zone (HCZ), 62
Harpham, Kevin, 19
Hedgeman, Anna, 155n48
Hegel, Georg W. F., 35, 40n43
Helms, Jesse, 8, 13–14, 241
Henderson, J. Raymond, 106–7
Heschel, Rabbi Abraham Joshua, 47, 158
Higginbotham, A. Leon, 68–69
Hitler, Adolf, 159, 180–81, 187, 197, 211, 216
Hooks, Bell, 116
Hoover, J. Edgar, 112, 128–32, 153–54, 230
Hurley, Ruby, xxv, 57, 66–71
Hussein, Saddam, xix, 48

I

Institute for Justice, 43
Ivory, Luther D., 30

J

Jackson, Bishop Harry R., Jr., 20–21
Jackson, Jesse L., xix, 37–38, 43, 47, 52–53, 75, 77, 159–60, 204
Jackson, Jimmy Lee, 213
Jackson, Mahalia, 171
Jakes, Bishop T. D., 37
James, Daniel "Chappie," 242
James, Roy, 194
Jefferson, Thomas, xiii–xiv, 241
Jenkins, William A., 185
John Birch Society (JBS), 4, 6, 14
Johnson, Lyndon B., 153n40, 166, 250
Johnson, Mordecai W., 192
Jones, Clarence B., xiv–xv, xix–xxxi, 17–18, 20, 25–27, 29–54, 56–57, 60–63, 70, 73–79, 83, 85, 87–88, 100, 102–3, 107, 111, 113, 115–18, 120, 122, 125, 27, 130, 145–50, 156–72, 174–83, 186, 190, 194–204, 206–8, 211–12, 219, 230, 237–38
Jones, Bob, Jr., 8
Jones, Richard, 81–82
Jones, William R., 89–90
Jordan, Vernon, 68
"Joshua generation," 89

K

Kaiser, Ernest, xx
Kennedy, Edward M., 243–44, 250
Kennedy, John F., 128–29, 151, 153, 165–66, 249–50
Kennedy, Robert F., 128–29, 153
Killens, John O., xx
King, Alberta Williams, 185
King, Alveda, 26, 237–38

King, Coretta Scott, xxvii, 108, 112, 123, 125, 129, 136–37, 139–42, 196, 207, 239–40, 242, 244, 252
King, Delia Lindsay, 184–85
King Holiday and Service Act (1994), 253, 256
King, James Albert, 184–85
King, Martin Luther, Jr. xiii–260
   and American civil religion, xiii–xiv, xxx, 247–54
   and King memorials, xiii, xxx–xxxi, 14–16, 19, 236–60
   and "kitchen experience," 223–24, 226
   and "Letter from the Birmingham City Jail" (1963), 5, 36, 45n63, 167
   and Montgomery Improvement association (MIA), 66, 190, 221
   and Southern Christian Leadership Conference (SCLC), 4–5, 15, 31, 92, 112, 125, 129, 151, 185, 194–95, 201, 206, 215, 241
   and *World House*, 86–87, 90–95, 98
King, Martin Luther, Sr., 123–24, 184n6, 185–86
King Papers Project, 108, 113–14
Ku Klux Klan (KKK), 3–4, 16, 19, 169, 190, 202, 229

L

L, William Pope, 79
LaHaye, Tim, 12–13, 47
Land, Richard, 12–13, 52–53
Landmark Legal Foundation (LLF), 43
Lee, Barbara, 58–59
Lee, Bernard, 127, 130
Lentz, Richard, 28
Leonard, Bill J., 7n22, 8
Levin, Rabbi Yehuda, 15
Levison, Stanley, xv, 32, 34, 35n21
Lewis, John, 17–18, 62, 89n46, 125

Lincoln, Abraham, 23, 241, 249–51, 253
Lischer, Richard, 235n50
Long, Bishop Eddie, 20–21, 37
Long, Michael G., 138–39
Los Angeles Bible College, 8
Lowery, Joseph E., 17, 89n46, 241–42
Lucy, Autherine, 67
Lyons, Henry L., Jr., 2

M

Maguire, Daniel C., 12–13
Marable, Manning, 135
Marshall, Thurgood, 33
Martin, Trayvon, 52, 53n89, 170
Marx, Karl, xiv
Matthews, Chris, 244
McDonald, Larry, 241, 250
McGuire, Meredith, 248, 252
McKissick, Floyd, 191n25
McNair, Denise, 220
Mecham, Evan, 14
Meredith, James, 199
Metzger, Tom, 161
Mikelson, Thomas, 227
Mills, Charles, 81
"Ministers and Marches" (1965), 11
Moral Majority, Inc., 1, 11–12
Morial, Marc H., 23
Morton, Bishop Paul, 37
"Moses generation," 89
Mother Pollard, 33
Muhammad, Elijah, 158, 160
Murray, Pauli, 155
Murtaugh, Arthur, 129
Mussolini, Benito A.A., xiv
Myrdal, Gunnar, 85

N

Nash, Diane, 155
Nation of Islam (NOI), 159
National Action Network (NAN), 24
National Association for the Advancement of Colored People (NAACP), 24, 35n21, 57, 63, 67–71, 151, 184

National Baptist Convention, USA, 63
National Black Republican Association (NBRA), 17–18
National Urban League, 23, 63
Negro American Labor Committee (NALC), 151
Nehru, Jawaharlal, 194
Newman, Isaiah DeQuincey, 68
New Right, 1–2, 10–11, 13, 16, 19–20
Niebuhr, Reinhold, xxvi, 35, 132–33, 135, 189n19
Nix, Robert, 251

O

Oates, Stephen B., 120, 122, 132
Obama, Barack H., xiii, xxx, 17, 22–23, 26–27, 41–42, 53, 78–79, 80n17, 89, 245–47, 252
Obama, Michelle, 62
Occupy Movement, 91, 171
Outlaw, Lucius T., 81
Owens, Jesse, 171

P

Palin, Sarah, xxii–xxiii, 25–26
Parks, Rosa L., 66
Paris, Peter J., 86, 90n48
Patterson, John, 3
Payne, Charles, 71
Pearman, Eric G., 207, 217
Pinn, Anthony, 95–96
Political Right, 1, 9, 13–14
postblackness, 73, 79, 83
postracism, 73, 79, 83
Poussaint, Alvin F., xx
Powell, Adam Clayton, Jr., 151n30
Powell, Colin, 80n17
Powers, Georgia Davis, 132
Praeger, Dennis, 107–8

R

Randolph, A. Philip, 34, 151–52, 154–56

Ratliff, Keith, Sr., 144–45
Rauschenbusch, Walter, xxvi, 124n12, 133–35, 193
Ray, James Earl, 8, 50, 219, 233
Reagan, Ronald, xiii, 14, 239–40, 244–47, 255
Reeb, James, 83n25
Reed, Ralph, 15–16
Rice, Condoleeza, 80n17
Rice, John R., 6–7
Robb, Thomas, 16
Robertson, Carole, 220
Robertson, Pat, 15, 48, 54
Robinson, Jo Ann, 66, 103, 124
Rogers, Taylor, 66
Roosevelt, Franklin D., xiii
Ross, Rosetta E., 137
Rushing, Byron, 143–44
Russell, Lord Bertrand, 137–38
Rustin, Bayard, xxvii, 34, 35n21, 122, 146, 150–56, 179, 189–90
Rutherford, William, 195

S

Satre, Jean Paul, 214
Saunders, Robert, 68
Schneier, Rabbi Marc, 161–62n16
Scholtes, Peter S., 137
Schubert, Franz, 259
Scott, Elsie, 58–59
Sharpton, Al, xix, 24, 26, 37–38, 43, 47, 52–53, 75, 77, 159–60, 204
Shores, Arthur D., 32
Smiley, Glenn, 179, 189–90
Smith, Gerald L. K., 6
Smith, Kenneth L., 133, 189
Smith, Noel, 7–8
Smith, Will, 80n17
Southern Baptist Convention (SBC), 4, 6, 12, 14, 52
Southern Baptist Theological Seminary, Louisville, KY, 4, 6
Southern Poverty Law Center (SPLC), 41, 177
Spencer, Bob, 8–9, 152n32

Spivak, Lawrence E., 191n25
St. Ambrose of Milan, 138
St. Augustine of Hippo, 138
St. Jerome, 138
Stevens, John Paul, 55–56, 59, 63
Strom, Kevin A., 19
Student Nonviolent Coordinating Committee (SNCC), 112
Styron, William, xx, 30n3,
Sullivan, William C., 130

T

Talmadge, Herman E., 3
Tea Party, xx, 21–22, 25–27, 42, 46
Terry, Robert, 43n55
Thelwel, Mike, xx
The Radical Right, 1, 4, 15, 19, 22, 27
Thielicke, Helmut, 208, 210–11
Thomas, Cal, xxii, 12–13
Thomas, Clarence, 80n17
Thoreau, Henry David, 182–83, 189, 195
Thurman, Howard, 83n25, 97
Thurman, Strom, 8, 152–54
Thurston, John, 130
Tides Foundation, 22n74
Till, Emmett L., 67
Toure, xxv, 79–80
Trevor-Roper, Hugh, xv
Truth and Reconciliation Commission (TRC), 118
Tubman, Harriet, 111, 242
Turner, Nat, xx–xxi, 30n3

V

Vietnam, xv, 92, 104
Viguerie, Richard, 1
Vivian, C. T., 135
Voting Rights Act (1965), 166, 246

W

Walker, Alice, 101, 136
Walker, David, 86
Walker, Wyatt Tee, 125, 127, 194
War Resister's League (WRL), 151
Washington, Booker T., 242
Washington, George, 14, 139, 241–42, 248–49, 253
Welch, Robert H. W., 4
Wells-Barnett, Ida B., 86
Weniger, Archer, 7
Wesley, Cynthia, 220
West, Cornel, 97n68, 205
West, Traci C., 137
White Citizens' Council (WCC), 3
White, Clifford, J., III, 241
Wiggins, William H., 239–42
Wilcox, Nathaniel, 142–43
Wiley, Christine, 144
Wiley, Dennis, 144
Wilkins, Roy, 151, 154
Williams, Adam D., 184–85
Williams, Jennie C. Parks, 184–85, 224
Williams, John A., xx, 30n3, 120
Williams, Willis, 185
Winfrey, Oprah, 41, 89n46, 168
Wink, Walter, 196, 201
Winkle, Rip Van, 168
Wise, Tim, 42
Woffard, Harris, 34n19
Women's Political Council, Montgomery, Ala. (WPC), 66
Wonder, Stevie, 239n8

X

X, Malcolm (Little), 38, 80n17, 86, 93, 206, 216–17

Y

Young Americans for Freedom (YAF), 241
Young, Andrew, xiv, 35n21, 127, 226, 239
Young, Robert Alexander, 86

Z

Z, Jay, 80n17

Zack, Naomi, 81
Zeitgeist, 39
Zepp, Ira G., Jr., 133

Zimmerman, George, 52
Zionists, 158

www.ingramcontent.com/pod-product-compliance
Lightning Source LLC
Chambersburg PA
CBHW021653230426
43668CB00008B/612